WONDER WOMAN

BY GEORGE PÉREZ

VOLUME 1

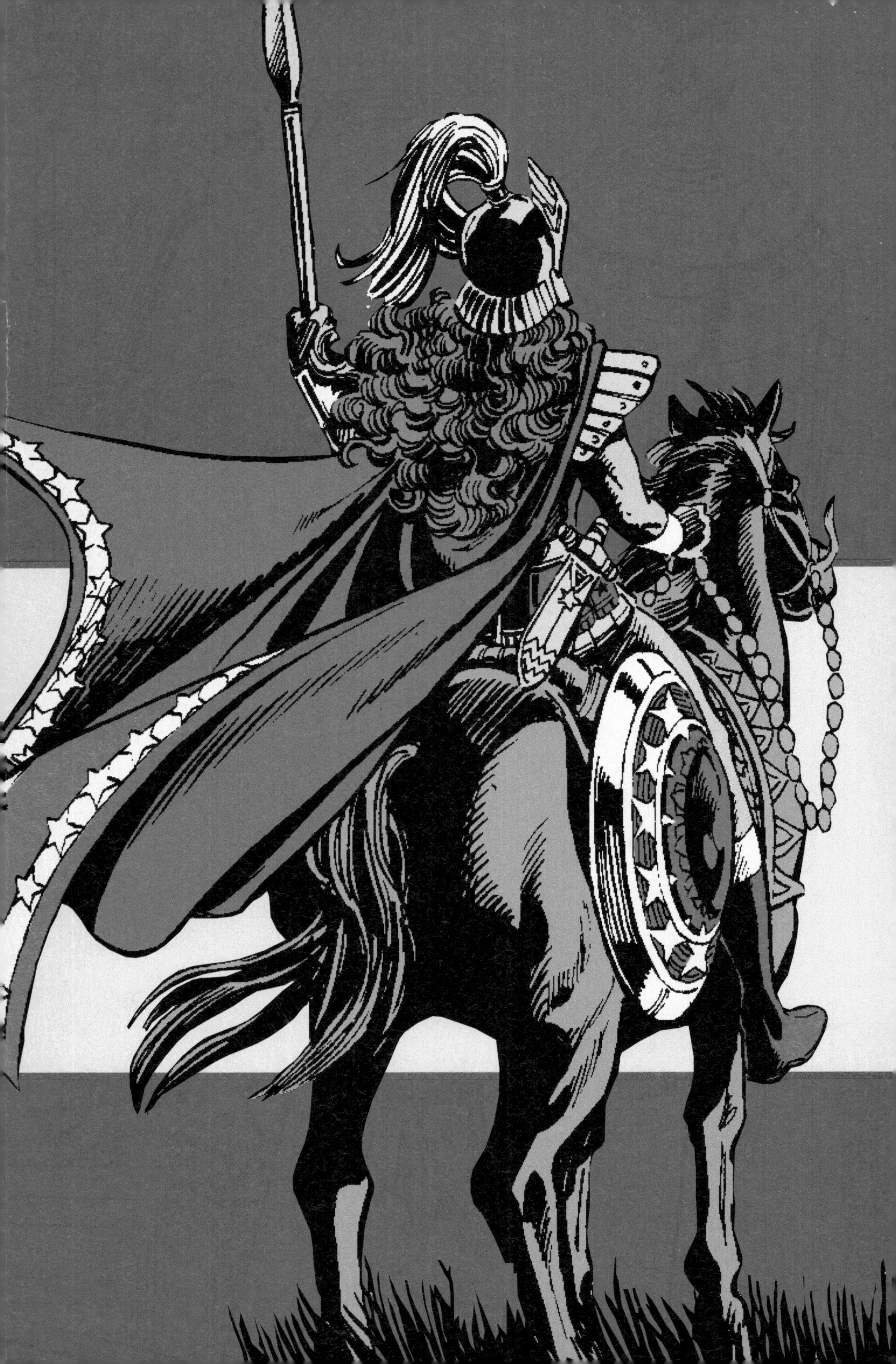

WONDER WOMAN

BY GEORGE PÉREZ
VOLUME 1

GEORGE PÉREZ LEN WEIN GREG POTTER
Writers

GEORGE PÉREZ
Penciller

BRUCE PATTERSON BOB SMITH GEORGE PÉREZ
Inkers

TATJANA WOOD CARL GAFFORD
Colorists

JOHN COSTANZA L.S. MACINTOSH
Letterers

GEORGE PÉREZ
Collection Cover Artist

WONDER WOMAN created by **WILLIAM MOULTON MARSTON**

SUPERMAN created by **JERRY SIEGEL** and **JOE SHUSTER**
By special arrangement with the Jerry Siegel family

WONDER WOMAN BY GEORGE PÉREZ

FSC
www.fsc.org

MIX
Paper from
responsible sources
FSC® C101537

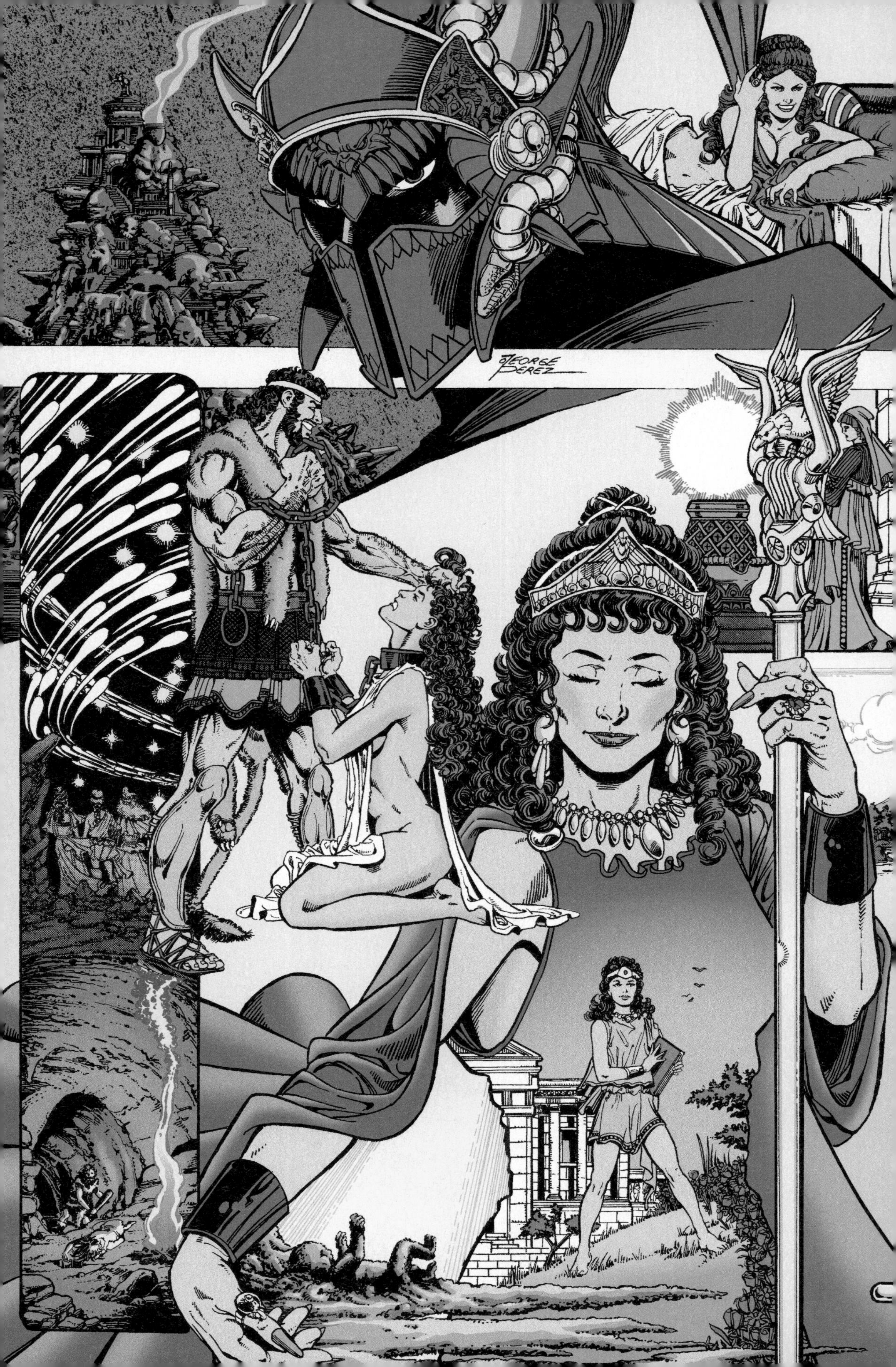
GEORGE PEREZ

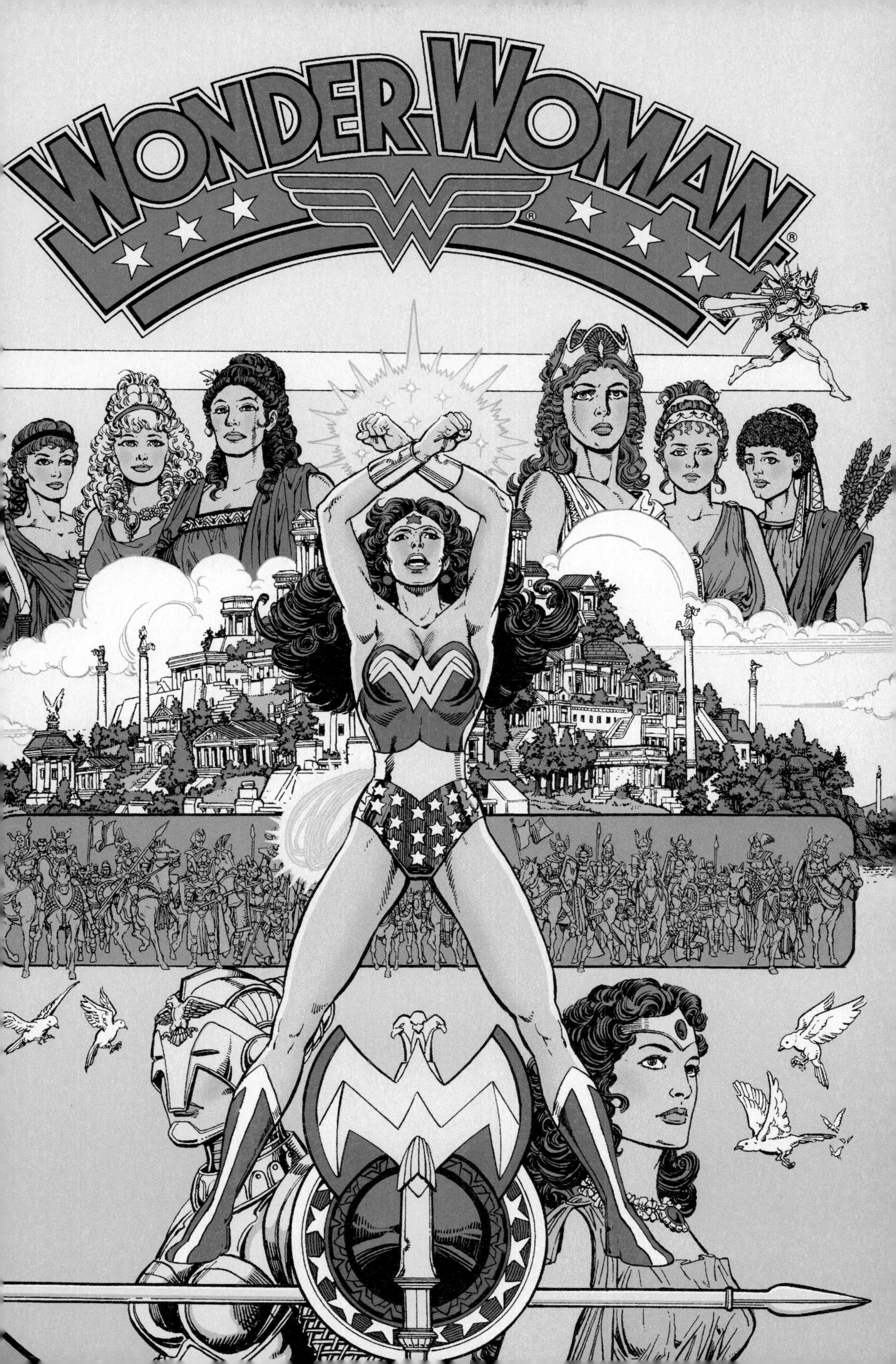

WONDER WOMAN

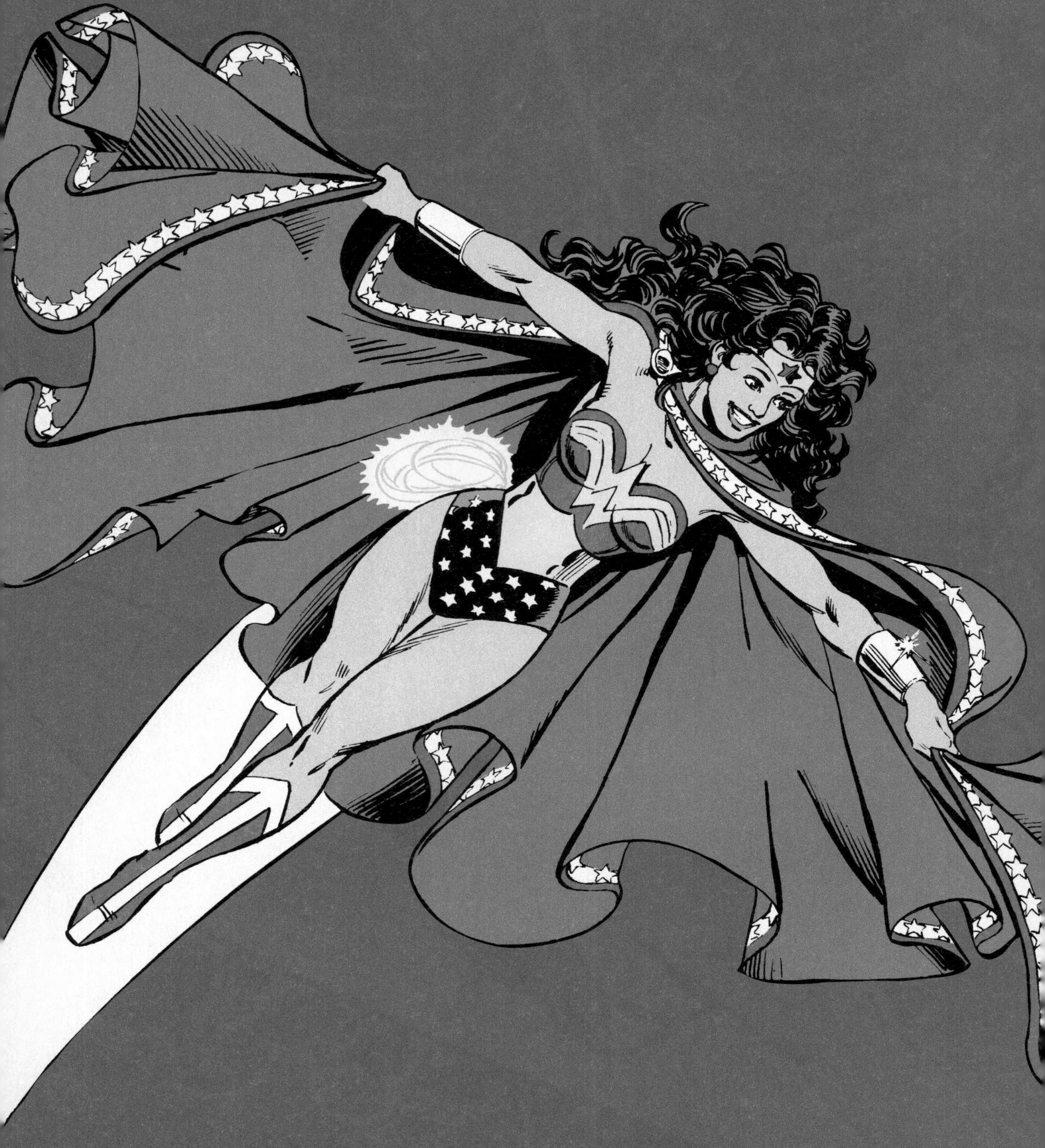

"THE GODS ARE DEAD, KILLED BY THE ONE GOD. BETWEEN THE MEN OF THE *NEW* AND THOSE OF ANCIENT TIMES THERE WILL NO LONGER BE A THOUGHT IN COMMON."
-- FERDINAND LOT

30,000 B.C.--TODAY, YOUR TRIBE CAST YOU OUT! THEY MOCKED YOU -- CALLED YOU USELESS...

...CALLED YOU AN ANIMAL!

ONLY YESTERDAY YOU WERE CALLED A MAN! YOU *HUNTED* WITH MEN AND *FOUGHT* WITH MEN.

THAT WAS BEFORE YOU MET THE SABERTOOTH...

...THE ONE WHO BESTED YOU...

...THE ONE WHO TOOK YOUR HAND!

NOW, YOU ARE A MAN *NO MORE.* FOR MEN ARE HUNTERS -- AND HUNTERS NEED HANDS!

THAT MAKES YOU AFRAID. BUT YOU MUST NOT SHOW YOUR FEAR.

REMEMBER WHAT THE TRIBE TEACHES...

...FEAR IS FOR WOMEN!

SO YOU HIDE YOUR FACE--QUELL YOUR TREMBLING.

STILL, SOMEHOW, SHE KNOWS!

AND WHEN SHE TOUCHES YOU...

...WHEN YOU HEAR HER SYMPATHETIC WHINING...

...YOU CURSE HER!

SO YOU PULL AWAY-- BUT SHE INSISTS!

YOU TRY TO IGNORE HER -- BUT HER WHIMPERING TAUNTS YOU...

...TEASES YOU...

...EMASCULATES YOU...

...MAKES YOU... SNAP!

AND WHEN YOUR TEMPER COOLS...

...WHEN THE ECHO OF HER SCREAM HAS BEEN SWALLOWED BY THE AIR...

...YOU HEAR IT!

A MUFFLED STIRRING WITHIN HER.

AND A VOICE--

--AS IF FROM THE EARTH ITSELF--

--WHISPERING--

--CALLING--

--BECKONING--

--MAKING SOMETHING HAPPEN...

AND IT MAKES YOU WANT TO...

...THAT YOU CANNOT UNDERSTAND!

...SCREAM!

②

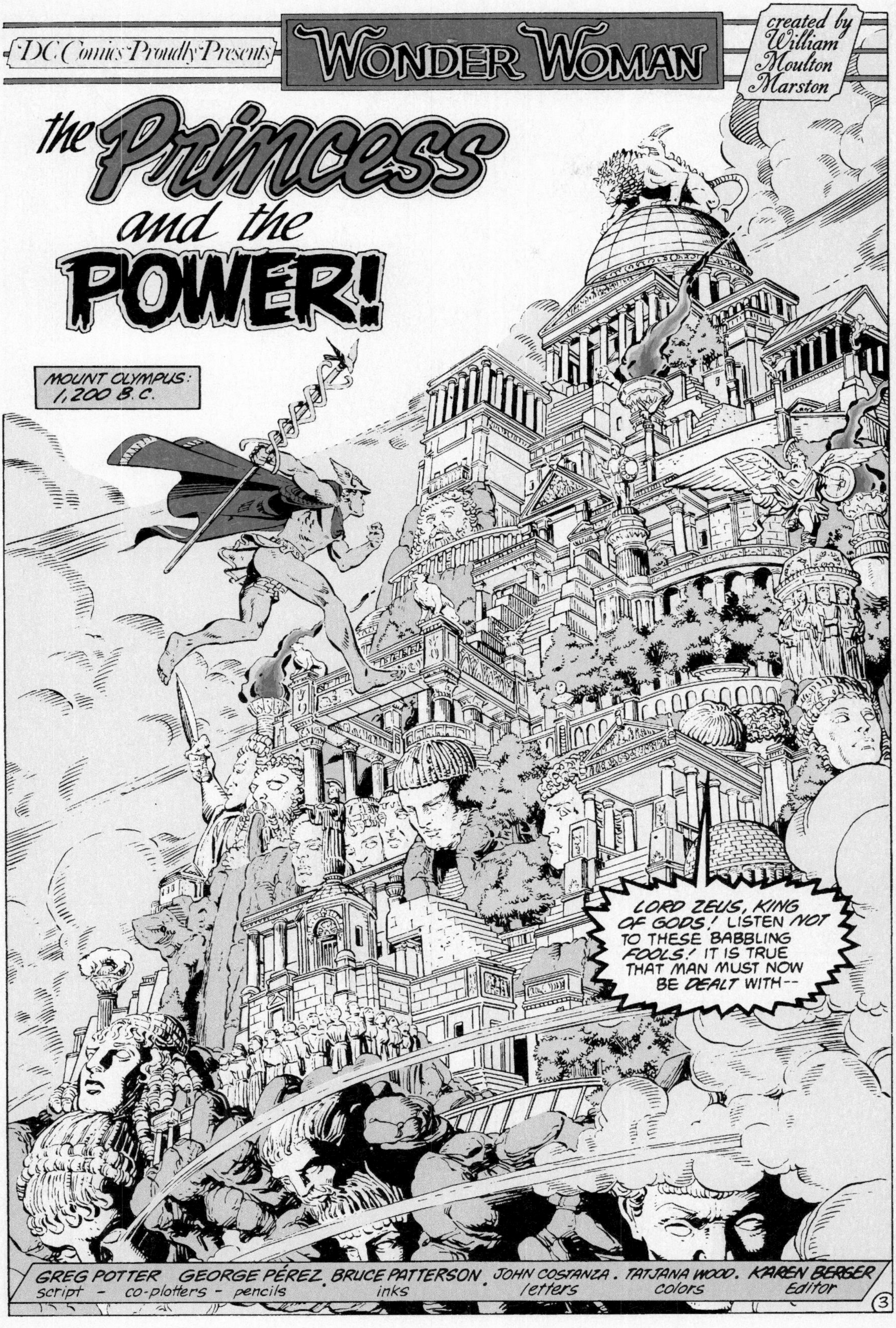
DC Comics Proudly Presents
WONDER WOMAN
created by William Moulton Marston
the Princess and the POWER!
MOUNT OLYMPUS: 1,200 B.C.
LORD ZEUS, KING OF GODS! LISTEN NOT TO THESE BABBLING FOOLS! IT IS TRUE THAT MAN MUST NOW BE DEALT WITH--
GREG POTTER script - GEORGE PÉREZ co-plotters - pencils . BRUCE PATTERSON inks . JOHN COSTANZA letters . TATJANA WOOD colors . KAREN BERGER Editor
3

--BUT IF THE GODS WISH TO SECURE THEIR POWER ON EARTH, HEED THE WORDS OF *YOUR SON*-- *ARES*-- *GOD OF WAR!*

MY HALF-SISTER *ARTEMIS* HAS PROPOSED TO CREATE A *NEW RACE OF MORTALS* ON EARTH-- A RACE WHICH, *SHE* CLAIMS, SHALL *MAKE MEN WORSHIP US AS NEVER BEFORE!* MY LORD, THIS PLAN IS *LUNACY!*

IF OLYMPUS *TRULY* DESIRES TO *OWN* MEN'S HEARTS-- IF *POWER* IS OUR *ULTIMATE AIM*-- THEN LET *ARES* DESCEND UPON THESE *WEAK-KNEED MORTALS...*

...AND WITH *THE DOGS OF WAR,* I SHALL *CRUSH* THEM INTO *ETERNAL SUBMISSION!*

NO, ARES. VIOLENCE WILL MAKE MAN *FEAR* US, NOT *FOLLOW* US. OUR INTENT WITH THIS *NEW RACE* IS TO SET AN *EXAMPLE* --TO SHOW MAN AND WOMAN'S TRUE PLACE WITH EACH OTHER--

--AS GAEA HAD MEANT IT TO BE!

FORCE IS ALL MEN UNDERSTAND! *FORCE* IS ALL THEY *WORSHIP!*

AND I AM *FORCE INCARNATE!*

LORD ZEUS--ARES' WAY SHALL *DESTROY* US ALL. IF MAN DIES...

...SHALL WE *NOT* ALSO *PERISH?*

THERE IS *TRUTH* IN MY SISTER'S WORDS, FATHER ZEUS. MEN *WORSHIP* THE GODS-- AND *THROUGH* THEIR *WORSHIP,* WE GROW STRONG.

WITHOUT THEIR GOOD WILL, WE SHALL BECOME *AS NOTHING* IN MAN'S WORLD!

SO, APOLLO-- YOU *AGREE* WITH *ARTEMIS!*

DO YOU, TOO, SEE THIS NEW RACE AS *FEMALE?*

DOES THEIR GENDER *TRULY MATTER*, LORD ZEUS? THEY SHALL BE AS *NO OTHER WOMEN* EVER BEFORE *SEEN* BY MAN! *STRONG...BRAVE... COMPASSIONATE!*

THEY SHALL BE OLYMPUS' GLORY--

WHAT ARE YOU *AFRAID* OF, ARES? THAT OLYMPUS SHALL BE REPRESENTED ON EARTH BY *WOMEN*?

OR THAT THESE NEW MORTALS SHALL BE ABLE TO *RESIST* EVEN *YOUR* BASE INFLUENCE?

NO MORTAL RESISTS *ARES*, ATHENA! MY *ULTIMATE DOMINA-TION* OF MAN IS *INEVITABLE!*

EVEN IN PROPHECY *NOTHING* IS INEVITABLE, ARES. MANKIND IS EVER BLESSED -- AND CURSED--WITH *THE POWER OF CHOICE!*

NAY, LORD! THEY SHALL BE OLYMPUS' *SHAME!*

ENOUGH!

YOU SPEAK AS IF MAN WILL SOMEDAY *FORGET* THE GODS! I SAY IT SHALL *NEVER COME TO PASS!*

IT *MATTERS LITTLE*, THEREFORE, WHETHER YOUR NEW RACE IS *BORN OR NOT!*

SETTLE THIS *TRIFLING* MATTER AMONG *YOUR-SELVES* -- AND BOTHER ZEUS WITH IT *NO MORE!*

HERA-- WILL YOU NOT SPEAK WITH LORD ZEUS? WE WOULD HAVE HIS *BLESSING* IN THIS VENTURE...AND HE WOULD LISTEN TO YOU.

MY HUSBAND IS *PROUD*-- AND YOUR WORDS HAVE STIRRED A *STORM* WITHIN HIM.

MY ADVICE TO YOU IS THIS: WALK NOT *LIGHTLY* INTO SUCH A *MAELSTROM!*

AND DO NOT ASK *YOUR QUEEN* TO TAKE SIDES *AGAINST HER LORD* WHILE HE STILL *RAGES!*

5

13

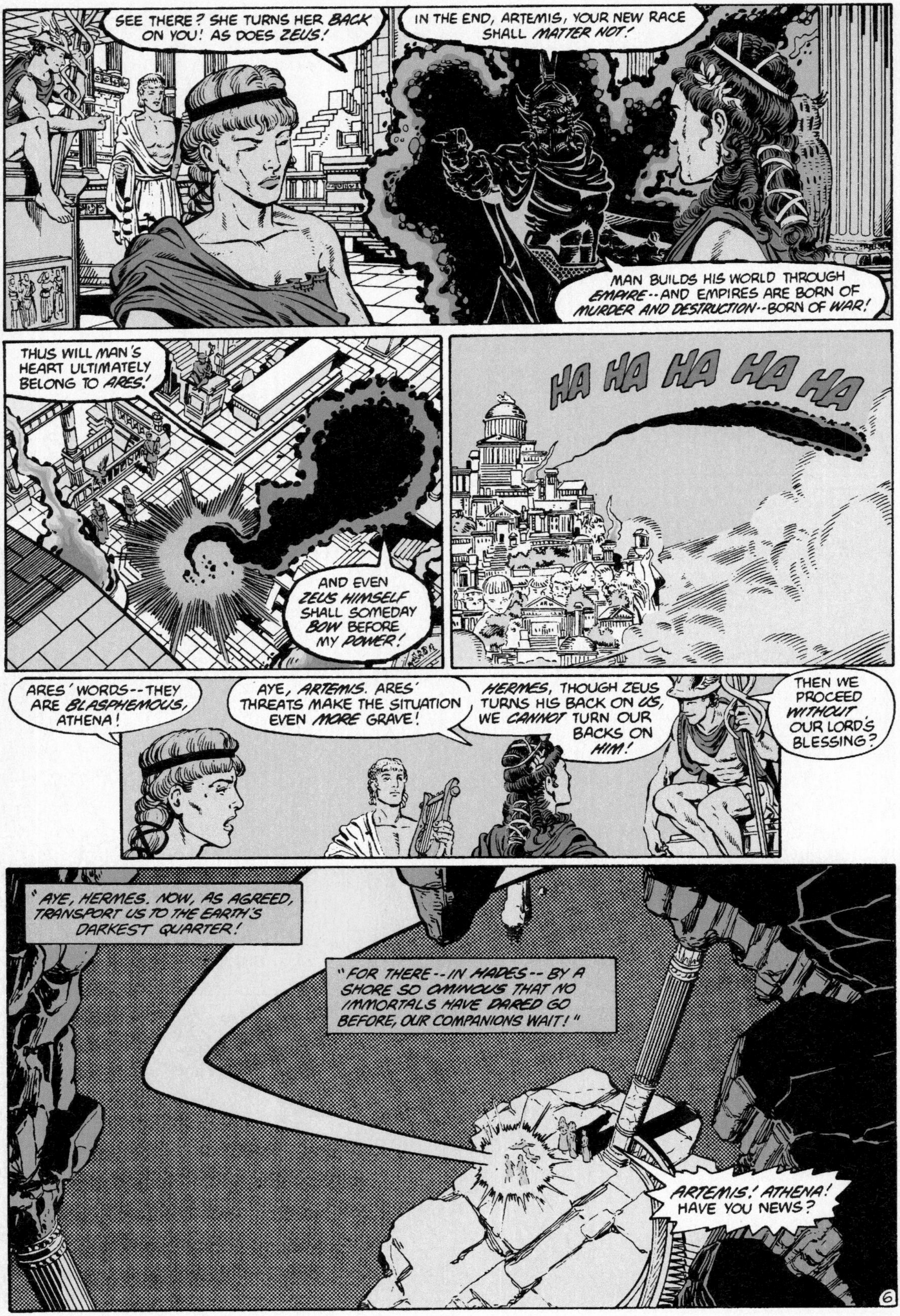
SEE THERE? SHE TURNS HER BACK ON YOU! AS DOES ZEUS!
IN THE END, ARTEMIS, YOUR NEW RACE SHALL MATTER NOT!
MAN BUILDS HIS WORLD THROUGH EMPIRE--AND EMPIRES ARE BORN OF MURDER AND DESTRUCTION--BORN OF WAR!
THUS WILL MAN'S HEART ULTIMATELY BELONG TO ARES!
AND EVEN ZEUS HIMSELF SHALL SOMEDAY BOW BEFORE MY POWER!
HA HA HA HA HA
ARES' WORDS--THEY ARE BLASPHEMOUS, ATHENA!
AYE, ARTEMIS. ARES' THREATS MAKE THE SITUATION EVEN MORE GRAVE!
HERMES, THOUGH ZEUS TURNS HIS BACK ON US, WE CANNOT TURN OUR BACKS ON HIM!
THEN WE PROCEED WITHOUT OUR LORD'S BLESSING?
"AYE, HERMES. NOW, AS AGREED, TRANSPORT US TO THE EARTH'S DARKEST QUARTER!
"FOR THERE--IN HADES--BY A SHORE SO OMINOUS THAT NO IMMORTALS HAVE DARED GO BEFORE, OUR COMPANIONS WAIT!"
ARTEMIS! ATHENA! HAVE YOU NEWS?
6

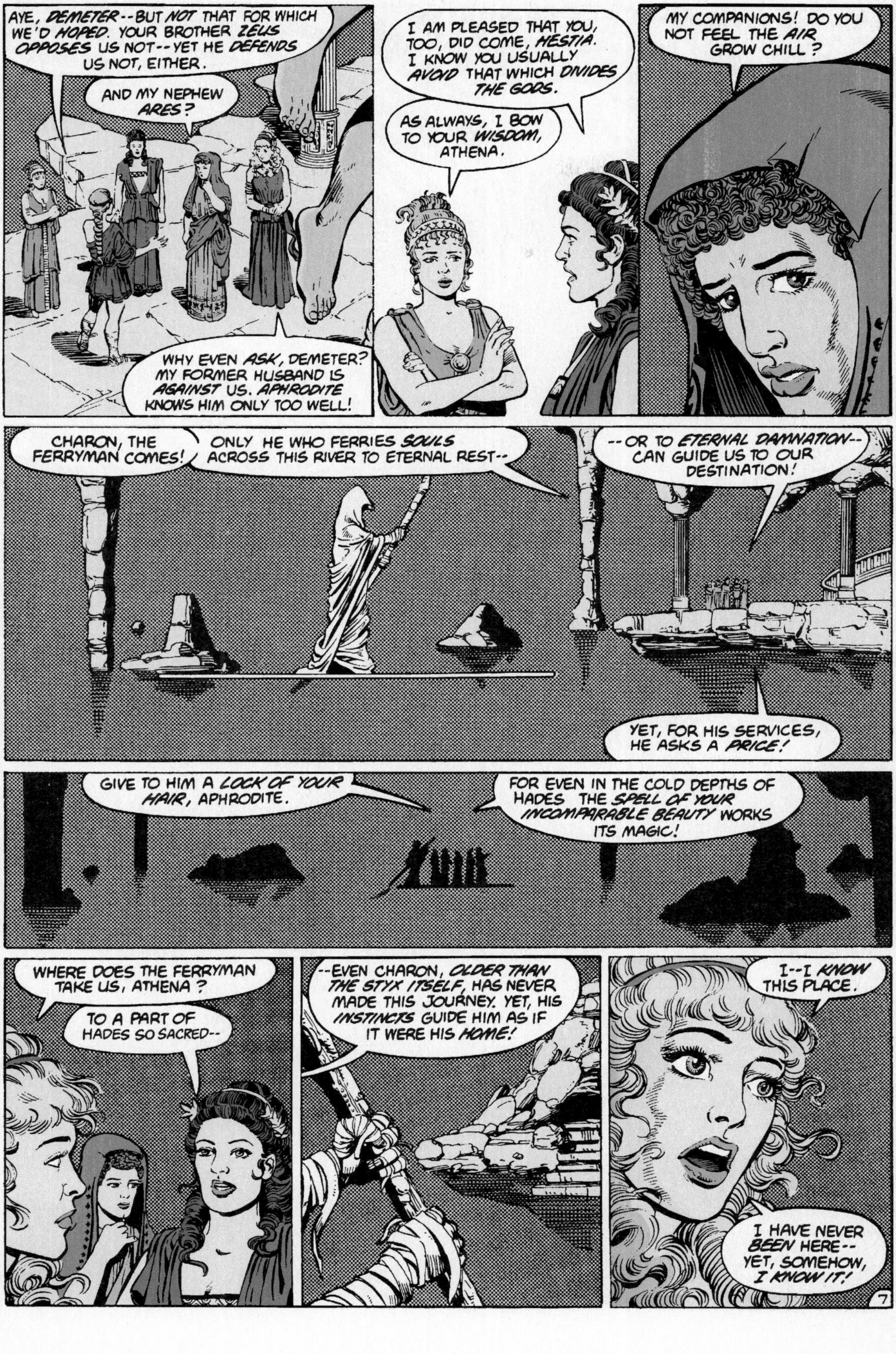
AYE, DEMETER--BUT NOT THAT FOR WHICH WE'D HOPED. YOUR BROTHER ZEUS OPPOSES US NOT--YET HE DEFENDS US NOT, EITHER.
AND MY NEPHEW ARES?
WHY EVEN ASK, DEMETER? MY FORMER HUSBAND IS AGAINST US. APHRODITE KNOWS HIM ONLY TOO WELL!
I AM PLEASED THAT YOU, TOO, DID COME, HESTIA. I KNOW YOU USUALLY AVOID THAT WHICH DIVIDES THE GODS.
AS ALWAYS, I BOW TO YOUR WISDOM, ATHENA.
MY COMPANIONS! DO YOU NOT FEEL THE AIR GROW CHILL?
CHARON, THE FERRYMAN COMES!
ONLY HE WHO FERRIES SOULS ACROSS THIS RIVER TO ETERNAL REST--
--OR TO ETERNAL DAMNATION--CAN GUIDE US TO OUR DESTINATION!
YET, FOR HIS SERVICES, HE ASKS A PRICE!
GIVE TO HIM A LOCK OF YOUR HAIR, APHRODITE.
FOR EVEN IN THE COLD DEPTHS OF HADES THE SPELL OF YOUR INCOMPARABLE BEAUTY WORKS ITS MAGIC!
WHERE DOES THE FERRYMAN TAKE US, ATHENA?
TO A PART OF HADES SO SACRED--
--EVEN CHARON, OLDER THAN THE STYX ITSELF, HAS NEVER MADE THIS JOURNEY. YET, HIS INSTINCTS GUIDE HIM AS IF IT WERE HIS HOME!
I--I KNOW THIS PLACE.
I HAVE NEVER BEEN HERE--YET, SOMEHOW, I KNOW IT!
7

AYE, APHRODITE. IT IS THE WELL OF REBIRTH--

--THE CAVERN OF SOULS!

IT IS, IN TRUTH, THE SOURCE FROM WHICH *ALL* LIFE ONCE SPRUNG!

IT IS THE WOMB OF *GAEA*-- MOTHER OF US ALL!

THOSE *LIGHTS* ARE SOULS OF WOMEN--

--THEIR LIVES CUT SHORT BY MAN'S FEAR AND IGNORANCE.

GAEA TOOK THEM UNDER HER CARE BEFORE SHE *LEFT* THIS PLANE.

NOW, THEY AWAIT *REBIRTH!*

THEIR NEW DESTINY BEGINS HERE! THEY HAVE WAILED IN LIMBO FOR *CENTURIES*-- SOON, THEY SHALL WAIL *NO MORE!*

SOON, THEY SHALL SING *THE SONG OF LIFE!*

ARTEMIS OPENS HER MOUTH...

8

16

...AND THE SKIES ABOVE FAIR GREECE YAWN WIDE...

...POURING THOUSANDS OF SOULS FROM GAEA'S WOMB!

IT IS *DONE*, GODDESSES. WE ARE ALL OF US *MIDWIVES* TO GAEA'S *NEW OFFSPRING!*

NOW LET US PRAY THAT THESE CHILDREN DO NOT *FAIL* US -- FOR THE FATE OF *MEN* AND *GODS* RESTS IN THEIR HANDS!

ATHENA... DO NOT GO YET. *LOOK!*

ONE *SOUL* YET *REMAINS* IN DARK LIMBO, BUT IT *WAILS NOT* LIKE THE OTHERS!

AYE, APHRODITE. THAT ONE HAS A *SPECIAL* DESTINY. BUT HER TIME IS *NOT YET COME!*

FOLLOW ME, *MIDWIVES.* WE HAVE MUCH STILL TO DO.

EARTH... A ONCE TRANQUIL LAKE BUBBLES WITH THE SOFT BREATH OF CREATION...

...UNTIL ITS SURFACE BURSTS...

...AND SHE WHO IS CALLED *HIPPOLYTE* BECOMES THE *FIRST* TO RISE AND KISS APOLLO'S SUN DRENCHED SKIES

BESIDE HER, HER SISTER *ANTIOPE* IS REBORN.

AND AROUND HER, THOUSANDS *MORE* RE-EMBODIED SOULS EMERGE -- EACH DRINKING JOY- FULLY THE BREATH OF *NEW LIFE!*

9

THE WATERS CHURN ANEW -- AND STILL *MORE* CHILDREN OF THE MIDWIVES ARE REBORN!

AMONG THEM IS MENALIPPE -- SHE WHOSE *ONENESS* WITH NATURE SHALL MAKE HER *ORACLE* OF THE GODS' NEW RACE.

AND AELLA -- WHOSE COURAGE SHALL BE AS THE HAWK'S --

-- YET WHOSE *HEART* IS SO EASILY *SWAYED.*

BUT THEN, AS THE BLESSED LAKE'S WATERS GROW STILL --

DAUGHTERS! ATTEND ME!

-- A VISION... AND THE NEW-BORN ARE SUDDENLY *HUSHED.*

YOU ARE A *CHOSEN RACE* -- BORN TO LEAD HUMANITY IN THE WAYS OF *VIRTUE* -- *THE WAY OF GAEA!* THROUGH YOU, ALL MEN SHALL KNOW US BETTER -- AND WORSHIP US ALWAYS!

HESTIA SHALL BUILD YOU A CITY AND WARM YOUR HEARTHS AND IT IS FAIR *APHRODITE* WHO GRANTS YOU *THE GREAT GIFT OF LOVE!*

FOREVERMORE, YOU SHALL FIND *STRENGTH* IN THESE GIFTS. THEY ARE YOUR MOST *SACRED BIRTHRIGHT* -- THEY ARE YOUR *POWER!*

THEREFORE DOES *ATHENA* GRANT YOU *WISDOM,* THAT YOU MAY BE GUIDED BY THE LIGHT OF *TRUTH* AND *JUSTICE!*

I, *ARTEMIS,* GRANT YOU SKILL IN THE *HUNT!* DEMETER SHALL MAKE YOUR FIELDS *FRUITFUL!*

"YOU, HIPPOLYTE, SHALL BE QUEEN OVER ALL MY DAUGHTERS!"

"ANTIOPE, YOU SHALL RULE BY YOUR SISTER'S SIDE!"

"SEE TO IT THAT THESE GIFTS WE GIVE ARE *NEVER ABUSED!*"

"AND WEAR YOU *BOTH* THESE SYMBOLS OF OUR TRUST -- *GAEA'S GIRDLE!* NEVER LET IT BE REMOVED!"

"NOW GO, MY DAUGHTERS! HENCEFORTH, YOU SHALL FORM A SACRED *SISTERHOOD!* HENCEFORTH, YOU SHALL BE *AMAZONS!*"

"AND *NONE* MAY RESIST YOUR POWER!"

THE ECHOES OF ARTEMIS' WORDS FADE-- AND THE WINDS OF TIME CARRY THE YEARS AWAY. BUT UPON THE GALE RIDE THE VOICES OF POETS!

LISTEN! FROM THEIR MOUTHS POUR WONDROUS TALES--TALES OF A CITY-STATE GOVERNED SOLELY BY WOMEN--OF A PLACE WHERE COMPASSION AND JUSTICE REIGN-- A PLACE THE POETS CALL THEMYSCIRA! IN THIS WAY, THE POWER AND THE GLORY OF THE AMAZONS IS SOON KNOWN THROUGH- OUT ALL GREECE!

YET, KINGS DO NOT LIKE POPULARITY--NOR DO THEY LIKE POWER--UNLESS IT IS THEIR OWN! THUS THE RULERS OF GREECE GROW JEALOUS OF THE AMAZONS. AND SO THE POETS ARE SEIZED--AND BRIBED--AND THREATENED.

NOW ARE TALES TOLD OF AMAZON ATROCITIES-- OF MURDERS, WARS AND THIEVERY! NOW DO THE GODESSES CRY FROM OLYMPUS' HEIGHTS! FOR THEIR DAUGHTERS HAVE BECOME OUTCASTS--REGARDED BY ALL MANKIND AS DIFFERENT...STRANGE...AND EVEN INHUMAN! NOW, MANKIND UNDERSTANDS THE AMAZONS NOT AT ALL. AND THAT WHICH MAN DOES NOT UNDERSTAND, HE FEARS!

MY DEAREST HERACLES-- MUST YOU LEAVE SO SOON?

AFTER ALL, IT IS NOT EVERYDAY THAT I PLY MY TRADE WITH A DEMI-GOD!

MY DALLIANCE WITH YOU WAS BUT A BRIEF RESPITE FROM THE TASKS MY RULER EURYSTHEUS HAS SET ME. I MUST GO.

BUT IN TRUTH, I SHALL BE GLAD WHEN MY LABORS ARE DONE. HERA HAS SET A MADNESS UPON ME WHICH BURNS MY SOUL-- AND IT SHALL NOT COOL UNTIL I HAVE DONE EURYSTHEUS' WILL!

COME BACK TO BED, MY HERO. EURYSTHEUS CAN WAIT--

--AND SO CAN THE AMAZON QUEEN WHO CALLS YOU "EURYSTHEUS' TRAINED DOG!"

SILENCE, WENCH! HERACLES IS NO MAN'S PET!

OOOH! SEE HOW HE *BARKS* AND *GROWLS!* HIPPOLYTE WAS *RIGHT*...

...YOU'D LOOK SO HANDSOME ON A *LEASH!*

I SAID *BE SILENT!*

NO WOMAN -- NOR MAN -- CAN SAY SUCH A THING ABOUT *HERACLES!*

HUSH, MY LOVER -- BE CONTENT!

I MERELY *REPEAT* WHAT I'VE HEARD... WHAT *EVERYONE* HAS HEARD...

...FROM THE LIPS OF THE *AMAZON QUEEN!*

HERACLES, YOUR LEGIONS ARE ASSEMBLED.

THEN LET US RIDE, *THESEUS!*

NO LONGER DO I DESIRE TO *PLEASE* WOMEN...

...ONLY TO *CONQUER* THEM!

"*EXCELLENT,* MY DEAR, *EXCELLENT!* YOUR LIES HAVE *STIRRED* SUCH HATRED WITHIN HIM!"

"*IRONIC,* IS IT NOT? ALMOST *LAUGHABLE!*"

"WHILE HE BURNS WITH *HERA'S* MADNESS..."

"YOUR SOUL BURNS AS MY SPIRIT CONSUMES YOU!"

"BUT THEN... YOU HAVE *SERVED YOUR PURPOSE.*"

ARES IS WELL *PLEASED!*

12

20

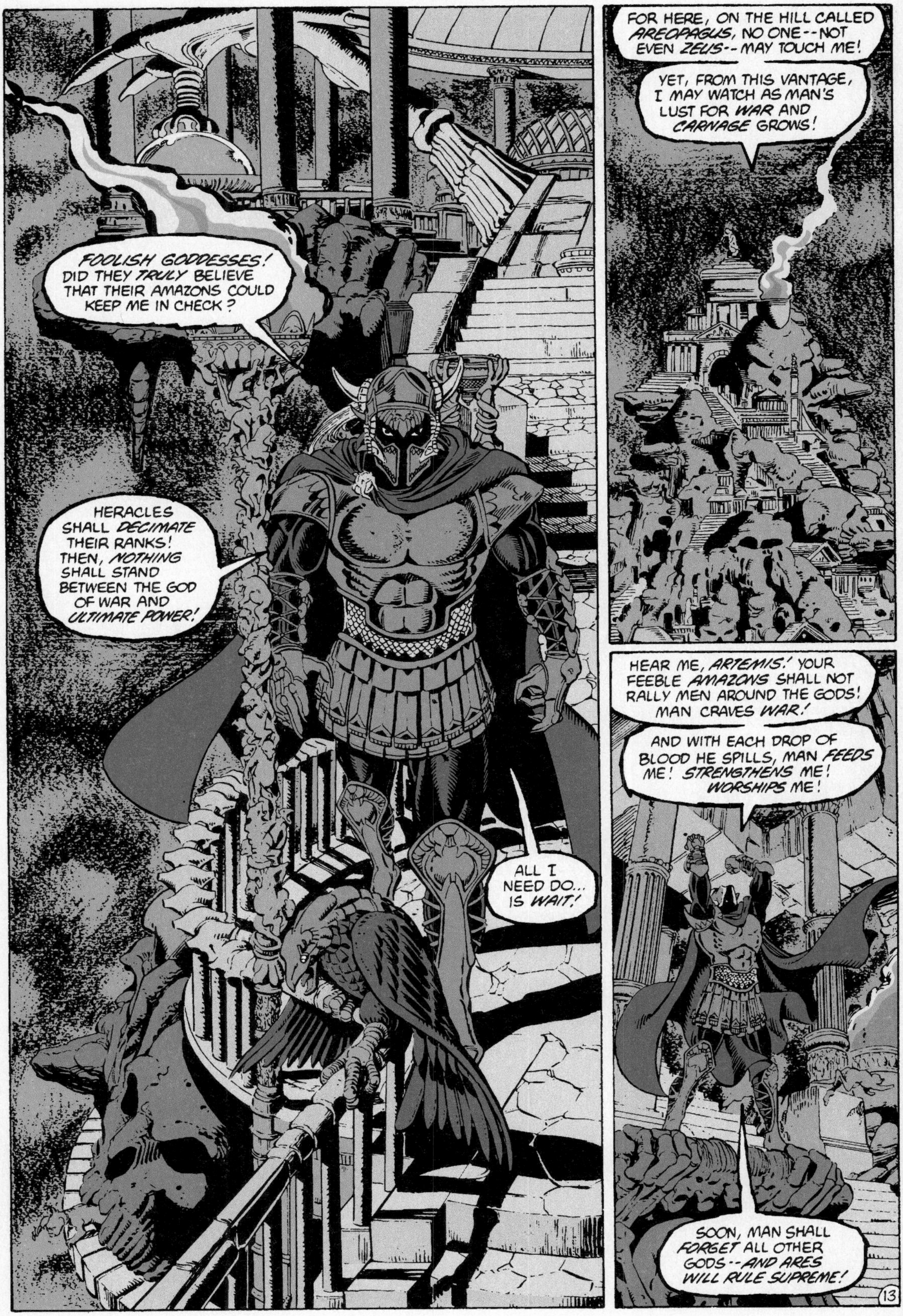
FOOLISH GODDESSES! DID THEY TRULY BELIEVE THAT THEIR AMAZONS COULD KEEP ME IN CHECK?
HERACLES SHALL DECIMATE THEIR RANKS! THEN, NOTHING SHALL STAND BETWEEN THE GOD OF WAR AND ULTIMATE POWER!
ALL I NEED DO... IS WAIT!
FOR HERE, ON THE HILL CALLED AREOPAGUS, NO ONE--NOT EVEN ZEUS--MAY TOUCH ME!
YET, FROM THIS VANTAGE, I MAY WATCH AS MAN'S LUST FOR WAR AND CARNAGE GROWS!
HEAR ME, ARTEMIS! YOUR FEEBLE AMAZONS SHALL NOT RALLY MEN AROUND THE GODS! MAN CRAVES WAR!
AND WITH EACH DROP OF BLOOD HE SPILLS, MAN FEEDS ME! STRENGTHENS ME! WORSHIPS ME!
SOON, MAN SHALL FORGET ALL OTHER GODS--AND ARES WILL RULE SUPREME!
13

IN TRUTH, *HERACLES* -- NEVER HAVE I SEEN YOU IN GREATER *AGONY!*

THE CLOSER WE TRAVEL TO THE AMAZONS' CITY, THE *HOTTER* YOUR *MADNESS* BURNS!

REMIND ME NOT OF HERA'S CURSE, *THESEUS!*

I THINK ONLY OF THE HARLOT *HIPPOLYTE* -- AND HER BRASH *BOASTS!*

FOR THERE AT LAST LIES *THEMYSCIRA!* SOON SHALL HIPPOLYTE'S *AMAZONS* KNOW THE PAIN OF UTTER DEFEAT!

YOU SEE, *THESEUS?* THEY HIDE IN THE TREES LIKE *VIPERS!*

I AM *HERACLES OF THEBES!* I DEMAND TO SEE YOUR QUEEN!

INTRUDERS! *HALT* AND BE RECOGNIZED!

"HIPPOLYTE *KNOWS* OF YOUR COMING, MIGHTY ONE.

"OUR QUEEN WOULD SPEAK WITH YOU IN YONDER CLEARING."

SO, *MENALIPPE* -- THAT WHICH YOU *FORETOLD* HAS COME TO PASS! THE ARMY OF *HERACLES* AWAITS WITHOUT OUR WALLS.

AYE, *ANTIOPE* -- AND I AM FILLED WITH *DREAD* THIS DAY!

NOT *I*, ORACLE.

I AM FILLED ONLY WITH *LUST FOR REVENGE!* MAN HAS *HUNTED* US FOR TOO LONG! I SAY WE *KILL* THIS LOT AS A *WARNING TO ALL!*

HUSH, AELLA... MURDER IS *ARES'* WAY, NOT OURS!

SO -- *YOU* ARE HIPPOLYTE.

AND *YOU* ARE THE FABLED *HERACLES.*

14

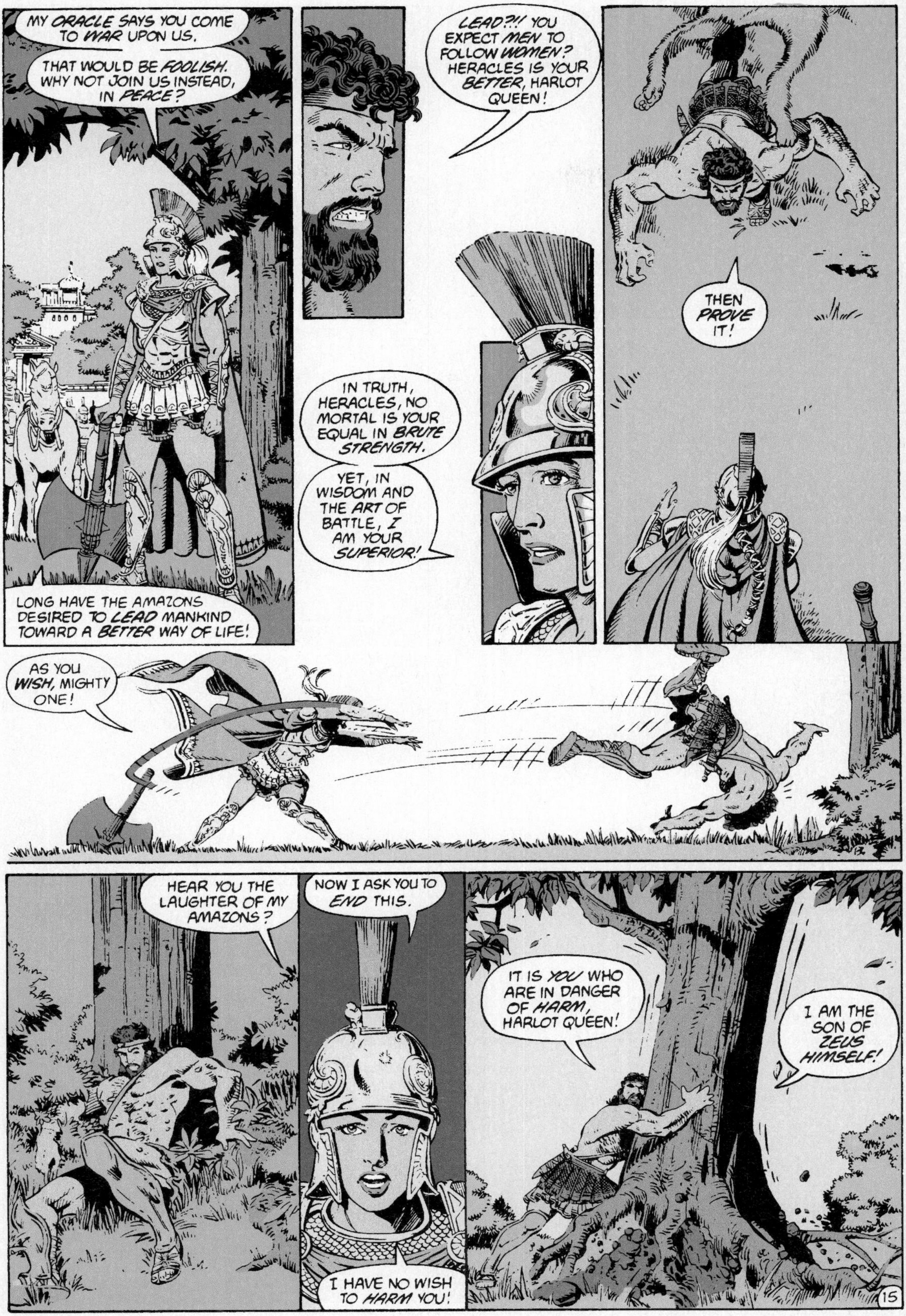

MY ORACLE SAYS YOU COME TO WAR UPON US.
THAT WOULD BE FOOLISH. WHY NOT JOIN US INSTEAD, IN PEACE?
LONG HAVE THE AMAZONS DESIRED TO LEAD MANKIND TOWARD A BETTER WAY OF LIFE!
LEAD?!! YOU EXPECT MEN TO FOLLOW WOMEN? HERACLES IS YOUR BETTER, HARLOT QUEEN!
IN TRUTH, HERACLES, NO MORTAL IS YOUR EQUAL IN BRUTE STRENGTH.
YET, IN WISDOM AND THE ART OF BATTLE, I AM YOUR SUPERIOR!
THEN PROVE IT!
AS YOU WISH, MIGHTY ONE!
HEAR YOU THE LAUGHTER OF MY AMAZONS?
NOW I ASK YOU TO END THIS.
I HAVE NO WISH TO HARM YOU!
IT IS YOU WHO ARE IN DANGER OF HARM, HARLOT QUEEN!
I AM THE SON OF ZEUS HIMSELF!
15

HIS *BLOOD*-- HIS *POWER*-- FLOWS THROUGH MY VEINS!

AYE, HERACLES! BUT YOUR *MOTHER* WAS A *MORTAL!*

AND MORTALS *MAKE MISTAKES!*

KRASH

SURRENDER OR DIE!

THE CHOICE IS YOURS!

AND WITH HIPPOLYTE'S WORDS, A STILLNESS FALLS OVER ALL-- AS WAR OR PEACE RESTS ON HERACLES' REPLY.

HA! BY ZEUS, GIRL-- HERACLES IS *IMPRESSED!*

MEN! LAY BACK!

THE AMAZONS ARE *WORTHY* ALLIES INDEED!

16

LAUGHTER -- THE UNIVERSAL LANGUAGE. HEALER OF DISCORD. MOTHER OF UNITY.

TONIGHT, ITS SONG DANCES BRIGHTLY BENEATH A FULL MOON...

...RISING MERRILY FROM THE LIPS OF MEN -- AND WOMEN.

THIS GATHERING IS HERACLES' IDEA -- A GESTURE OF GOOD WILL TOWARD THE WOMEN HE NOW CALLS FRIENDS!

YET, NOT ALL AMAZONS ARE CONTENT THIS NIGHT.

THESEUS AND ANTIOPE SEEM SO HAPPY!

BUT, I HAVE READ THE SIGNS. THEY FORETOLD DISASTER ON ON THIS DAY!

"HOW COULD I HAVE BEEN SO WRONG?"

HERACLES... I REJOICE UNTO MY VERY SOUL!

THIS IS HOW MEN AND WOMEN SHOULD FACE ONE ANOTHER-- NOT WITH SWORDS, BUT WITH LOVE, LAUGHTER, AND EQUALITY.

I SHOULD NEVER HAVE LISTENED TO MENALIPPE!

ORACLES SEE ONLY WHAT MIGHT BE. MORTALS CREATE THEIR OWN DESTINIES.

AND WHEN I GAZE UPON YOUR BEAUTY, FAIR HIPPOLYTE...

...I FEEL THAT MY DESTINY MUST BE EVERMORE AT YOUR SIDE!

HERACLES, I --

SPEAK NOT, MY QUEEN. DRINK WITH ME.

TO THE UNITY OF MAN AND WOMAN!

DRINK!

WHY... MY INCOMPARABLE HIPPOLYTE! DOES MY POTION DISPLEASE YOU?

ALLOW GALLANT HERACLES TO RELIEVE YOU...

...OF YOUR MISERY!

17

SEMI-CONSCIOUSNESS: IT IS LIKE A SEA OF TAR THROUGH WHICH HIPPOLYTE STRIVES TO SURFACE.

AND FROM SOMEWHERE BEYOND THE INKY BLACKNESS, SHE HEARS THE WOEFUL CRIES OF HER AMAZON SISTERS!

THEY WAIL AS HERACLES' MEN TAKE UP ARMS AGAINST THEM!

WAIL AS THEIR HOMES ARE TORCHED, THEIR BODIES RAVAGED, THEIR PRIDE STRIPPED AWAY!

AND FAINTLY, RISING ABOVE THE CHAOS AND BRUTALITY, IS ANOTHER SOUND...

...THE COLD AND DISTANT ECHO OF ARES' LAUGHTER!

I SEE YOU ARE FINALLY COMING TO YOUR SENSES, MY QUEEN!

GOOD!

HOW STUPID YOU HAVE BEEN! DID YOU TRULY BELIEVE I WOULD BE YOUR ALLY?

NO WOMAN IS HERACLES' EQUAL! AND NO WOMAN WITHHOLDS HERSELF FROM HERACLES' EMBRACE-- EVEN IF SHE MUST BE READIED BY DRUG AND CHAIN!

NOW, I HAVE MADE YOU A REAL WOMAN!

THIS GIRDLE I TAKE AS A PRIZE-- A SYMBOL OF MY CONQUEST!

HOW DEARLY I WOULD LIKE TO BREAK YOU FURTHER...TO SEE YOU BEG AND PLEAD!

ALAS, EURYSTHEUS' MADNESS LEADS ME ON! I LEAVE FOR TROY TONIGHT.

FAREWELL, AMAZON QUEEN! IT HAS BEEN MOST....AMUSING!

GODDESSES OF OLYMPUS! I BEG YOU-- FORGIVE ME! I HAVE FAILED YOU!

18

NO, DAUGHTER... ...YOU HAVE BETRAYED ONLY YOURSELF.

EXAMINE YOURSELF, HIPPOLYTE -- EXAMINE YOUR RACE. ONCE, THE AMAZONS DREAMED OF *LEADING* MANKIND!

BUT YOU CHOSE TO *WITHDRAW* FROM HUMANITY -- *TO IGNORE THE PURPOSE FOR WHICH YOU WERE CREATED* -- AND YOU GREW *BITTER* AND *CORRUPT*.

HAVE YOU FORGOTTEN THE *SOURCE* OF YOUR POWER? HAVE YOU FORGOTTEN THE *EXAMPLE* YOU WERE TO SET?

PLEASE, ATHENA! *FREE ME!*

I YEARN TO TAKE *REVENGE* UPON THIS...*HERACLES!*

BLOODY VENGEANCE IS *NOT* THE ANSWER, DAUGHTER!

IT IS TIME FOR YOU TO *CLEANSE YOUR SOUL* -- TIME TO *REDEDICATE* YOURSELF TO THAT WHICH *GAEA* GAVE YOU! *ONLY THEN* SHALL YOU BE FREE!

"LOOK UPON MY FACE, HIPPOLYTE! SEE THERE THE TRUTH OF WHAT I SAY!"

"THEN, AS I LEAVE YOU..."

EH?

YOU! AMAZON! WHAT *BLASPHEMOUS TRICKERY* ARE YOU --

BY THE GODS!

GREETINGS, BROTHER.

THIS IS WHAT YOU DESIRE, IS IT NOT?

THEN YOU SHALL HAVE IT...

"...BATHE IN THE LIGHT OF MY WISDOM!"

...BUT NOT AS YOU IMAGINED!

YOUR KIND SHALL IMPRISON MINE *NO MORE!*

19

27

NOW, SUDDENLY, HIPPOLYTE IS EVERYWHERE--SURPRISING HER CAPTORS--FREEING HER SISTERS-- SOUNDING THE CALL TO ARMS! YET, WITH THAT CALL, SHE WHISPERS A CAUTION...

"AMAZONS, REMEMBER THE SOURCE OF OUR POWER-- REMEMBER GAEA'S WAY!"

BUT THEY HEED THEIR QUEEN *NOT!*

FOR THEIR SOULS BOIL WITH *RAGE*-- THEIR WEAPONS, LIKE THE FANGS OF MADDENED DOGS, *DRINK DEEP* OF THEIR ENEMIES -- AND THE GROUND AT THEIR FEET IS SOON COVERED WITH *CRIMSON!*

AND LIKE SOME CRAZED, BLOODTHIRSTY *BEAST,* THE BATTLE GROWS OUT OF *CONTROL!*

THEN DOES *HORROR* SCREAM WITHIN HIPPOLYTE'S HEAD! FOR HER EYES ARE FILLED WITH SIGHTS OF *BLASPHEMY*--

--OF SISTERS WHO KILL WITH *HEARTLESS* PRECISION...

...OF *ONE* SISTER WHO KILLS...

...WITH EYES OF *SPARKLING* PLEASURE!

WHEN IT FINALLY *ENDS*-- WHEN THE SCREAMS OF THE ENEMY HAVE BEEN *SILENCED*--

-- THE VICTORY CRIES OF THE AMAZONS BUFFET HIPPOLYTE LIKE A COLD AND CALLOUS WIND.

WELL DONE, MY SISTERS! NOW LET US RIDE AFTER *HERACLES*! LET US *SACK* HIS HOME AND *RECLAIM* YOUR GIRDLE!

THEN, WE SHALL *SLIT* HIS ACCURSED THROAT FROM *EAR TO EAR*!

NO, ANTIOPE. *NEVER* VENGEANCE-- *NEVER AGAIN*!

ATHENA HAS SPOKEN TO ME. SHE WAITS FOR US BY THE SHORES OF THE AEGEAN.

ATHENA?!!

WHERE WAS SHE WHEN HERACLES MURDERED HALF MY SISTERS? WHERE WAS *SHE* WHEN MANKIND *SHUNNED* US, *HOUNDED* US-- *HUNTED* US?

RENOUNCE ATHENA, MY SISTER! *AVENGE* YOUR AMAZON DEAD!

THAT IS *ARES'* WAY, ANTIOPE. WE ACHIEVE NO GLORY BY EMBRACING THE *DARK GOD'S* POWER!

ARE YOU SO *NAIVE,* MENALIPPE? *ARES* IS NOT OUR ENEMY! WE *NEED* THE GOD OF WAR MERELY TO *SURVIVE*!

HIPPOLYTE, I GIVE YOU MY *GIRDLE*! FROM THIS DAY FORWARD, I TAKE *NOTHING* FROM OLYMPUS.

NO, ANTIOPE! I *BEG* YOU-- COME WITH US!

I CANNOT. MAY THE *FATES* BE WITH YOU, HIPPOLYTE!

I SHALL ALWAYS LOVE YOU!

THE HOOFBEAT OF *ANTIOPE* AND HER FOLLOWERS FADE INTO *NOTHINGNESS*...

㉑

...AND THEN, THE LONG WALK TO THE AEGEAN.

MY DAUGHTERS-- YOU HAVE *FAILED* US! YOU HAVE FORGOTTEN THE *SOURCE* OF YOUR POWER-- FORGOTTEN THE *TRUST* PLACED IN YOU!

FOR THESE FAILURES, YOU MUST DO A *PENANCE!* ONE IN WHICH THERE IS *NEW HONOR*-- NEW *RESPONSIBILITY!* WE SHALL SEND YOU TO AN ISLAND-- BENEATH WHICH LIES AN *UNSPEAKABLE EVIL!*

YOU SHALL BE THE *JAILERS* OF THAT EVIL! AS LONG AS YOU REMAIN THERE AND *SHIRK NOT* YOUR NEW CHARGE-- YOU SHALL LIVE AS *IMMORTALS* AND YOUR SOULS SHALL *AGAIN* BECOME *PURE.*

"YET, YOU MUST *EVERMORE* WEAR THE *SYMBOLS* OF YOUR FORMER *BONDAGE*-- AS A REMINDER NEVER TO ERR AGAIN!"

GODDESS-- WHERE *IS* THIS ISLAND?

FOR THIS AID, WE THANK YOU, GOD OF THE SEAS!

I AM *GLAD* TO HELP!

ARES DID *MURDER* MY OWN SON, DEMETER.

"WHERE MAN MAY NOT EASILY *DISCOVER* IT. IT APPEARS A *PARADISE!* AND SO IT *SHALL* BE-- AS LONG AS YOU GUARD ITS *VILE SECRET* WELL...

"...AND LET NO *MORTAL* MAN TRESPASS ITS GROUNDS!"

"BUT ATTEND YOU NOW!

"POSEIDON CLEARS A PATH TO YOUR NEW HOME!"

"BESIDES, THE *ORACLES* TELL ME THAT YOUR *AMAZONS* ARE MORE THAN THEY SEEM-- THAT UPON *ONE* OF THEIR KIND RESTS NOT ONLY THE *FUTURE* OF THE GODS...

"...BUT OF ALL *MANKIND!*"

22

THE DAYS BRING *FATIGUE,* THE NIGHTS ARE BITTER *COLD*-- AND AT EVERY TURN, THE FOLLOWERS OF HIPPOLYTE FEAR THAT POSEIDON'S *TUNNEL* WILL SUDDENLY *FALTER*-- AND COME *THUNDERING DOWN* AROUND THEM! YET, THROUGHOUT THEIR *THREE MONTHS'* JOURNEY, THE WATERY PATHWAY *HOLDS.* AND AS THEIR FEET TOUCH THE *SOIL* OF PARADISE ISLAND, EACH AMAZON KNOWS THE GIFT OF *IMMORTALITY!* THEREBY ARE THEY *REJUVENATED*-- AND SET THEMSELVES, HEART AND SOUL, TO WORK...

...BUILDING...

...CLEARING...

...PLANNING...

...KEEPING THEIR ARTS AND HISTORY ALIVE...

...ERECTING GREAT HALLS OF JUSTICE...

...SCULPTING *ICONS* TO THE GLORY OF THE GODS!

THUS DO THE *CENTURIES* PASS AND UPON THE GROUNDS OF *PARADISE,* THE AMAZON NATION RENEWS ITS SENSE OF *PURPOSE* AND *DISCIPLINE.*

...STILL THERE ARE THOSE WHO *FALL IN BATTLE!* FOR THE EVIL *SECRET* WITHIN THE ISLAND IS NOT EASY TO CONTAIN!

FOR THOUGH THE AMAZONS KNOW *IMMORTALITY*-- THOUGH THEY NEVER AGE OR HUNGER...

AND THE *BURDEN* OF THE AMAZONS' *RESPONSIBILITY* IS HEAVY INDEED!

23

OUTSIDE, BEYOND THE SEAS, THE WORLD OF MAN CHANGES. GREAT CIVILIZATIONS RISE AND FALL.

BUT THE AMAZONS KNOW *NOTHING* OF THIS. THEY HEAR ONLY THE VOICES OF THE OLD GODS GROW MORE DISTANT --AS IF OLYMPUS ITSELF WERE BEING SWALLOWED IN THE CLOUDS!

UNTIL FINALLY, OF ALL WHO DID ONCE COMMUNE WITH THE GODS, ONLY *MENALIPPE* REMAINS ABLE.

THUS IT IS THAT ON THIS FATEFUL NIGHT, DURING THE 30TH CENTENNIAL OF PARADISE ISLAND, THE ORACLE OF THE AMAZONS DOES WHAT HER QUEEN REQUESTS...

TELL ME--DO THE SIGNS SAY ANYTHING ABOUT THIS FEELING WITHIN ME?

WHAT *IS* THIS STRANGE *YEARNING* WHICH HOLDS ME SO?--THAT HAS HAD ME IN ITS GRIP LO THESE *MANY MONTHS!*

BE AT *PEACE*, HIPPOLYTE! YOU FEEL THE CALL OF A *GREAT DESTINY!*

KNOW THAT YOU--AND *ALL* ORIGINAL AMAZONS-- ARE *REINCARNATIONS!* ALL OF US KNEW LIFE *BEFORE* THE MIDWIVES PLUCKED US FROM GAEA'S *WOMB.*

BUT *ONLY YOU*, MY QUEEN, WERE *PREGNANT* AT THE TIME OF YOUR DEATH! NOW, YOU HEAR THE CALL OF YOUR *UNBORN DAUGHTER!*

THIS *YEARNING*, THEN-- IT IS A YEARNING --*FOR MY CHILD.!!?*

MENALIPPE!

"AYE! AND IF YOU WOULD SATISFY IT, FOLLOW *ARTEMIS'* BIDDING!"

"GO AT SUNRISE TO THE SHORE--AND KNEEL THERE!"

"THEN, FROM THE CLAY OF PARADISE, FORM YOU AN IMAGE!"

"YOUR HEART SHALL RACE WITH ANTICIPATION-- BUT STEADY YOURSELF..."

"...AND SHAPE THE IMAGE WITH *CARE!*"

"THEN OPEN YOURSELF TO FAIR *ARTEMIS*-- THAT THE *MID-WIFE* OF ALL OLYMPUS MAY ENTER YOU!"

24

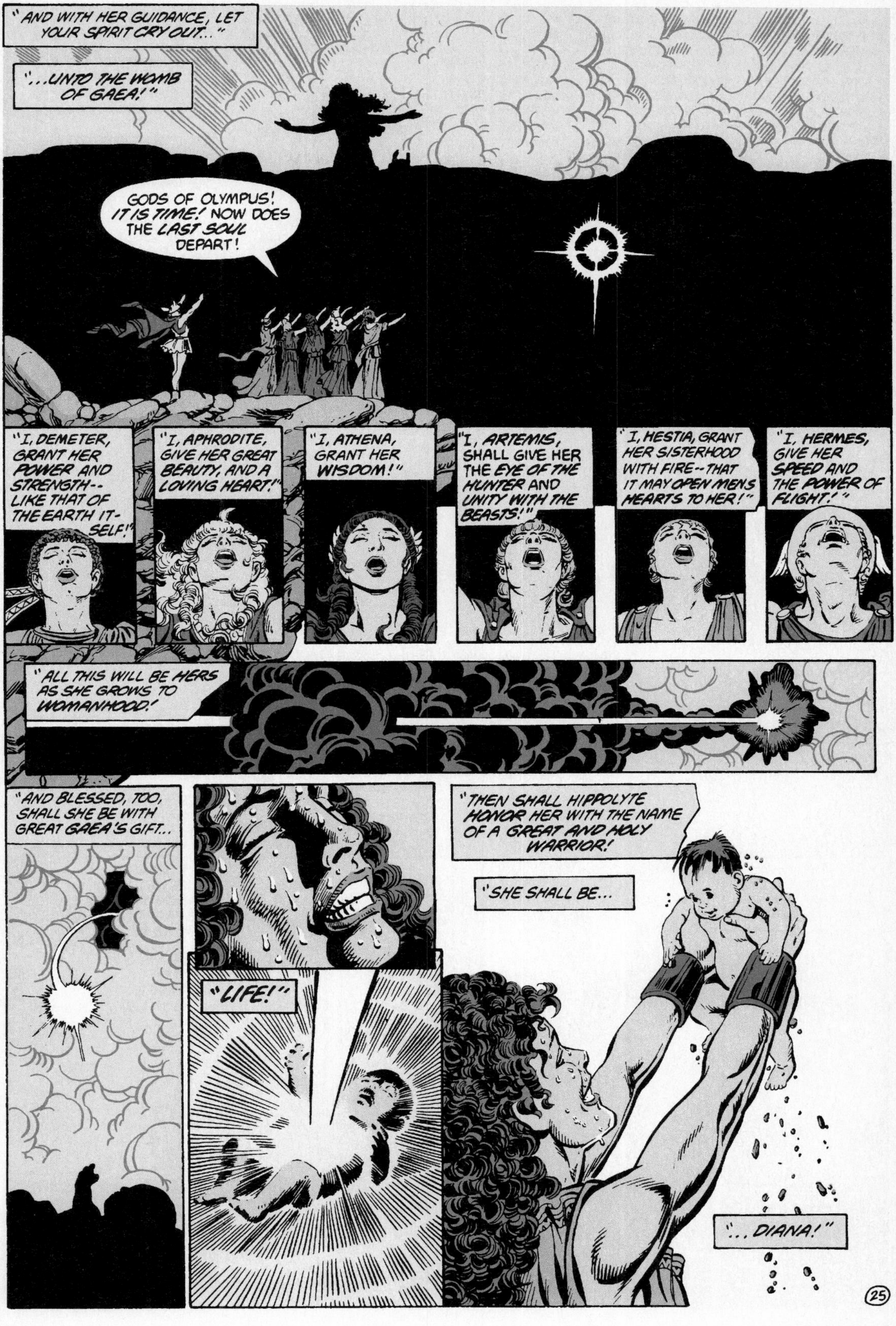
"AND WITH HER GUIDANCE, LET YOUR SPIRIT CRY OUT..."
"...UNTO THE WOMB OF GAEA!"
GODS OF OLYMPUS! IT IS TIME! NOW DOES THE LAST SOUL DEPART!
"I, DEMETER, GRANT HER POWER AND STRENGTH-- LIKE THAT OF THE EARTH IT-SELF!"
"I, APHRODITE, GIVE HER GREAT BEAUTY, AND A LOVING HEART!"
"I, ATHENA, GRANT HER WISDOM!"
"I, ARTEMIS, SHALL GIVE HER THE EYE OF THE HUNTER AND UNITY WITH THE BEASTS!"
"I, HESTIA, GRANT HER SISTERHOOD WITH FIRE--THAT IT MAY OPEN MENS HEARTS TO HER!"
"I, HERMES, GIVE HER SPEED AND THE POWER OF FLIGHT!"
"ALL THIS WILL BE HERS AS SHE GROWS TO WOMANHOOD!
"AND BLESSED, TOO, SHALL SHE BE WITH GREAT GAEA'S GIFT...
"LIFE!"
"THEN SHALL HIPPOLYTE HONOR HER WITH THE NAME OF A GREAT AND HOLY WARRIOR!
"SHE SHALL BE...
"...DIANA!"
25

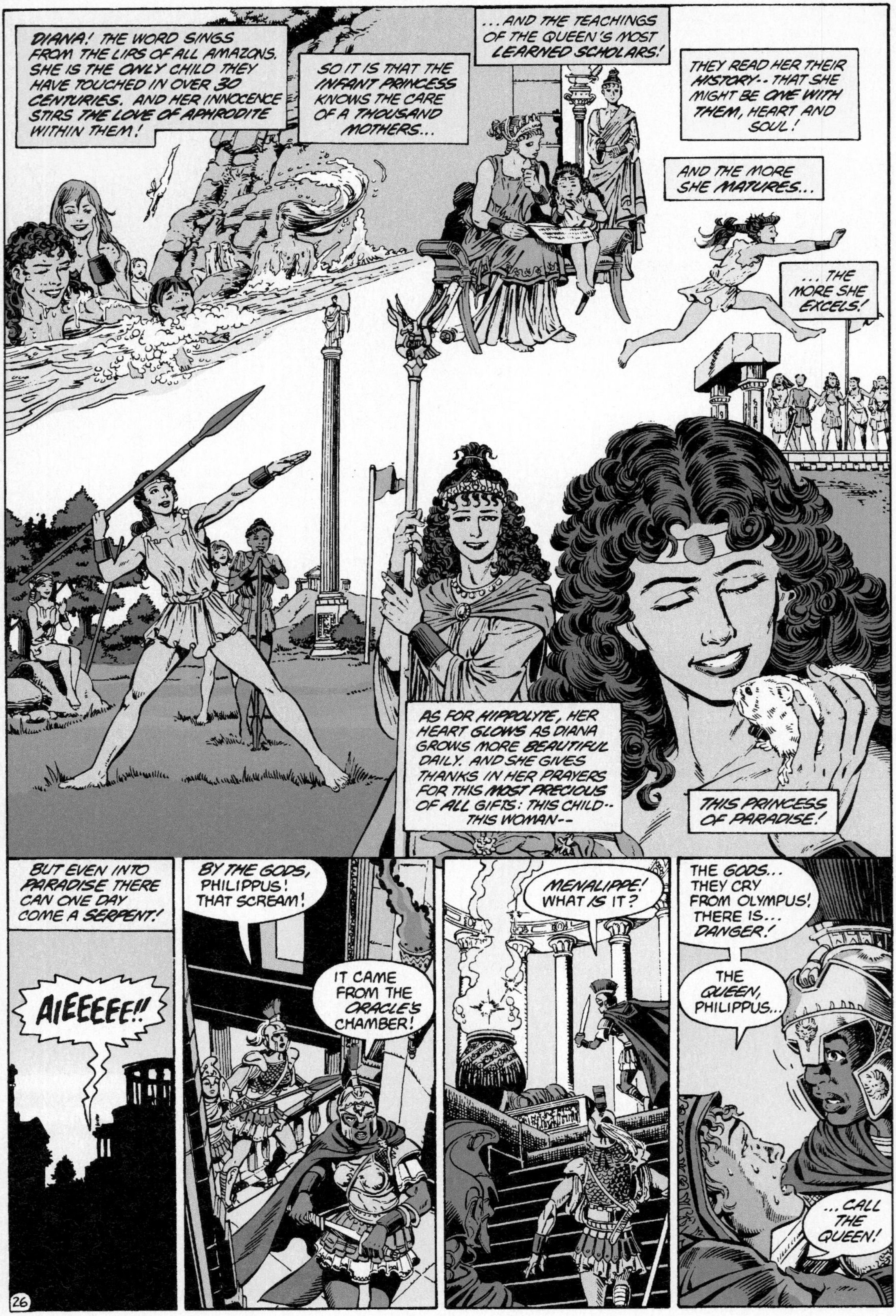
DIANA! THE WORD SINGS FROM THE LIPS OF ALL AMAZONS. SHE IS THE ONLY CHILD THEY HAVE TOUCHED IN OVER 30 CENTURIES. AND HER INNOCENCE STIRS THE LOVE OF APHRODITE WITHIN THEM!
SO IT IS THAT THE INFANT PRINCESS KNOWS THE CARE OF A THOUSAND MOTHERS...
...AND THE TEACHINGS OF THE QUEEN'S MOST LEARNED SCHOLARS!
THEY READ HER THEIR HISTORY--THAT SHE MIGHT BE ONE WITH THEM, HEART AND SOUL!
AND THE MORE SHE MATURES...
...THE MORE SHE EXCELS!
AS FOR HIPPOLYTE, HER HEART GLOWS AS DIANA GROWS MORE BEAUTIFUL DAILY. AND SHE GIVES THANKS IN HER PRAYERS FOR THIS MOST PRECIOUS OF ALL GIFTS: THIS CHILD--THIS WOMAN--
THIS PRINCESS OF PARADISE!
BUT EVEN INTO PARADISE THERE CAN ONE DAY COME A SERPENT!
AIEEEEE!!
BY THE GODS, PHILIPPUS! THAT SCREAM!
IT CAME FROM THE ORACLE'S CHAMBER!
MENALIPPE! WHAT IS IT?
THE GODS... THEY CRY FROM OLYMPUS! THERE IS... DANGER!
THE QUEEN, PHILIPPUS...
...CALL THE QUEEN!
26

FOOTFALLS ECHO THROUGH THE PALACE. THEN, MENALIPPE TELLS HER TALE -- OF THE GODS CRYING OUT IN TERROR -- OF ARES GONE INSANE -- HIS MIGHT MULTIPLIED A THOUSAND-FOLD -- HIS BEING DRAWN MAGNET-LIKE TO SOME TERRIBLE POWER WITHIN MAN'S WORLD!

THIS "POWER", MENALIPPE -- WHAT IS ITS NATURE?

I KNOW NOT, MY QUEEN!

BUT WITH IT, ARES MAY CONSUME THE VERY EARTH ITSELF -- AND EVEN PARADISE SHALL NOT BE SPARED!

AND WHAT OF THE GODS?

NO, I -- I KNOW NOT WHY. BUT WE ARE COMMANDED TO CHOOSE A CHAMPION -- THE VERY BEST AMONG US! SHE SHALL PROVE HERSELF THROUGH TOURNAMENT AND THE TRIAL OF FLASHING THUNDER!

SHE ALONE CAN SAVE US AND SHE ALONE SHALL FACE ARES IN THE WORLD OF MAN!

CAN THEY NOT STOP MAD ARES?

IF THE GODS WILL IT, IT SHALL BE DONE! PROCLAIM IT THROUGH-OUT PARADISE! THERE SHALL BE A TOURNAMENT ON THE 'MORROW!

AND THERE--

-- SHALL A CHAMPION BE BORN!

AYE. A CHAMPION. YET HOW CAN EVEN THE BEST OF US SUCCEED...

MOTHER, I -- FORGIVE ME. I OVERHEARD YOU BY YOUR LEAVE, I WISH TO BE INCLUDED IN THIS TOURNAMENT.

NO, DIANA! YOU ARE BUT A CHILD!

...WHERE THE GODS DARE NOT GO?

I AM AN AMAZON, MOTHER! I WEAR THE MARK, LIKE ALL MY SISTERS!

I HAVE NO INTENSION OF LOSING YOU, DAUGHTER -- EVER! THE ANSWER IS NO!

BUT...

SILENCE! I AM YOUR QUEEN AS WELL AS YOUR MOTHER! AND I HAVE SPOKEN!

IT IS SO... UNFAIR! WAS I BORN ONLY TO BE CODDLED LIKE SOME ETERNAL INFANT?

AM I NOT AN AMAZON? AM I NOT A WOMAN?

OH, GODS OF OLYMPUS! THOUGH I LOVE PARADISE, I YEARN FOR MORE FROM MY LIFE...

...I YEARN FOR PURPOSE!

AYE, DIANA! AND PURPOSE YOU SHALL HAVE! THE TIME HAS COME!

27

35

MORNING:

OUR HERALDS DID SPREAD THE NEWS *SWIFTLY*, MY QUEEN! OUR TWO-HUNDRED *FINEST* WARRIORS HAVE ASSEMBLED...

...TO ACCEPT *THE GODS' CHALLENGE!* BUT, BY YOUR LEAVE, WHY HAVE YOU COMMANDED THEM TO COME *MASKED?*

FOR *THREE THOUSAND* YEARS, THESE AMAZONS HAVE LIVED AS *SISTERS!* NOW, I CALL UPON THEM TO *COMPETE FIERCELY!*

NO AMAZON SHALL *HESITATE* BECAUSE SHE VIES AGAINST A *DEAR FRIEND* -- OR BECAUSE SHE *SYMPATHIZES* WITH ANOTHER'S *TURMOIL.*

THE *SALUTE* IS GIVEN --

--*THE GAMES BEGIN!*

ALL THROUGH THE DAY, AMAZONS PROVE THEIR PROWESS IN CONTESTS OF SKILL AND STRATEGY!

EACH KNOWS THE *SERIOUSNESS* OF THIS TOURNAMENT...

...AND *EACH* PERFORMS AS ONLY AN ATHLETE OF *THREE-THOUSAND YEARS'* EXPERIENCE CAN!

BUT *ONE* THRILLS MORE THAN THE OTHERS. SHE IS KEENEST OF EYE, MOST FLEET OF FOOT..

...AND HER *MIGHT* IS BEYOND COMPARE!

28

ON THE FINAL DAY THIS AMAZON HAS INDEED BESTED ALL-- AND HER SISTERS ROAR THEIR APPROVAL!

SISTER, YOU HAVE PROVEN YOURSELF *CHAMPION* THIS DAY. NOW, IF THE GODS BE PLEASED, YOU SHALL PASS THE *FINAL TEST*-- THAT OF THE *FLASHING THUNDER!*

I AWARD YOU NOW THESE *SILVER BRACELETS!*

"BY THEM, ALL SHALL KNOW YOU AS *THE MOST WORTHY* AMONG US!"

"NOW LET US SEE YOUR FACE..."

...THAT WE, AND THE GODS, MIGHT *SMILE* UPON IT!

GREAT HERA! *IT CANNOT BE!*

I'M *SORRY,* MOTHER-- BUT *ATHENA HERSELF* SPOKE TO ME AS I SAT BY HER STATUE!

I *KNOW* THAT WHAT I DO IS *RIGHT!*

DIANA?!!

NO! I FORBID THIS!

HUSH, MY QUEEN! YOU MUSTN'T!

THE PRINCESS *WON* HER PLACE RIGHT- FULLY. YOU CANNOT FIGHT THE *WILL OF THE GODS!*

29

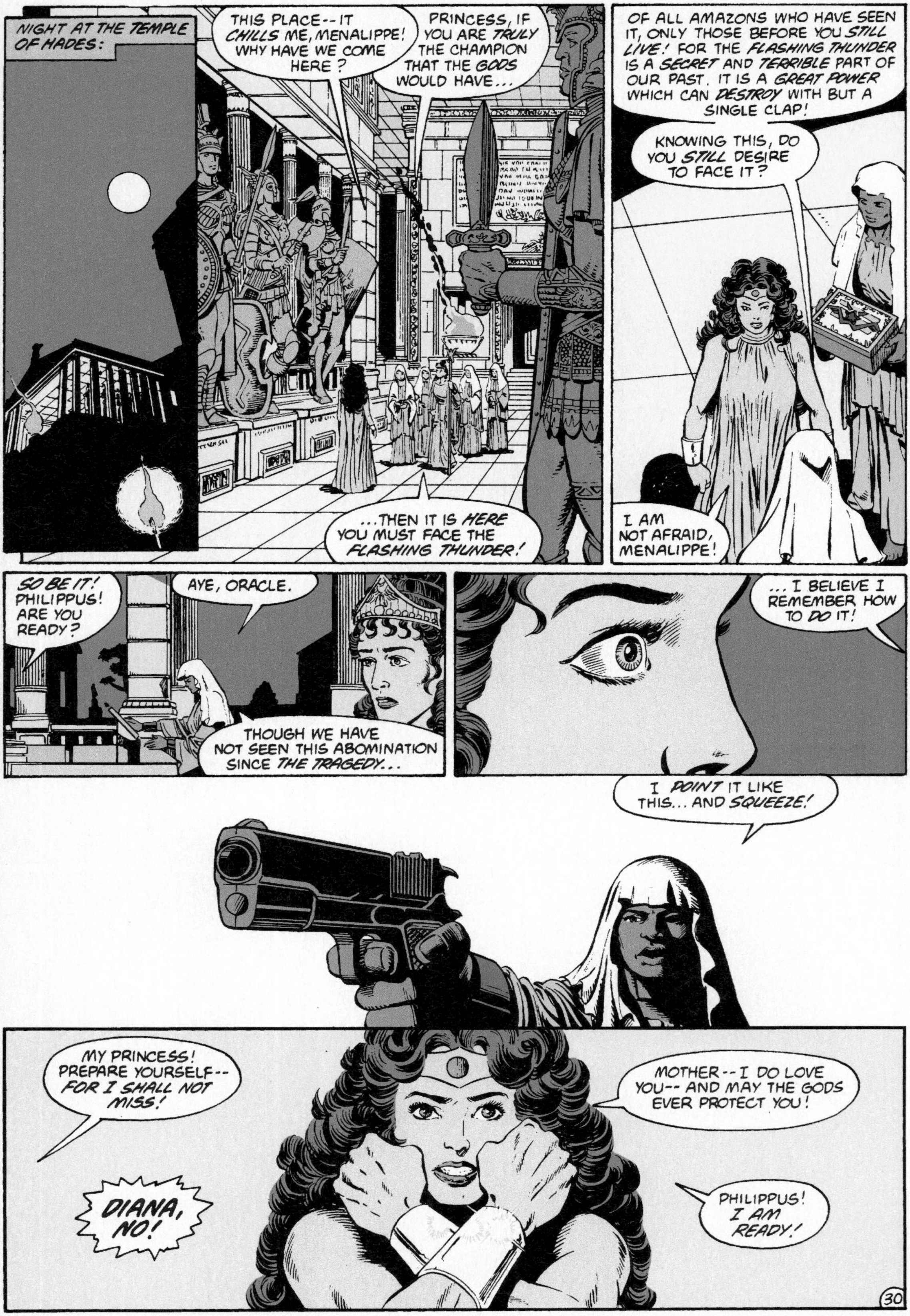
NIGHT AT THE TEMPLE OF HADES:
THIS PLACE--IT CHILLS ME, MENALIPPE! WHY HAVE WE COME HERE?
PRINCESS, IF YOU ARE TRULY THE CHAMPION THAT THE GODS WOULD HAVE...
...THEN IT IS HERE YOU MUST FACE THE FLASHING THUNDER!
OF ALL AMAZONS WHO HAVE SEEN IT, ONLY THOSE BEFORE YOU STILL LIVE! FOR THE FLASHING THUNDER IS A SECRET AND TERRIBLE PART OF OUR PAST. IT IS A GREAT POWER WHICH CAN DESTROY WITH BUT A SINGLE CLAP!
KNOWING THIS, DO YOU STILL DESIRE TO FACE IT?
I AM NOT AFRAID, MENALIPPE!
SO BE IT! PHILIPPUS! ARE YOU READY?
AYE, ORACLE.
THOUGH WE HAVE NOT SEEN THIS ABOMINATION SINCE THE TRAGEDY...
...I BELIEVE I REMEMBER HOW TO DO IT!
I POINT IT LIKE THIS... AND SQUEEZE!
MY PRINCESS! PREPARE YOURSELF-- FOR I SHALL NOT MISS!
MOTHER--I DO LOVE YOU-- AND MAY THE GODS EVER PROTECT YOU!
DIANA, NO!
PHILIPPUS! I AM READY!
30

GREAT HERA!

BY THE GODS! WHAT IS THAT THING? WHERE DID IT COME FROM?

THIS IS NO TIME FOR TALES OF HORROR, MY DAUGHTER!

YOU ARE ALIVE! THAT IS ALL THAT MATTERS!

BUT MOTHER, I --

HUSH! KNOW THAT THE GODS ARE WITH YOU...

NOW IS THE PLAN OF THE GODDESSES CLEAR, DIANA! YOU WERE BORN INTO THIS WORLD TO BE THE MOST HONORED AMONG ALL AMAZONS! HENCE-FORTH, YOUR WARRIOR'S GARB SHALL PROCLAIM YOUR HONOR!

LOOK NOW UPON THE STANDARD FROM WHICH WE SHALL WEAVE THAT GARB...

...AS AM I!

...THE STANDARD OF THE WARRIOR FOR WHOM YOU WERE NAMED...

...SHE WHO DIED NOBLY THAT THE AMAZON RACE MIGHT LIVE!

"AMAZONS! HEAR YOUR QUEEN! EVEN AS APOLLO'S SUN GIVES BIRTH TO THIS GLORIOUS DAY, I HAVE GATHERED YOU HERE...

...TO WITNESS A BIRTH OF ANOTHER KIND!

"THE CHAMPION HAS BEEN CHOSEN...

.." THE GODS HAVE BEEN SATISFIED!"

31

39

THERE IS A MOMENT OF SILENCE. THEN, DIANA RAISES HER BRACELETS... AND SMILES.

FROM A THOUSAND AMAZON THROATS, A MIGHTY CHEER RISES TO THE HEAVENS!

AND ON A MOUNTAIN CALLED OLYMPUS, FIVE GODDESSES KNOW JOY!

ONLY HIPPOLYTE SMILES NOT-- FOR HER THOUGHTS ARE OF ARES -- AND OF THE WORDS SHE SPOKE JUST DAYS BEFORE...

"HOW CAN EVEN THE BEST OF US SUCCEED... WHERE THE GODS DARE NOT GO?"

AND SO THE QUEEN PULLS HER CLOAK AROUND HER... AND SHIVERS 'NEATH APOLLO'S SUN!

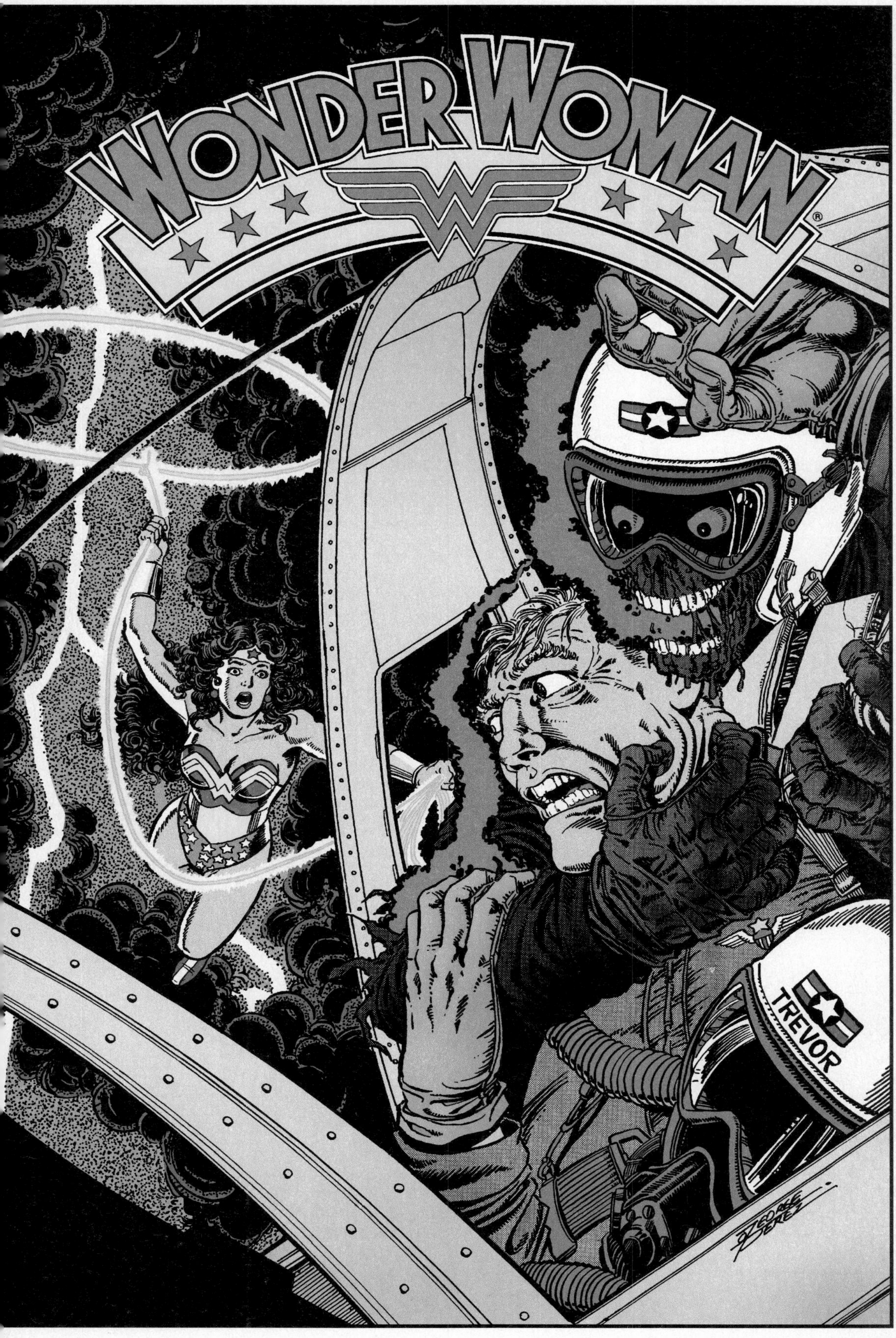
WONDER WOMAN
TREVOR
GEORGE PEREZ

"THUNDERSTORMS MAKE ME *NERVOUS.*

"THE LIGHT...THE NOISE...LIKE GUNSHOTS.

"WHEN I WAS A KID, I THOUGHT GUNS WERE *MACHO.*

"MAYBE THAT'S WHY I JOINED THE *AIR FORCE.*

"BUT IN THE MILITARY, I SAW WHAT GUNS *DO* TO PEOPLE. IT MADE ME *SICK.*

"IT MADE ME *GROW UP.*"

THIS IS A *RESTRICTED* AREA, SIR.

MAY I SEE YOUR *CLEARANCE?*

"NOT THAT I'M *AFRAID* OF GUNS. I FACED *PLENTY* IN 'NAM.

"WHAT I'M AFRAID OF IS PUTTING *LUNATICS* BEHIND THE TRIGGERS. THREE YEARS AGO, I TOLD THAT TO A *CONGRESSIONAL INVESTIGATION COMMITTEE.*

"AND I NAMED *NAMES!*

"EVER SINCE THAT DAY, LT. CANDY HAS BEEN *WORRIED* ABOUT ME.

"SOMETIMES SHE ACTS MORE LIKE MY *MOTHER* THAN MY *ATTACHE.*

"I TOLD ETTA NOT TO *WORRY.* THEY CAN'T *TOUCH* ME. I'M A GODDAMN *WAR HERO!*

"'BUT I DON'T *TRUST* HIM, STEVIE,' SHE SAID, 'AND I DON'T LIKE *LEAVING* YOU WITH HIM!'

"SHE WAS TALKING ABOUT KOHLER-- GENERAL *GERARD KOHLER.* NOW THERE'S A *LUNATIC* FOR YOU!' I TOLD THE COMMITTEE THAT.

"FOR MY HONESTY, THEY LET KOHLER SENTENCE ME TO A *DESK.* THREE YEARS AGO.

"NOW, SUDDENLY, THE GENERAL WANTS TO SEE ME--IN MY FLIGHT SUIT--AT MIDNIGHT.

"WHAT'S HE UP TO?"

"WHAT DOES HE WANT WITH A *RENEGADE FLYBOY* WHO *HATES* HIS *GUTS?*"

COLONEL *TREVOR* TO SEE YOU, SIR.

SEND HIM IN, SERGEANT.

COLONEL STEPHEN TREVOR REPORTING AS ORDERED, GENERAL KOHLER.

AT EASE, COLONEL. AND WIPE THAT *SMIRK* OFF YOUR FACE. IF I HAD HAD MY WAY, YOU'D HAVE BEEN STRIPPED OF YOUR WINGS *YEARS* AGO!

BLEEDING HEARTS DON'T BELONG IN THE SERVICE OF THIS COUNTRY.

BECAUSE I *CHOSE* TO CALL YOU, TREVOR! MY ORDERS WERE TO PICK A *SPECIAL* PILOT FOR THIS MISSION. *YOU* FIT MY REQUIREMENTS.

THEN MAY I ASK *WHY* YOU'VE CALLED ME, SIR?

TAKE THIS. INSIDE ARE YOUR *ORDERS* AND *COORDINATES*. THE TOP BRASS WANTS TO SHOW OFF ITS NEW, MODIFIED *"PHANTOM"* TO SOME FOREIGN MUCKETY-MUCKS.

GIVE 'EM A GOOD SHOW, TREVOR.

BEGGING THE GENERAL'S PARDON, BUT THIS HARDLY CALLS FOR A PILOT OF MY EXPERIENCE. BESIDES, THE PHANTOM ISN'T EVEN THAT *NEW*.

AND THESE COORDINATES... THERE'S *NOTHING OUT THERE!*

STOW IT, TREVOR! NO ONE *CARES* WHAT *YOU* THINK! NOT ANYMORE!

YOU'LL FLY THAT PHANTOM *AS ORDERED* AND YOU'LL DO IT WITH YOUR *MOUTH SHUT!*

AND REMEMBER-- THE PHANTOM IS A *FIGHTER* PLANE. SO MANEUVER IT LIKE A *WAR* MACHINE!

YOU ARE *CAPABLE* OF THAT, AREN'T YOU, COLONEL?

YES, SIR.

GOOD. NOW GET OUT OF HERE.

JUST THE *SMELL* OF YOU MAKES MY *STOMACH* CRAWL!

"I STIFFEN UP INSIDE. NOT BECAUSE MY SALUTE IS A *MOCKERY*... OR EVEN BECAUSE I HATE HIM...

"BUT BECAUSE *SOMETHING* ABOUT ALL THIS IS JUST NOT *RIGHT!*"

43

"SOME WOULD SAY MY SUSPICIONS DON'T MATTER-- THAT ANY *GOOD* SOLDIER WOULD JUST FOLLOW ORDERS.

"BUT THERE AREN'T MANY *GOOD* SOLDIERS UNDER THE THUMB OF SOMEONE LIKE *KOHLER.*

"AND I'M SURPRISED THAT WHEN WE WERE IN 'NAM...

"...*SOMEONE* DIDN'T *FRAG* HIM!"

CAPTAIN SLADE? I UNDERSTAND YOU'RE TO *ACCOMPANY* ME ON THIS CHICKEN ASSIGNMENT.

"CHICKEN" ASSIGNMENT, SIR?

I AM DOING WHAT MY SUPERIOR OFFICERS *TELL* ME, SIR! I UNDERSTAND THAT I AM TO FOLLOW *YOUR* DIRECTIVES WHILE IN THIS AIRCRAFT.

I UNDERSTAND THAT THAT IS THE *GENERAL'S* WISH.

THAT IS ALL I *NEED* TO UNDERSTAND. IT IS ALL *YOU* NEED TO UNDERSTAND...

...*SIR!*

"YEAH. THUNDERSTORMS MAKE ME NERVOUS.

"AND SO DO GUNG-HO CO-PILOTS!"

THE HIGH-AND-MIGHTY *COLONEL TREVOR!* A *DOVE* IN A NEST OF *HAWKS!*

A MAN RULED BY *NONE* BUT HIS *OWN* CONSCIENCE.

ALL THAT WILL SOON *CHANGE,* COLONEL! FOR TONIGHT, I SHALL *BREAK* YOUR ACCURSED WILL!

TONIGHT, YOU SHALL DO THE BIDDING OF *ARES,* GOD OF WAR!

"SURELY THE GODS MUST BE IN *TURMOIL* THIS NIGHT!

"THEIR AGONY *RENDS THE VERY DARKNESS*...

"... AND *RAGES* LIKE SOME *WILD BEAST* 'ROUND THE STATUE OF *NOBLE ARTEMIS!*

"GRANT ME THE *COURAGE* OF THE *HUNTER*, O *SILENT ARTEMIS*."

FOR I AM *FRIGHTENED* BY THIS NIGHT-- FRIGHTENED BY THE *MISSION* I AM CALLED TO PERFORM.

FRIGHTENED THAT I MIGHT *FAIL!*

A FIRE IN THE SKY!

Greg Potter & *George Pérez*   *Bruce Patterson*   *costanza*   *Tatjana Wood*   *Karen Berger*
script, co-plotters, pencils   inks   letters   colors   Editor

④

PRINCESS DIANA LOOKS *UNEASY*, QUEEN HIPPOLYTE.

FOR TONIGHT, THE GODS SHALL *REVEAL* TO YOUR DAUGHTER THE *NATURE* OF HER DREAD MISSION...

...A MISSION WHICH WILL PIT HER AGAINST A *GOD GONE MAD!*

BUT TAKE HEART, MY QUEEN, FOR THE GODS HAVE ALSO PROMISED HER A *SPECIAL WEAPON*-- ONE WHICH SHALL AID HER MIGHTILY IN BATTLE!

THOUGH WHAT *KIND* OF WEAPON COULD AFFECT HER FOUL ENEMY *ARES*, I CANNOT GUESS.

DIANA HAS *ACCEPTED* THE GODS' CALLING...

"...AND NOW, FOR HER, THERE IS NO TURNING BACK!"

HEPHAESTUS! IS IT *READY?*

YOUR IMPATIENCE BEGINS TO *ANNOY* ME, *ARTEMIS!* IF YOU WOULD HAVE ME FORGE THIS *WEAPON,* LEAVE ME TO MY WORK!

BE NOT *ANGRY,* MY FORMER HUSBAND. *ARTEMIS'* WORDS SPRING FROM THE FEAR WE *ALL* FEEL-- AND FROM THE *URGENCY* OF YOUR TASK!

APHRODITE SPEAKS TRUE. THERE IS A CHAMPION ON EARTH WHO AWAITS THIS WEAPON.

HER NAME IS *DIANA, PRINCESS OF THE AMAZONS*-- AND UPON HER SHOULDERS RESTS OUR *ONE* HOPE FOR *SALVATION!*

HOPE! SALVATION! YOU GRASP AT *STRAWS* LIKE DROWNING CHILDREN!

BUT THIS WEAPON SHALL BRING DIANA *GREAT* POWER! THROUGH IT, I SHALL GIVE HER REIN O'ER THE *FIRES OF TRUTH*--

--THAT THE HEARTS AND THOUGHTS OF *ALL MEN* MAY BE OPENED UNTO HER!

I TAKE NO STOCK IN YOUR FOOLISH SCHEMES, HESTIA; I DO THIS TASK OUT OF *HATRED* FOR ARES--*NOT* FOR ANY OTHER REASON.

DO YOU TRULY BELIEVE I WOULD SO READILY HELP ONE WHO HAS *BETRAYED* ME?

PLEASE, HEPHAESTUS. THIS IS NOT THE *TIME!*

TIME! SOON, THERE SHALL *BE* NO TIME FOR THE GODS. *ARES* SHALL SEE TO THAT! FOR IF *ZEUS HIMSELF* CANNOT CONTROL THE GOD OF WAR, SURELY YOU, TOO, SHALL *FAIL!*

BUT I AM OLD... AND TIRED... AND *CARE NOT.*

I CARE ONLY THAT I MIGHT MEET MY FATE WITHOUT *PAIN!*

6

47

HERE, THEN, ARTEMIS--TAKE YOUR *LASSO OF TRUTH*.

I HAVE FORGED IT FROM THE GIRDLE OF *GAEA HERSELF*--

-- SO THAT NO GOD NOR MORTAL MAY *EVER* BREAK ITS BONDS!

NOW DOES OUR FATE REST IN THE HANDS OF A *CHILD*. AND YET, THIS IS A CHILD WHOSE LOVE FOR US HAS *NEVER* FALTERED!

"HERE IS THE GREAT TASK-- TO SAVE US FROM THE HORROR...

"...OF *OBLIVION!*"

GREAT HERA!

THAT *BOLT*-- AS IF FROM THE *HEART OF ARTEMIS HERSELF!* AND UPON THE GROUND...

A ROPE OF *PUREST GOLD!* CAN *THIS* BE THE WEAPON THE GODS HAVE PROMISED?

INDEED IT *IS*, CHILD!

BY ATHENA'S MANTLE! IT *CANNOT* BE! NOT FOR *CENTURIES* HAS ANY AMAZON LAID EYES UPON HIM!

GREETINGS, *PRINCESS DIANA!*

I AM HERMES, MESSENGER OF THE GODS!

HAVE YOU COME TO *LEAD* ME ON MY MISSION, HERMES?

AH! WOULD THAT I *COULD*, PRINCESS-- FOR YOU ARE *FAIR* INDEED!

BUT I MAY NOT STAY AWAY FROM OLYMPUS LONG-- FOR MY POWER TO *OPERATE* IN YOUR WORLD IS NOT WHAT IT *ONCE* WAS.

THEREFORE, I CAN GUIDE YOU ONLY AS FAR AS YOUR *FIRST* CLUE!

CLUE? I DO NOT UNDERSTAND.

YOU ARE NOT *MEANT* TO... *YET!*

COME, TAKE MY HAND

THOUGH I GAVE YOU THE *POWER OF FLIGHT* WHEN YOU WERE BORN, I NOW TAKE YOU TO A PLACE...

...WHERE EVEN *EAGLES* CANNOT SOAR!

GONE! *BOTH* OF THEM!

AM I NOT EVEN GIVEN THE CHANCE TO BID MY OWN DAUGHTER *FAREWELL*, MENALIPPE?

CONCERN YOURSELF *NOT* WITH THAT, MY QUEEN. PRAY, INSTEAD, THAT YOU MAY TAKE HER IN YOUR ARMS *ONCE MORE*--WHEN ARES IS AT LAST *DEFEATED!*

HANSCOM AIR FORCE BASE, THIS IS COLONEL TREVOR. I'M AT COORDINATE NINE ZERO FIVE. DO YOU READ ME, OVER? OVER?

LOOKS LIKE WE LOST 'EM, COLONEL.

8

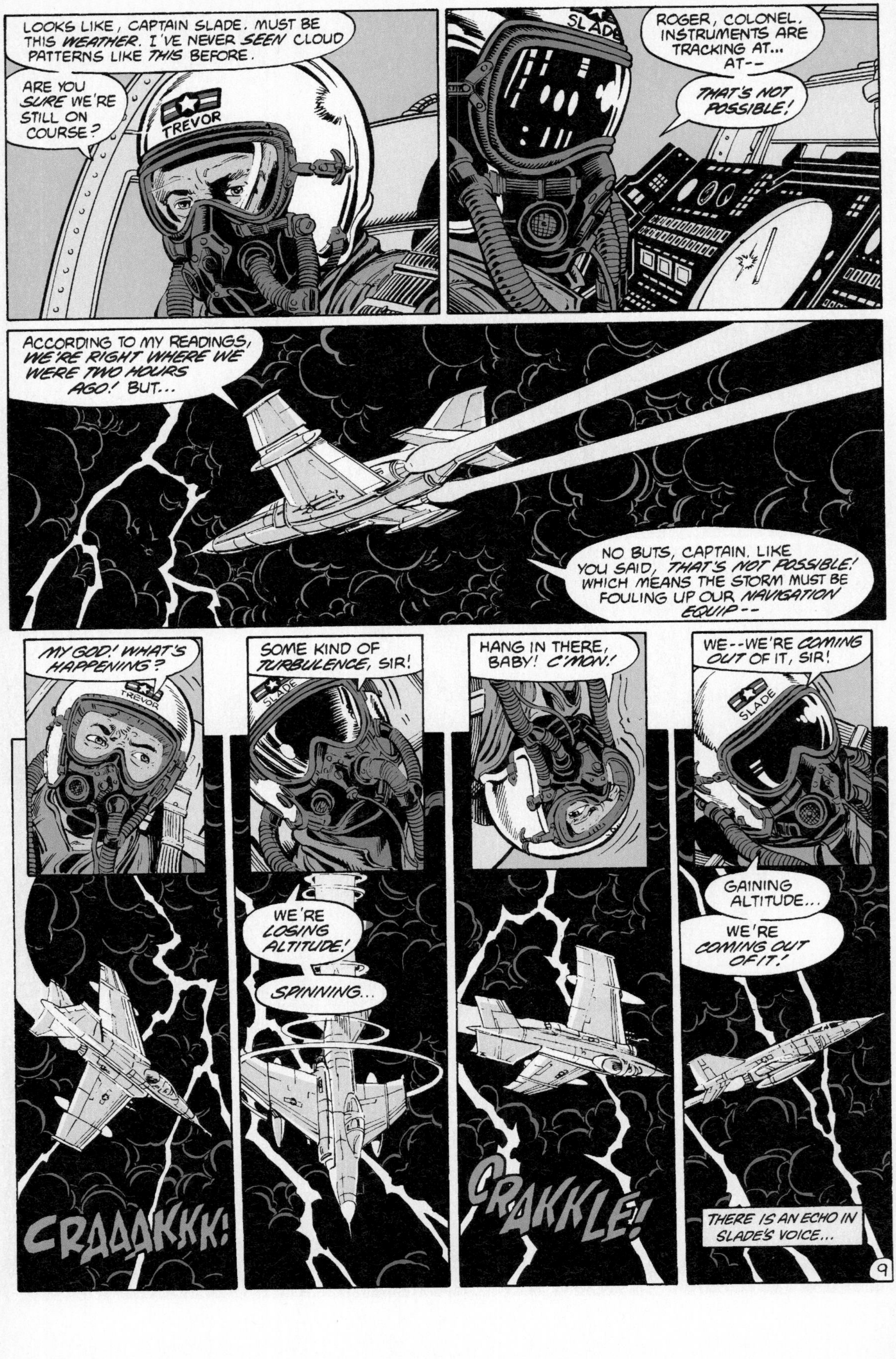
LOOKS LIKE, CAPTAIN SLADE. MUST BE THIS WEATHER. I'VE NEVER SEEN CLOUD PATTERNS LIKE THIS BEFORE.
ARE YOU SURE WE'RE STILL ON COURSE?
TREVOR
SLADE
ROGER, COLONEL. INSTRUMENTS ARE TRACKING AT... AT--
THAT'S NOT POSSIBLE!
ACCORDING TO MY READINGS, WE'RE RIGHT WHERE WE WERE TWO HOURS AGO! BUT...
NO BUTS, CAPTAIN. LIKE YOU SAID, THAT'S NOT POSSIBLE! WHICH MEANS THE STORM MUST BE FOULING UP OUR NAVIGATION EQUIP--
MY GOD! WHAT'S HAPPENING?
TREVOR
CRAAAKKK!
SOME KIND OF TURBULENCE, SIR!
SLADE
WE'RE LOSING ALTITUDE!
SPINNING...
HANG IN THERE, BABY! C'MON!
CRAKKLE!
WE--WE'RE COMING OUT OF IT, SIR!
SLADE
GAINING ALTITUDE...
WE'RE COMING OUT OF IT!
THERE IS AN ECHO IN SLADE'S VOICE...
9

...LIKE BONES RATTLING WITHIN A *HOLLOW GRAVE*...

...LIKE THE WINDS WHICH NOW MOAN ABOVE THE *ROTTING CORPSE* OF THIS ONCE BEAUTIFUL HILLTOP!

BY *THE GODS,* HERMES! WHERE HAVE YOU BROUGHT ME? AND WHAT *DISASTER* HAS BEFALLEN THIS WRETCHED PLACE?

THE DISASTER IS CALLED *ARES,* MY PRINCESS. FOR THIS IS *AREOPAGUS--* ONCE THE *HOME* OF THE WAR-GOD.

HIS *FETID PRESENCE* TURNED THIS HILL'S GRASS TO *STONE--* DECIMATED ITS TREES-- *FOULED* ITS AIR!

NOW, EVEN THE WALLS OF ARES' *OWN PALACE* LIE *CRUMBLING* IN THE WAKE OF HIS DEPARTURE. FOR THE GOD OF WAR HIDES SOME- WHERE IN *MAN'S WORLD--* PLOTTING THE *DESTRUCTION* OF US ALL!

COME! IT IS INTO THE *MAW* OF THIS *EVIL PLACE* THAT YOU AND I MUST GO!

⑩

BUT FEAR NOT-- FOR THE LIGHT FROM MY *CADUCEUS* SHALL *LEAD* US!

IT IS DIFFICULT *NOT* TO *FEAR*, HERMES. I HAVE ALWAYS BELIEVED THAT THE GODS *PROTECTED* THE AMAZONS-- THAT THEIR *POWER* AND *MIGHT* WERE LIKE A *SHIELD!*

BUT *HERE*-- WITHIN THESE *DREAD* WALLS -- I FEEL STRANGELY *ALONE!*

BE *TRUTHFUL* WITH ME, *HERALD* -- ARE MY FEELINGS *GROUNDLESS?* OR ARE THE GODS NOT QUITE AS *OMNIPOTENT* AS MENALIPPE ONCE TAUGHT ME?

HUSH, MY BEAUTIFUL DAUGHTER, THOUGHTS SUCH AS THOSE WILL TURN YOUR *HAIR* TO *GRAY!*

ATTEND INSTEAD THE *MOANS* EMANATING FROM *YON* CAVERN!

GO THEN... FOLLOW THE LIGHT BUT FOLLOW IT *ALONE!*

FOR THE ONE YOU ARE ABOUT TO MEET IS A *DEADLY* SORT. AND IF SHE SHOULD SEE ME, SHE WOULD BLAST MY FORM TO ATOMS!

BUT *YOU*, MY PRINCESS, ARE A *STRANGER* TO HER-- AND SHE HATES YOU *NOT.* AT LEAST, NOT *YET!*

SISTER! ARE YOU *ILL?* WHY DO YOU *WAIL* SO?

YOU CALL ME "*SISTER*"? WOE TO ANY WHO THINK THEY BE *KIN* TO SUCH AS *I!* GO AWAY, LITTLE ONE. LEAVE *HARMONIA* TO HER SOLITUDE!

FOR SOLITUDE IS THE ONLY *SOLACE* I HAVE EVER FOUND IN THIS LIFE!

FORGIVE ME, SISTER HARMONIA, BUT I *CANNOT* LEAVE YOU ALONE. I HAVE BEEN SENT TO-- TO RECEIVE A *CLUE* FROM YOU!

A *CLUE?* WHAT *KIND* OF CLUE?

TO THE WHEREABOUTS OF *ARES*, GOD OF WAR!

I SEE. AND WHAT WOULD A *BABE-IN-ARMS* LIKE *YOU* KNOW OF ARES?

11

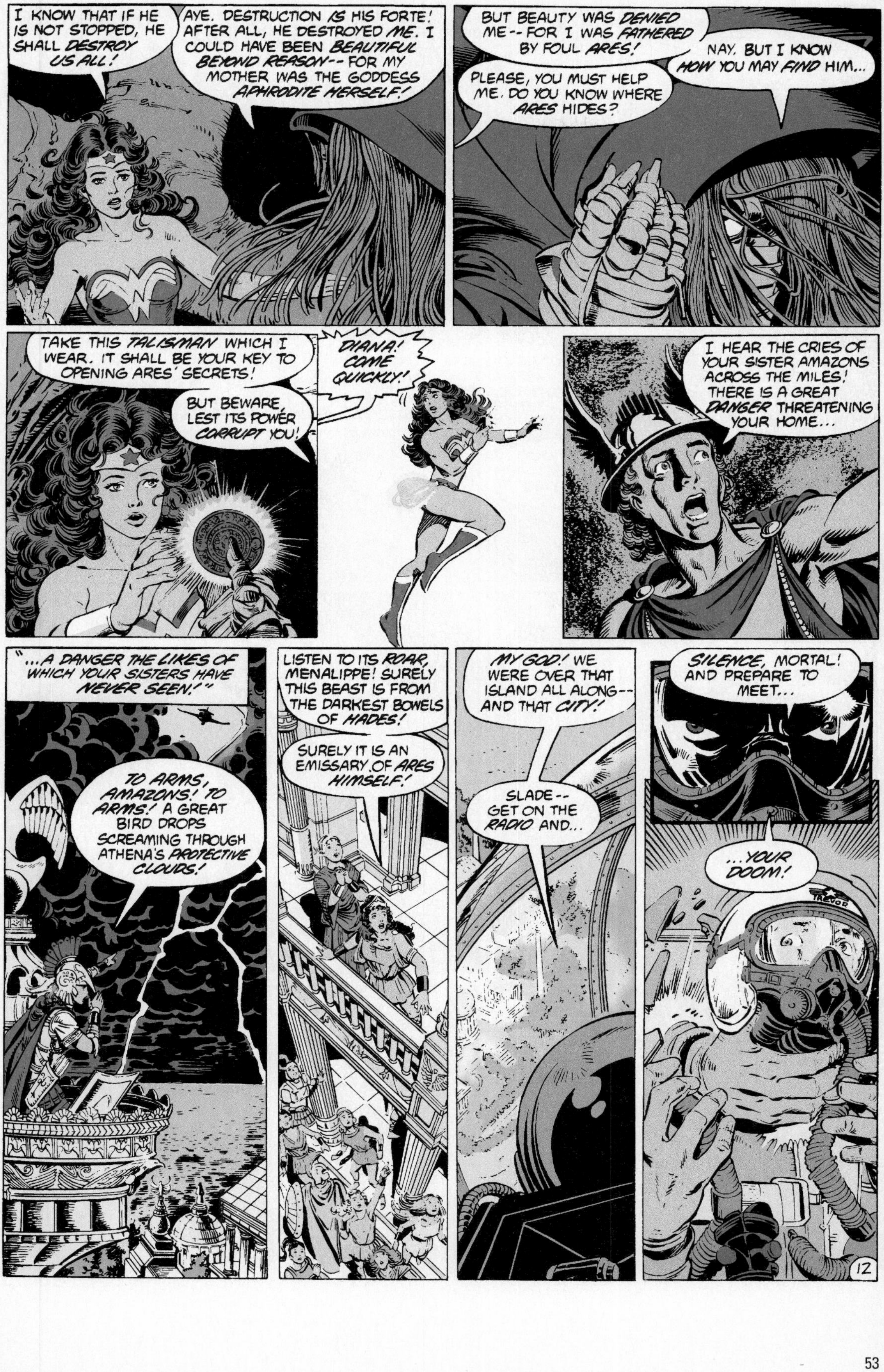
I KNOW THAT IF HE IS NOT STOPPED, HE SHALL DESTROY US ALL!
AYE. DESTRUCTION IS HIS FORTE! AFTER ALL, HE DESTROYED ME. I COULD HAVE BEEN BEAUTIFUL BEYOND REASON-- FOR MY MOTHER WAS THE GODDESS APHRODITE HERSELF!
BUT BEAUTY WAS DENIED ME-- FOR I WAS FATHERED BY FOUL ARES!
PLEASE, YOU MUST HELP ME. DO YOU KNOW WHERE ARES HIDES?
NAY, BUT I KNOW HOW YOU MAY FIND HIM...
TAKE THIS TALISMAN WHICH I WEAR. IT SHALL BE YOUR KEY TO OPENING ARES' SECRETS!
BUT BEWARE, LEST ITS POWER CORRUPT YOU!
DIANA! COME QUICKLY!
I HEAR THE CRIES OF YOUR SISTER AMAZONS ACROSS THE MILES! THERE IS A GREAT DANGER THREATENING YOUR HOME...
"...A DANGER THE LIKES OF WHICH YOUR SISTERS HAVE NEVER SEEN!"
TO ARMS, AMAZONS! TO ARMS! A GREAT BIRD DROPS SCREAMING THROUGH ATHENA'S PROTECTIVE CLOUDS!
LISTEN TO ITS ROAR, MENALIPPE! SURELY THIS BEAST IS FROM THE DARKEST BOWELS OF HADES!
SURELY IT IS AN EMISSARY OF ARES HIMSELF!
MY GOD! WE WERE OVER THAT ISLAND ALL ALONG-- AND THAT CITY!
SLADE-- GET ON THE RADIO AND...
SILENCE, MORTAL! AND PREPARE TO MEET...
...YOUR DOOM!
TREVOR
12

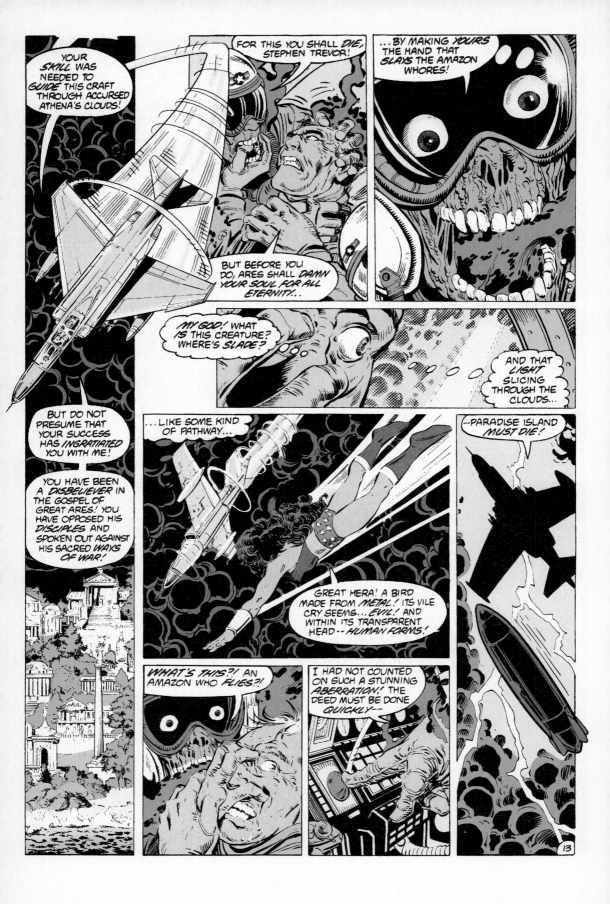

YOUR **SKILL** WAS NEEDED TO **GUIDE** THIS CRAFT THROUGH ACCURSED ATHENA'S CLOUDS!

FOR THIS YOU SHALL **DIE**, STEPHEN TREVOR!

...BY MAKING **YOURS** THE HAND THAT **SLAYS** THE AMAZON **WHORES!**

BUT BEFORE YOU DO, ARES SHALL **DAMN** YOUR SOUL FOR ALL ETERNITY...

MY **GOD!** WHAT **IS** THIS CREATURE? WHERE'S **SLADE?**

AND THAT **LIGHT** SLICING THROUGH THE CLOUDS...

BUT DO NOT PRESUME THAT YOUR SUCCESS HAS **INGRATIATED** YOU WITH ME!

YOU HAVE BEEN A **DISBELIEVER** IN THE GOSPEL OF GREAT **ARES!** YOU HAVE OPPOSED HIS **DISCIPLES** AND SPOKEN OUT AGAINST HIS SACRED **WAYS OF WAR!**

...LIKE SOME KIND OF PATHWAY...

GREAT **HERA!** A BIRD MADE FROM **METAL!** ITS VILE CRY SEEMS...**EVIL!** AND WITHIN ITS TRANSPARENT HEAD-- **HUMAN FORMS!**

--PARADISE ISLAND **MUST DIE!**

WHAT'S THIS?! AN AMAZON WHO **FLIES?!**

I HAD NOT COUNTED ON SUCH A STUNNING **ABERRATION!** THE DEED MUST BE DONE **QUICKLY--**

13

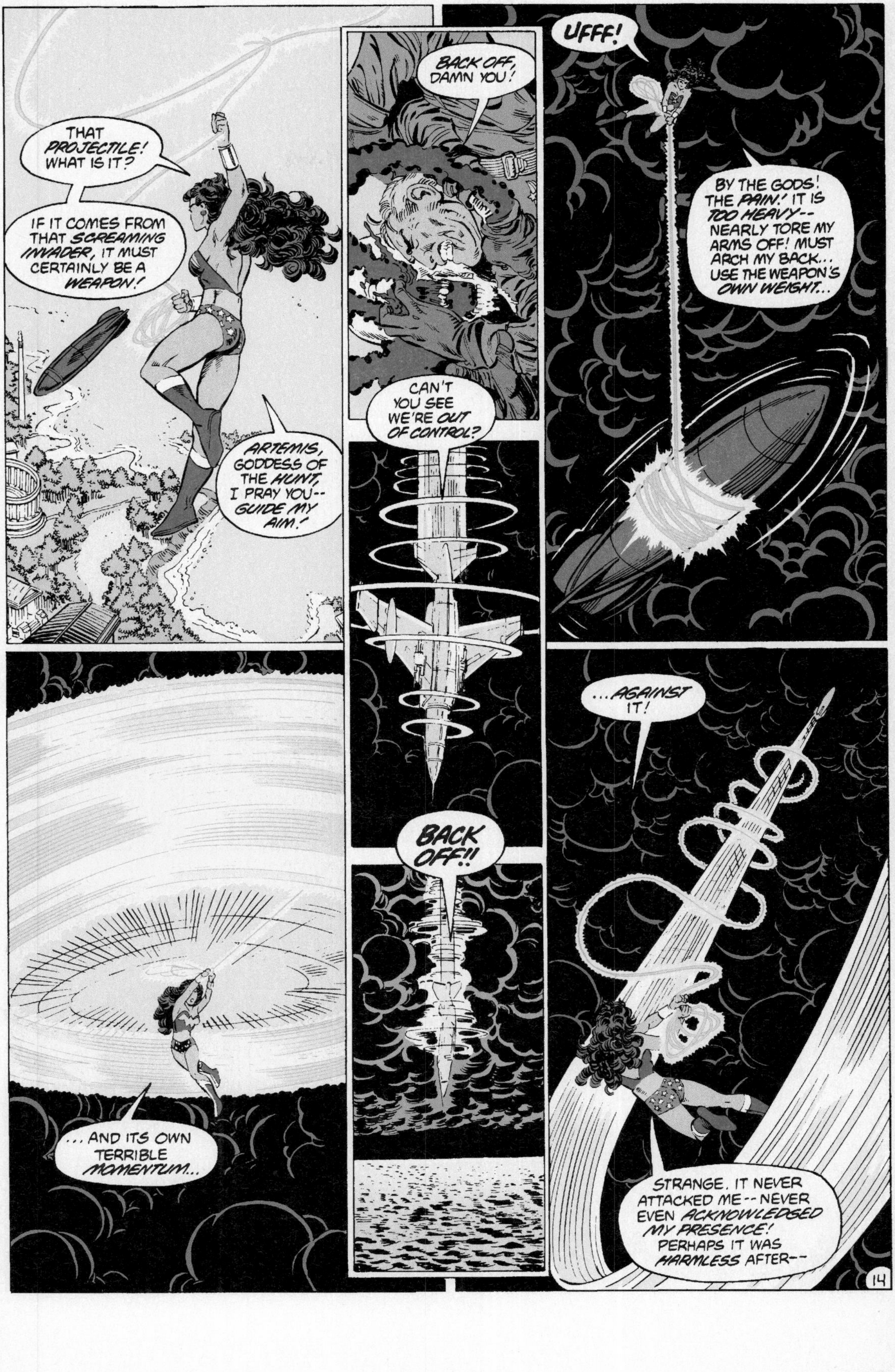

THAT PROJECTILE! WHAT IS IT?
IF IT COMES FROM THAT SCREAMING INVADER, IT MUST CERTAINLY BE A WEAPON!
ARTEMIS, GODDESS OF THE HUNT, I PRAY YOU-- GUIDE MY AIM!
BACK OFF, DAMN YOU!
CAN'T YOU SEE WE'RE OUT OF CONTROL?
BACK OFF!!
UFFF!
BY THE GODS! THE PAIN! IT IS TOO HEAVY-- NEARLY TORE MY ARMS OFF! MUST ARCH MY BACK... USE THE WEAPON'S OWN WEIGHT...
...AND ITS OWN TERRIBLE MOMENTUM...
...AGAINST IT!
STRANGE. IT NEVER ATTACKED ME-- NEVER EVEN ACKNOWLEDGED MY PRESENCE! PERHAPS IT WAS HARMLESS AFTER--
14

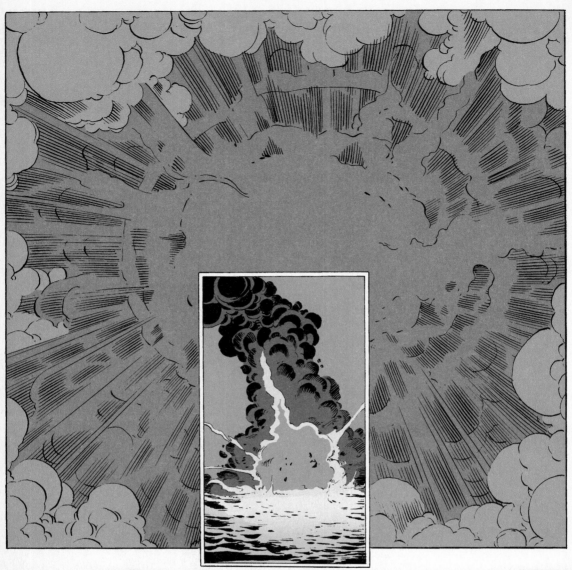

BY THE GODS! WHAT FOUL DEMON COULD *CONCEIVE* SUCH POWER?

A POWER THAT CAN *BURN* THE SKY ITSELF!

WERE IT NOT FOR *DIANA*, PARADISE WOULD HAVE *PERISHED* IN THAT AWESOME FIRE--!

AYE, DIANA HAS INDEED PROVEN HERSELF *WORTHY* OF THE GODS' TRUST!

BUT WAIT! *LOOK!*

15

"SHE DIVES TOWARD THE CHURNING SEA!"

BEFORE THE INVADER SANK BENEATH POSEIDON'S WAVES, I HEARD A VOICE FROM WITHIN IT!

IT TAUNTED ME...SPOKE OF PARADISE ISLAND'S DOOM!

SURELY SUCH AN ENTITY MUST BE AN EMISSARY FROM ARES HIMSELF!

AND PERHAPS IT CAN TELL ME MORE OF HIS MASTER PLAN!

BY THE GODS! THAT THING--DISINTEGRATING BEFORE MY EYES!

I FEAR I AM TOO LATE!

DIANA! STAY AWAY FROM THAT ONE!

FOR HE IS A WICKED BEAST-- AND HIS VERY TOUCH WOULD MELT YOUR SOUL!

THEMIS, DEITY OF THE SEAS!

DO NOT LOOK SO STARTLED, CHILD. LIKE THE GREAT POSEIDON, I HAVE LONG TAKEN AN INTEREST IN YOUR KIND!

BEHOLD, AMAZON PRINCESS-- WITHIN THIS PROTECTIVE SHELL, I HAVE GATHERED FOR YOU-- THE MAN!

SO THIS IS WHAT MAN LOOKS LIKE! STRANGE, HIS IMAGE IS NOBLE--LIKE THAT OF THE GODS THEMSELVES!

YET, HE CAME TO PARADISE RIDING WITHIN THE METAL BIRD'S SKULL! SURELY, HE MUST BE MY ENEMY!

I DO HEAR YOUR THOUGHTS, MY CHILD. BELIEVE ME-- YOU HAVE MUCH TO LEARN. QUELL YOUR ANGER AND TAKE THE MAN ASHORE!

16

ELSEWHERE:

WHERE IS KOHLER, DAMMIT!

I DEMAND TO SEE KOHLER!

G-GENERAL HILLARY!

WHAT A PLEASANT SURPRISE, GENERAL! WE DIDN'T EXPECT--

STOW IT, CORPORAL! WHERE'S YOUR COMMANDING OFFICER?

I--

NEVER MIND! I'LL FIND HIM MYSELF! WHEN DID YOU SAY TREVOR REPORTED TO KOHLER, LT. CANDY?

MIDNIGHT, SIR! IT WAS SO IRREGULAR THAT I THOUGHT I SHOULD CHECK WITH YOU.

DAMN GLAD YOU DID, LIEUTENANT! I KNEW NOTHING ABOUT ANY MISSION! KOHLER'S MY SUBORDINATE-- AND I'LL BE HANGED IF I'LL LET HIM SEND PILOTS TO GOD-KNOWS-WHERE WITHOUT CONSULTING ME!

OPEN THAT DOOR, SERGEANT!

I WANT TO SEE KOHLER'S FACE WHEN I--

I--

GOOD GOD!

GOOD, LOVING GOD!

KOHLER

17

THE ISLAND OF HEALING--NOT TWENTY OAR-STROKES AWAY FROM *PARADISE ISLAND.*

HERE, CENTURIES AGO, THE AMAZONS BUILT A SHELTER-- A PLACE WHERE THEY MIGHT, IF NEED BE, HOUSE SHIP-WRECK VICTIMS.

HERE, COME ALL WHO ARE IN PAIN, BE THEY AMAZON, ANIMAL...OR EVEN MAN!

WHY DO WE WASTE OUR *BEST PHYSICIAN'S* SKILLS ON THIS... *CREATURE?* I SAY THROW HIM BACK INTO THE SEA!

SILENCE, PHILIPPUS! WOULD YOU HAVE US *MURDER* A DEFENSE-LESS MORTAL?

SUCH VIOLENCE IS *MAN'S WAY*--NOT OURS!

I DO NOT UNDERSTAND, MOTHER. WE HAVE NEVER GIVEN MAN REASON TO *HATE* US. WHY SHOULD THEY NOW ATTACK OUR HOME?

DO YOU NOT REMEMBER OUR *HISTORY,* MY DAUGHTER? MEN HAVE *ALWAYS* HATED US-- BECAUSE WE WOULD NEVER BOW TO THEIR *DOMINATION!*

AYE! I REMEMBER--*BECAUSE I WAS THERE!* THE LAST MAN I LAID EYES UPON *BOUND* ME, *FORCED HIS WILL* UPON ME--AND THEN, SMILING, *SPAT IN MY FACE!*

BECAUSE DIANA TELLS US THAT IT IS *THE GODS' WILL.*

DO YOU NO LONGER TRUST THE *GODS,* PHILIPPUS?

I WILL *NEVER* UNDERSTAND WHY WE SHOULD SAVE ANY *MALE!*

18

THEMIS IS NO GOD! SHE IS BUT A GOD'S MESSENGER! I TRUST HER NOT!

BUT THESE *EMBLEMS* THAT THE MAN WORE-- HAVE YOU NOTICED? THEY *MATCH* MY WARRIOR'S GARB! SURELY THIS IS NO *COINCIDENCE*!

SURELY THE GODS THEM-SELVES HAVE HAD A *HAND* IN THIS DAY'S EVENTS!

AYE. AND IT IS OBVIOUS THAT *ONE* OF THOSE GODS IS *ARES*! ONLY *HIS* POWER COULD HAVE BREACHED OUR DEFENSES!

STILL, POSEIDON IS ARES' *ENEMY*.

HE WOULD NOT HAVE *SENT* THEMIS UNLESS SAVING THIS MAN'S LIFE WOULD *HELP* US!

YOU ARE INDEED FILLED WITH *WISDOM*, DIANA!

BUT THEN, WAS IT NOT *I* WHO *GAVE* YOU THAT GIFT?

THOUGH YOU AND YOUR SISTERS HAVE NOT SEEN ME IN OVER *3,000* YEARS, PHILIPPUS, I HAVE *ALWAYS* BEEN WITH YOU. FOR THE *FAITH* OF YOUR KIND HAS BEEN THE GODS' EVER-PRESENT *JOY*!

ATHENA!

DIANA-- YOU ARE NOW PREPARED FOR YOUR MISSION!

SHOULD YOU *FAIL*, NEITHER GOD NOR AMAZON NOR EVEN *MAN* SHALL *SURVIVE* YOU!

HAVE YOU *HARMONIA'S* AMULET?

YES, MY LADY. BUT SHE DID NOT EXPLAIN ITS *USE*.

NOR *CAN* SHE-- FOR HER MIND IS *ADDLED*. THE AMULET IS BUT *ONE-HALF* OF A POWERFUL *TALISMAN*. YOU MUST FIND THE *OTHER* HALF. IT IS THE ONLY WAY TO LOCATE AND *DEFEAT* ARES!

19

NOW TAKE THE HAND OF HERMES. HE SHALL GUIDE YOU TO *MAN'S WORLD*-- WHERE YOUR DESTINY AWAITS!

A MOMENT, I PRAY YOU, BEFORE WE DEPART!

GOODBYE, MOTHER. I AM *FRIGHTENED*-- YET, I SHALL REMEMBER THE POWER WITHIN ME WHENEVER I THINK OF *YOU!*

SISTERS! FAREWELL!

BY THE POWERS THE GODS HAVE GRANTED ME, I SHALL *NOT FAIL!*

HAIL, PRINCESS! HAIL, DIANA!

I SHALL MISS YOU, MY SISTERS...

I SHALL MISS YOU *ALL!*

HERMES, I AM READY!

THEN *HOLD TIGHT* TO THE MAN, DIANA.

HIS INNERMOST THOUGHTS SHALL BE OUR *COMPASS*...

...GUIDING US TO THE PLACE *WHENCE HE CAME!*

FOR TODAY, PRINCESS, SHALL YOU WALK...AMONG MORTALS!

WORRY NOT, MY QUEEN! DIANA'S CAUSE IS *JUST!* THE GODS SHALL *PROTECT* HER!

THE GODS ARE *FRIGHTENED* OF ARES! SOMEHOW HE HAS BECOME *MORE POWERFUL* THAN THEY! AND MY DAUGHTER IS BUT A *CHILD!*

I WISH I COULD *BELIEVE* THAT, *PHILIPPUS.* BUT EVEN *YOU* MUST SENSE A *SHIFT* IN THE ORDER OF THINGS.

MENALIPPE-- YOU ARE OUR *ORACLE!* WHAT DOES THE *FUTURE* HOLD FOR YOUR PRINCESS?

20

ARES' POWER HAS *CLOUDED* THE DAYS TO COME, MAKING THEM IMPOSSIBLE FOR EVEN *MY* EYES TO SEE!

"BUT WHATEVER BEFALLS DIANA...WHATEVER *PERILS* LIE AHEAD...

"...WHATEVER THE *PURPOSE* FOR SAVING THE MAN WHO FELL FROM THE SKY, DIANA SHALL FIGHT WITH HONOR!

"AND IF *DEATH* BE HER DESTINY...

"...THEN MAY WE ALL FACE OUR FATES AS BRAVELY AS SHE NOW FACES *HERS!*"

SO KOHLER GOES OUT IN *GRAND STYLE.* IF THE POOR *BUZZARD* DESERVED ANY PITY, I'D GIVE IT TO HIM.

STOW THE *EDITORIAL* COMMENTS, COLONEL MICHAELIS.

WE ALL KNOW THAT YOU'RE TREVOR'S *CLOSEST* FRIEND.

DIDN'T HE *TELL* YOU ABOUT HIS MEETING WITH KOHLER?

NO, SIR. HE JUST CALLED ME TO TAKE HIS *OFFICE DUTIES* FOR AWHILE.

I HOPE YOU DON'T THINK *HE* HAD ANYTHING TO DO WITH THE GENERAL'S *DEATH!*

OF COURSE HE DIDN'T! STEVE TREVOR IS THE *FINEST OFFICER* I'VE EVER KNOWN!

MAYBE. BUT HE'S GOT SOME *DAMNED STICKY* QUESTIONS TO ANSWER!

THE MORTAL THEY CALL *KOHLER* SERVED OUR CAUSE WELL!

AYE! HIS LOVE OF *AGGRESSION* MADE HIM A *WILLING PAWN* IN OUR GAME!

NOW, KOHLER IS *NO MORE!* HIS FRAIL FORM WAS DESTROYED BY HIS OWN BURNING SOUL!

IT IS *UNFORTUNATE* THAT THE OTHER MORTAL, *SLADE,* FAILED SO MISERABLY!

21

AYE, BROTHER *PHOBOS*. STILL, THERE ARE *THOUSANDS MORE* WHOM WE CONTROL! THIS PITIFUL *AMAZON* STANDS NOT A *CHANCE* AGAINST US!

AGREED, *DEIMOS!* OUR FATHER *ARES* MEANS TO RULE *ALL HUMANITY!!* AND WITH THE TWO OF *US* BY HIS SIDE, HIS WISH SHALL *CERTAINLY* BE FULFILLED!

SOON, WE SHALL *CRUSH* ALL WHO OPPOSE HIM UNDER OUR HEELS...

...AND THE *FIRST* TO FEEL OUR POWER SHALL BE THE *PRINCESS DIANA!*

22

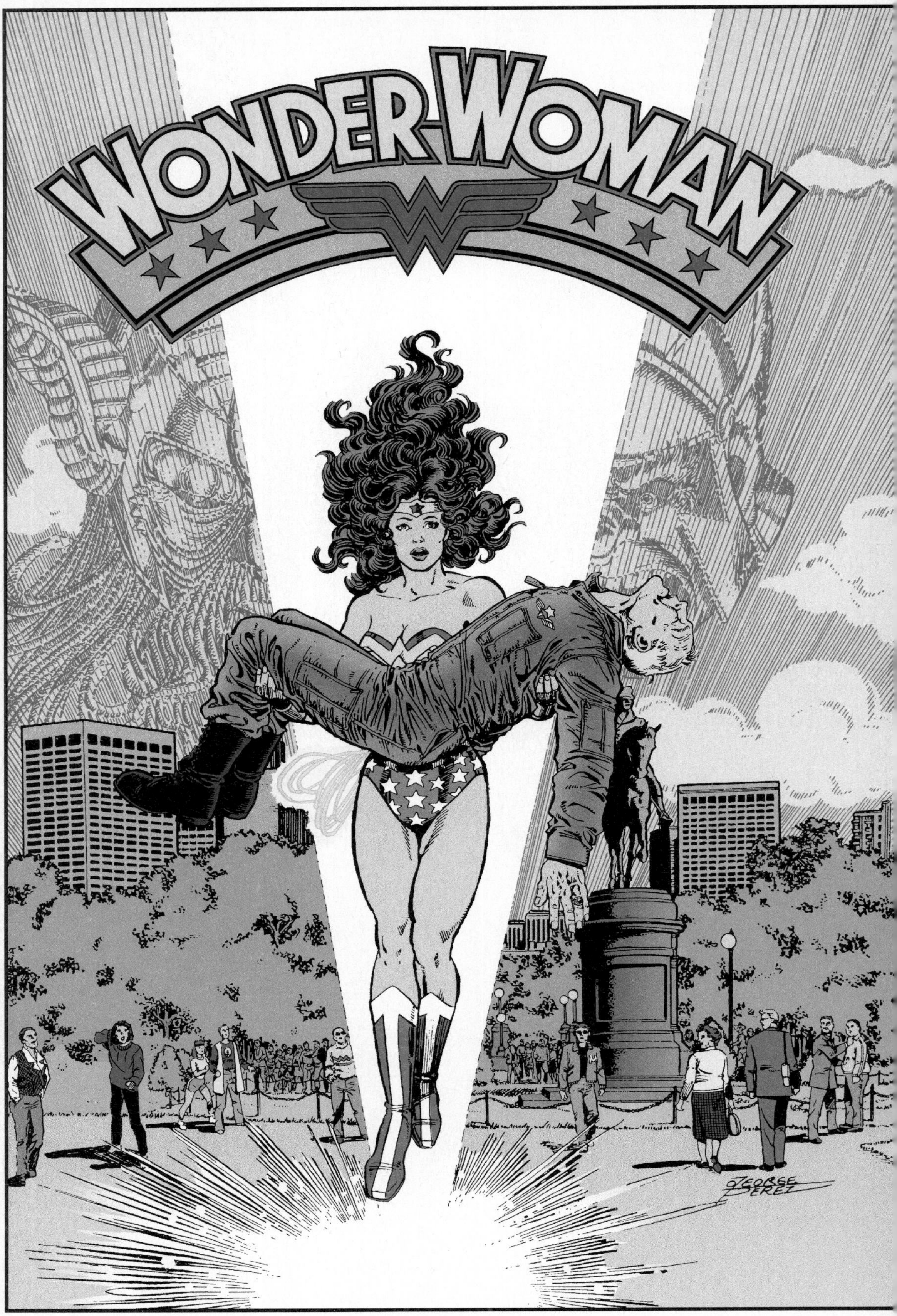
WONDER WOMAN
GEORGE PEREZ

DC Comics Proudly Presents

WONDER WOMAN

created by William Moulton Marston

IT SPRAWLS BELOW HER IN THE LATE AFTERNOON SUN LIKE SOME GREAT GROTESQUE TAPESTRY, ALL BRIGHT LIGHTS AND JAGGED EDGES, ALL GLITTER AND NOISE, HAUNTINGLY BEAUTIFUL YET MOCKINGLY REMOTE...

IT IS THE CITY OF BOSTON IN THE STATE OF MASSACHUSETTS IN THE COUNTRY SHE NOW KNOWS IS CALLED THE UNITED STATES OF AMERICA--

--AND THE PRINCESS DIANA, CHOSEN OF THE AMAZONS, CARRIED HENCE BY THE NOBLE HERMES, SWIFTEST OF ALL THE GODS, WONDERS IF SHE WILL EVER TRULY BE ABLE TO UNDER-STAND IT!

GEORGE PÉREZ: plotter & artist
BRUCE D. PATTERSON: inker
JOHN COSTANZA . TATJANA WOOD
letterer   colorist
and KAREN BERGER: editor
warmly welcome
LEN WEIN: scripter

"DEADLY ARRIVAL!"

IT IS SO *EXQUISITE,* HERMES-- AND YET SO *DISTURBING!*

HOW COULD A *RACE* CAPABLE OF SUCH WANTON *DESTRUCTION* CREATE SOMETHING SO BREATHTAKINGLY *BEAUTIFUL?*

JUDGE THEM NOT TOO *HARSHLY,* DIANA.

THIS IS A TIME OF GREAT *TENSION* FOR THE HUMAN RACE!

--AND THAT MAKES HIM *AFRAID--*

MAN APPEARS TO HAVE LOST HIS *WAY* UPON THIS EARTH--

--FOR HE CAN FEEL THE FRIGID FINGERS OF *ARES* CLOSING ABOUT HIS QUIVERING THROAT IN A *DEATH-GRIP!*

REPENT! TOGETHER WE SHALL FALL

THAT IS WHY I HAVE *BROUGHT* YOU HERE TO MAN'S WORLD, MY DAUGHTER--

--THAT YOU MIGHT ULTIMATELY PUT AN *END* TO ARES' *MADNESS.*

GREAT *HERA!* THAT *METAL BIRD--* LIKE THE ONE THAT ALMOST DESTROYED *PARADISE ISLAND--!*

THE ONE FLOWN BY THE *MAN* WE LEFT *BEHIND* HERE--!

DO NOT *DISMISS* THE MAN SO *LIGHTLY,* DAUGHTER--

--FOR, OF *ALL* WHO DWELL HERE, 'TIS *HIS* FATE WHICH SHALL MOST CLOSELY INTERTWINE WITH *YOURS!*

BUT *HOW,* GREAT HERMES?

MORE THAN THAT I CANNOT *SAY,* DIANA--!

NOW *COME--* LET US SET YOU UPON YOUR PROPER *PATH!*

2

HANSCOM AIR FORCE BASE, CONCORD, MASSACHUSETTS:

SPECIFICALLY, THE STERILE CORRIDORS OF THE BASE HOSPITAL--

--WHERE A ONE-MAN ASSAULT FORCE IS EVEN NOW LANDING...

GENERAL HILLARY-- PLEASE WAIT--!

THE HELL I WILL!

I WANT TO SEE TREVOR-- AND I MEAN NOW!

RIGHT THIS WAY, SIR!

DETAILS, DOCTOR?

NOT MANY, GENERAL. NIGHT NURSE FOUND TREVOR IN ONE OF THE BEDS WHILE MAKING ROUNDS. NO IDEA HOW HE GOT THERE.

HE'D OBVIOUSLY BEEN IN SOME SORT OF ACCIDENT. BUT HIS WOUNDS-- EVEN THE INTERNAL INJURIES-- WERE ALREADY HEALING!

HE'S BEEN UNDER ARMED GUARD EVER SINCE!

HE'S BEEN WHAT--?!?

GENERAL TOLLIVER, WHAT'S GOING ON HERE?

GENERAL HILLARY!

GOOD TO SEE YOU AGAIN, SIR--

--BUT I'M AFRAID COLONEL TREVOR IS UNDER ARREST!

TREVOR?!? IN GOD'S NAME, MAN-- WHY?

PLEASE DON'T BE OBTUSE, GENERAL.

NOT ONLY HAS TREVOR RETURNED WITHOUT THE "PHANTOM" JET HE ALLEGEDLY COMMANDEERED--

--BUT HE IS ALSO WANTED FOR QUESTIONING REGARDING THE BRUTAL MURDER OF GENERAL GERARD KOHLER--

--A MURDER, I MIGHT ADD, WITH WHICH YOU ARE INTIMATELY FAMILIAR!

BEGGING THE GENERAL'S *PARDON*-- BUT THAT'S NOT *POSSIBLE!*

COLONEL TREVOR WAS *ORDERED* TO FLY THAT PLANE BY *GENERAL KOHLER* HIMSELF.

THERE IS NO *RECORD* OF THAT, LT. CANDY. DID YOU *SEE* THESE SUPPOSED *ORDERS?*

UH...NO...

"COLONEL TREVOR WILL UNDERGO *QUESTIONING* WHEN HE FINALLY *RECOVERS CONSCIOUSNESS.*

THEN MY DECISION *STANDS!*

"*UNTIL* THEN, HE REMAINS MY *PRISONER!*"

HARVARD UNIVERSITY:

WHERE A *GLISTENING* SHAFT OF *UNNATURAL LIGHT* LANCES THROUGH THE *GATHERING TWILIGHT*--

--CARRYING WITH IT TWO *EXTRAORDINARY* TRAVELERS...

WHY HAVE WE *COME* HERE, HERMES? WHAT *IS* THIS PLACE?

A PLACE OF *HIGHER LEARNING*, DIANA.

HERE YOU SHALL MEET THE *ONE* WHO IS TO BECOME YOUR *MENTOR* AND *GUIDE* THROUGH *MAN'S WORLD.*

WITH HER *BESIDE* YOU, YOU SHALL FINALLY LEARN THE SECRETS OF *THIS*--

--MAD *HARMONIA'S* TALISMAN!

I REGRET I CANNOT AID YOU ANY *FURTHER*, DAUGHTER--BUT KNOW YOU HAVE MY *BLESSINGS.*

GO NOW-- AND TAKE *WITH* YOU THE HOPES OF THE *GODS* THEMSELVES!

"FOR THE *FATE* OF GODS AND MEN ALIKE NOW RESTS UPON YOUR *EFFORTS!*

"*FARE THEE WELL*, DIANA... FARE THEE WELL..."

4

WHILE, ACROSS CAMPUS...

GOT THOSE *BOOKS* YOU WANTED, PROFESSOR KAPATELIS.

WHERE D'YOU WANT ME TO *PUT* 'EM?

THREE *GUESSES,* ELIOT--AND THE FIRST TWO DON'T *COUNT.*

NEXT TO THE *OTHERS,* RIGHT?

AND HERE YOUR PARENTS THINK THEY *WASTED* THE MONEY FOR YOUR *EDUCATION!*

DID YOU GET EVERYTHING I *ASKED* FOR?

OH, YE OF LITTLE *FAITH*--! BUT IF *DEAN MARSDEN* OKAYED THE *PURCHASE* OF THESE--

--HOW COME I HAD TO *SNEAK* 'EM IN?

ELIOT, OH ELIOT--WHERE'S YOUR SENSE OF *ADVENTURE?*

HIGHER *LEARNING* HAS ALWAYS REQUIRED SOME MEASURE OF HIGHER *RISK!*

HEY, DON'T TELL *ME* ABOUT RISK, PROFESSOR.

I'M WORKING FOR *YOU,* REMEMBER--?

-- THE PROFESSOR WITH THE HIGHEST PERCENTAGE OF *TEACHING ASSISTANT CASUALTIES* ON CAMPUS.

SEE YOU *TOMORROW,* PROFESSOR--IF THEY HAVEN'T *ARRESTED* ME BY THEN!

POOR ELIOT... BOY SEEMS TO HAVE DEVELOPED A *TWITCH* SINCE HE STARTED WORKING FOR ME!

NOW WHERE WAS THAT VOLUME ON-- AH-*HAH!*

COME TO *MATER,* YOU ELUSIVE LITTLE INCUNABULUM, YOU--

--OOOOO

NO--!!

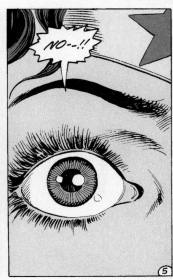

NO--!!

⑤

NO--?

THANKS. LOOKS LIKE I OWE YOU ONE FOR SAVING MY *EPIDERMIS!*

CUTE *COSTUME.* ARE YOU WITH THE *FOUNDER'S DAY* CELEBRATION?

⟨ ARE YOU *WELL, SISTER?* ⟩

⟨ YOUR *WORLD--* AND I-- HAVE *NEED* OF YOU! ⟩

WHAT THE--? SHE'S SPEAKING SOME SORT OF *GIBBERISH--* MIXED WITH *ANCIENT GREEK--!*

PLEASE--*SLOW DOWN!* I CAN'T *UNDERSTAND* YOU!

HOW DO I MAKE HER *UNDERSTAND--?*

PERHAPS...

EH--?! WHAT IS THAT?

IT LOOKS LIKE AN AMULET OF SOME SORT, ANCIENT IN DESIGN--

--YET GLEAMING AS IF IT WERE NEW!

AND WHEN SHE TURNS HER HAND, IT--IT DISAPPEARS!

--AS IF IT EXISTS ON ONLY ONE PLANE OF REALITY--!

WHATEVER THIS AMULET IS, IT'S NOT OF THIS EARTH--

--AND YET, IT'S SO BEAUTIFUL, SO COMPELLING--!

PLEASE, MAY I TOUCH--

--IT--

SLENDER FINGERS BRUSH BURNISHED METAL--

--AND, FOR PROFESSOR JULIA KAPATELIS, THE WORLD SUDDENLY EXPLODES INTO FIRE AND FANTASY!

< GREAT HERA! >

IMAGES FLASH THROUGH HER MIND LIKE QUICKSILVER--

--IMAGES OF HUNGRY CHURNING SEAS AND MAGNIFICENT WARRIOR WOMEN--

--OF WHISPERED VOICES AND A GOLDEN KISS--

--AND YET, DESPITE THE TURMOIL, THERE IS HOPE AND A SENSE OF BELONGING...

...AYE, THIS TUMBLES THROUGH THE MIND OF JULIA KAPATELIS IN LESS THAN AN INSTANT--

-- ALL THIS AND ONE THING MORE --

-- A STIRRING OF PRIDE AND PURPOSE UNLIKE ANYTHING SHE HAS FELT BEFORE --

-- AND THEN IN A WINK, IT IS GONE!

MY HEAD IS SPINNING -- AND YET IT FEELS SO CLEAR!

IT'S AS IF SOME HIDDEN DOOR HAD BEEN OPENED IN MY MIND --!

⟨DO YOU UNDERSTAND NOW?⟩

⟨CAN YOU HELP ME?⟩

I DON'T KNOW WHO YOU ARE, SISTER --

-- BUT I DO KNOW I'D BETTER FIND OUT!

AND THIS AMULET IS SOMEHOW THE KEY TO IT ALL --

-- ONCE WE CAN LEARN WHAT IT UNLOCKS!

HER WORDS ARE STRANGE -- BUT HER MEANING IS CLEAR!

SHE INTENDS TO HELP ME -- AS HERMES FORETOLD!

⟨MY GREEK IS A LITTLE RUSTY --⟩

⟨-- BUT IF WE'RE GOING TO WORK TOGETHER, KIDDO -- I NEED TO KNOW YOUR NAME!⟩

⟨MY... NAME?⟩

⟨PLEASE -- CALL ME DIANA!⟩

9

SOMEWHERE:

AMIDST THE DEEPEST DARKNESS IMMORTAL MIND CAN CONCEIVE, A MONSTROUS FIGURE STANDS HUNCHED BEFORE HIS EARTHEN POOL OF OMNISCIENCE--

--AND IS DISPLEASED BY WHAT HE SEES...

SO-- THE FLEET-FOOTED HERMES HAS LED THE PRINCESS DIANA TO ONE WHO MAY AID HER IN HER QUEST!

WE MUST CRUSH THE CURSED AMAZON-- NOW!

--BEFORE SHE CAN BECOME AN ANNOYANCE!

MY WILY BROTHER DEIMOS WOULD TAKE TIME TO PLAN, TO SCHEME BEFORE HE STRUCK--

--BUT PHOBOS HAS NO NEED FOR SUCH AMENITIES!

I SHALL STRIKE WHILE THE MOMENT IS HOT--

--THEN HUMBLY ACCEPT THE PRAISE OF OUR FATHER ARES FOR TAKING SUCH INITIATIVE!

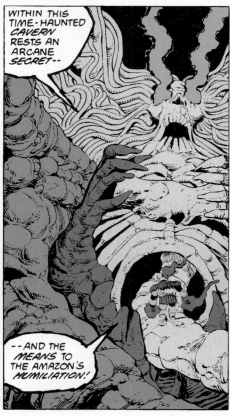

WITHIN THIS TIME-HAUNTED CAVERN RESTS AN ARCANE SECRET--

--AND THE MEANS TO THE AMAZON'S HUMILIATION!

FOR HERE, PULSING WITH AN UNHOLY LIFE OF ITS OWN--

--LURKS THE HEART OF THE GORGON!!

10

AYE, ANCIENT AND *EVIL* IS THE GORGON'S HEART--

--THE STUFF OF WRITHING *NIGHTMARES*--

--AND YET IT IS MINE TO *CONTROL* WITH IMPUNITY--

--TO *SHAPE* AT MY MOST CASUAL *WHIM*--

--INTO THE *OBJECT* OF THE AMAZON'S *DESTRUCTION!*

THERE-- 'TIS *DONE!* MATCH YOUR WICKED WILES AGAINST *THIS,* BROTHER DEIMOS--

--IF YOU *CAN!*

ELSEWHERE:

WELCOME, MY CHILDREN...

...TO THE HOUSE OF *DEIMOS!*

SOON, ALL YOU HAVE *WORKED* AND *WAITED* FOR--

--ALL THAT I HAVE *PROMISED* YOU--

--WILL AT LAST BE *YOURS!*

FOR THE *HOUR* AT LAST IS *UPON* US, MY CHILDREN!

THE MOMENT IS *COME* FOR US --TO *STRIKE!!*

11

FOR YEARS WE HAVE WATCHED *HELPLESSLY* AS THIS GREAT NATION HAS BEEN OVERRUN BY *IMBECILES*--

--BY THOSE WHO DO NOT *LOVE* THIS COUNTRY AS *WE* DO--

--BY THOSE WHO SEEK TO *SUBVERT* ALL THAT WHICH WE *BELIEVE!*

IF THIS *NATION* IS TO BE STRONG, *WE* MUST BE STRONG--

-- STRONG ENOUGH TO *CRUSH* THOSE WHO WOULD *DEFY US!*

NOTHING MUST BE PERMITTED TO *INTERFERE* WITH OUR PLAN TO PROTECT OUR *COUNTRY*--

--TO PROTECT OUR *POWER!*

GO NOW, MY CHILDREN -- AND DO WHAT *MUST* BE DONE!

MAKE THEM *FEAR* US -- FOR THEIR FEAR SHALL GIVE YOU *STRENGTH!*

BOSTON AT RUSH HOUR:

WHERE *ROUTE TWO*, AS EVER, HAS BECOME A *PARKING LOT* FOR THE DURATION...

HONK HONK!

C'MAHN, YOU *IDIOTS*--! WHADDAYA WAITIN' FOR--?

< SUCH *NOISE*--! SUCH *TUMULT*--! HOW CAN PEOPLE *LIVE* LIKE THIS?>

< HOW CAN THEY *THINK*?>

< IT IS A *COMMON* OCCURRENCE, DIANA. YOU'LL GET *USED* TO IT. >

< GUESS THEY DON'T HAVE *TRAFFIC JAMS* WHEREVER IT IS *YOU* COME FROM... >

...LUCKY STIFF!

BOY... IT MUST REALLY BE A *PARADISE!*

12

HANSCOM AIR FORCE BASE, MILITARY HOSPITAL:

QUIT STALLING, TREVOR-- I WANT SOME STRAIGHT ANSWERS!

AND I'D SINCERELY LOVE TO GIVE THEM TO YOU, GENERAL TOLLIVER--

--BUT I CAN'T REMEMBER EVERYTHING THAT HAPPENED TO ME AFTER MY PLANE WENT DOWN!

THEN TRY A LITTLE HARDER, COLONEL!

I DO REMEMBER RANDOM IMAGES...

...BEING ATTACKED BY MY CO-PILOT, FOR INSTANCE... THEN SPOTTING SOME UNCHARTED ISLAND...

AND, STRANGEST OF ALL, BEING CARRIED IN THE ARMS OF THE MOST BEAUTIFUL WOMAN I'VE EVER SEEN...

...A WOMAN WHO COULD FLY...

DELUSION, TREVOR-- ALL OF IT PURE DELUSION--! NO ONE WOULD EVER BELIEVE SUCH AN OUTLANDISH STORY--

--AND, WITH KOHLER DEAD, NO ONE COULD POSSIBLY PROVE IT!

REGARDLESS, WE CANNOT TAKE THAT CHANCE--!

WHAT ARE YOU TALKING ABOUT, GENERAL?

THAT, COLONEL TREVOR, IS SOMETHING YOU WILL NEVER KNOW!

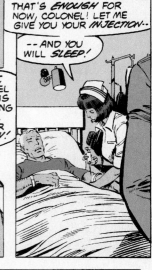

THAT'S ENOUGH FOR NOW, COLONEL! LET ME GIVE YOU YOUR INJECTION--

--AND YOU WILL SLEEP!

YEAH-- PERMANENTLY, I'LL BET! I SAW YOU FILL THAT SYRINGE WITH AIR, SISTER-- --AND I HAVE NO INTENTION OF DYING FROM AN INDUCED EMBOLISM!

WHOK!

UUNNHH!

NEVERTHELESS, COLONEL-- --YOU ARE GOING TO DIE!!

HUNNFF!!

WE HAVE COME MUCH TOO FAR, FOOL--

BROK!

--TO PERMIT YOU TO INTERFERE WITH OUR MASTER PLAN!

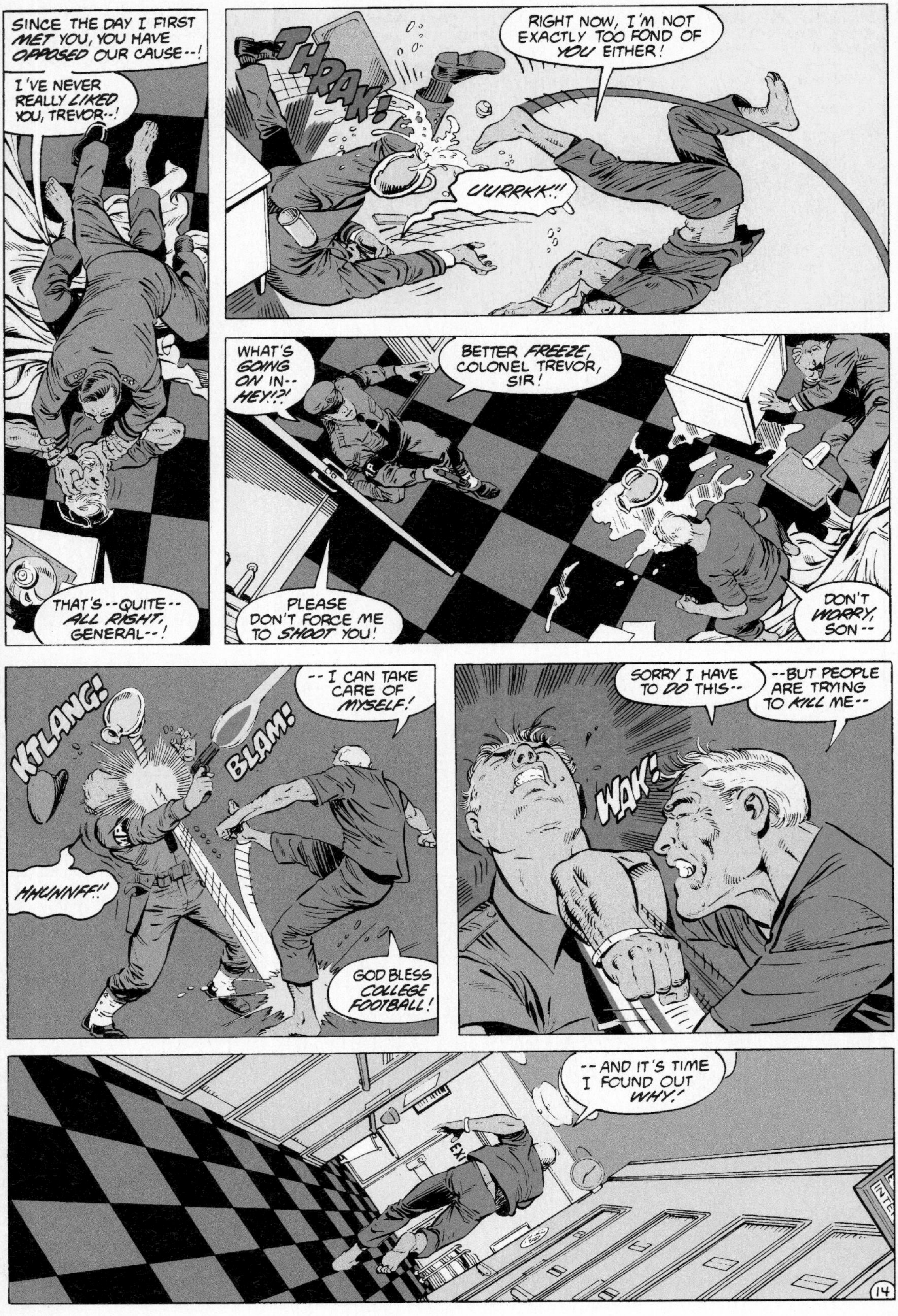
SINCE THE DAY I FIRST MET YOU, YOU HAVE OPPOSED OUR CAUSE--!
I'VE NEVER REALLY LIKED YOU, TREVOR--!
THRAK!
RIGHT NOW, I'M NOT EXACTLY TOO FOND OF YOU EITHER!
UURRKK!!
THAT'S--QUITE--ALL RIGHT, GENERAL--!
WHAT'S GOING ON IN-- HEY!?!
BETTER FREEZE, COLONEL TREVOR, SIR!
PLEASE DON'T FORCE ME TO SHOOT YOU!
DON'T WORRY, SON--
--I CAN TAKE CARE OF MYSELF!
KTLANG!
BLAM!
HHUNNFF!!
GOD BLESS COLLEGE FOOTBALL!
SORRY I HAVE TO DO THIS--
--BUT PEOPLE ARE TRYING TO KILL ME--
WAK!
--AND IT'S TIME I FOUND OUT WHY!
14

SECURITY, THIS IS *SIMMONS!* BLOCK ALL THE *EXITS!*

COLONEL TREVOR IS TRYING TO--

BLAM!

SORRY, SERGEANT-- --BUT *NO ONE* CAN BE PERMITTED TO *INTERFERE!*

ABSOLUTELY *NO ONE!*

BEACON HILL, THE HOME OF PROFESSOR JULIA KAPATELIS:

ISN'T IT A LITTLE *LATE* TO BE MAKING *DELIVERIES?*

HEY, MINE NOT TO REASON *WHY,* KIDDO.

I JUST DO WHAT I'M *TOLD--!*

GEE, WONDER WHAT'S *INSIDE* THIS THING?

MAKES NO *NOISE* WHEN I *SHAKE* IT--!

MOM WILL PROBABLY *KILL* ME IF I OPEN IT--

--BUT THE PACKAGE *IS* ADDRESSED TO *KAPATELIS*--

--AND *I AM* A *KAPATELIS*--

AH, WHAT THE *HECK--!* SHE CAN ONLY KILL ME *ONCE--!*

--VANESSA KAPATELIS--

--BUT, HEY, WHAT'S A DIFFERENT FIRST NAME BETWEEN *FRIENDS?*

WOW-- *RADICAL!*

IT'S A *DOLL*-- THE *UGLIEST* DOLL I'VE EVER *SEEN--!*

MOM WILL POSITIVELY *LOVE* IT!

15

79

THE APARTMENT OF LT. ETTA CANDY:

HE DID *WHAT?!?*

COLONEL MICHAELIS, THAT'S JUST NOT *POSSIBLE!*

I DON'T *CARE* WHAT SECURITY SAID! COLONEL TREVOR SIMPLY WOULDN'T *DO* SUCH A THING!

YOU'RE HIS *BEST FRIEND--!*

CAN'T YOU *HELP* HIM?

I'M DOING WHAT I *CAN,* LIEUTENANT--

--BUT HE'S ACCUSED OF *MURDERING* A GUARD DURING HIS *ESCAPE!*

HANG IN THERE, ETTA... I'LL BE IN *TOUCH.*

I CAN'T BELIEVE THIS IS *HAPPENING--* NOT TO COLONEL TREVOR--!

HE'S THE MOST *HONEST,* MOST *ETHICAL,* MOST-- *DECENT* PERSON I'VE EVER KNOWN!

NO MATTER *WHAT* HE'S ACCUSED OF, I KNOW HE DIDN'T *DO* IT!

HE'S BEING *SET UP* SOMEHOW-- BUT BY *WHO?*

AND, MORE IMPORTANT, *WHY?*

IF ONLY I KNEW-- WHERE HE *WAS--*

--MAYBE I COULD *HELP* HIM SOME--

--MMPPHH!

SORRY TO BE SO ROUGH, LIEUTENANT-- HOPE I DIDN'T *HURT* YOU--!

COLONEL TREVOR?!? WH-WHAT'S *HAPPENING,* SIR?

THEY SAY YOU'VE GONE *CRAZY--* MURDERED A *GUARD--!*

DON'T *BELIEVE* IT, ETTA-- NOT A *WORD!*

PEOPLE ARE TRYING TO *KILL* ME, ETTA-- TRYING TO GET ME *OUT OF THE WAY--*

--AND YOU'VE GOT TO HELP ME FIND OUT *WHY!!*

16

ALSO ELSEWHERE:

‹WELCOME, MY CHILDREN...›

‹...TO THE HOUSE OF DEIMOS!›

‹SOON, ALL YOU HAVE WORKED AND WAITED FOR--›

‹--WILL AT LAST BE YOURS!›

‹--ALL THAT I HAVE PROMISED YOU--›

‹FOR THE HOUR AT LAST IS UPON US, MY CHILDREN!›

‹THE MOMENT IS COME FOR US--TO STRIKE!›

‹FOR YEARS WE HAVE WATCHED HELPLESSLY AS THIS GREAT NATION HAS BEEN OVERRUN BY IMBECILES--›

‹--BY THOSE WHO DO NOT LOVE THIS COUNTRY AS WE DO--›

‹--BY THOSE WHO SEEK TO SUBVERT ALL THAT WHICH WE BELIEVE!›

‹IF THIS NATION IS TO BE STRONG, WE MUST BE STRONG--›

‹--STRONG ENOUGH TO CRUSH THOSE WHO WOULD DEFY US!›

‹NOTHING MUST BE PERMITTED TO INTERFERE WITH OUR PLAN TO PROTECT OUR COUNTRY--›

‹--TO PROTECT OUR POWER!›

‹GO NOW, MY CHILDREN--AND DO WHAT MUST BE DONE!›

* TRANSLATED FROM THE RUSSIAN.

‹MAKE THEM FEAR US--FOR THEIR FEAR SHALL GIVE YOU STRENGTH!›*

⑰

THE KAPATELIS HOME:

‹THESE BOOKS SHOULD HELP US GET A HANDLE ON YOU.›

‹I STILL CAN'T BELIEVE YOU'RE ABLE TO CARRY THEM ALL. YOU MUST REALLY WORK OUT.›

‹WORK... OUT...?›

‹NEVER MIND. I'LL TRY TO EXPLAIN LATER.›

NESSIE? NESSIE, I'M HOME!

BE RIGHT DOWN!

‹I THINK YOU'LL LIKE MY DAUGHTER. SHE'S MUCH LIKE YOU SEEM--›

‹--HEADSTRONG, FIERCELY INDEPENDENT--!›

NESSIE, I'D LIKE YOU TO MEET DIANA.

HI. LOVE YOUR COSTUME.

PART OF THE FOUNDER'S DAY CELEBRATION, HUH?

I'VE NEVER SEEN ANOTHER WOMAN QUITE LIKE HER...

SHE'S SO YOUNG... SO VULNERABLE...

...SO BEAUTIFUL...

NESSIE, DIANA WILL BE STAYING WITH US FOR A LITTLE WHILE.

OH...UH... GREAT...

HOW... UH... LONG IS A LITTLE WHILE?

I REALLY DON'T KNOW, HONEY. DIANA DOESN'T SPEAK ENGLISH.

I'LL HAVE TO TUTOR HER BEFORE WE ACTUALLY GET DOWN TO BUSINESS.

GEE-- THANKS!

THANKS A LOT!

‹PLEASE FORGIVE MY DAUGHTER, DIANA. SHE'S NOT USUALLY LIKE THAT.›

‹BUT I'VE BEEN SO BUSY LATELY... PAID HER SO LITTLE ATTENTION...›

‹SOMETIMES I JUST DON'T UNDERSTAND THAT GIRL.›

18

YEAH, BRIAN, I *KNOW* WE WERE SUPPOSED TO *STUDY* TOGETHER--

--AND I'M *SORRY.*

BRUCE IS BACK!

NO TRESPASSING VIOLATORS WILL BE SKINNED

BUT THE *ALGEBRA TEST* ISN'T TILL *FRIDAY*-- SO WE CAN STILL DO IT *TOMORROW* NIGHT, OKAY?

YEAH, I WANNA SEE YOU *TOO*--

--BUT MOM IS ON THE *RAMPAGE* AGAIN--

--AND I'VE GOT THIS *AWESOME HEADACHE*--

--AND WE'VE GOT THIS--AH-- *SICK AUNT* VISITING--

--AND THE *LAST* THING I WANT IS FOR MY *BOYFRIEND* TO MEET A *FOX* LIKE HER!

MIDNIGHT IN THE KAPATELIS HOME:

LIGHTS BURN BRIGHT IN THE STUDY--

--AS JULIA *MARVELS* AT THE SPEED AND *ALACRITY* WITH WHICH HER NEW STUDENT *CONSUMES* HER FIRST LESSONS--

-- *ABSORBING* IN MERE MINUTES THE RUDIMENTS OF A LANGUAGE THAT EVEN THE *NATIVES* CAN BARELY UNDERSTAND...

WHILE, IN THE *LIVING ROOM,* A *POUTING* VANESSA, LIKE MOST OF AMERICA, HAS FINALLY *DOZED OFF* IN FRONT OF *JOHNNY CARSON*--

-- HAVING COMPLETELY *FORGOTTEN* THE GROTESQUE *STATUE* DELIVERED FOR HER *MOTHER* ONLY HOURS *BEFORE*--

--A *STATUE* WHOSE *COLD EYES* NOW BEGIN TO *GLOW*--

--WITH A *CRUEL* AND *UNNATURAL LIFE!*

⑲

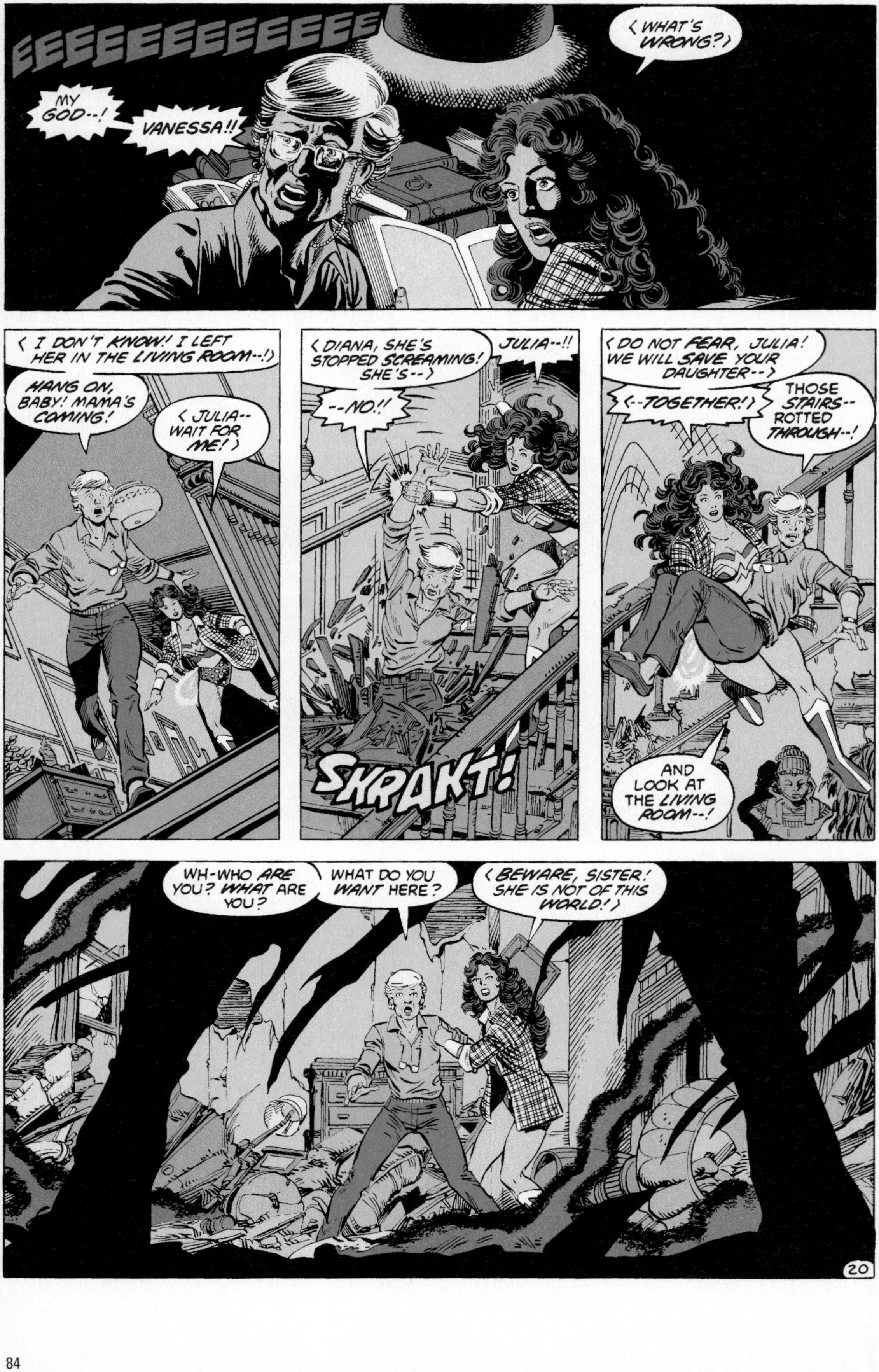
EEEEEEEEEEEEE
⟨ WHAT'S WRONG?⟩
MY GOD--!
VANESSA!!
⟨ I DON'T KNOW! I LEFT HER IN THE LIVING ROOM--!⟩
HANG ON, BABY! MAMA'S COMING!
⟨ JULIA-- WAIT FOR ME!⟩
⟨ DIANA, SHE'S STOPPED SCREAMING! SHE'S--⟩
JULIA--!!
--NO!!
SHRAKT!
⟨ DO NOT FEAR, JULIA! WE WILL SAVE YOUR DAUGHTER--⟩
⟨--TOGETHER!⟩
THOSE STAIRS-- ROTTED THROUGH--!
AND LOOK AT THE LIVING ROOM--!
WH-WHO ARE YOU? WHAT ARE YOU?
WHAT DO YOU WANT HERE?
⟨ BEWARE, SISTER! SHE IS NOT OF THIS WORLD!⟩
20

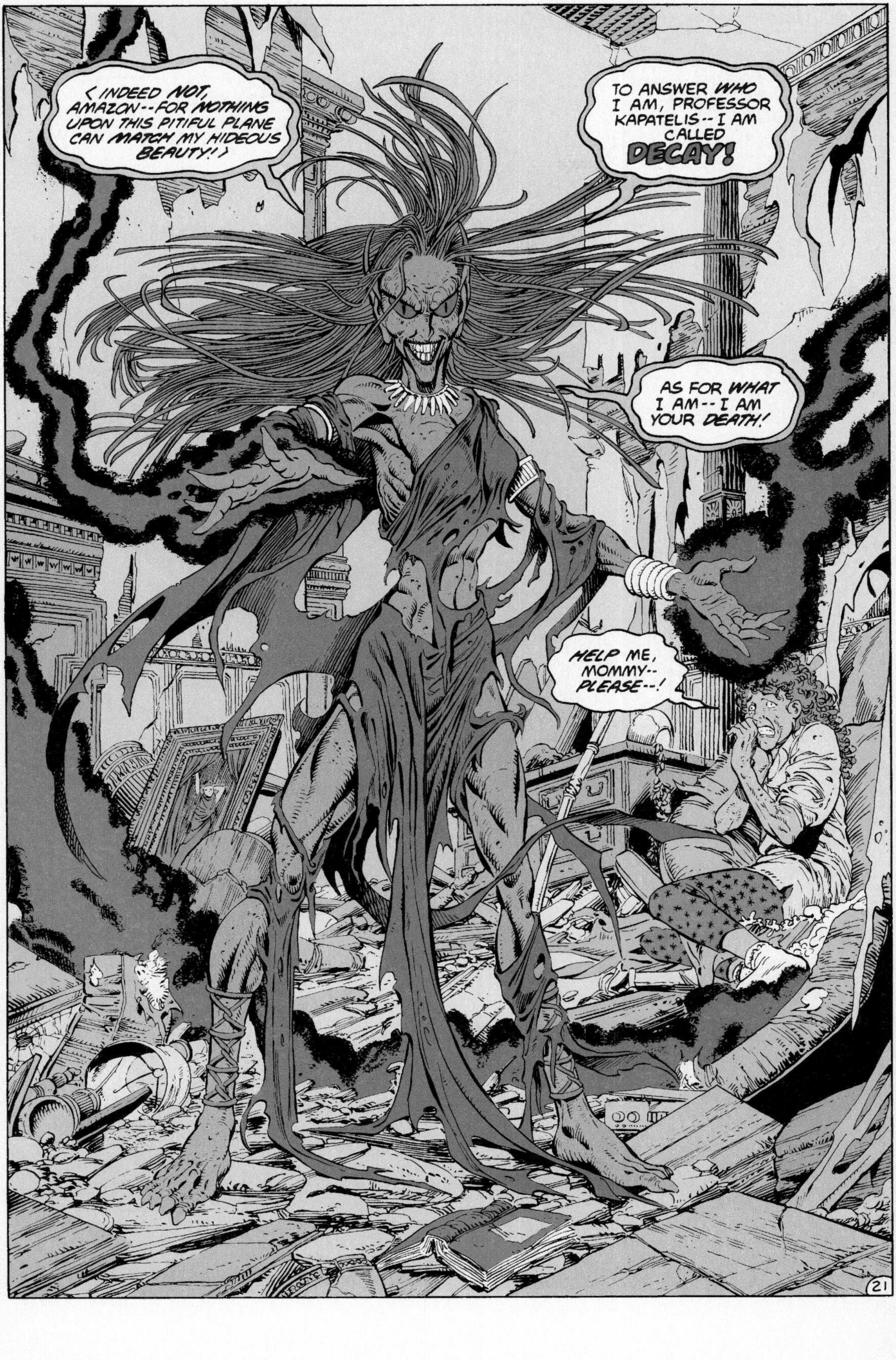

< INDEED NOT, AMAZON--FOR NOTHING UPON THIS PITIFUL PLANE CAN MATCH MY HIDEOUS BEAUTY! >
TO ANSWER WHO I AM, PROFESSOR KAPATELIS--I AM CALLED DECAY!
AS FOR WHAT I AM--I AM YOUR DEATH!
HELP ME, MOMMY--PLEASE--!
21

I'M SO OLD, MOMMY-- SO UGLY AND OLD--!

WHAT'S WRONG WITH ME--?

I DON'T KNOW, BABY--BUT MAMA WILL SAVE YOU--!

‹ JULIA-- NO! DO NOT APPROACH HER! ›

" ‹ HOW IRONIC, AMAZON-- THAT THIS NEW REFUSE SHOULD BECOME YOUR FINAL RESTING PLACE! › "

OH... MY... GOD...

‹ INDEED NOT, AMAZON-- FOR IT IS YOU I SEEK! ›

‹ STEP FORWARD, PRINCESS-- AND FEEL MY FATAL TOUCH! ›

‹ VERY WELL THEN, AMAZON-- I WILL COME TO YOU! ›

‹ AS MY MOTHER--THE MEDUSA-- TURNED MEN TO STONE, SO SHALL I RENDER THEM TO DUST! ›

22

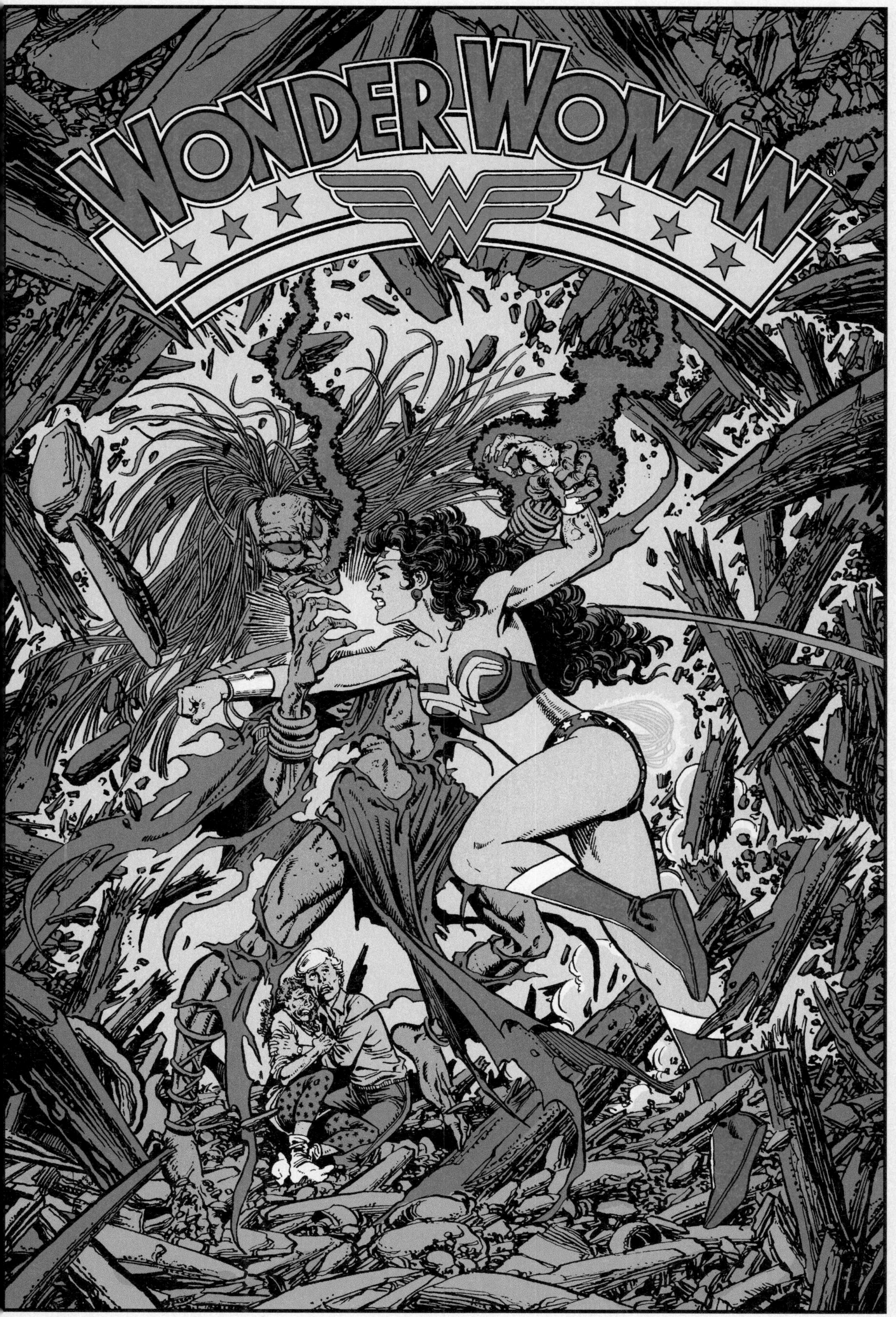
WONDER WOMAN

DC Comics Proudly Presents

WONDER WOMAN

created by William Moulton Marston

A LONG DAY'S JOURNEY INTO FRIGHT!

George Pérez . Len Wein . Bruce D. Patterson . costanza . Tatjana Wood
plotter / penciller   scripter   inker   letterer   colorist

Karen Berger, editor

THIRTY SECONDS AGO, IT WAS THE COMFORTABLY APPOINTED SUBURBAN BOSTON HOME OF PROFESSOR JULIA KAPATELIS AND HER DAUGHTER VANESSA...

FIFTEEN SECONDS AGO, IT BECAME A BATTLEGROUND -- AN ARENA OF CONFRONTATION BETWEEN THE DISPLACED PRINCESS DIANA, DAUGHTER OF THE AMAZONS, AND THE CREATURE CALLED DECAY, DAUGHTER OF THE MEDUSA...

AND NOW, AS DECAY'S ARCANE POWER BRINGS THE BUILDING CRASHING DOWN INTO RUIN, IT APPEARS IT IS ABOUT TO BECOME THE AMAZING AMAZON'S FINAL RESTING PLACE...

...OR IS IT?

WITH THE EXTRAORDINARY *SPEED* THAT IS HER *BIRTHRIGHT*--

--A GIFT FROM THE NOBLE *HERMES*, SWIFTEST OF ALL THE GODS--

--*DIANA* BECOMES A BLUR OF MOTION, CARRYING THE HAPLESS WOMEN FROM THEIR DEVASTATED *HOME*--

--EVEN AS IT CRUMBLES INTO *DUST* AND *ASH* BEHIND THEM!

WHAT THE HECK WAS ALL THAT *NOISE*?

CRIPES! LOOK AT THE *TREES*--!

SO *OLD*-- ALMOST *ROTTEN*--!

HEY--*LOOK!* THE *KAPATELIS* PLACE HAS *CAVED IN*--!

I'VE HEARD OF *TERMITES*--

--BUT THIS IS *RIDICU-LOUS!*

< A MOMENT *LONGER*-- AND DECAY WOULD SURELY HAVE *SLAIN* US! >

< ARE YOU *INJURED*, JULIA? >

NO, I--I'M *FINE*, DIANA. BUT *VANESSA*--!

WHAT HAS THAT MONSTER *DONE* TO HER?

ONLY THAT WHICH I SHALL *SOON* DO TO *YOU*, PROFESSOR--AND TO THAT PITIFUL *AMAZON* AS WELL!

< COME YE *FORTH*, O MIGHTY *PRINCESS*--IF YOU *DARE!* >

2

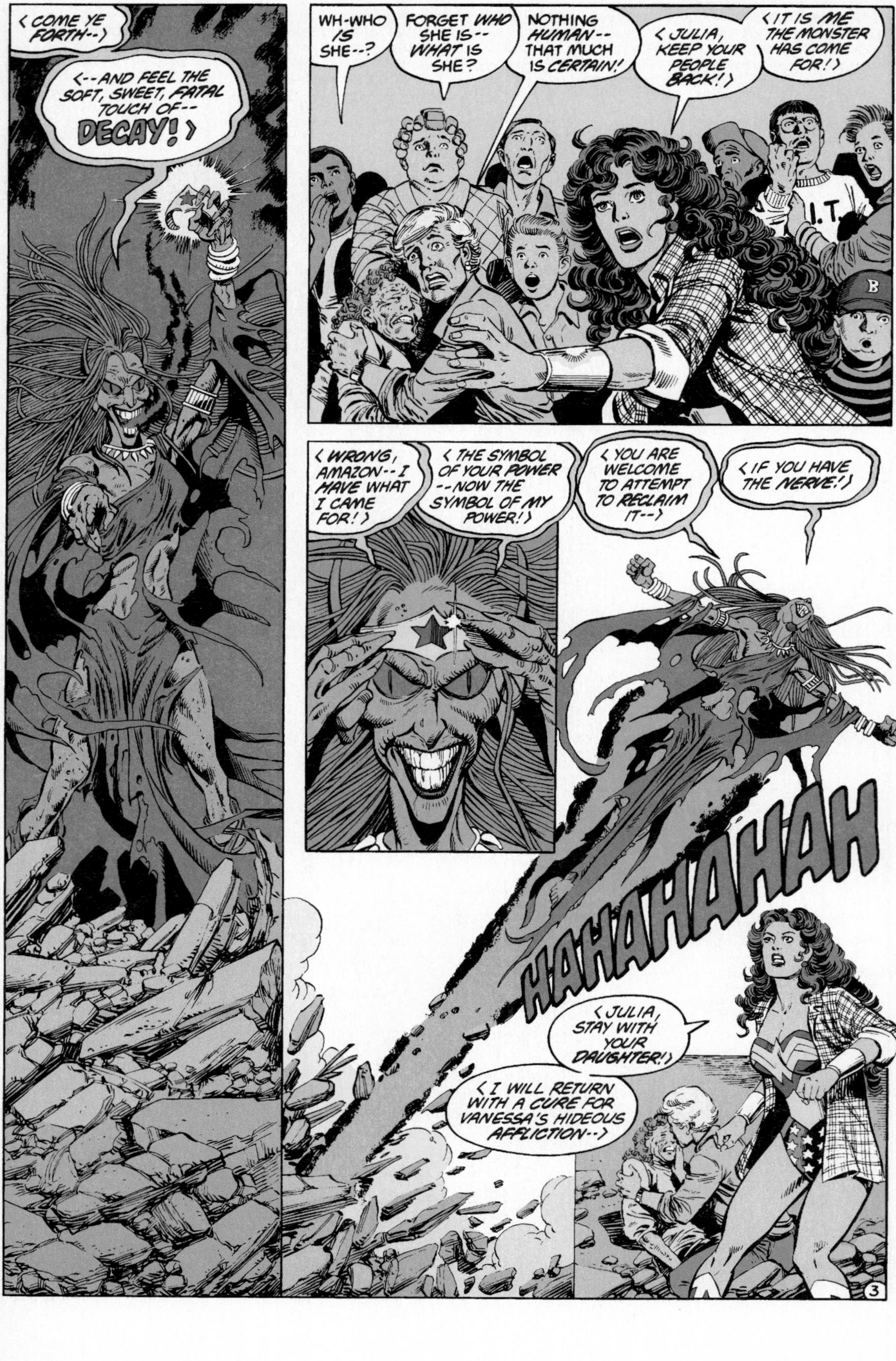

< COME YE FORTH-- >
<--AND FEEL THE SOFT, SWEET, FATAL TOUCH OF-- DECAY! >
WH-WHO IS SHE--?
FORGET WHO SHE IS-- WHAT IS SHE?
NOTHING HUMAN-- THAT MUCH IS CERTAIN!
< JULIA, KEEP YOUR PEOPLE BACK! >
< IT IS ME THE MONSTER HAS COME FOR! >
I.T.
B
< WRONG, AMAZON--I HAVE WHAT I CAME FOR! >
< THE SYMBOL OF YOUR POWER --NOW THE SYMBOL OF MY POWER! >
< YOU ARE WELCOME TO ATTEMPT TO RECLAIM IT-- >
< IF YOU HAVE THE NERVE! >
HAHAHAHAHAH
< JULIA, STAY WITH YOUR DAUGHTER! >
< I WILL RETURN WITH A CURE FOR VANESSA'S HIDEOUS AFFLICTION-- >
3

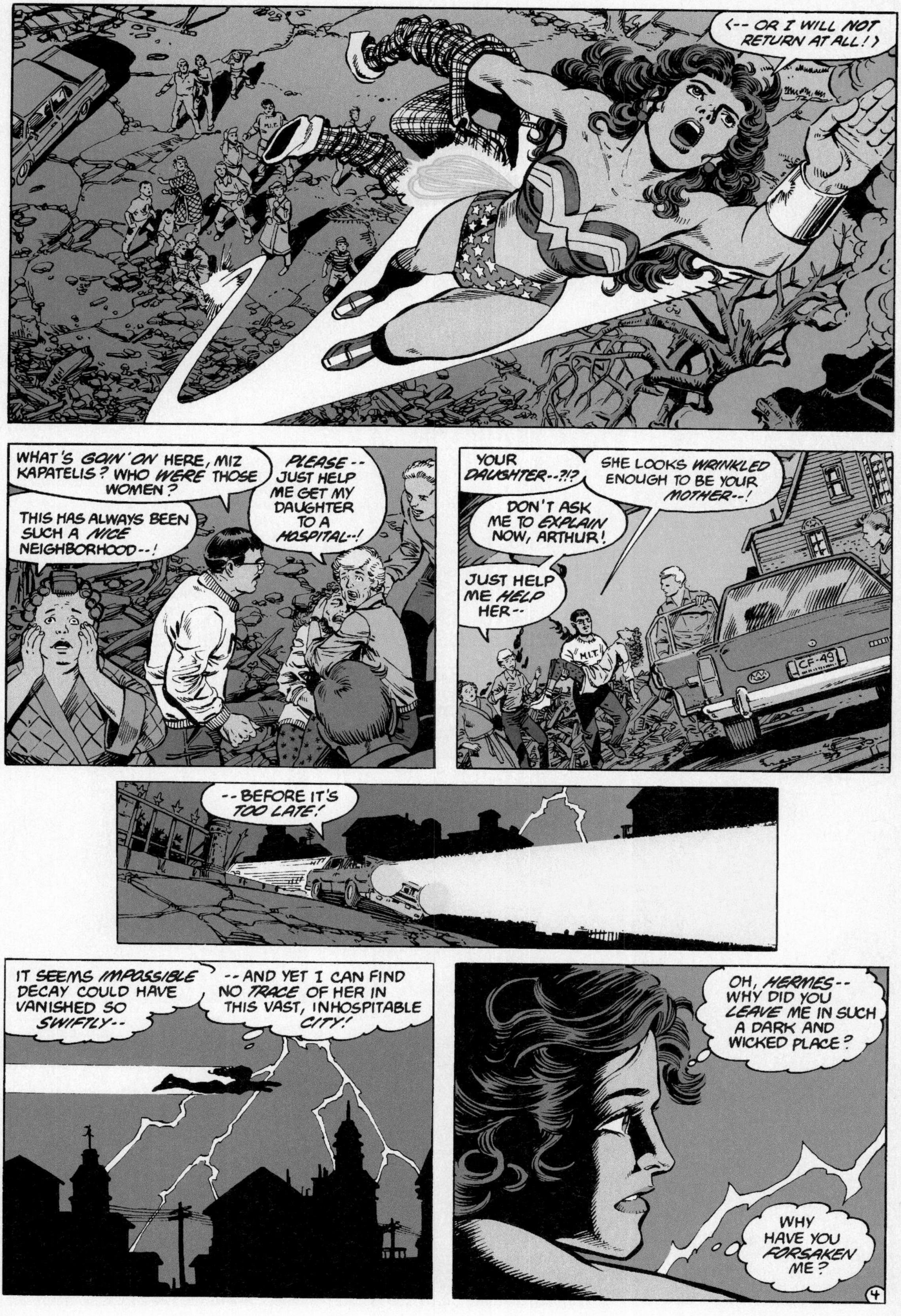
<-- OR I WILL NOT RETURN AT ALL! >
WHAT'S GOIN' ON HERE, MIZ KAPATELIS? WHO WERE THOSE WOMEN?
THIS HAS ALWAYS BEEN SUCH A NICE NEIGHBORHOOD--!
PLEASE-- JUST HELP ME GET MY DAUGHTER TO A HOSPITAL--!
YOUR DAUGHTER--?!?
SHE LOOKS WRINKLED ENOUGH TO BE YOUR MOTHER--!
DON'T ASK ME TO EXPLAIN NOW, ARTHUR!
JUST HELP ME HELP HER--
CF-49
--BEFORE IT'S TOO LATE!
IT SEEMS IMPOSSIBLE DECAY COULD HAVE VANISHED SO SWIFTLY--
--AND YET I CAN FIND NO TRACE OF HER IN THIS VAST, INHOSPITABLE CITY!
OH, HERMES-- WHY DID YOU LEAVE ME IN SUCH A DARK AND WICKED PLACE?
WHY HAVE YOU FORSAKEN ME?
4

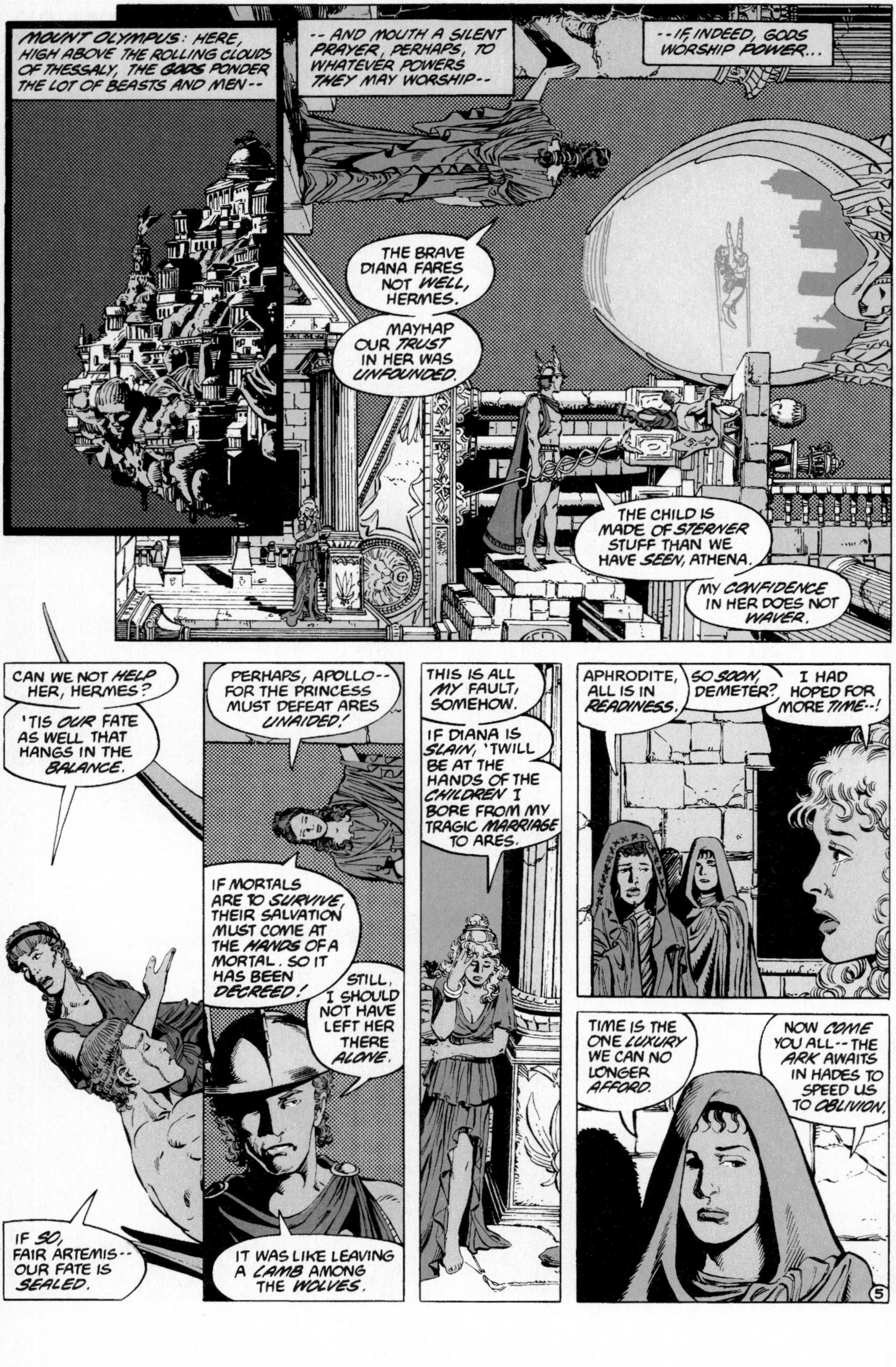
MOUNT OLYMPUS: HERE, HIGH ABOVE THE ROLLING CLOUDS OF THESSALY, THE GODS PONDER THE LOT OF BEASTS AND MEN--
-- AND MOUTH A SILENT PRAYER, PERHAPS, TO WHATEVER POWERS THEY MAY WORSHIP--
--IF, INDEED, GODS WORSHIP POWER...
THE BRAVE DIANA FARES NOT WELL, HERMES.
MAYHAP OUR TRUST IN HER WAS UNFOUNDED.
THE CHILD IS MADE OF STERNER STUFF THAN WE HAVE SEEN, ATHENA.
MY CONFIDENCE IN HER DOES NOT WAVER.
CAN WE NOT HELP HER, HERMES?
'TIS OUR FATE AS WELL THAT HANGS IN THE BALANCE.
IF SO, FAIR ARTEMIS-- OUR FATE IS SEALED.
PERHAPS, APOLLO-- FOR THE PRINCESS MUST DEFEAT ARES UNAIDED!
IF MORTALS ARE TO SURVIVE, THEIR SALVATION MUST COME AT THE HANDS OF A MORTAL. SO IT HAS BEEN DECREED!
STILL, I SHOULD NOT HAVE LEFT HER THERE ALONE.
IT WAS LIKE LEAVING A LAMB AMONG THE WOLVES.
THIS IS ALL MY FAULT, SOMEHOW.
IF DIANA IS SLAIN, 'TWILL BE AT THE HANDS OF THE CHILDREN I BORE FROM MY TRAGIC MARRIAGE TO ARES.
APHRODITE, ALL IS IN READINESS.
SO SOON, DEMETER?
I HAD HOPED FOR MORE TIME--!
TIME IS THE ONE LUXURY WE CAN NO LONGER AFFORD.
NOW COME YOU ALL-- THE ARK AWAITS IN HADES TO SPEED US TO OBLIVION.
5

HANSCOM AIR FORCE BASE: HERE, THE LIGHTS ARE DARK NOW, SHADOWS OVERLAPPING SHADOWS--

--AS ONE SHADOW MOVES WITH A WILL OF ITS OWN...

HMMM

THE COLONEL WAS RIGHT!

TRYON

TREVOR,S

REF. 001353 DEF
ARES PROJECT &
SECURITY CODE

SOMETHING IS DEFINITELY NOT KOSHER HERE.

JUST WHAT EXACTLY IS THE ARES PROJECT?

TOP SECRET

A - At

I DON'T UNDERSTAND ANY OF THIS--

GEN. TOLLIVER

--BUT COLONEL TREVOR WILL--

--ONCE I SHOW HIM THESE PHOTOS!

NOW ALL I HAVE TO DO IS GET OUT OF HERE WITHOUT BEING--

--SEEN--

LIEUTENANT CANDY?!?

'SCUSE ME, MA'AM--?

Y-YES, SERGEANT--?! WH-WHAT IS IT?

SORRY IF I STARTLED YA, MA'AM--

--BUT I THOUGHT YOU MIGHT WANNA SEE THIS!

ROT RIOT

...HERE WITH A SPECIAL REPORT...

6

NOW WHAT?

MORE ARMS SALES TO THE AY-RABS--?

HUSH, SOLDIER! THIS LOOKS IMPORTANT--!

...JANET KASEL, HERE IN BOSTON COMMON, WHERE THE LOCAL FOLIAGE HAS SUDDENLY BEGUN TO ROT AS IF DISEASED...

...WHILE, NEARBY, JUST MOMENTS AGO, A NEWLY OPENED PARKING GARAGE COLLAPSED UNDER ITS OWN WEIGHT, KILLING TWO PEOPLE...

BOTH PHENOMENA HAVE BEEN ATTRIBUTED TO THE BIZARRE GLOWING OBJECT OBSERVED FLYING OVER THE CITY, CAPTURED HERE BY OUR OWN TRAFFIC COPTER...

FRED, WE HAVE JUST RECEIVED WORD THAT THIS MYSTERIOUS DECAY HAS BEGUN TO SPREAD THROUGHOUT THE CITY...

BACK TO YOU AT THE STUDIO.

THANK YOU, JANET. WE'LL HAVE MORE ON THIS INCREDIBLE SITUATION AS SOON AS IT COMES IN.

IN OTHER NEWS TONIGHT, THE SEARCH GOES ON FOR ACCUSED KILLER COLONEL STEPHEN TREVOR...

THE CONTROVERSIAL COLONEL TREVOR IS BEING SOUGHT IN CONNECTION WITH THE DIS-APPEARANCE OF AN AIR FORCE FIGHTER JET--

-- AND HE IS THE PRIMARY SUSPECT IN THE MURDERS OF SEVERAL MILITARY PERSONNEL.

FILE FOOTAGE

WELL, THAT'S JUST ABOUT ENOUGH OF THAT GARBAGE!

SEE YOU TOMORROW, SERGEANT.

G'NIGHT, MA'AM-- AND DON'T WORRY.

I DON'T BELIEVE THE COLONEL DID IT NEITHER.

⑦

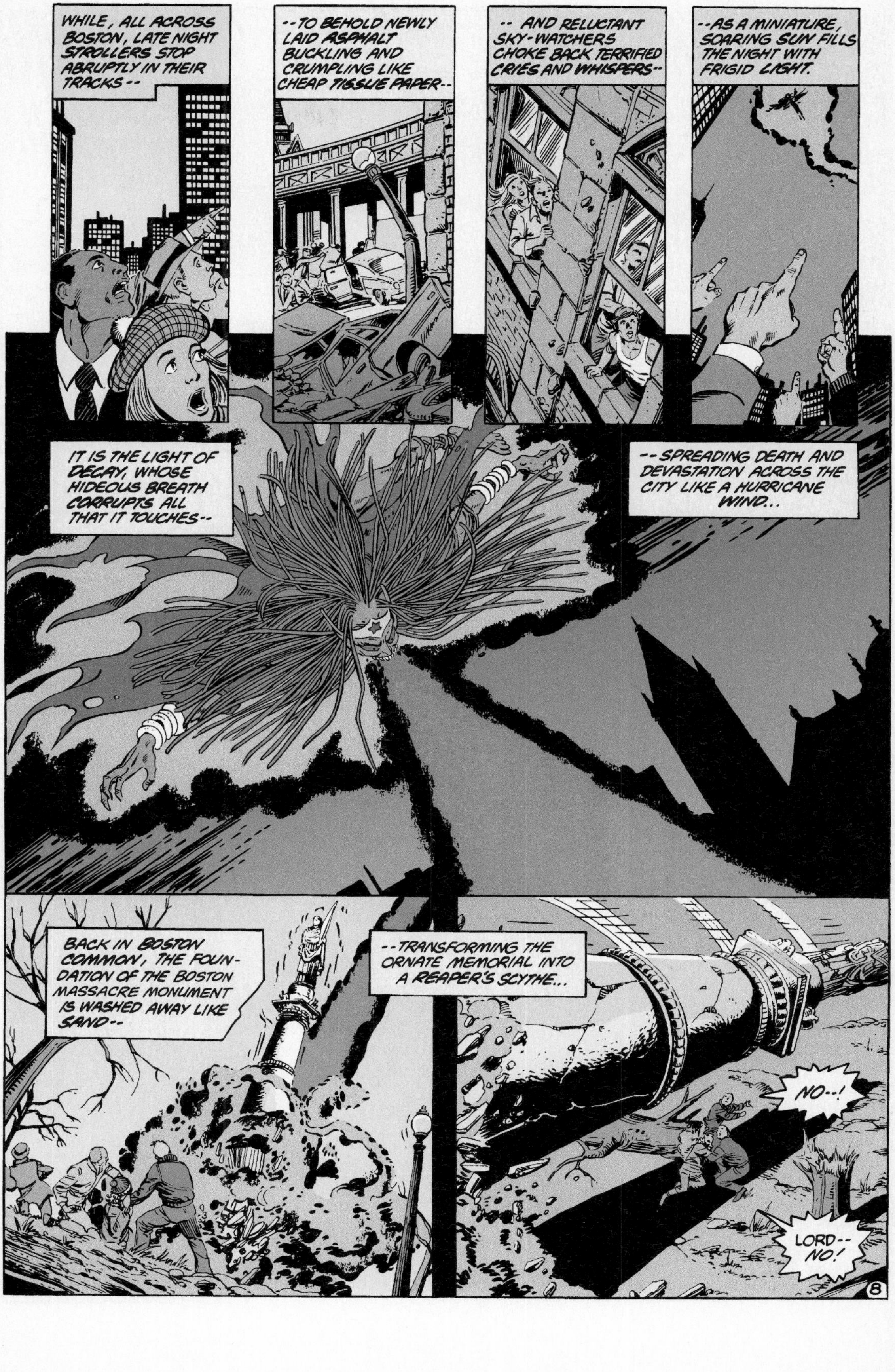
WHILE, ALL ACROSS BOSTON, LATE NIGHT STROLLERS STOP ABRUPTLY IN THEIR TRACKS--
--TO BEHOLD NEWLY LAID ASPHALT BUCKLING AND CRUMPLING LIKE CHEAP TISSUE PAPER--
-- AND RELUCTANT SKY-WATCHERS CHOKE BACK TERRIFIED CRIES AND WHISPERS--
--AS A MINIATURE, SOARING SUN FILLS THE NIGHT WITH FRIGID LIGHT.
IT IS THE LIGHT OF DECAY, WHOSE HIDEOUS BREATH CORRUPTS ALL THAT IT TOUCHES--
--SPREADING DEATH AND DEVASTATION ACROSS THE CITY LIKE A HURRICANE WIND...
BACK IN BOSTON COMMON, THE FOUNDATION OF THE BOSTON MASSACRE MONUMENT IS WASHED AWAY LIKE SAND--
--TRANSFORMING THE ORNATE MEMORIAL INTO A REAPER'S SCYTHE...
NO--!
LORD-- NO!
8

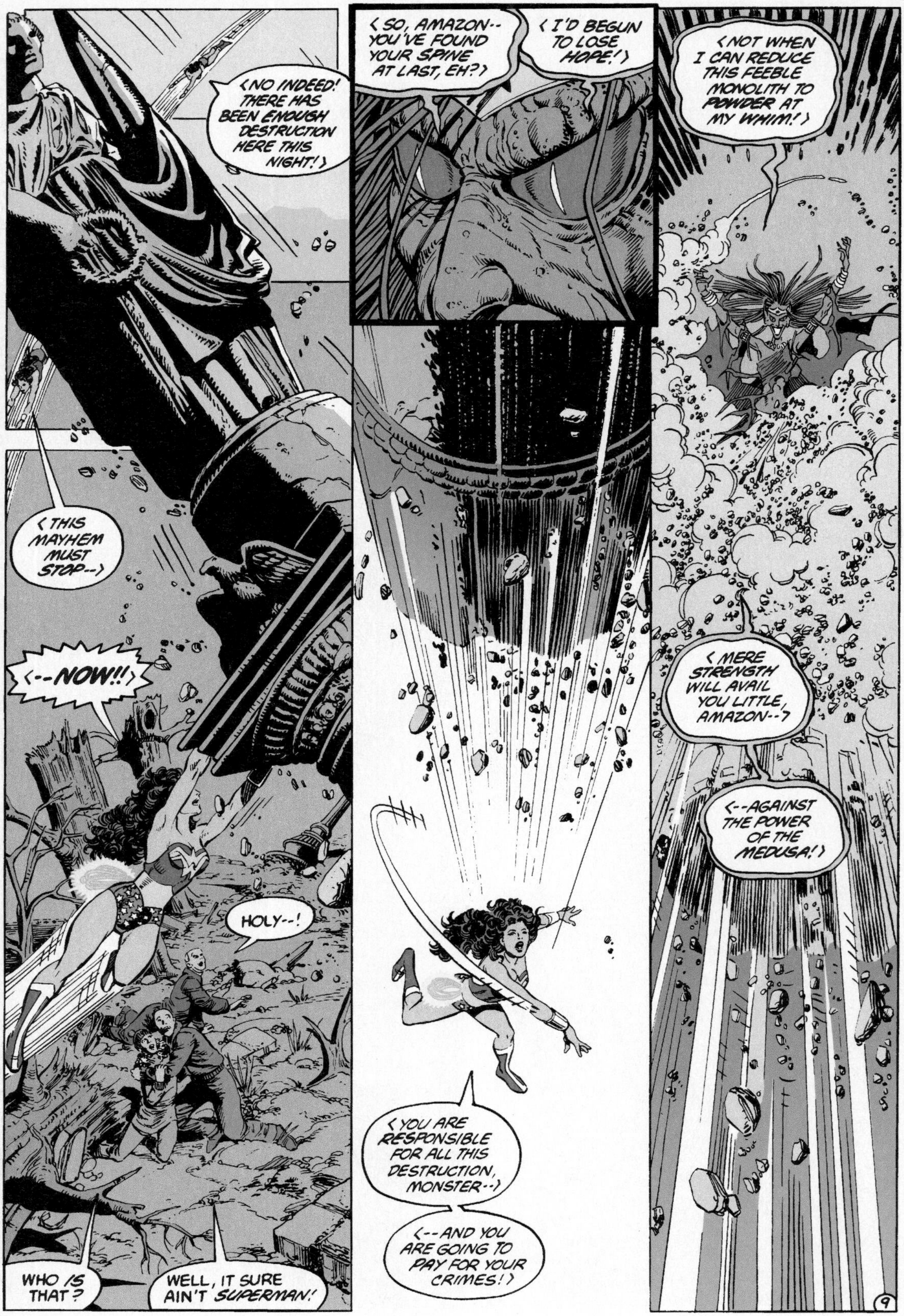

< NO INDEED! THERE HAS BEEN ENOUGH DESTRUCTION HERE THIS NIGHT! >
< SO, AMAZON-- YOU'VE FOUND YOUR SPINE AT LAST, EH? >
< I'D BEGUN TO LOSE HOPE! >
< NOT WHEN I CAN REDUCE THIS FEEBLE MONOLITH TO POWDER AT MY WHIM! >
< THIS MAYHEM MUST STOP-- >
< --NOW!! >
HOLY--!
WHO IS THAT?
WELL, IT SURE AIN'T SUPERMAN!
< YOU ARE RESPONSIBLE FOR ALL THIS DESTRUCTION, MONSTER-- >
< --AND YOU ARE GOING TO PAY FOR YOUR CRIMES! >
< MERE STRENGTH WILL AVAIL YOU LITTLE, AMAZON-- >
< --AGAINST THE POWER OF THE MEDUSA! >
9

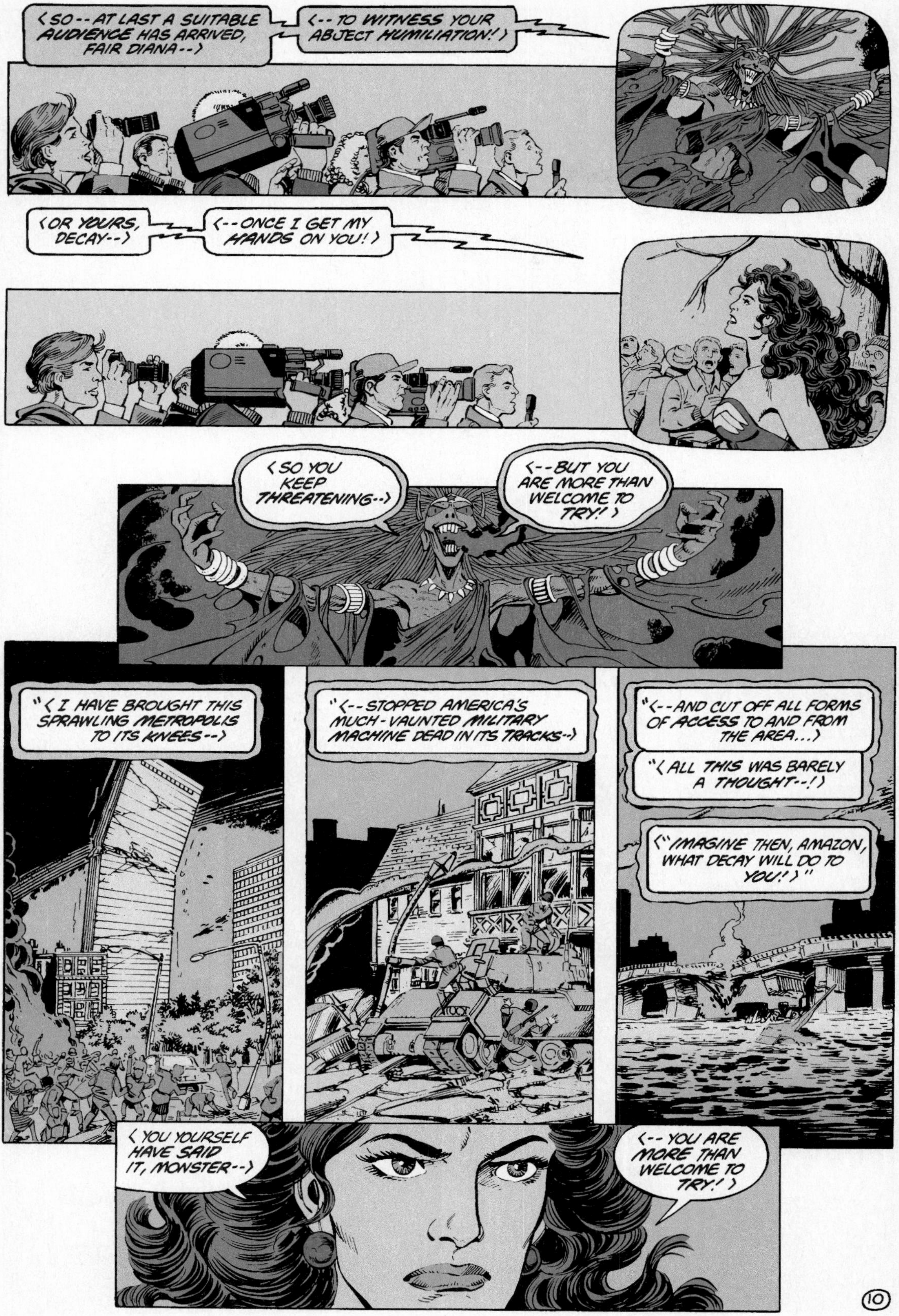

⟨SO--AT LAST A SUITABLE AUDIENCE HAS ARRIVED, FAIR DIANA--⟩
⟨--TO WITNESS YOUR ABJECT HUMILIATION!⟩
⟨OR YOURS, DECAY--⟩
⟨--ONCE I GET MY HANDS ON YOU!⟩
⟨SO YOU KEEP THREATENING--⟩
⟨--BUT YOU ARE MORE THAN WELCOME TO TRY!⟩
"⟨I HAVE BROUGHT THIS SPRAWLING METROPOLIS TO ITS KNEES--⟩
"⟨--STOPPED AMERICA'S MUCH-VAUNTED MILITARY MACHINE DEAD IN ITS TRACKS--⟩
"⟨--AND CUT OFF ALL FORMS OF ACCESS TO AND FROM THE AREA...⟩
"⟨ALL THIS WAS BARELY A THOUGHT--!⟩
⟨"IMAGINE THEN, AMAZON, WHAT DECAY WILL DO TO YOU!⟩"
⟨YOU YOURSELF HAVE SAID IT, MONSTER--⟩
⟨--YOU ARE MORE THAN WELCOME TO TRY!⟩
10

〈 DEFEND YOURSELF, DECAY--OR PERISH! 〉

SHEESH! YOU UNDERSTAND WHAT SHE'S SAYIN'?

NO WAY, MAN--IT'S ALL GREEK TO ME!

〈 AT LAST, AMAZON--YOU'VE COME CLOSE ENOUGH TO FEEL MY FATAL POWER! 〉

〈 I FEEL NOTHING, MONSTER--SAVE AN ALL-CONSUMING RAGE! 〉

〈 AYE, RAGE THAT HAS BLINDED YOU TO THE TRUTH-- 〉

〈 --AND LEFT YOU VULNERABLE TO THE DEATH-GRIP OF DECAY--! 〉

FEEL SO WEAK-- MY SKIN-- STARTING TO WRINKLE--!

〈 FOR MY SAKE, AMAZON-- SUFFER! 〉

〈 FOR THE SAKE OF MY MASTER --DIE!! 〉

〈 NO-- WILL NOT SURRENDER--! 〉

〈 WILL NEVER ADMIT--DEFEAT--! 〉

I ALLOWED MY TEMPER TO OVERCOME ME--

--AND THAT GAVE DECAY THE ADVANTAGE--!

〈 IT IS FINISHED, AMAZON! 〉

〈 SOON YOU WILL BE ONE WITH THE EARTH AND THE DUST ONCE MORE! 〉

11

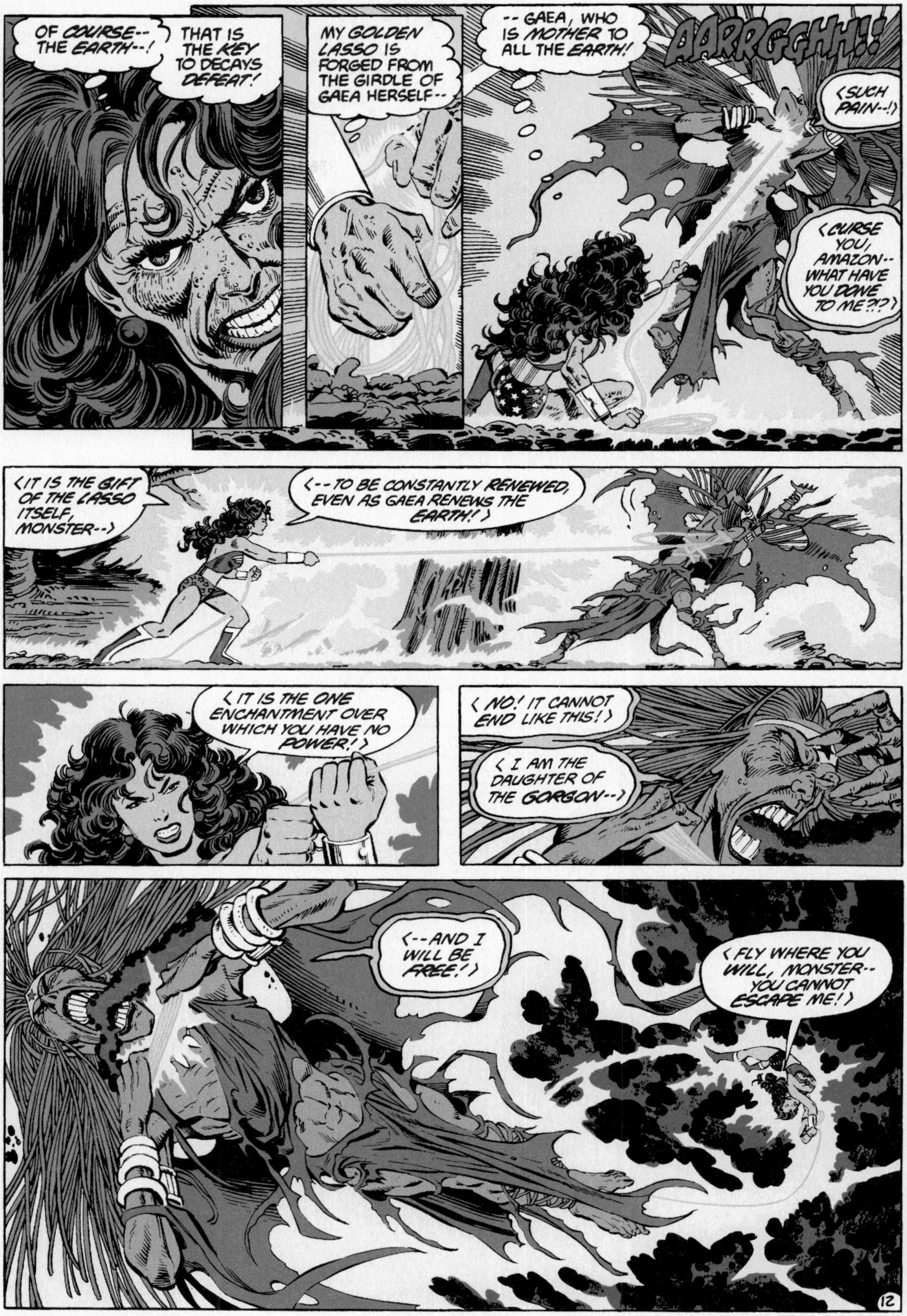
OF COURSE-- THE EARTH--!
THAT IS THE KEY TO DECAYS DEFEAT!
MY GOLDEN LASSO IS FORGED FROM THE GIRDLE OF GAEA HERSELF--
-- GAEA, WHO IS MOTHER TO ALL THE EARTH!
AARRGGHH!!
<SUCH PAIN--!>
<CURSE YOU, AMAZON-- WHAT HAVE YOU DONE TO ME?!?>
<IT IS THE GIFT OF THE LASSO ITSELF, MONSTER-->
<--TO BE CONSTANTLY RENEWED, EVEN AS GAEA RENEWS THE EARTH!>
<IT IS THE ONE ENCHANTMENT OVER WHICH YOU HAVE NO POWER!>
<NO! IT CANNOT END LIKE THIS!>
<I AM THE DAUGHTER OF THE GORGON-->
<--AND I WILL BE FREE!>
<FLY WHERE YOU WILL, MONSTER-- YOU CANNOT ESCAPE ME!>
12

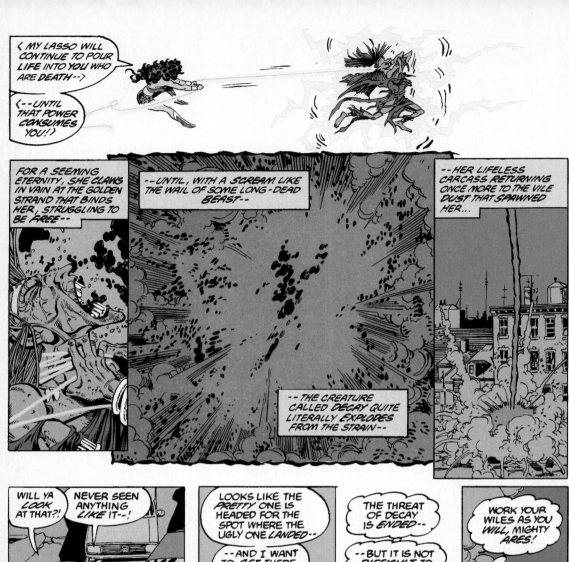

‹ MY LASSO WILL CONTINUE TO POUR LIFE INTO YOU WHO ARE DEATH-- ›

‹ --UNTIL THAT POWER CONSUMES YOU! › ›

FOR A SEEMING ETERNITY, SHE CLAWS IN VAIN AT THE GOLDEN STRAND THAT BINDS HER, STRUGGLING TO BE FREE--

--UNTIL, WITH A SCREAM LIKE THE WAIL OF SOME LONG-DEAD BEAST--

-- THE CREATURE CALLED DECAY QUITE LITERALLY EXPLODES FROM THE STRAIN--

--HER LIFELESS CARCASS RETURNING ONCE MORE TO THE VILE DUST THAT SPAWNED HER...

WILL YA LOOK AT THAT?!

NEVER SEEN ANYTHING LIKE IT--!

YOU SURE THEY AIN'T SHOOTIN' A MOVIE HERE?

COME ON, HOWIE-- LET'S MOVE IT!!

LOOKS LIKE THE PRETTY ONE IS HEADED FOR THE SPOT WHERE THE UGLY ONE LANDED--

--AND I WANT TO GET THERE BEFORE SHE DOES!

THE THREAT OF DECAY IS ENDED--

--BUT IT IS NOT DIFFICULT TO GUESS WHO SENT HER!

WORK YOUR WILES AS YOU WILL, MIGHTY ARES!

13

IN THE FINAL *ACCOUNTING*, THE VICTORY WILL BE *MINE!*

WHUMP WHUMP WHUMP

BY *HERA!* THE *FLASHING THUNDER*--!

AM I SO SOON UNDER *ATTACK* ONCE MORE?

C'MON, SISTER-- DON'T *COVER UP!*

SMILE NICE FOR THE CAMERA, *SWEETIE*-- YOU'RE ON NATIONAL *TV!*

GET *READY*, STUDIO-- I'M GONNA TRY FOR AN *INTERVIEW!*

'SCUSE ME, *MISS*

YOUR *NAME*

GOT A *BOYFRIEND*

WE WERE *WONDERING*

TELL *US*

UNDER *CONTRACT*

YOUR *OWN SERIES*

WH-WHAT ARE THEY *SAYING?* WHAT DO THEY *WANT?*

JULIA--! SHE WOULD UNDER- STAND--!

MUST *FIND* HER AGAIN-- BEFORE I LOSE MY *MIND*--!

HEY-- *WAIT!*

WE NEED TO *KNOW*--!

WHO *ARE* YOU?

WHATEVER THEIR INTENTIONS WERE MATTERS NOT TO *ME!*

ALL THAT MUST *CONCERN* ME NOW IS *ARES!*

14

ELSEWHERE:

IN THAT ARCANE NETHER-REGION BETWEEN HADES AND THE HEAVENS...

DEIMOS--PLEASE! I DID NOT MEAN TO--!

OF COURSE NOT, BROTHER PHOBOS-- YOU NEVER DO!

AND YET, IN YOUR HUNGER TO IMPRESS OUR FATHER ARES, YOU COULD HAVE RUINED EVERYTHING!

I SHOULD DESTROY YOU FOR YOUR INCREDIBLE STUPIDITY!

BUT NOW IS THE MOMENT TO CALCULATE, NOT ACT ON UNREASONING IMPULSE!

WH-WHAT ARE YOU GOING TO DO TO ME, BROTHER DEIMOS?

I HAVE SERVED OUR FATHER WELL!

AYE-- IN THE PAST, PERHAPS.

YOUR PAWN DECAY NEVER STOOD A CHANCE AGAINST A CHILD OF GAEA SUCH AS THE PRINCESS DIANA--

--AND SUCH THOUGHTLESS-NESS COULD WELL HAVE JEOPARDIZED OUR FATHER'S MASTER PLAN!

WERE IT UP TO ME, THIS FOOLISH ACT WOULD HAVE BEEN YOUR LAST--

NOOOOOOOO

--BUT IT IS FOR MIGHTY ARES TO MAKE THAT DECISION--

--AND, FOR SOME INEXPLICABLE REASON, HE SEEMS TO HAVE NEED OF YOU!

JUST BE GRATEFUL, DEAR BROTHER, THAT YOU HAVE LANDED MERELY IN A FOUNTAIN OF BILE--

--AND NOT SOMETHING, SHALL WE SAY, MORE PERMANENT!

BUT ARES' DAY OF GLORY WILL SOON BE UPON US--

--AND WE MUST ALL BE PREPARED!

15

102

HALFWAY ACROSS BOSTON, CAROLE BENNETT STARES AT THE PHOTO ON HER DESK AND CHUCKLES SOFTLY TO HERSELF...

AS CITY EDITOR, SHE REALIZES THAT, IF TONIGHT'S NEWS IS HANDLED RIGHT, THE BOSTON GLOBE-LEADER COULD BE MAKING JOURNALISTIC HISTORY...

SHE ACTUALLY FLEW? LIKE A BIRD? LIKE SUPERMAN?

YOU'RE ABSOLUTELY SURE OF THIS? THIS ISN'T JUST MORE SWAMP GAS OR ANOTHER SIGHTING OF THE ABOMINABLE SNOWMAN?

CAROLE, TAKE A LOOK FOR YOURSELF, OKAY?

YOU REMEMBER WHEN SUPERMAN HIT METROPOLIS -- HOW THE PLANET LATCHED ONTO HIM --!

THEIR CIRCULATION ZOOMED. THIS COULD BE OUR CHANCE.

COULD BE, MAX -- BUT WE'RE GONNA NEED A NAME FOR OUR NEW SUPERSTAR.

HOW ABOUT SUPER-WOMAN?

HOW ABOUT BEING SERIOUS.

HMM -- THIS SYMBOL ON HER CHEST -- LOOKS LIKE A CROSS BETWEEN A BIRD AND SOME SORT OF STYLIZED DOUBLE-W.

WELL, BIRD-WOMAN IS OUT -- THERE'S ALREADY A HAWKWOMAN.

SO LET'S THINK ABOUT THE DOUBLE-W.

I MEAN, SUPERMAN HAS AN S ON HIS CHEST FOR IDENTIFICATION -- SO WHY NOT A DOUBLE-W FOR HER?

WE'RE GONNA NEED SOMETHING CATCHY, SOMETHING EASY TO REMEMBER --

-- AND, BOYS AND GIRLS, I THINK I'VE GOT IT...

BOSTON GLOBE-LEADER

WONDER WOMAN!

MYSTERY HEROINE SAVES CITY FROM DEADLY DEMON OF DESTRUCTION

"...A WBST NEWS-BREAK! LAST NIGHT'S AMAZING BATTLE OVER BOSTON COMMON SEEMS TO HAVE INTRODUCED TO OUR CITY A NEW HEROINE OF ASTONISHING POWER!"

"THE NEWSPAPERS HAVE ALREADY DUBBED HER WONDER WOMAN, AND THAT APPEARS TO BE THE PERFECT NAME FOR HER.

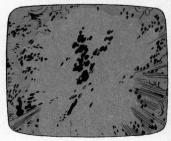

"SINGLE-HANDEDLY, THIS WONDER WOMAN SAVED BOSTON FROM THE MONSTER WHO CALLED HERSELF DECAY, EVEN AS..."

16

WHILE, IN THE WOODLANDS *NORTH* OF BOSTON, A SMALL SEDAN SNAKES ITS WAY UP A WINDING MOUNTAIN TRAIL...

THIRTY-TWO DOLLARS? THIRTY-TWO DOLLARS FOR ONE SACK OF GROCERIES?

I THINK I'M GONNA BE *SICK.*

COLONEL TREVOR, SIR-- I'M *BACK.*

I'LL TELL YOU, SIR-- CONSIDERING THE COST OF *FOOD* THESE DAYS, WE REALLY SHOULD CONSIDER GIVING OURSELVES *UP!*

AT LEAST, IN *JAIL,* WE'D GET FED FOR *FREE!*

COLONEL?

IN *HERE,* ETTA-- SLOWLY LOSING MY *MIND!*

WHAT *IS* IT, SIR? WHAT'S *WRONG?*

JUST GET *IN* HERE -- AND LISTEN TO *THIS!*

REMEMBER THAT *WOMAN* I TOLD YOU ABOUT, ETTA-- THAT *ANGEL* I FANTASIZED WHO *SAVED* ME FROM MY *PLANE CRASH?*

WELL, SHE *WASN'T* A FANTASY -- WASN'T A *HALLUCINATION!*

THERE SHE IS ON THE *TV,* ETTA-- IN THE *FLESH.*

AND, IF YOU'LL PARDON MY *SAYING* SO, COLONEL-- JUDGING FROM THAT *COSTUME* --

--*LOTS* OF *FLESH,* INDEED!

YOU *SEE,* ETTA-- I *WASN'T* GOING CRAZY! MY MYSTERIOUS ANGEL OF MERCY IS *REAL!*

AND SHE MAY BE THE *ONLY* ONE WHO *KNOWS* WHAT REALLY *HAPPENED* TO ME THAT NIGHT.

I HAVEN'T GOT ANY *CHOICE,* ETTA. SOMEHOW, I'VE GOT TO *FIND* HER!

17

WHILE, AT MERCY GENERAL HOSPITAL...

YOU CAN'T KEEP *AVOIDING* ME, DOCTOR -- I WANT TO KNOW THE *TRUTH!*

WHAT THE HELL IS WRONG WITH MY *DAUGHTER?*

TO BE *HONEST,* PROFESSOR KAPATELIS -- I HAVE ABSOLUTELY NO *IDEA!*

THE *AGING PROCESS* APPEARS TO BE IN *REMISSION* -- BUT SINCE WE DON'T KNOW WHAT *CAUSED* IT, WE CAN'T *CURE* IT!

SHE'S TERRIBLY *WEAK* -- AND WE'RE TERRIBLY *FRUSTRATED!*

HAVE *FAITH,* JULIA -- VANESSA WILL *RECOVER* FROM THIS -- -- *SOMEHOW.*

JULIA, THERE'S AN ARMY OF *REPORTERS* DOWN THE HALL. WANT ME TO RUN *INTERFERENCE?*

YES, ARTHUR -- *PLEASE!* I -- I JUST CAN'T *SPEAK* TO THEM RIGHT NOW.

I HAVE TO BE BY *MYSELF* FOR A WHILE -- TRY TO THINK THIS *THROUGH!*

EITHER *THAT* -- OR LOSE MY *MIND.*

THIS IS ALL SO *INSANE...UNNATURAL AGING...MONSTROUS CREATURES...*

I -- I DON'T KNOW HOW TO *DEAL* WITH IT -- DON'T KNOW IF *ANYONE* COULD DEAL WITH IT.

I FEEL HELPLESS AND USELESS AND...

...AND...

GOD, I DON'T KNOW *WHAT* I FEEL...

...OUTSIDE OF *EMPTY.*

EH?

DID SOMEONE *CALL* --?

THOUGHT I HEARD A *VOICE* -- FROM BEYOND THAT *DOOR.*

HELLO?

WHO --?

DIANA --?!? THANK GOD YOU'RE *BACK!* HAVE YOU *LEARNED* ANYTHING? A *CURE* FOR VANESSA'S *CONDITION?*

PLEASE -- *TELL* ME!

18

OH -- I FORGOT. YOU STILL DON'T SPEAK MUCH *ENGLISH*, DO YOU?

‹THE *AMULET*--?‹? WHAT ABOUT--?›

‹OF COURSE, I SHOULD HAVE *REALIZED* -- SOMEHOW IT'S CREATED SOME SORT OF PSYCHIC *BONDING* BETWEEN US.›

‹I STILL DON'T KNOW EXACTLY WHAT'S *GOING ON* HERE--BUT I DO KNOW THERE'S SOME-THING OUT THERE THAT HURT MY *DAUGHTER*--›

‹SO, LIKE IT OR *NOT*, DIANA, FROM THIS POINT *FORWARD*--›

‹--THIS IS *MY* FIGHT, TOO.›

‹--SOME-THING THAT HAS TO BE *STOPPED*!›

THUS, SHORTLY, IN THE KAPATELISES' WINTER HOME...

‹ARE YOU *COLD*, DIANA? YOU DO GET COLD, RIGHT?›

‹HOLD ON, I'LL GET YOU SOMETHING *WARM* TO WEAR.›

‹THANK *GOD*, AT LEAST SOMETHING ABOUT YOU IS *NORMAL*. TODAY A CHILL, TOMORROW THE *SNIFFLES*.›

‹OKAY, LET'S GET DOWN TO *CASES*...›

‹THE *INSCRIPTION* ON THIS AMULET OBVIOUSLY MEANS *SOMETHING*, BUT WE DON'T KNOW *WHAT*.›

‹STILL, I'M *SURE* I'VE SEEN THE DESIGNS ON IT *BEFORE*--SOMEPLACE IN ONE OF MY *BOOKS*.›

‹LET'S SEE, THAT'S *TEN THOUSAND* BOOKS AT *TEN MINUTES* A BOOK...›

‹BETTER SIT DOWN AND *READ* SOMETHING, DIANA. THIS MIGHT TAKE A WHILE.›

‹WHAT WE NEED TO DO IS *CONNECT* THIS AMULET WITH VARIOUS PREVIOUS DESIGNS...›

‹...CHART THE *RELATIVE* SIZE AND SHAPE...›

‹...THEN MAKE THE *APPROPRIATE* COMPARISONS...›

‹DEFINITELY THE STUFF OF *MYSTERY*!›

‹UNFORTUNATELY, I NEVER WAS A FAN OF *ELLERY QUEEN*.›

19

< I REALIZE YOU STILL DON'T SPEAK OUR LANGUAGE, DIANA, BUT PERHAPS IF YOU COULD INDICATE-->

DIANA?

DIANA?

OH, GREAT-- NOW WHAT?

WELL, SHE CAN'T HAVE GONE FAR.

DIANA?

SNAKT

EH?

WHO--?!?

YOU!?!

<YOU!!?!>

20

MISS, *PLEASE*-- DON'T *RUN!*

I HAVEN'T COME HERE TO *HURT* YOU!

...PLEASE...

WHO... *ARE* YOU?

WHAT... DO YOU... *WANT*... WITH ME?

WHERE YOU GET... WEAPON OF... *FLASHING THUNDER*...?

YOU CAN *SPEAK?* THANK *GOD!*

LOOK, YOU SAVED ME *ONCE,* WONDER WOMAN -- YOU'VE *GOT* TO HELP ME *AGAIN!*

PLEASE-- I REALLY *NEED* YOU.

NO! STAY... *BACK!*

YOU *HEARD* WHAT SHE SAID, COLONEL -- BETTER *LISTEN* TO HER!

DON'T BE SURPRISED I *RECOGNIZE* YOU, MISTER! COLONEL STEPHEN TREVOR IS RATHER *FAMOUS* THESE DAYS.

OR SHOULD I SAY *INFAMOUS?*

NOW BACK AWAY FROM HER-- *SLOWLY!*

PLEASE, YOU DON'T *UNDER-STAND*--!

I *KNOW* THIS WOMAN! SHE SAVED MY LIFE WHEN A *MONSTER* TRIED TO MAKE ME CRASH MY *AIRCRAFT!*

I KNOW IT SOUNDS *CRAZY*-- BUT EVERY WORD OF IT IS *TRUE.*

I HATE TO *ADMIT* IT, BUT CONSIDER-ING EVERYTHING *ELSE* THAT'S HAPPENED LATELY, THAT SOUNDS UNCOMFORTABLY *PLAUSIBLE.*

IS *TRUE*...BUT YOU CAME *FIRST* TO PARADISE ISLAND... AS *MESSENGER OF DEATH*...

WHY SHOULD... WE *BELIEVE* YOU... *NOW?*

BECAUSE MY LIFE *DEPENDS* ON IT!

21

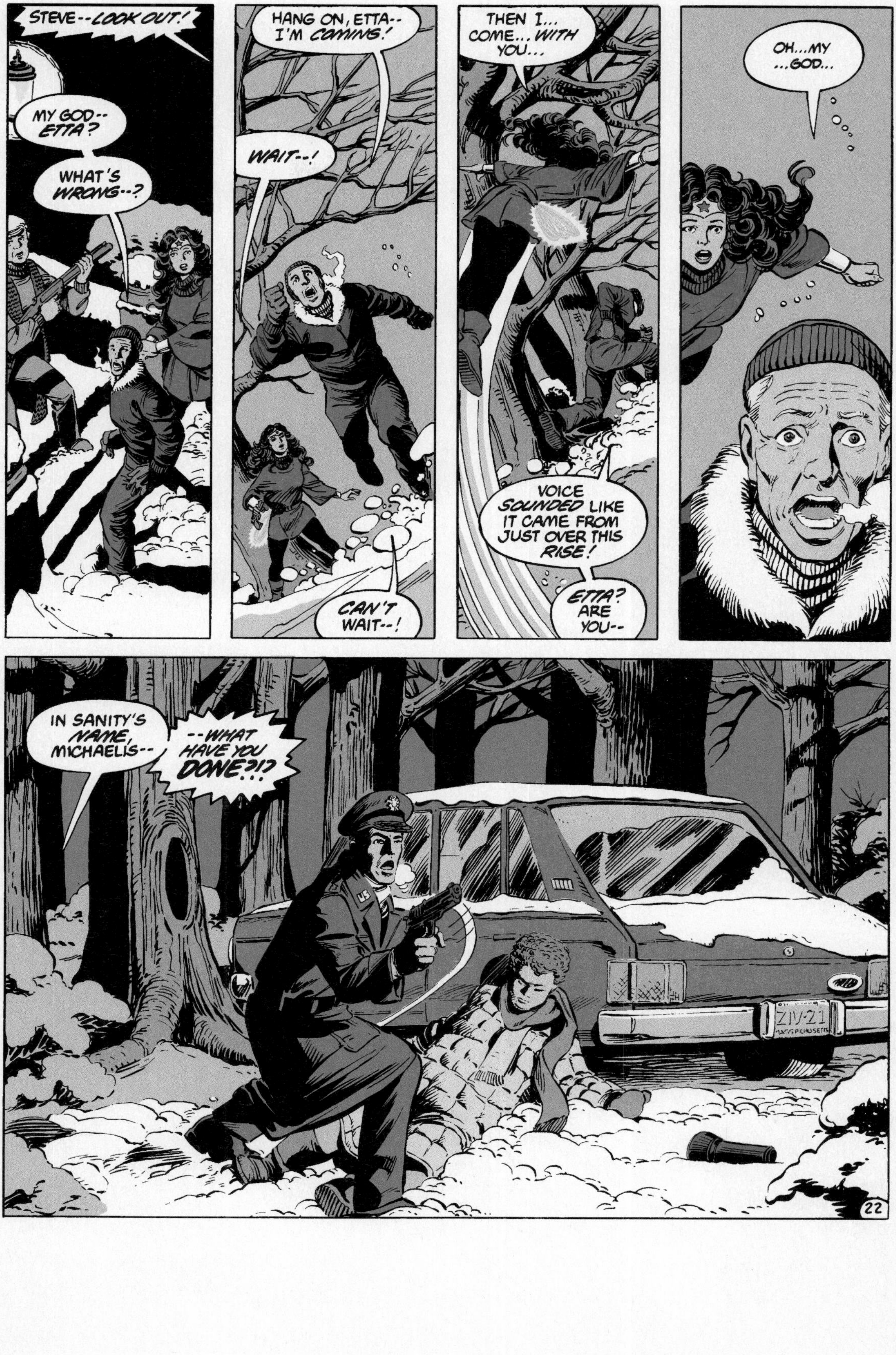
STEVE--LOOK OUT!
MY GOD--ETTA?
WHAT'S WRONG--?
HANG ON, ETTA--I'M COMING!
WAIT--!
CAN'T WAIT--!
THEN I... COME... WITH YOU...
VOICE SOUNDED LIKE IT CAME FROM JUST OVER THIS RISE!
ETTA? ARE YOU--
OH...MY ...GOD...
IN SANITY'S NAME, MICHAELIS--
--WHAT HAVE YOU DONE?!?
ZIV-21
MASSACHUSETTS
22

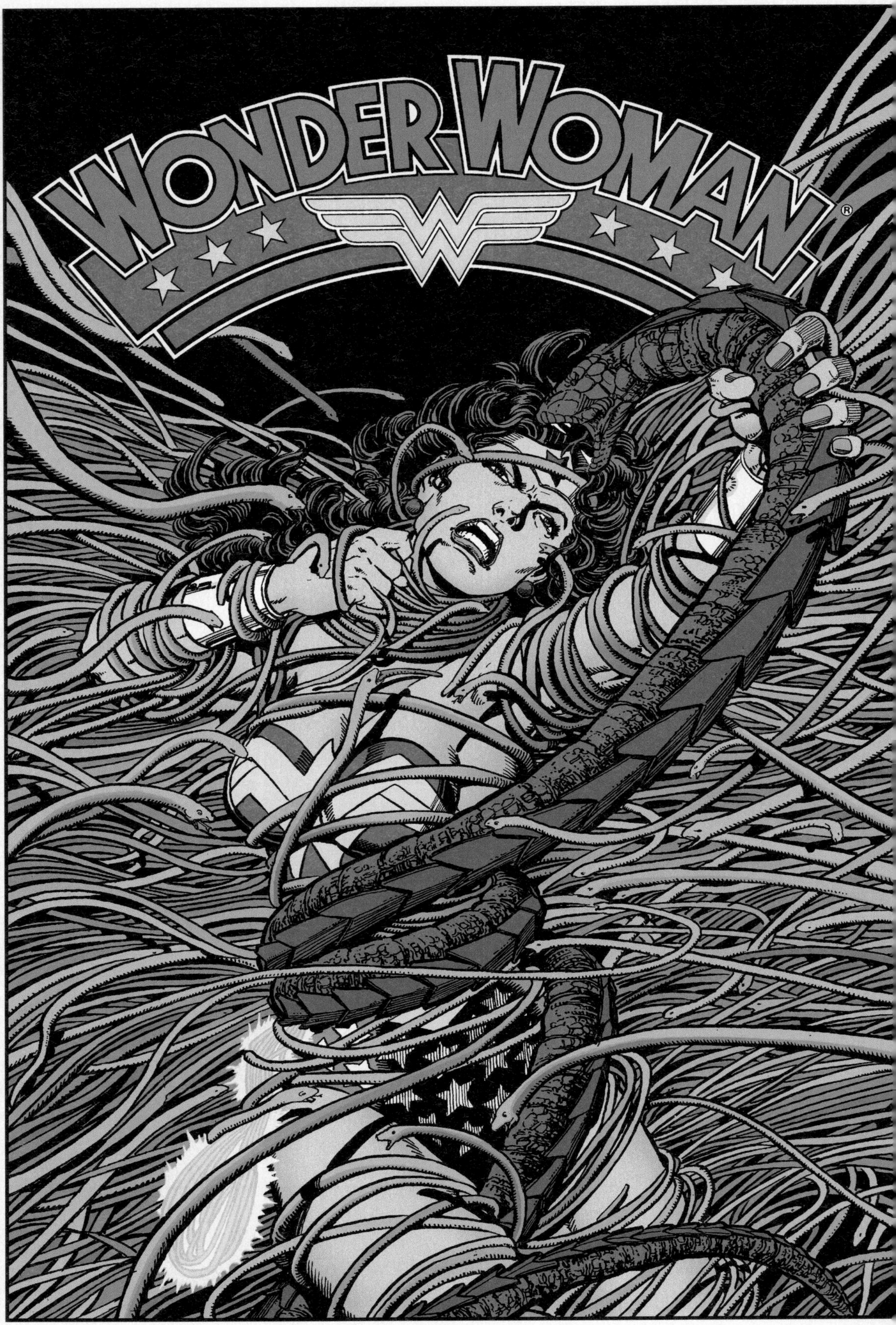
WONDER WOMAN®

THERE IS NO LAUGHTER IN THE HALLS OF *PARADISE* TONIGHT...

ALL ACROSS THE ISLAND, SOMBER AMAZONS WAIT PATIENTLY AS THE ORACLE *MENALIPPE* ATTEMPTS COMMUNION WITH THE GODS WHO HAVE SO LONG PROTECTED THEM...

IS THERE ANY *WORD* YET, SISTER?

NONE -- AND THE WAR-GOD ARES' INFLUENCE GROWS STRONGER ACROSS ALL THE *EARTH*.

NOW, EVEN THE *FLOWERS* ARE DYING.

AND UNLESS MENALIPPE CAN LEARN THE REASON *WHY*, SISTERS--

--WE ALL SOON MAY *FOLLOW!*

THE OLYMPIAN MISTS ARE *CLOUDED*, MY QUEEN.

NEVER HAVE THE SIGNS BEEN SO DIFFICULT TO *DECIPHER!*

YOU ARE *HIDING* SOMETHING FROM ME, MENALIPPE-- I CAN *FEEL* IT!

SPEAK, ORACLE -- TELL ME THE FATE OF MY *DAUGHTER!*

I *SWEAR,* HIPPOLYTE-- I KNOW *NOTHING* OF THE FATE OF THE *PRINCESS DIANA!*

I SENSE ONLY THAT THE *TIME OF RECKONING* IS NEARLY AT HAND.

"*EVEN THE DEMONS* WE'VE HELD CAPTIVE FOR CENTURIES IN THE VERY *BOWELS* OF PARADISE ISLAND ARE IN DANGER OF BEING *RELEASED!*"

I DO NOT *UNDERSTAND* IT, MY QUEEN...

WHY WON'T APOLLO ANSWER HIS WAYWARD DAUGHTERS?

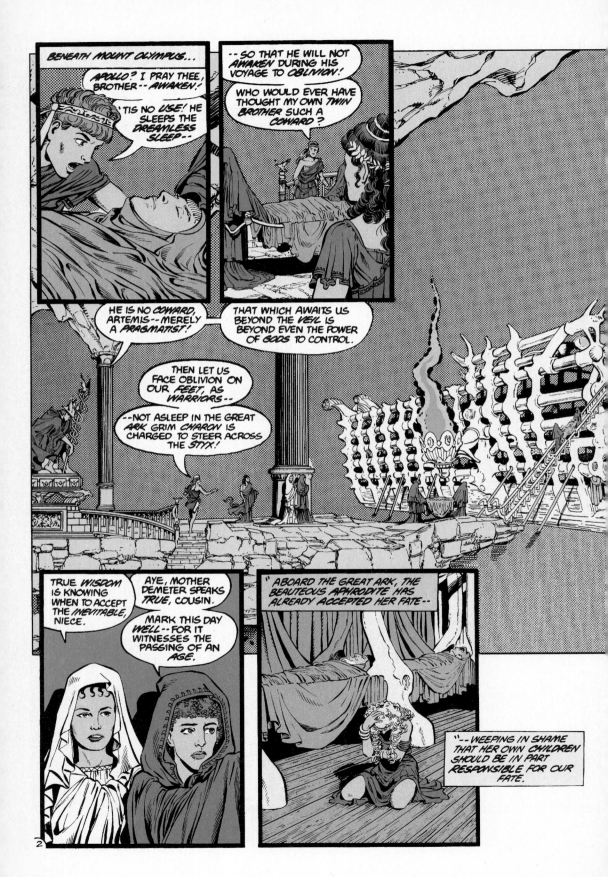

BENEATH MOUNT OLYMPUS...

APOLLO? I PRAY THEE, BROTHER-- AWAKEN!

'TIS NO USE! HE SLEEPS THE DREAMLESS SLEEP--

--SO THAT HE WILL NOT AWAKEN DURING HIS VOYAGE TO OBLIVION!

WHO WOULD EVER HAVE THOUGHT MY OWN TWIN BROTHER SUCH A COWARD?

HE IS NO COWARD, ARTEMIS-- MERELY A PRAGMATIST!

THAT WHICH AWAITS US BEYOND THE VEIL IS BEYOND EVEN THE POWER OF GODS TO CONTROL.

THEN LET US FACE OBLIVION ON OUR FEET, AS WARRIORS--

--NOT ASLEEP IN THE GREAT ARK GRIM CHARON IS CHARGED TO STEER ACROSS THE STYX!

TRUE WISDOM IS KNOWING WHEN TO ACCEPT THE INEVITABLE, NIECE.

AYE, MOTHER DEMETER SPEAKS TRUE, COUSIN.

MARK THIS DAY WELL-- FOR IT WITNESSES THE PASSING OF AN AGE.

"ABOARD THE GREAT ARK, THE BEAUTEOUS APHRODITE HAS ALREADY ACCEPTED HER FATE--

"-- WEEPING IN SHAME THAT HER OWN CHILDREN SHOULD BE IN PART RESPONSIBLE FOR OUR FATE.

2

BUT IT CANNOT SIMPLY *END* LIKE THIS, PERSEPHONE! THERE MUST BE SOME OTHER *WAY*--!

INDEED, DEMETER-- *ATHENA* STANDS WITH *ARTEMIS!*

THOUGH THE *GODS* MAY WELL HAVE LOST FAITH IN *MAN*--

--'TIS THE PRINCESS DIANA'S FAITH IN *US* THAT MUST ULTIMATELY PROVE OUR *SALVATION!*

"COME NOW, CHILD-- THE FERRYMAN IS WAITING!"

FOR THE *MOMENT* AT LEAST--LET THE FERRYMAN *WAIT!*

3

MAN'S WORLD:

...ALL ACROSS THE GLOBE TODAY, TENSIONS RAN HIGH...

SUMMIT COLLAPSE

...AS THE PROPOSED SUMMIT MEETING BETWEEN EAST AND WEST COLLAPSED MERE HOURS BEFORE THE CONFERENCE WAS TO BEGIN...

"...WHILE, IN THE MIDDLE EAST, NEW FIGHTING BROKE OUT JUST MOMENTS AFTER A TEMPORARY TRUCE WAS DECLARED...

"...AND IN NICARAGUA, UNEXPECTED REBEL RAIDS WERE RESPONSIBLE FOR HEAVY CASUALTIES...

"INTERNATIONAL TERRORISM ALSO RAN RAMPANT TODAY, RESULTING IN NUMEROUS DEATHS AT FRENCH AND BELGIAN AIRPORTS...

"...WHILE IN LOCAL NEWS, ALLEGED MURDERER COLONEL STEPHEN TREVOR IS STILL AT LARGE--

"--AMIDST RAMPANT RUMORS THAT TREVOR IS ACTUALLY A SOVIET SPY...

SPY?

"AT A PRESS CONFERENCE EARLIER TODAY, GENERAL SAM TOLLIVER CLAIMED TO POSSESS EVIDENCE PROVING TREVOR'S GUILT--

"--AND SWORE HE WOULD NOT REST UNTIL TREVOR'S APPREHENSION...

" MEANWHILE, THE IDENTITY OF THE INCREDIBLE WONDER WOMAN WHO SAVED BOSTON FROM THE CREATURE CALLED DECAY REMAINS A MYSTERY...

WONDER WOMAN

"A SIZABLE REWARD HAS BEEN OFFERED TO ANYONE WHO KNOWS HER CURRENT WHEREABOUTS..."

‹IS SHE ALL RIGHT, DIANA?›

4

⟨IT IS MERELY A SUPERFICIAL *BUMP*, JULIA.⟩

⟨I HAVE RELIEVED THE *PAIN*--AND IT HAS ALREADY BEGUN TO *HEAL*.⟩

DON'T KNOW WHAT SHE *DID* TO ME--BUT SHE SHOULD *BOTTLE* IT!

MY HEAD FEELS *GREAT*.

NOW THAT WE KNOW LT. CANDY WILL *SURVIVE*, IT'S TIME WE GOT A FEW *ANSWERS*.

EXACTLY WHAT THE HELL *HAPPENED* OUT THERE?

I'M AFRAID IT'S ALL *MY* FAULT, PROFESSOR KAPATELIS.

WHEN I *STARTLED* ETTA, SHE SLIPPED AGAINST THE *CAR* AND BUMPED HER *SKULL*.

SORRY I *TRACKED* YOU OUT HERE, STEVE--BUT I WANTED TO *HELP*!

NO REASON TO *APOLOGIZE*, MICHAELIS-- FOR BEING MY *FRIEND*.

SO WHAT DO WE DO *NOW*?

GOOD *QUESTION*.

I THINK IT ALL DEPENDS ON THE LOVELY *LADY* HERE.

⟨I STILL DO NOT UNDERSTAND ALL THAT HAS *HAPPENED* HERE--⟩

⟨--BUT I TRULY BELIEVE NOW THAT WHICH FLEET HERMES *TOLD* ME!⟩

⟨I NEED YOU, STEPHEN TREVOR.⟩

⟨IT SEEMS WE NEED EACH *OTHER*.⟩

I STILL CAN'T UNDER- STAND A WORD SHE'S *SAYING*.

I CAN! IT APPEARS TO BE SOME FORM OF ANCIENT *GREEK*--

--AND GREEK'S *ONE* LANGUAGE I SPEAK *FLUENTLY*!

SWELL! THEN MAYBE *YOU* CAN ASK HER WHAT'S GOING ON.

I THINK *I* CAN EXPLAIN THAT, LT. CANDY.

APPARENTLY, IT HAS SOME- THING TO DO WITH--

--*THIS*,!!

THIS ANCIENT *TALISMAN*--!

NO, IT *DOESN'T!* I THOUGHT *THIS* WAS BEHIND EVERYTHING--

THIS FILE I STOLE FROM *GENERAL TOLLIVER'S* OFFICE.

IT'S CALLED THE *ARES PROJECT!*

PROJECT: ARES THE ARES PROJECT

⑤

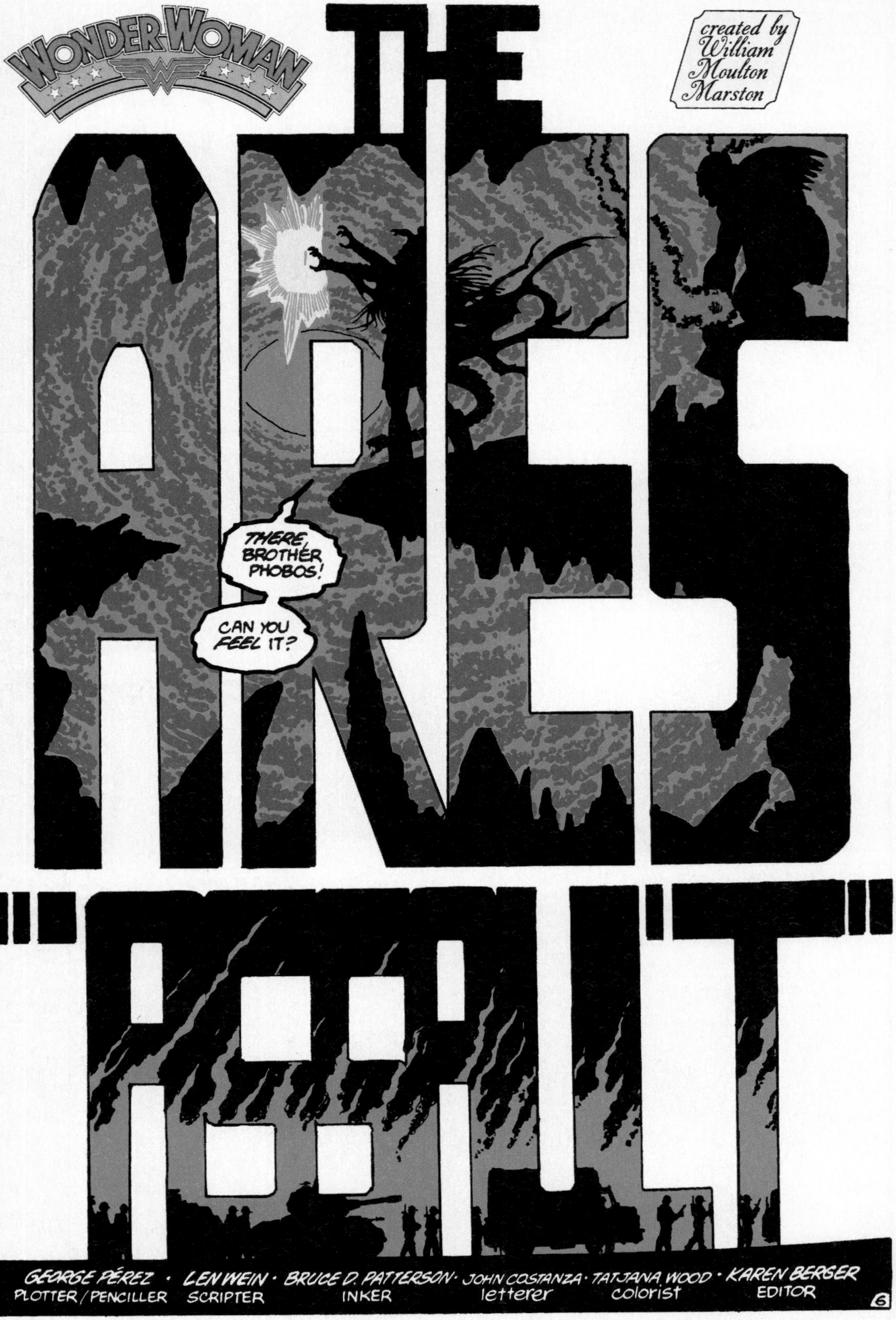
WONDER WOMAN
created by William Moulton Marston
THE ARES "AFFAIR"
THERE, BROTHER PHOBOS!
CAN YOU FEEL IT?
GEORGE PÉREZ · PLOTTER/PENCILLER
LEN WEIN · SCRIPTER
BRUCE D. PATTERSON · INKER
JOHN COSTANZA · letterer
TATJANA WOOD · colorist
KAREN BERGER · EDITOR
6

CAN YOU *FEEL* THAT FATEFUL TINGLE OF EAGER *ANTICIPATION?*

TOUCH THE *TALISMAN,* DEAR BROTHER-- AND KNOW THE MOMENT AT LAST IS *UPON US!*

THE MOMENT WHEN OUR FIERCE FATHER'S *MASTER PLAN* WILL FINALLY BEAR *FRUIT!*

"*EVEN NOW,* ON OPPOSITE SIDES OF THE EARTH, THE GREAT MILITARY POWERS ARE MASSING THEIR FORCES...

"*GENERALS WHO HAVE LONG WORSHIPPED* OUR FATHER NOW LEAD THEIR TROOPS INTO COMBAT FOR REASONS THEY DO NOT FULLY *COMPREHEND...*

"..*AND YET ARE WILLING TO FIGHT TO THE DEATH TO OBEY!*"

DO YOU NOT FEEL THE *RUSH* IN THE AIR, BROTHER PHOBOS-- THE POWERFUL *SURGE* OF ARES' ASCEN- DANCY?

LIFE IS TRULY *SWEET!*

FOR *YOU* PERHAPS, BROTHER DEIMOS--

-- BUT *PHOBOS* NOW FEELS A LUMBERING *FAILURE* IN HIS WAR- GOD FATHER'S EYES--

-- AND I INTEND TO *DO* SOMETHING TO *CORRECT* THAT SITUATION!

⑦

HOURS LATER, AT THE WINTER HOME OF JULIA KAPATELIS, AFTER ONE OF THE LONGEST NIGHTS IN THE COLLECTIVE MEMORY OF THOSE WHO ARE HIDING THERE...

EUREKA! IT'S FINISHED!

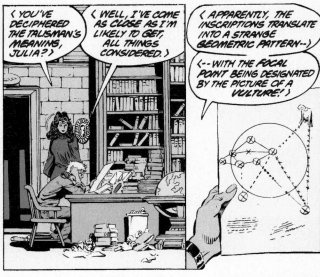

‹ YOU'VE DECIPHERED THE TALISMAN'S MEANING, JULIA? ›

‹ WELL, I'VE COME AS CLOSE AS I'M LIKELY TO GET, ALL THINGS CONSIDERED. ›

‹ APPARENTLY, THE INSCRIPTIONS TRANSLATE INTO A STRANGE GEOMETRIC PATTERN-- ›

‹ --WITH THE FOCAL POINT BEING DESIGNATED BY THE PICTURE OF A VULTURE! ›

‹ EXACTLY WHAT THAT MEANS, THOUGH, I COULDN'T BEGIN TO TELL YOU! ›

‹ AND FRANKLY, AT THIS PARTICULAR MOMENT, I'M TOO THOROUGHLY EXHAUSTED TO EVEN THINK ABOUT IT! ›

‹ WAKE ME SOMETIME BEFORE THE NEXT MILLENNIUM, OKAY? ›

‹ SLEEP WELL, SISTER-- YOU HAVE EARNED YOUR REST. ›

‹ THE REST OF THE TASK IS MINE TO ACCOMPLISH. ›

JULIA KAPATELIS IS TRULY AN EXTRAORDINARY WOMAN.

NO AMAZON COULD HAVE SOLVED THE PUZZLE MORE SWIFTLY-- OR MORE INGENIOUSLY.

THIS PATTERN LOOKS STRANGELY FAMILIAR TO ME--!

IF I COULD ONLY PLACE IT--!

PERHAPS THE OTHERS CAN HELP ME.

THEN AGAIN-- PERHAPS NOT.

ALL OF THEM-- ASLEEP.

WHAT A STRANGE WORLD THIS IS TO WHICH HERMES DELIVERED ME...

...POPULATED BY BEINGS UNLIKE ANY I HAD EVER KNOWN ON PARADISE ISLAND...

8

THIS *ETTA CANDY*, FOR EXAMPLE--!

SHE IS A *WOMAN*, EVEN AS *I* AM--

--AND YET SHE IS SO *STOUT*, SO *UNFIT*--!

SHE SEEMS *WIDE* ENOUGH TO BE *TWO* OF ME!

AND THIS MAN, *MICHAELIS*--

--WHO SPEAKS MY *NATIVE TONGUE* AS DOES *JULIA*--

--AND WHO ALSO WEARS A *GOLDEN BAND* UPON HIS FINGER-- AS DOES *JULIA.*

IS IT A *MARK* OF SOME SORT-- A *SIGN* OF SOME SECRET *UNION*--?

AND *THEN*, OF COURSE, THERE IS THE ONE CALLED *TREVOR*--!

NOBLE HERMES TOLD ME OUR *FATES* WERE IRREVOCABLY *INTERTWINED*--

--BUT *HOW?*

WILL I LEARN THE *TRUTH* BEFORE IT IS *TOO LATE?*

PERHAPS THE ANSWER LIES IN THIS *DIAGRAM*--

--THE SECRET OF MAD *HARMONIA'S* TALISMAN!

IF I COULD BUT--

GREAT HERA.!!

THOSE MARKINGS ON TREVOR'S *CHART*--!

THEY ARE A *MIRROR IMAGE* OF THE TALISMAN'S *INSCRIPTION*--!

< BY GAEA'S GIRDLE! >

< SUDDENLY ARES' PLAN IS CLEAR TO ME! >

9

ELSEWHERE:

MY GOD! THEY'VE BREACHED THE OUTER DEFENSES!

GET ME HQ! I'VE GOT TO--

BLAM!

C'MON, MEN-- MOVE IT!!

RIGHT THIS WAY, GENERAL...

"IT'S WAITING FOR YOU!"

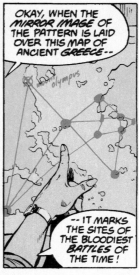

OKAY, WHEN THE MIRROR IMAGE OF THE PATTERN IS LAID OVER THIS MAP OF ANCIENT GREECE--

Mount Olympus

-- IT MARKS THE SITES OF THE BLOODIEST BATTLES OF THE TIME!

YET THE SAME PATTERN, WHEN LAID OVER A MAP OF THE MODERN WORLD--

--INDICATES SITES OF VARIOUS NUCLEAR BASES OR OTHER SUSPECTED ATTACK FACILITIES!

AND THE VULTURE RESTS OVER THE LOCATION OF MOUNT OLYMPUS ON THE OLD MAP--

--AND A POINT IN THE UPPER MIDWESTERN UNITED STATES ON THE NEW MAP--

--THAT MUST BE THE FOCAL POINT OF THIS ARES PROJECT!

GENERAL HILLARY-- THIS IS COLONEL MICHAELS!

YOU'VE GOT TO LISTEN TO ME, SIR!

THE SECURITY OF THE NATION --MAYBE THE WORLD--COULD BE AT STAKE!

CALM DOWN, MICHAELIS --AND START FROM THE BEGINNING!

BUT I'M WARNING YOU--

--IF THIS IS SOME HARE-BRAINED SCHEME TO HELP YOUR BUDDY TREVOR, I'LL--

GENERAL HILLARY, IT JUST CAME OVER THE WIRE!

ONE OF OUR OWN DEFENSE BASES HAS JUST BEEN COMMAN- DEERED BY RENEGADE U.S. TROOPS!

WHAT--?!?

GEN HILLARY

10

I'VE NEVER HEARD OF ANYTHING *LIKE* IT, SIR!

APPARENTLY, THEY HAD HAD *INSIDE HELP* FROM SOLDIERS ALREADY ON THE BASE!

...MY... *GOD*...

THE BASE IS COMPLETELY UNDER THEIR *CONTROL* NOW--!

AND, SIR--THEY'VE SET THE *MISSILES* AT THE *READY POINT!*

GENERAL?

SIR?

WHAT *IS* IT, COLONEL? WHAT'S *WRONG?*

I CAN'T *BELIEVE* IT!

WE'RE *TOO LATE!*

GENERAL TOLLIVER AND HIS TROOPS HAVE TAKEN OVER A *MISSILE* BASE!

DAMN!

IF OUR *RESEARCH* IS CORRECT, THE *SAME* THING IS PROBABLY HAPPENING IN *RUSSIA* EVEN AS WE SPEAK!

ALL TOLLIVER HAS TO DO IS PRESS A *BUTTON*--TO START WORLD WAR *THREE!!*

WE'VE GOT TO GET IN THERE AND *STOP* HIM!

BUT *HOW?*

THAT... IS MY... JOB...!

THE SECRET TO FINDING... THE *OTHER* HALF OF... MAD HARMONIA'S *AMULET*...RESTS IN THIS... *MIRROR.*

FOR IT IS BUT... A *REFLECTION* OF THE HALF I HOLD... AN EXACT *REVERSAL!*

IF THE IMAGES ARE *JOINED*...THE TALISMAN IS ONCE AGAIN *COMPLETE*... AND IT SHALL LEAD ME AT LAST... TO *ARES!*

THEN WHAT ARE WE *WAITING* FOR? LET'S GET GOING!

SHE SPEAKS *ENGLISH* NOW!?

WHEN DID SHE LEARN TO *SPEAK* ENGLISH?

IF ONE *LISTENS*... ONE *LEARNS.*

NOW I MUST TAKE... MY *LEAVE.*

NOT WITHOUT *ME*, YOU DON'T.

JULIA--*NO!* THIS IS *MY* BATTLE ALONE--!

THE *HELL* IT IS! MY *DAUGHTER* LIES NEAR *DEATH*--THE WORLD STANDS ON THE BRINK OF *NUCLEAR DESTRUCTION*--!

I HAVE JUST AS MUCH *STAKE* IN THIS AS *YOU* DO, SISTER-- AND I WON'T BE *DENIED!*

I'M WITH THE *PROFESSOR*, PRETTY LADY-- I'VE GOT A *FAMILY* OF MY OWN TO PROTECT!

AND I STASHED SOME SURPLUS *WEAPONRY* IN THE TRUNK OF MY CAR FOR JUST SUCH AN *EMERGENCY!*

YOU NEVER CEASE TO *AMAZE* ME, MATTHEW.

USED TO BE A *BOY SCOUT*, STEVE-- I'M ALWAYS *PREPARED.*

GLAD TO *HEAR* IT, SIR-- WHERE'S MY WEAPON?

IF I'M FIT TO SERVE IN THIS MAN'S AIR FORCE, I'M FIT TO CARRY A *WEAPON*, COLONEL!

WELL, SIR? TIME IS *WASTING!*

YOUR--?

BETTER *GIVE* IT TO HER, MICHAELIS.

SHE'S BEEN MY *AIDE* LONG ENOUGH FOR ME TO *KNOW* WHEN NOT TO *ARGUE* WITH HER!

BUT--!

12

ARE *THESE* BEINGS TYPICAL *EXAMPLES* OF THE RACE MY MOTHER SO *FEARED*?

FOR CREATURES SO *FRAIL*, THERE IS STILL A STRANGE *NOBILITY* ABOUT THEM.

IS IT MERELY THEIR INSTINCT FOR *SURVIVAL* THAT DRIVES THEM-- OR SOMETHING MORE *PROFOUND*?

WHATEVER THE *TRUTH*, MY MISSION IS *CLEAR*--

-- AND THE TWO *IMAGES* OF THE TALISMAN MUST BE *JOINED*!

READY WHENEVER *YOU* ARE, DIANA!

THEN LET IT BE *DONE*!

ARE YOU *SURE* ABOUT THIS, SIR?

I MEAN, PUTTING SUCH *BLIND FAITH* IN SOMEONE WE HARDLY *KNOW*--!

I CAN'T *EXPLAIN* IT, ETTA. MAYBE IT'S BECAUSE SHE SAVED MY *LIFE*--

-- OR MAYBE IT'S SOMETHING *MORE*!

AS *CORNY* AS THIS MAY SOUND...

...SHE REMINDS ME OF MY *MOTHER*.

THEN THE *TALISMAN* TOUCHES THE *SILVERED GLASS*--

-- AND, FOR FIVE FRAGILE *SOULS*, THE UNIVERSE ABRUPTLY TURNS INSIDE *OUT*!

123

13

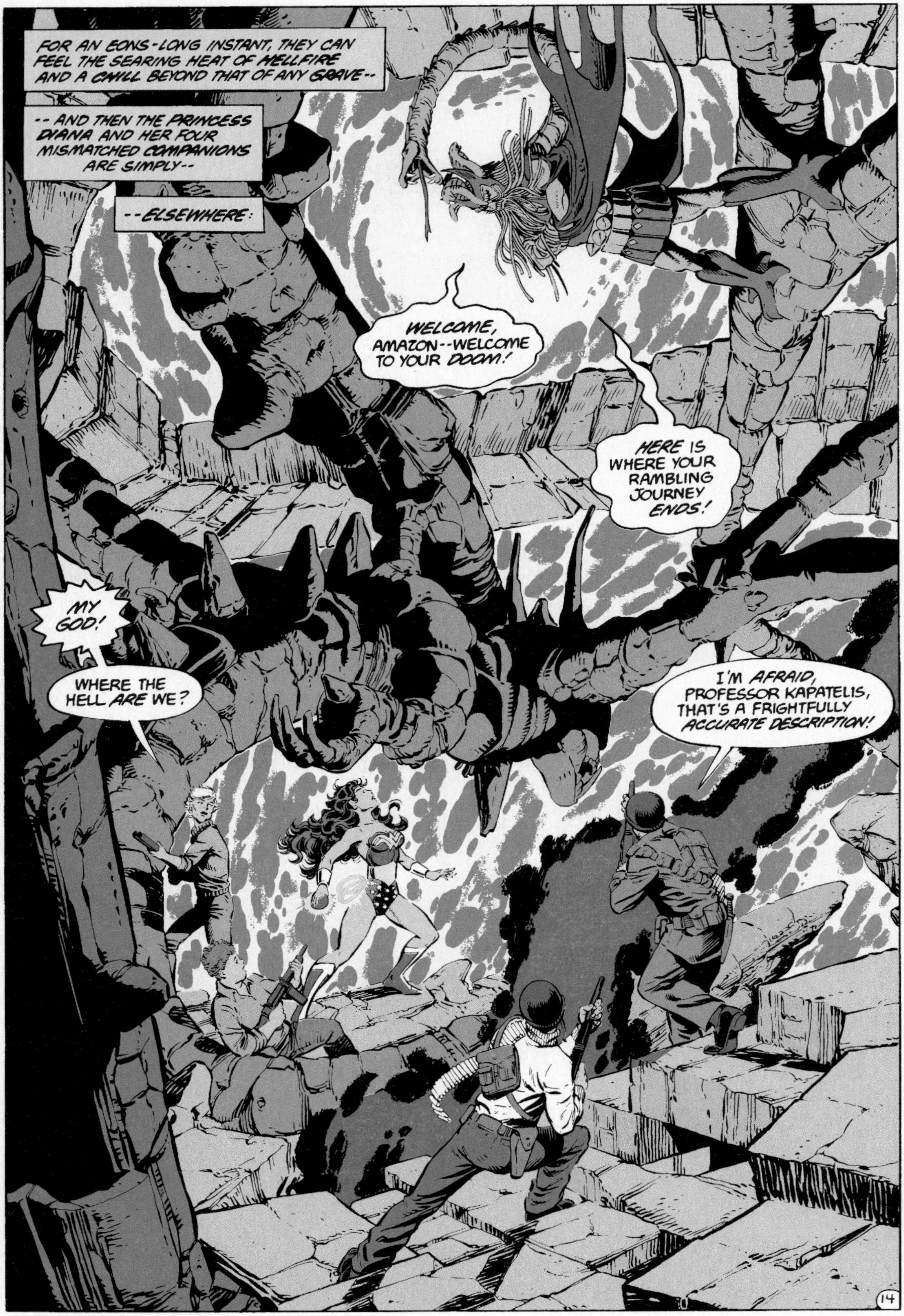
FOR AN EONS-LONG INSTANT, THEY CAN FEEL THE SEARING HEAT OF HELLFIRE AND A CHILL BEYOND THAT OF ANY GRAVE--
-- AND THEN THE PRINCESS DIANA AND HER FOUR MISMATCHED COMPANIONS ARE SIMPLY--
--ELSEWHERE:
WELCOME, AMAZON--WELCOME TO YOUR DOOM!
HERE IS WHERE YOUR RAMBLING JOURNEY ENDS!
MY GOD!
WHERE THE HELL ARE WE?
I'M AFRAID, PROFESSOR KAPATELIS, THAT'S A FRIGHTFULLY ACCURATE DESCRIPTION!
14

‹YOU'VE COME FOR THIS, HAVE YOU NOT, DEAR PRINCESS-- THE OTHER HALF OF MAD HARMONIA'S AMULET?›

‹WELL, COME AND TAKE IT THEN, CHILD...›

‹...IF YOU CAN!›

EH? MY HALF OF THE AMULET-- IT SEEMS SOMEHOW DRAWN TO ITS MATE--!

DIANA, WHO IS THIS MONSTER?

OH, PERMIT ME TO INTRODUCE MYSELF, PROFESSOR!

I AM DEIMOS, SON OF ARES, MASTER OF DUPLICITY--

--AND SOVEREIGN OF THE SERPENTS!

‹GREAT HERA!›

LORD-- NO! THE AMULET--!

I CAUGHT IT-- I CAN FEEL IT!

I JUST CAN'T SEE IT!

COLONEL, THE SNAKES ON THAT DEMON'S HELMET-- THEY'RE ALIVE!

SO I'VE NOTICED, ETTA--!

BUT JUST LET ME GET A BEAD ON 'EM--

"..AND THAT'S ONE PROBLEM I CAN CORRECT!"

SPAKOW

15

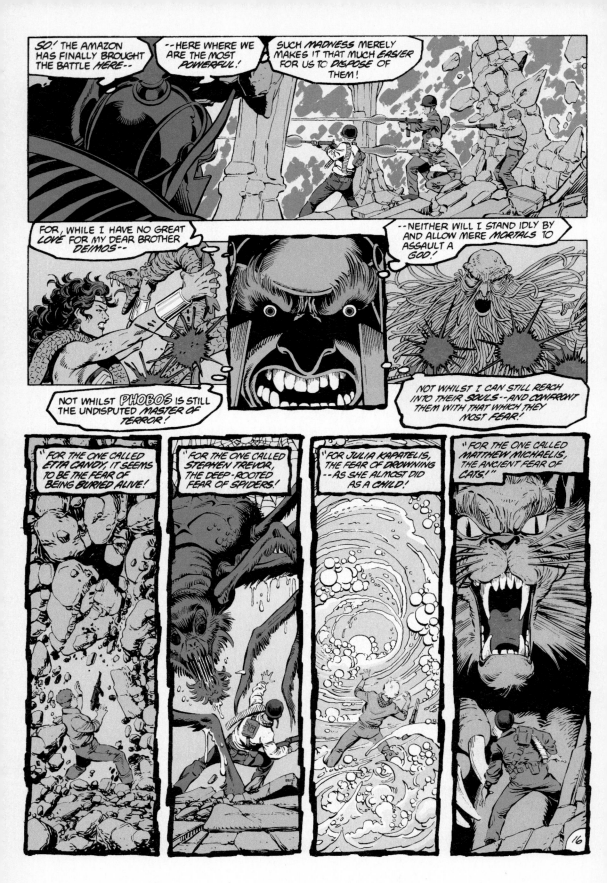

SO! THE AMAZON HAS FINALLY BROUGHT THE BATTLE *HERE*--

--HERE WHERE WE ARE THE MOST *POWERFUL*!

SUCH *MADNESS* MERELY MAKES IT THAT MUCH *EASIER* FOR US TO *DISPOSE* OF THEM!

FOR, WHILE I HAVE NO GREAT *LOVE* FOR MY DEAR BROTHER *DEIMOS*--

--NEITHER WILL I STAND IDLY BY AND ALLOW MERE *MORTALS* TO ASSAULT A *GOD*!

NOT WHILST *PHOBOS* IS STILL THE UNDISPUTED *MASTER OF TERROR*!

NOT WHILST I CAN STILL REACH INTO THEIR *SOULS*--AND *CONFRONT* THEM WITH THAT WHICH THEY *MOST FEAR*!

"FOR THE ONE CALLED *ETTA CANDY*, IT SEEMS TO BE THE FEAR OF BEING *BURIED ALIVE*!

"FOR THE ONE CALLED *STEPHEN TREVOR*, THE DEEP-ROOTED FEAR OF *SPIDERS*!

"FOR *JULIA KAPATELIS*, THE FEAR OF *DROWNING* --AS SHE ALMOST DID AS A *CHILD*!

"FOR THE ONE CALLED *MATTHEW MICHAELIS*, THE ANCIENT FEAR OF *CATS*!"

16

‹IN ATHENA'S NAME-- ENOUGH!›

‹THIS INSANITY CAN BE ALLOWED TO GO NO FURTHER!›

‹THESE MANIFEST FEARS ARE ONLY AS REAL AS WE MAKE THEM--?›

‹--AND A TRUE AMAZON KNOWS NO FEAR!›

STEVE, THE PRETTY LADY HAS THE RIGHT IDEA! WE'VE GOT TO TRADE OFF!

YOU HELP ONE OF THE OTHERS, BUDDY--AND LET ME HANDLE YOUR NIGHTMARE!

GOT IT, MATT--ON MY WAY!

THANK THE FATES JULIA IS STILL BREATHING!

IN THE BRIEF TIME I'VE KNOWN HER, SHE HAS COME TO MEAN MUCH TO ME!

MY GOD, ETTA-- HANG ON!

I'M COMING TO SAVE YOU!

INDEED, MORTAL?

BUT WHO SHALL SAVE YOU?

ANOTHER ONE--?!? 17

127

IF I REMEMBER MY *MYTHOLOGY* RIGHT, HE'S DEIMOS' BROTHER *PHOBOS*!

THOUGH, RIGHT *NOW*, HE'S JUST *CANNON FODDER*!

WHAT--?!?

C'MON, STEVE -- GET ETTA *OUTTA* HERE!

I CAN'T HOLD THIS BRUISER BACK FOR *LONG*!

IT'S *OKAY*, MATT-- I'VE *GOT* HER!

AND *NOW*, FOOLISH MORTALS-- *I* HAVE *YOU*!

AARRGGHH.!!

< YOUR COMPANIONS ARE *VALIANT* INDEED, PRINCESS--> <--BUT HOPELESSLY *MISMATCHED* AGAINST SUCH AS *WE*! >

< THREATEN US AS YOU WILL, GRIM GODLING! >

< THE DAUGHTER OF HIPPOLYTE DOES NOT FEAR YOU! >

< INDEED, AMAZON-- IT SEEMS YOU ARE *FRIGHTENED* OF VERY LITTLE! >

< THEN PERHAPS IT IS TIME YOU *LEARNED* FEAR, CHILD-->

< --TIME YOU *TASTED* THE *SERPENT'S KISS*! >

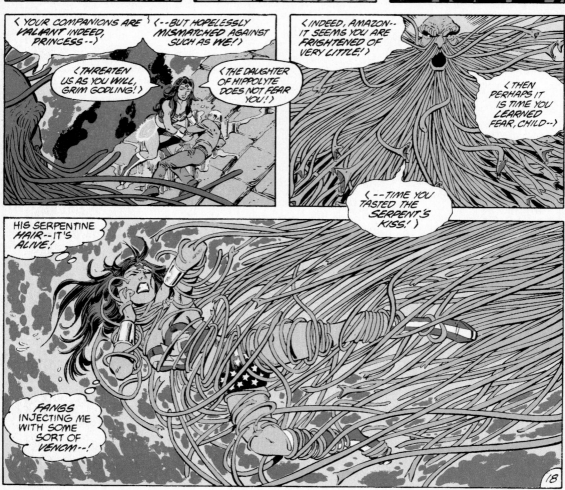

HIS SERPENTINE *HAIR*--IT'S *ALIVE*!

FANGS INJECTING ME WITH SOME SORT OF *VENOM*--!

18

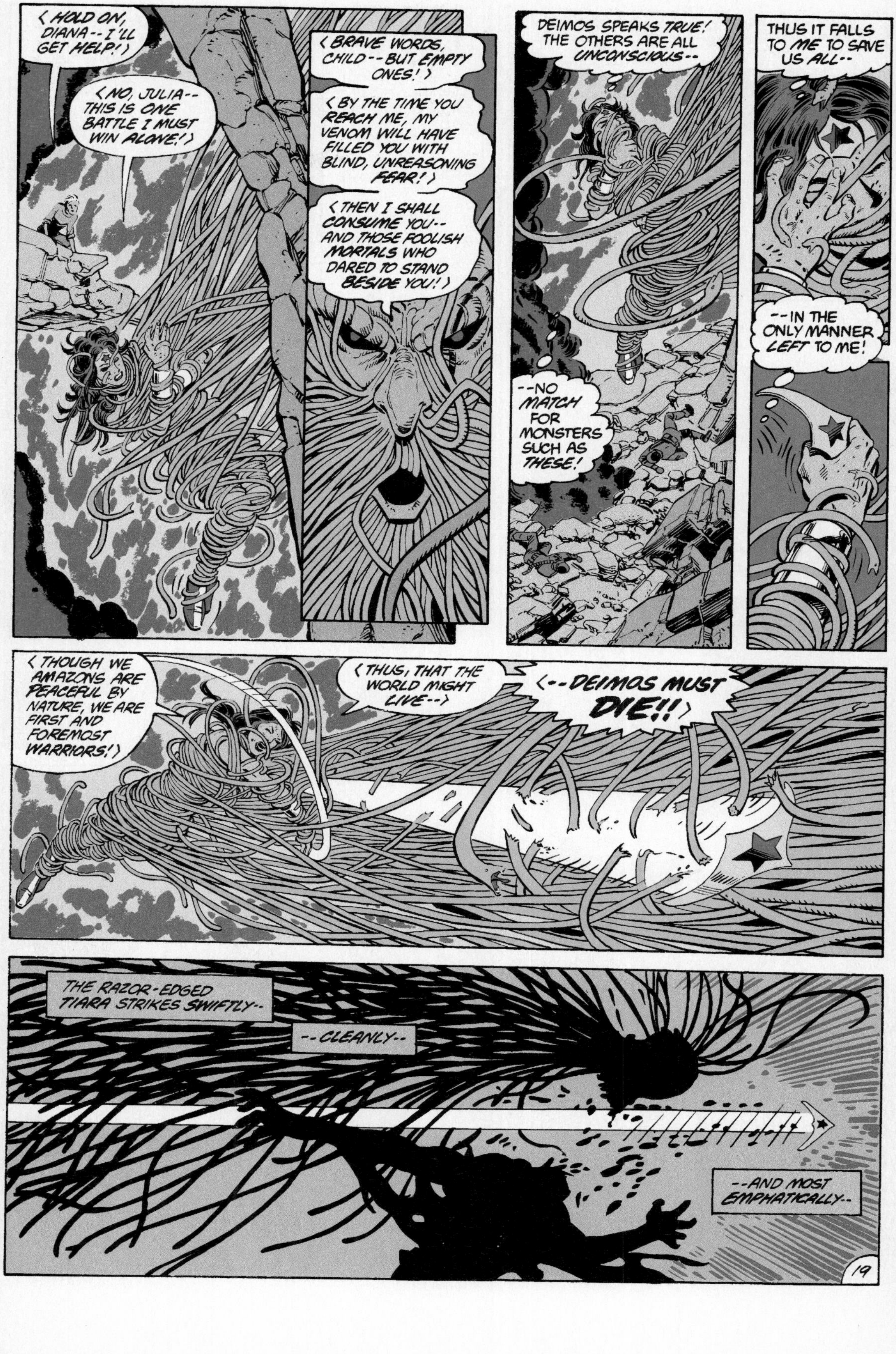

⟨ HOLD ON, DIANA -- I'LL GET HELP! ⟩
⟨ NO, JULIA -- THIS IS ONE BATTLE I MUST WIN ALONE! ⟩
⟨ BRAVE WORDS, CHILD -- BUT EMPTY ONES! ⟩
⟨ BY THE TIME YOU REACH ME, MY VENOM WILL HAVE FILLED YOU WITH BLIND, UNREASONING FEAR! ⟩
⟨ THEN I SHALL CONSUME YOU -- AND THOSE FOOLISH MORTALS WHO DARED TO STAND BESIDE YOU! ⟩
DEIMOS SPEAKS TRUE! THE OTHERS ARE ALL UNCONSCIOUS --
-- NO MATCH FOR MONSTERS SUCH AS THESE!
THUS IT FALLS TO ME TO SAVE US ALL --
-- IN THE ONLY MANNER LEFT TO ME!
⟨ THOUGH WE AMAZONS ARE PEACEFUL BY NATURE, WE ARE FIRST AND FOREMOST WARRIORS! ⟩
⟨ THUS, THAT THE WORLD MIGHT LIVE -- ⟩
⟨ -- DEIMOS MUST DIE!! ⟩
THE RAZOR-EDGED TIARA STRIKES SWIFTLY --
-- CLEANLY --
-- AND MOST EMPHATICALLY --
19

--CUTTING THE MAD GOD DEIMOS OFF IN MID-TAUNT--

--PUTTING AN END TO HIS ENDLESS LIFE IN LESS THAN THE SPACE OF A HEART-BEAT--

...MY... GOD...

--IF GODS, IN FACT, CAN TRULY DIE!

〈NOT A NOBLE END, EVEN FOR SUCH AS HE--〉

〈--BUT HE LEFT ME NO OTHER CHOICE!〉

〈YOUR FAITH IN ME HAS BEEN JUSTIFIED, FLEET HERMES.〉

〈BOTH HALVES OF MAD HARMONIA'S AMULET AT LAST ARE MINE!〉

NO! ONCE THE AMAZON JOINS THE AMULET, SHE SHALL DESTROY ME!

I MUST FLEE WHILE I STILL CAN!

BUT REST YE EASY, BROTHER DEIMOS--!

I SWEAR, SOME DAY SOON, YOU SHALL BE AVENGED!

ARE YOU... WELL, MY FRIENDS?

ABOUT AS WELL AS CAN BE EXPECTED, DIANA-- ALL THINGS CONSIDERED!

IT WAS SO DARK, STEVE... SO COLD...

HUSH... IT'S OKAY. YOU'RE SAFE NOW, ETTA. YOU'RE SAFE.

WELL, DIANA--LOOKS LIKE WE'VE GOT WHAT YOU CAME HERE FOR.

SO NOW WHAT DO WE DO?

IF YOU HAVE TO GO DEEPER INTO THIS HELLHOLE, LADY-- WE'RE READY!

NOT ENTHU- SIASTIC, MIND YOU-- BUT READY!

I DO NOT THINK... THAT WILL BE... NECESSARY.

THOUGH I HAVE NEVER BEFORE LED OTHERS INTO BATTLE--

-- I AM BLESSED TO STAND BESIDE WARRIORS SUCH AS THESE!

20

NOW, COME, JULIA-- --IT IS TIME... THE *HALVES* OF THE AMULET... WERE FINALLY *JOINED!*

THIS--AH-- ISN'T GOING TO *HURT,* IS IT?

READY WHEN *YOU* ARE, SISTER!

SLOWLY, TENTATIVELY, THE TWO ORNATE DISCS APPROACH ONE ANOTHER...

THERE IS A SOFT METALLIC *TIK* AS THEY *TOUCH*--

--AND THEN, ONCE MORE, THE FIVE WAYFARERS *VANISH*--

--TO REAPPEAR INSTANTANEOUSLY IN A WHOLLY *DIFFERENT* KIND OF *HELL!*

WH-WHERE ARE WE?

GOOD LORD-- IT'S THE *MISSILE BASE!*

WELCOME, COLONEL TREVOR! WE'VE BEEN *EXPECTING* YOU!

WHO--?!?

WHO *ELSE?*

WE WERE *WARNED* YOU WOULD SOON BE *AMONG* US, COLONEL! I COMMEND YOUR *EFFORTS!*

YOU CAN *STOW* THE COMPLIMENTS, GENERAL TOLLIVER! WHAT DO YOU INTEND TO *DO* WITH US?

WHY, WHAT WE DO WITH *ALL TRAITORS,* OF COURSE...

WE INTEND TO PUT YOU ALL UP AGAINST A *WALL*--

--AND *SHOOT* YOU!

21

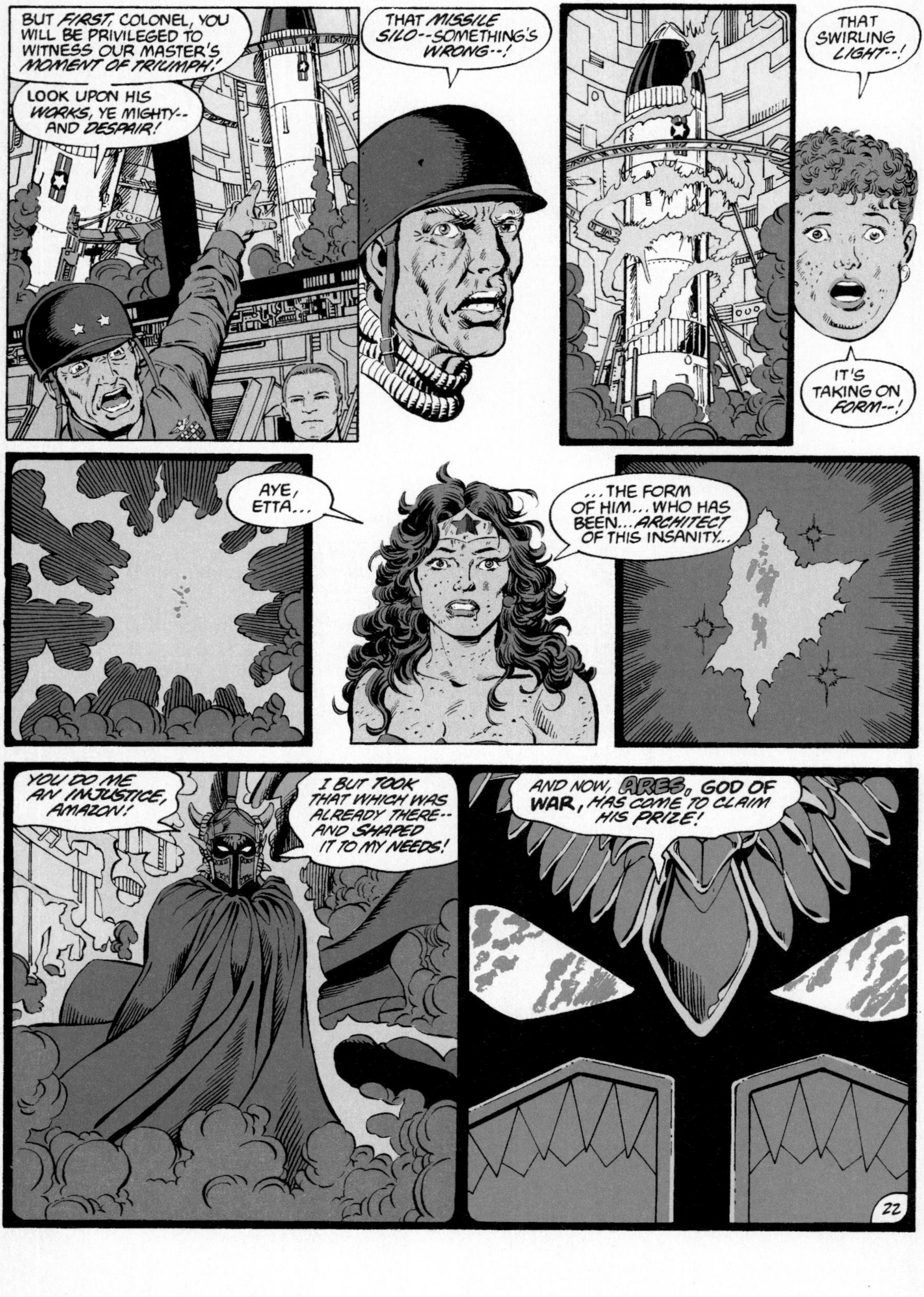
BUT FIRST, COLONEL, YOU WILL BE PRIVILEGED TO WITNESS OUR MASTER'S MOMENT OF TRIUMPH!
LOOK UPON HIS WORKS, YE MIGHTY-- AND DESPAIR!
THAT MISSILE SILO--SOMETHING'S WRONG--!
THAT SWIRLING LIGHT--!
IT'S TAKING ON FORM--!
AYE, ETTA...
...THE FORM OF HIM... WHO HAS BEEN... ARCHITECT OF THIS INSANITY...
YOU DO ME AN INJUSTICE, AMAZON!
I BUT TOOK THAT WHICH WAS ALREADY THERE-- AND SHAPED IT TO MY NEEDS!
AND NOW, ARES, GOD OF WAR, HAS COME TO CLAIM HIS PRIZE!
22

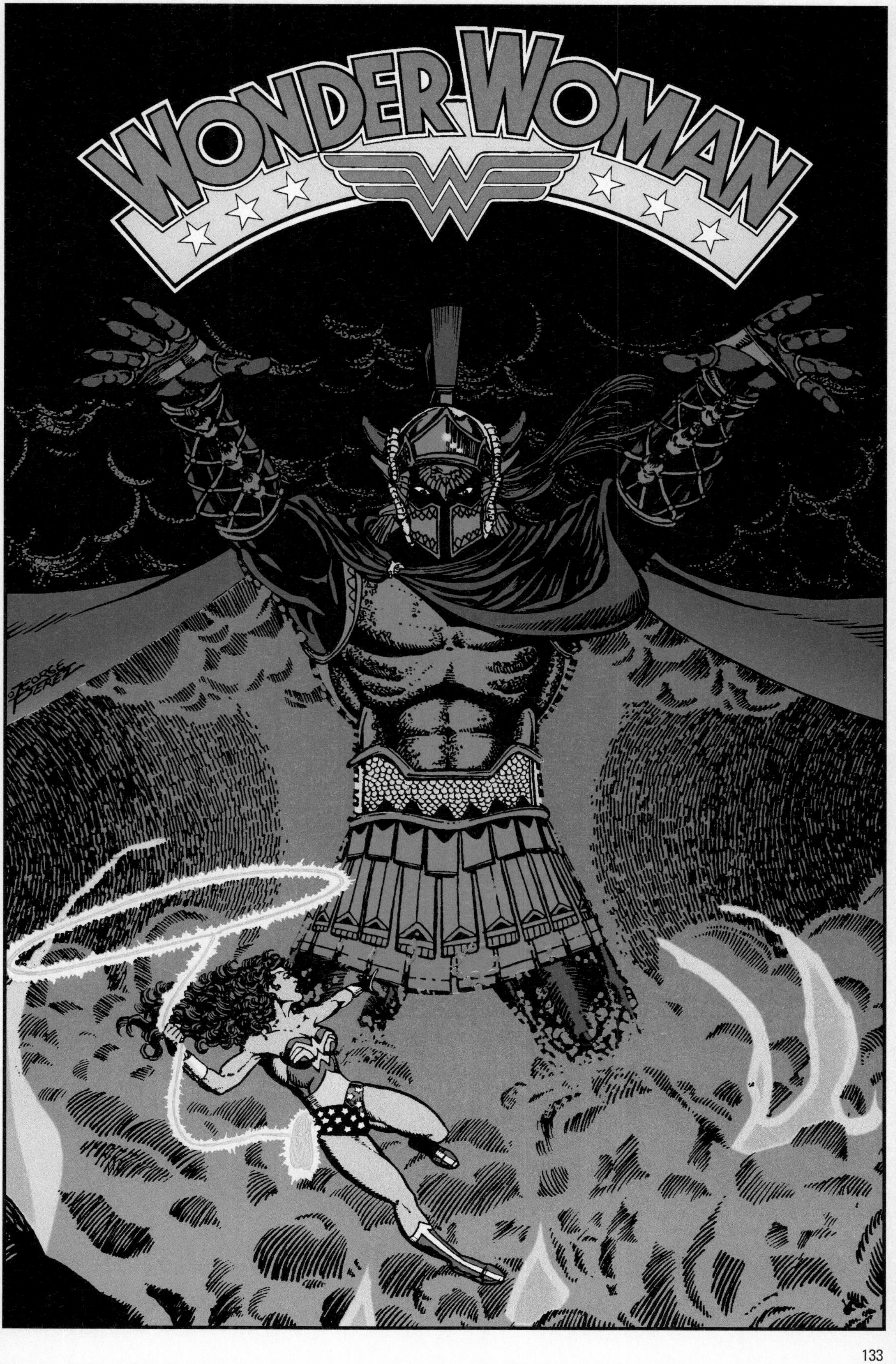
WONDER WOMAN
©GEORGE PÉREZ

"WE INTERRUPT OUR REGULAR PROGRAMMING TO BRING YOU A SPECIAL CHANNEL 35 NOW-NEWS BULLETIN! HERE IS ANCHOR-WOMAN CONNIE CONLEY IN OUR NEWSROOM WITH AN UPDATE REPORT..."

"REPORTS ARE STILL COMING IN CONCERNING THIS MORNING'S ASTONISHING TAKEOVER OF A FEDERAL MISSILE BASE BY A BAND OF RENEGADE MILITARY PERSONNEL LED BY AIR FORCE GENERAL SAMUEL TOLLIVER..."

"APPARENTLY, TOLLIVER AND HIS TROOPS HAD INSIDE HELP IN ACCOMPLISHING THEIR INFILTRATION-- THOUGH NO SPECIFIC DETAILS ARE YET KNOWN. WE SWITCH YOU NOW TO CHAUNCEY STARK, LIVE IN WASHINGTON..."

SPECIAL NEWS BULLETIN TV35

TOLLIVER

FILE TAPE

"THANK YOU, CONNIE. A HURRIED PRESS CONFERENCE HAS BEEN CALLED HERE TO REPORT ON THE PRESIDENT'S RECENT EFFORTS TO DISSUADE GENERAL TOLLIVER FROM HIS PLANS TO LAUNCH A NUCLEAR MISSILE STRIKE DIRECTLY AT MOSCOW..."

"MISTER REAGAN HAS ATTEMPTED REPEATEDLY TO TALK WITH TOLLIVER, WHO CLAIMS CERTAIN KNOWLEDGE OF SOVIET PLANS TO LAUNCH A NUCLEAR FIRST STRIKE AGAINST AMERICA..."

"SINCE WE WERE NOT REACTING QUICKLY ENOUGH, ACCORDING TO TOLLIVER, HE CLAIMS HE HAS NO CHOICE BUT TO PROTECT AMERICA IN HIS OWN WAY AT THIS TIME. TOLLIVER REFUSES TO RESPOND TO ANY FURTHER COMMUNICATION..."

"THOUGH MEETINGS WERE HELD EARLIER TODAY TO DEAL WITH THE TOLLIVER AFFAIR-- WHICH GENERAL JOHN HILLARY CALLS THE ARES ASSAULT-- THE GOVERNMENT HAS NO OFFICIAL STATEMENT FOR THE PRESS, AND THE RESULTS OF THE MEETINGS REMAIN UNKNOWN."

"MEANWHILE, RUMORS HAVE REACHED US THAT A RENEGADE SOVIET GENERAL AND HIS TROOPS HAVE NOW TAKEN CONTROL OF A RUSSIAN MISSILE SILO AT THIS TIME. THE SOVIETS HAVE REFUSED TO SUBSTANTIATE THESE RUMORS..."

"CHANNEL 35 WILL KEEP YOU INFORMED OF ANY LATE-BREAKING DEVELOPMENTS IN THIS DESPERATE SITUATION AS THEY OCCUR. MEANWHILE, WE NOW RETURN YOU TO 'ME AND THE CHIMP'..."

SOVIET SIEGE

SPECIAL NEWS BULLETIN TV35

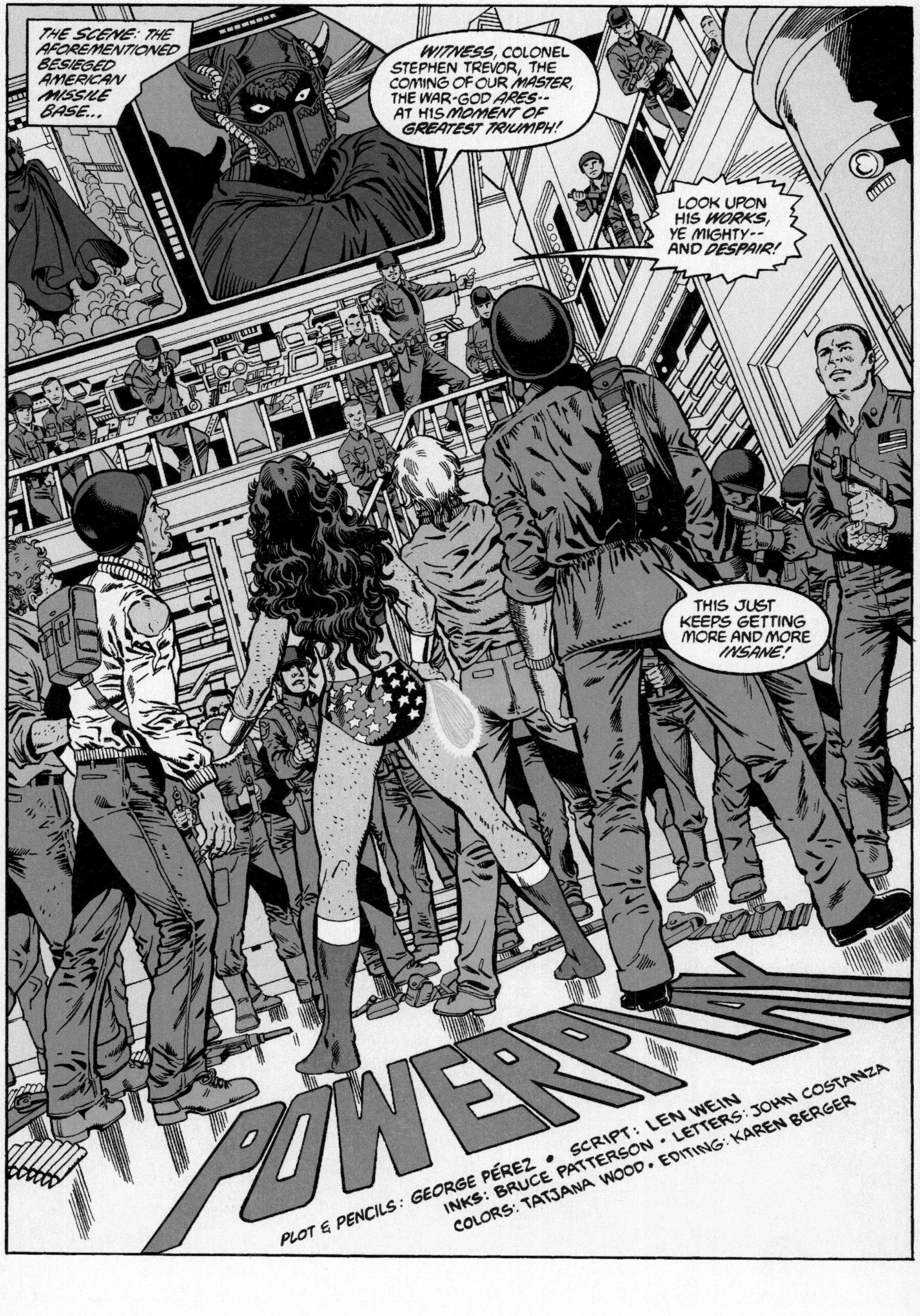
THE SCENE: THE AFOREMENTIONED BESIEGED AMERICAN MISSILE BASE...
WITNESS, COLONEL STEPHEN TREVOR, THE COMING OF OUR MASTER, THE WAR-GOD ARES--AT HIS MOMENT OF GREATEST TRIUMPH!
LOOK UPON HIS WORKS, YE MIGHTY--AND DESPAIR!
THIS JUST KEEPS GETTING MORE AND MORE INSANE!
POWERPLAY
PLOT & PENCILS: GEORGE PÉREZ • SCRIPT: LEN WEIN
INKS: BRUCE PATTERSON • LETTERS: JOHN COSTANZA
COLORS: TATJANA WOOD • EDITING: KAREN BERGER

THIS *INSANITY* IS OF MANKIND'S OWN *DEVISING*, COLONEL *MICHAELIS!* I MERELY TOOK THE *RAW MATERIAL* OFFERED ME -- AND SHAPED IT TO MY OWN *NEEDS!*

THIS IMPENDING *CONFLICT* SHALL BE THE GOD OF BATTLE'S SINGLE MOST EXQUISITE *MOMENT*, MY *CHILDREN* --

-- THE *MOMENT* OF THE AMAZONS' FATAL *FAILURE* AND MY FELLOW *GODS'* DESTRUCTION!

DWELL ON THAT, DAUGHTER OF *HIPPOLYTE* -- IN THESE PRECIOUS FEW MOMENTS LEFT TO YOU!

HAHAHAHAHA

I'VE GOT TO BE *DREAMING* THIS --!

THEN THAT MAKES *TWO* OF US, SIR.

I'VE *READ* ABOUT THE *GODS* --

-- BUT TO ACTUALLY *SEE* ONE --?!?

‹IT MAY WELL BE THE *LAST* THING WE EVER SEE, JULIA --!›

I'VE GOT AN *IDEA*, STEVE.

JUST LISTEN *CLOSE...*

ONCE I REACH THE *MASTER CONTROL ROOM*, THIS *KEY* WILL ENABLE ME TO *LAUNCH* THE *DOOMSDAY MISSILES* --

-- AND AT LAST BRING OUR *MASTER'S* PLAN TO *FRUITION!*

"FROM THE VERY *BEGINNING*, YOU AND YOUR KIND HAVE STOOD *AGAINST* US, COLONEL TREVOR -- THE ONE OUR MASTER CALLS THE *AMAZON PRINCESS DIANA* HAS EVEN *SLAIN* HIS SON *DEIMOS* -- BUT IN THE END, WE WILL *TRIUMPH!* "

WHEN I GIVE THE *WORD*, PROFESSOR KAPATELIS --I TELL DIANA TO *RUSH* TOLLIVER.

NO... I *CANNOT...* YOUR LIVES WOULD BE... IN *DANGER...*

AND THEY AREN'T *NOW?*

WE'RE *DEFINITELY* GOING TO DIE *OTHERWISE*, DIANA --

-- SO JUST DO WHAT MICHAELIS *SAYS!*

3

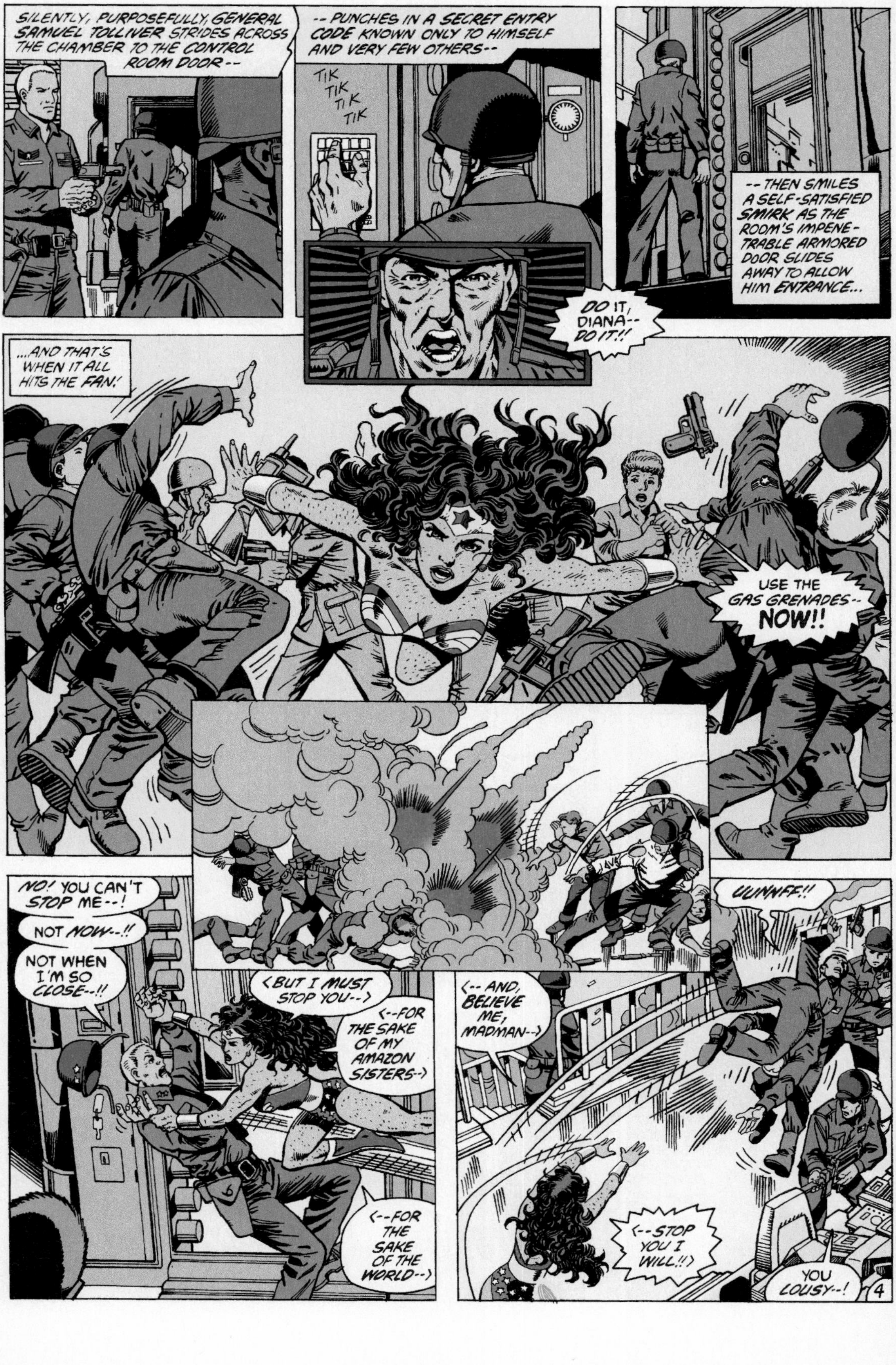
SILENTLY, PURPOSEFULLY, GENERAL SAMUEL TOLLIVER STRIDES ACROSS THE CHAMBER TO THE CONTROL ROOM DOOR--
--PUNCHES IN A SECRET ENTRY CODE KNOWN ONLY TO HIMSELF AND VERY FEW OTHERS--
TIK TIK TIK TIK
--THEN SMILES A SELF-SATISFIED SMIRK AS THE ROOM'S IMPENE-TRABLE ARMORED DOOR SLIDES AWAY TO ALLOW HIM ENTRANCE...
DO IT, DIANA-- DO IT!!
...AND THAT'S WHEN IT ALL HITS THE FAN!
USE THE GAS GRENADES-- NOW!!
NO! YOU CAN'T STOP ME--!
NOT NOW--!!
NOT WHEN I'M SO CLOSE--!!
<BUT I MUST STOP YOU-->
<--FOR THE SAKE OF MY AMAZON SISTERS-->
<--FOR THE SAKE OF THE WORLD-->
<--AND, BELIEVE ME, MADMAN-->
UUNNFF!!
<--STOP YOU I WILL!!>
YOU LOUSY--!
4

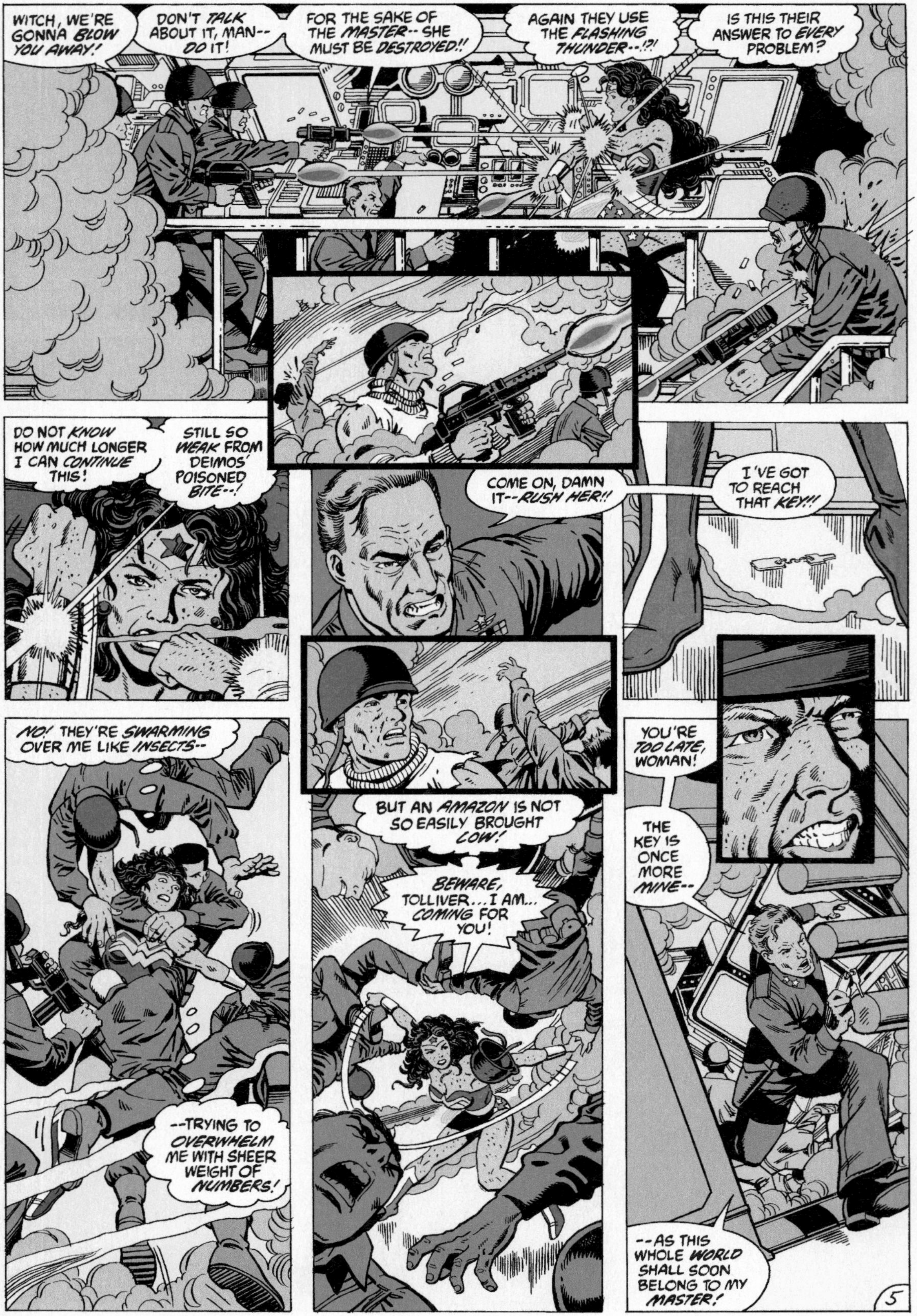
WITCH, WE'RE GONNA BLOW YOU AWAY!
DON'T TALK ABOUT IT, MAN-- DO IT!
FOR THE SAKE OF THE MASTER-- SHE MUST BE DESTROYED!!
AGAIN THEY USE THE FLASHING THUNDER--!?!
IS THIS THEIR ANSWER TO EVERY PROBLEM?
DO NOT KNOW HOW MUCH LONGER I CAN CONTINUE THIS!
STILL SO WEAK FROM DEIMOS' POISONED BITE--!
COME ON, DAMN IT--RUSH HER!!
I'VE GOT TO REACH THAT KEY!!
NO! THEY'RE SWARMING OVER ME LIKE INSECTS--
--TRYING TO OVERWHELM ME WITH SHEER WEIGHT OF NUMBERS!
BUT AN AMAZON IS NOT SO EASILY BROUGHT LOW!
BEWARE, TOLLIVER... I AM... COMING FOR YOU!
YOU'RE TOO LATE, WOMAN!
THE KEY IS ONCE MORE MINE--
--AS THIS WHOLE WORLD SHALL SOON BELONG TO MY MASTER!
5

FLAM!

NO! GOTTA REACH TOLLIVER--!

ONCE THAT DOOR SEALS BEHIND HIM-- HE'S WON!

EH? SOMEONE BEHIND ME--!

MY GOD, ETTA-- Y-YOU KILLED THAT MAN--!

COMES WITH THE TERRITORY, PROFESSOR.

WELL, YOU WON'T LIVE LONG ENOUGH TO WORRY ABOUT IT, LADIES--

YOU DO IT-- BUT YOU NEVER GET USED TO IT!

--IF YOU DON'T KEEP YOUR EYES OPEN!

GREAT HERA! COLONEL TREVOR HAS FOLLOWED TOLLIVER THROUGH THAT DOOR--!

LOOKS LIKE WE'RE THE ONLY ONES LEFT STANDING!

EITHER OF YOU SEEN STEVE AND DIANA?

THERE! COLONEL MICHAELIS --LOOK!

SWEET SISTER-- LOOK AT HER MOVE!

DIANA--WAIT!

WHAT'S WRONG?!

MUST REACH...TOLLIVER AND TREVOR...

...BEFORE IT IS... TOO LATE...

〈CURSE YOU, ARES --FOR YOUR COWARDICE!〉

〈THIS IS THE DAY I WAS BORN FOR--〉

〈--THE DAY FOR WHICH THE GODS GRANTED ME THIS POWER--!〉

〈WHY DO YOU HIDE BEHIND A MISERABLE MAD MORTAL?〉

〈DIANA!?!〉

〈WHY WILL YOU NOT FACE ME, ARES?〉

WHAT IS SHE DOING UP THERE?

〈DIANA?〉

〈WHAT'S HAPPENING?〉

〈DIANA?〉

6

139

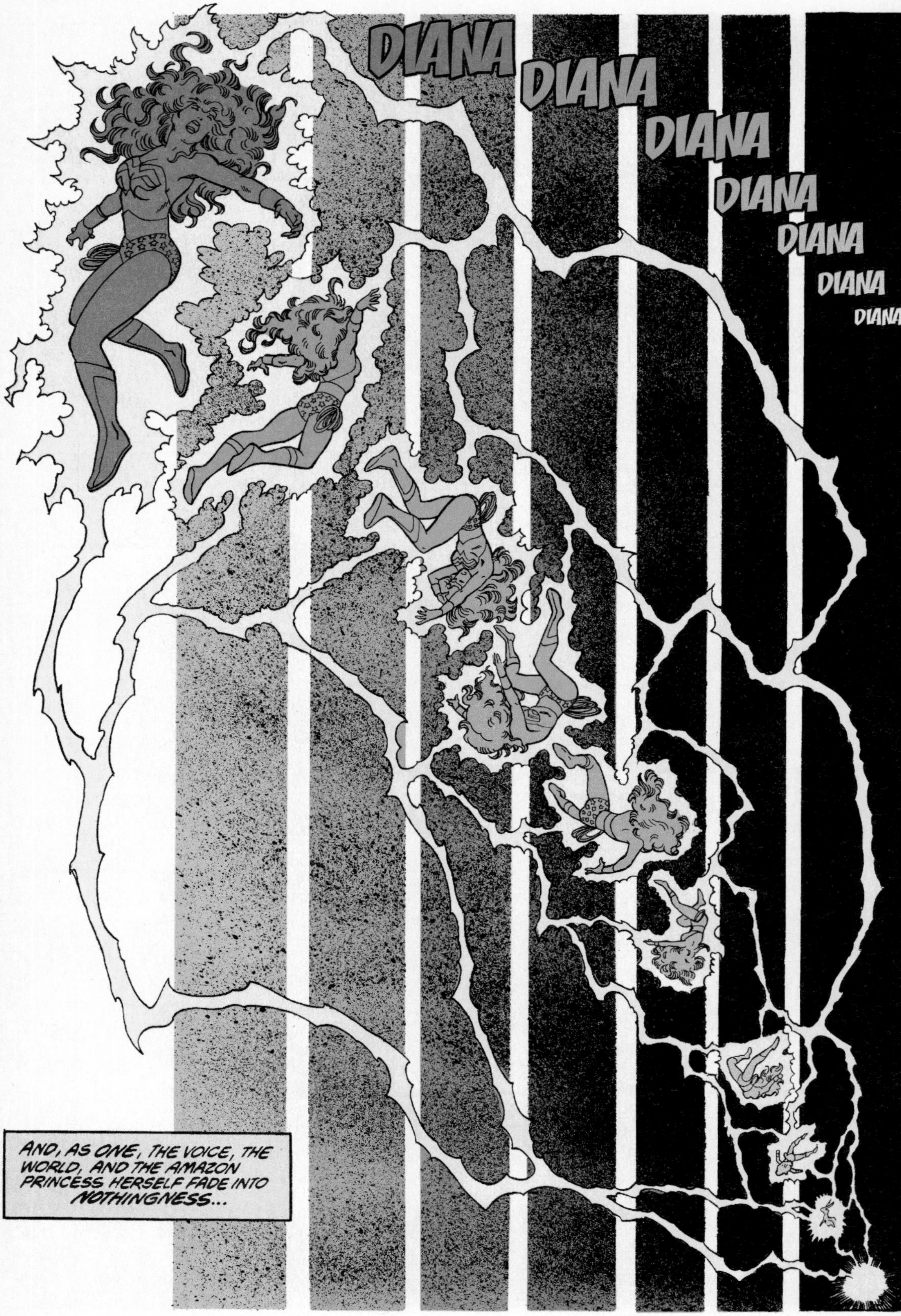
DIANA
DIANA
DIANA
DIANA
DIANA
DIANA
DIANA
AND, AS ONE, THE VOICE, THE WORLD, AND THE AMAZON PRINCESS HERSELF FADE INTO NOTHINGNESS...

HIS FOOTSTEPS ECHOING LIKE METALLIC *THUNDER*, COLONEL STEVE TREVOR RACES SWIFTLY, YET CAUTIOUSLY, THROUGH THE HEAVILY-ARMORED CHAMBER--

--HIS HEART POUNDING WILDLY IN HIS CHEST, HIS *BREATH* CAUGHT COLD IN HIS THROAT--

--KNOWING THE FATE OF ALL *MANKIND* NOW DEPENDS ON WHAT HE *DOES* HERE--

-- AND PRAYING HE'S EQUAL TO THE TASK...

OKAY, GENERAL-- *HOLD IT!*

YOU'RE *TOO LATE*, TREVOR!

I'VE ALREADY *OVERRIDDEN* THE FAILSAFE SYSTEMS AND ACTIVATED THE *LAUNCH CODES!*

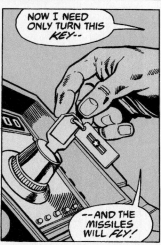

NOW I NEED ONLY TURN THIS *KEY*--

--AND THE MISSILES WILL *FLY!*

TOLLIVER-- *NO!* STAY AWAY FROM THAT--

DAMN!

MIGHTY ARES, *PROTECT* YOUR FAITHFUL SERV--

AARRGGHH!!

DIDN'T *WANT* TO KILL HIM-- BUT HE GAVE ME NO CHOICE--!

NOW I HAVE TO *DEACTIVATE* THE LAUNCH CODES *WITHOUT* HIM!

BETTER REMOVE THE *KEY*, JUST IN CASE, BEFORE--

--EH?

LEAVE... IT... ALONE!

OH... MY... GOD...

NOT *AGAIN!!*

8

AT FIRST, THERE IS ONLY THE *DARKNESS,* COMPLETE, ALL-ENCOMPASSING--

-- THEN COMES THE *THUNDER*--

--AND THE BLINDING BURSTS OF *LIGHT*--

--THE RANDOM *ERUPTIONS* OF EXPLOSIVE FORCE THAT RUMBLE SAVAGELY THROUGH THE SHADOWS--

--ECHOING LIKE THE CACKLE OF DEMONIC LAUGHTER--

--AND ROUSING THE *PRINCESS DIANA* FROM HER NUMBED SLEEP--

--TO BEHOLD THE LIVING EMBODIMENT OF *NIGHTMARE*--

--THE BLACK, BLEAK, BELLIGERENT VISAGE OF THE *WAR-GOD ARES*--

--HE WHO IS NOW *POWER INCARNATE!*

< YOU *CHALLENGED* ME, AMAZON-- AND I HAVE *ANSWERED!* >

< NOW STAND AND FACE ME-- OR *CRAWL* LIKE THE COWARD YOU ARE! >

‹WHY, WAR-GOD? WHY ARE YOU DOING THIS, TO US--›

‹--TO THE WORLD?›

‹TO FULFILL THE ANCIENT PROPHECY, AMAZON--!›

‹AS URANUS WAS SLAIN BY HIS SON CHRONOS, WHO IN TURN WAS SLAIN BY HIS SON ZEUS--›

‹--NOW SHALL I SLAY MY OWN FATHER AND THUS BECOME MORE POWERFUL THAN HE EVER WAS!›

‹AND THE GREAT CATACLYSM I AM ABOUT TO UNLEASH SHALL BE THE FINAL TESTAMENT TO MY POWER!›

‹BEHOLD, AMAZON-- AND WITNESS THE DEATH OF A WORLD!›

‹DESPITE HIS BEST EFFORTS, YOUR COMRADE TREVOR IS NO MATCH FOR MY PAWN TOLLIVER--›

‹--OR THE DEMONIC SPIRIT THAT NOW ANIMATES TOLLIVER'S CORPSE!›

‹HIS DEFEAT IS IMMINENT, CHILD--›

‹--MY VICTORY INEVITABLE!›

‹ALL ACROSS THE WORLD, MY INFLUENCE GROWS STRONGER..›

‹--MORTAL TORMENTING MORTAL OVER SOMETHING SO INSIGNIFICANT AS THE COLOR OF ONE'S SKIN--›

‹--EVEN AS MY FOREMOST SOVIET WORSHIPPER PREPARES TO TURN A KEY THAT WILL LAUNCH A MISSILE--›

‹--WHICH WILL SIGNAL THE FINAL CONFLAGRATION!›

‹ATHENA PROTECT US!›

‹SHE CANNOT HELP YOU, AMAZON--›

10

‹ -- NO MORE THAN SHE HAS HELPED YOUR SISTER AMAZONS.! ›

‹ LOOK CLOSELY NOW, CHILD OF HIPPOLYTE--! ›

‹ --OBSERVE THE WITHERED TREES AND DYING FLOWERS OF YOUR ONCE-BEAUTIFUL HOMELAND, PARADISE ISLAND--! ›

‹ BEHOLD THE WARRIOR-WOMAN PHILLIPUS AS SHE MAKES HER WAY THROUGH A LANDSCAPE THAT SPEAKS OF NOTHING SAVE DESPAIR-- ›

‹ --AND WITNESS THE END OF MY HALF-SISTER ARTEMIS' DREAM.! ›

HIPPOLYTE, MY QUEEN--

--HAS THERE BEEN ANY NEW WORD FROM THE PRINCESS DIANA?

NONE THUS FAR, PHILLIPUS--

--AND WE CONTINUE TO GROW OLDER AND MORE FRAIL WITH EACH PASSING MOMENT!

I FEAR MY NOBLE DAUGHTER HAS FAILED IN HER SWORN MISSION TO STOP THE WAR-GOD'S MADNESS--

--AND WE SHALL ALL PAY THE PRICE OF HER FAILURE!

DO NOT DESPAIR, FAIR HIPPOLYTE--IT IS NOT ENDED YET!

"IF DIANA WERE TRULY DEAD, WE WOULD LONG SINCE HAVE JOINED HER!

DIANA

"AND, SO LONG AS THE PRINCESS YET LIVES, THERE IS HOPE!"

11

‹PHILLIPUS *SPEAKS* TRUE, WAR-*GOD!*›   ‹SO LONG AS *LIFE* REMAINS, THERE IS *ALWAYS* HOPE--›

‹--AND SO LONG AS THERE IS *HOPE,* THERE CAN BE *VICTORY!*›

‹*DEFEND* YOURSELF, ARES! YOUR TIME OF *RECKONING* HAS COME AT--›

AARRGHH!!

‹*FOOLISH* CHILD, YOU ARE IN MY *REALM* NOW--›

‹--AND THUS YOU ARE *MINE*--›

‹--TO *TOY* WITH AS I PLEASE!›

‹I *COULD* DESTROY YOU WITH BUT A *SINGLE* THOUGHT--›

‹--BUT THAT WOULD BE TOO *QUICK,* TOO *PAINLESS* BY COMPARISON!›

‹I WOULD MUCH RATHER SEE YOU *SUFFER* FOR A TIME--›

‹--UNTIL YOU HAVE LEARNED A LITTLE *HUMILITY!*›

‹YOU ARE-- TRULY *MAD*--!›

‹*PERHAPS,* AMAZON-- BUT I AM ALSO *GREATEST* OF ALL THE *GODS!*›

‹*ACKNOWLEDGE* ME AS SUCH, CHILD--›

‹--OR DIE IN *UNIMAGINABLE AGONY!*›

12

CAN'T BREATHE--!

LOSING CONSCIOUSNESS--!

MAD HARMONIA'S AMULET-- MY ONLY CHANCE--!

ARES' OWN SAD DAUGHTER CLAIMED IT IS POSSESSED OF AWESOME POWER--

-- AND PERHAPS ONLY POWER SPAWNED BY ARES HIMSELF CAN HOPE TO DEFEAT HIM!

UUNNHH!!

THERE! THE BLOW BROKE ARES' GRIP-- BUT IT ALSO ENRAGED HIM!

NOW THE DARKNESS ITSELF HAS BEGUN TO BURN-- IGNITED BY HIS FURY!

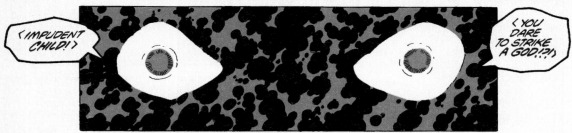

‹IMPUDENT CHILD!›

‹YOU DARE TO STRIKE A GOD!?!›

‹SUCH ARROGANCE MUST NOT GO UNPUNISHED!›

‹'TWAS THE GODS WHO MADE YOU, AMAZON--›

‹-- AND YOU CAN BE UNMADE AGAIN IN AN INSTANT!›

HHUUNNFF!!

13

146

‹ FLAMES LEAPING ALL AROUND ME-- SEARING MY SKIN WITHOUT BURNING IT--! ›

‹ HERA HELP ME! ›

‹ MY FELLOW GODS CANNOT HELP YOU, AMAZON-- THEY CANNOT EVEN HELP THEMSELVES! ›

‹ FOR THE FIRST TIME IN YOUR YOUNG LIFE-- YOU ARE TRULY ALONE! ›

‹ EVEN YOUR COMRADES ARE OTHERWISE OCCUPIED, CHILD-- ›

‹ --STRUGGLING DESPERATELY TO UNDO TOLLIVER'S WORK! ›

ATTAGIRL, ETTA--YOU'VE DONE IT!

DONE WHAT?

SHE'S OVERRIDDEN THE BASE'S OUTER SECURITY SYSTEMS, DOC.

WITH ANY LUCK, SOMEONE IN THE ARRIVING ASSAULT FORCE WILL KNOW HOW TO DEACTIVATE ALL THE MISSILES.

AND IF THEY DON'T--?

I WAS HOPING NO ONE WOULD ASK--!

WE'RE RUNNING OUT OF TIME, COLONEL MICHAELIS.

ONCE THOSE MISSILES ARE LAUNCHED, ARES WINS!

YOU'VE GOT TO THINK POSITIVELY, ETTA.

SO LONG AS WE'RE STILL BREATHING--

"--THIS PARTICULAR WAR IS FAR FROM OVER!"

14

147

MY GOD, WHAT..?!?

IT'S TOLLIVER'S TROOPS--!

THEY DON'T KNOW WHEN TO STAY DEAD!

GET DOWN, LADIES, BEFORE THEY--

--UUNNHH!!

⟨GREAT HERA!⟩

⟨NOOOOO!!⟩

⟨YOU COULD NOT EVEN SAVE THOSE THREE FOOLS-- AND YET YOU EXPECT TO SAVE A WORLD?⟩

⟨BE SERIOUS, CHILD-- ADMIT YOUR INADEQUACIES!⟩

WHY HAVE THE GODS BROUGHT ME HERE IF ONLY TO SEE ME FAIL?

WHY WILL THEY NOT ANSWER ME?

AND DO YOU FIND ANSWERS IN THE BLACK WATERS OF THE RIVER STYX, FAIR ARTEMIS?

THE PRINCESS DIANA HAS FAILED US, ATHENA.

DESPITE OUR FERVENT HOPES, SHE PROVED NOT STRONG ENOUGH TO BEST THE WAR-GOD!

YOU MUST HAVE FAITH, ARTEMIS.

WE MUST ALL HAVE FAITH THAT OUR DAUGHTER WILL REALIZE THE TRUE POWER THAT IS HERS.

THE GREAT ARK OF CHARON AWAITS, SISTERS.

WE CAN NO LONGER DELAY OUR JOURNEY TO OBLIVION!

NO! WE HAVE PLACED OUR TRUST IN THE CHILD DIANA-- AND SHE STILL SURVIVES!

THE CONFLICT IS NOT YET OVER!

AYE, PERSEPHONE-- ATHENA SPEAKS TRUE! TELL THE FERRYMAN TO WAIT.

WE SHALL SEE THIS THROUGH-- TO THE BITTER END!

15

FOR AN INTERMINABLE INSTANT, THE AMAZON PRINCESS KNEELS AMIDST THE RIPPLING FLAMES--

--ARES' MOCKING INSULTS ECHOING ENDLESSLY IN HER EARS--

--THEN, SLOWLY, HESITANTLY AT FIRST, SHE RISES ONCE MORE TO HER FEET--

--HER HAND CLUTCHING THE GLEAMING WEAPON SHE CARRIES EVER AT HER SIDE--

--A GREAT GOLDEN LASSO--

--FORGED BY THE GOD HEPHAESTUS FROM THE GIRDLE OF THE EARTH-MOTHER GAEA HERSELF!

< CURSE YOU, AMAZON-- STAY DOWN! >

< DO YOU NOT KNOW WHEN YOU HAVE BEEN BESTED? >

< NOT SINCE HERACLES FIRST PUT US IN CHAINS HAS AN AMAZON BEEN BESTED, WAR-GOD! >

< I HAVE BEEN CHARGED BY THE GODS OF OLYMPUS TO PUT AN END TO YOUR MAD SCHEME-- >

<--AND WITH THEIR AID OR WITHOUT IT, PUT AN END TO IT I SHALL! >

< YOU WILL NOT LIVE SO LONG, CHILD! >

< I HAVE PLAYED WITH YOU LONG ENOUGH-- >

<--NOW THE GAME IS DONE! >

< IS IT, ARES? >

< WE SHALL SEE! >

< AMAZON-- NO!! >

< YOU KNOW NOT WHAT YOU DO! >

16

LIKE THE COILS OF SOME SURREAL SERPENT, THE STRANDS OF THE GOLDEN LASSO ENCIRCLE THE WAR-GOD'S *TORSO*--

--GROWING TIGHTER, EVER TIGHTER, UNTIL ARES *SCREAMS*--

--AND THE NETHER WORLD GOES SUDDENLY MAD--

--ITS VIOLENT CONVULSIONS KNOCKING THE AMAZON PRINCESS BACK OFF HER *FEET*--

--SENDING HER SPRAWLING, BARELY ALIVE...

17

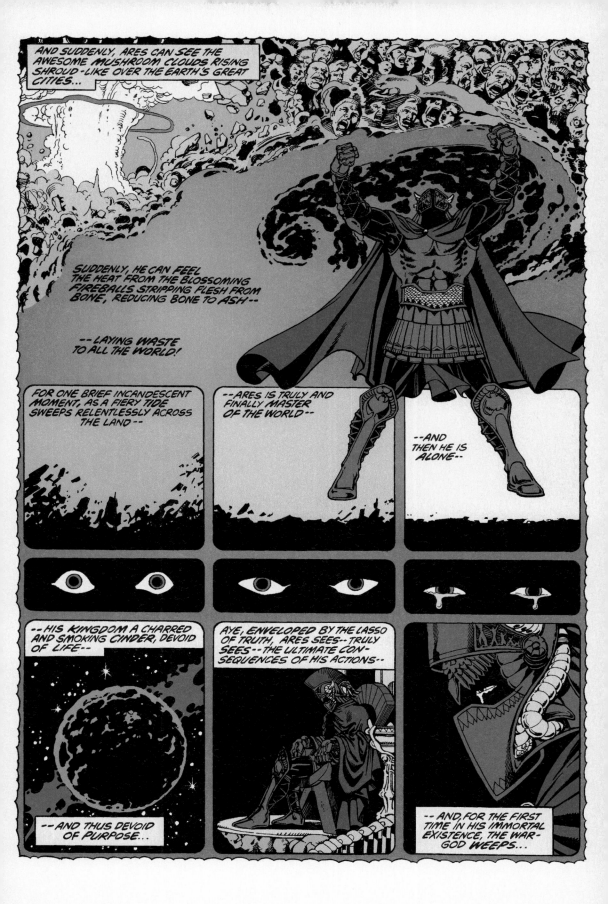

AND SUDDENLY, ARES CAN SEE THE AWESOME MUSHROOM CLOUDS RISING SHROUD-LIKE OVER THE EARTH'S GREAT CITIES...

SUDDENLY, HE CAN FEEL THE HEAT FROM THE BLOSSOMING FIREBALLS STRIPPING FLESH FROM BONE, REDUCING BONE TO ASH--

--LAYING WASTE TO ALL THE WORLD!

FOR ONE BRIEF INCANDESCENT MOMENT, AS A FIERY TIDE SWEEPS RELENTLESSLY ACROSS THE LAND--

--ARES IS TRULY AND FINALLY MASTER OF THE WORLD--

--AND THEN HE IS ALONE--

-- HIS KINGDOM A CHARRED AND SMOKING CINDER, DEVOID OF LIFE--

--AND THUS DEVOID OF PURPOSE...

AYE, ENVELOPED BY THE LASSO OF TRUTH, ARES SEES--TRULY SEES--THE ULTIMATE CON-SEQUENCES OF HIS ACTIONS--

-- AND, FOR THE FIRST TIME IN HIS IMMORTAL EXISTENCE, THE WAR-GOD WEEPS...

151

FOR, WITHOUT THOSE ALIVE TO WORSHIP HIM, ARES' POWER SWIFTLY WANES--

--HIS GREAT PALACE AREOPAGUS GROWING MORE AND MORE DECAYED--

--UNTIL, AT LAST, IT CRUMBLES INTO NOTHINGNESS--

-- CARRYING THE WAR-GOD WITH IT DOWN INTO THE VILE DUST WHENCE HE FIRST SPRUNG--

-- UNMOURNED, UNHONORED, AND UNSUNG...

‹ NO...IT CANNOT BE...›

‹ MY DREAMS OF GLORY... ALL COME AT LAST TO THIS.....?!?›

‹ IT IS THE TRUTH, MIGHTY ARES-- BELIEVE IT--!›

‹ FOR YOUR OWN SAKE-- FOR THE SAKE OF US ALL--›

‹--YOU MUST STOP THIS MADNESS BEFORE IT IS TOO LATE!›

‹ AYE, CHILD--THERE IS NO OTHER CHOICE!›

‹ HAND ME MY DAUGHTER HARMONIA'S TALISMAN!›

‹ AND LET THE BALANCE BE RESTORED!›

YOU...CAME... CLOSE... TREVOR...

...BUT... VICTORY... IS...MINE...!

NO! CAN'T LET YOU--

UUNNHH!!

FOOL...YOU...HAVE... NO...CHOICE...!

THE...KEY... IS...MINE...

...AND...THE... WORLD... BELONGS...TO... ARES...!

LAUNCH

NO--I BLEW IT--!

THE MISSILES WILL--

--WILL--

--NOTHING--

THEY DIDN'T LAUNCH--!

WHAT...HAPPENED..?

WHAT... WENT... WRONG...?

THIS...WAS...TO... BE...OUR... MOMENT...OF... TRIUMPH...

...THE...DAWN... OF...THE...AGE... OF...ARES...!

WHY...HAS...THE... POWER...ABANDONED... ME...WHEN...I...NEEDED ...IT...MOST..?

WHY...HAS...MY... LORD...FORSAKEN... ME...?

20

‹ TOLLIVER IS GONE -- AS IS HIS SOVIET COUNTER-PART! ›

‹ THE THREAT IS ENDED! THE BALANCE RESTORED! ›

‹ FROM THIS MOMENT FORTH, MAN MUST DECIDE HIS OWN DESTRUCTION! ›

‹ HIS CAPACITY FOR BLOODSHED IS GREAT, AND THIS SHALL KEEP ME STRONG--7

‹ --BUT I SHALL NEVER AGAIN TAKE AN ACTIVE ROLE IN MAN'S DEMISE! ›

‹ IT SEEMS THOSE DAYS ARE PAST! ›

‹ THERE IS A DIFFERENCE BETWEEN DESTRUCTION AND OBLIVION, CHILD-- ›

‹ --AND IT FALLS TO YOU TO TEACH IT TO MAN-- ›

‹ --TO SAVE MAN FROM HIMSELF! ›

‹ WE SHALL SEE IF YOU ARE EQUAL TO IT! ›

‹ AND IF YOU ARE NOT, DIANA--THEN BEWARE! ›

‹ FOR THE WORLD SHALL HEAR FROM ME AGAIN! ›

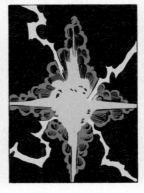

21

AND, FOR THE MOMENT AT LEAST, THE LIGHTS IN MAN'S WORLD GROW BRIGHTER ONCE MORE...

NEVER SEEN ANYTHING *LIKE* IT, GENERAL HILLARY, SIR--

--MINUTE WE *BROKE IN* HERE, TOLLIVER'S BOYS ALL WENT UP LIKE *TORCHES*-- JUST LIKE GENERAL *KOHLER!*

MUST'A BEEN SOME KIND'A FREAKY *SUICIDE* PACT--!

ANY *OTHER* CASUALTIES, SON?

"*JUST ONE,* SIR--

"BUT I'M AFRAID IT'S A *BAD* ONE...

"*COLONEL TREVOR'S* BUDDY, COLONEL *MATTHEW MICHAELIS*--!

"SEEMS HE *BOUGHT* IT WHILE SAVING LIEUTENANT *CANDY* AND THAT KAPATELIS WOMAN--!

"HE WAS ONE OF THE *BEST,* SIR--HE'LL BE *MISSED!*"

INDEED HE WILL, SON! AND *SPEAKING* OF TREVOR--

WHERE *IS* HE, LIEUTENANT?

HE HAS A *HEAP* OF *EXPLAINING* TO DO!

I'M RIGHT HERE, GENERAL--

EH?

--AND RIGHT NOW, I'M NOT VERY *HAPPY!*

FOR GOD'S SAKE, WILL SOMEBODY PLEASE *HELP* ME WITH HER?!?

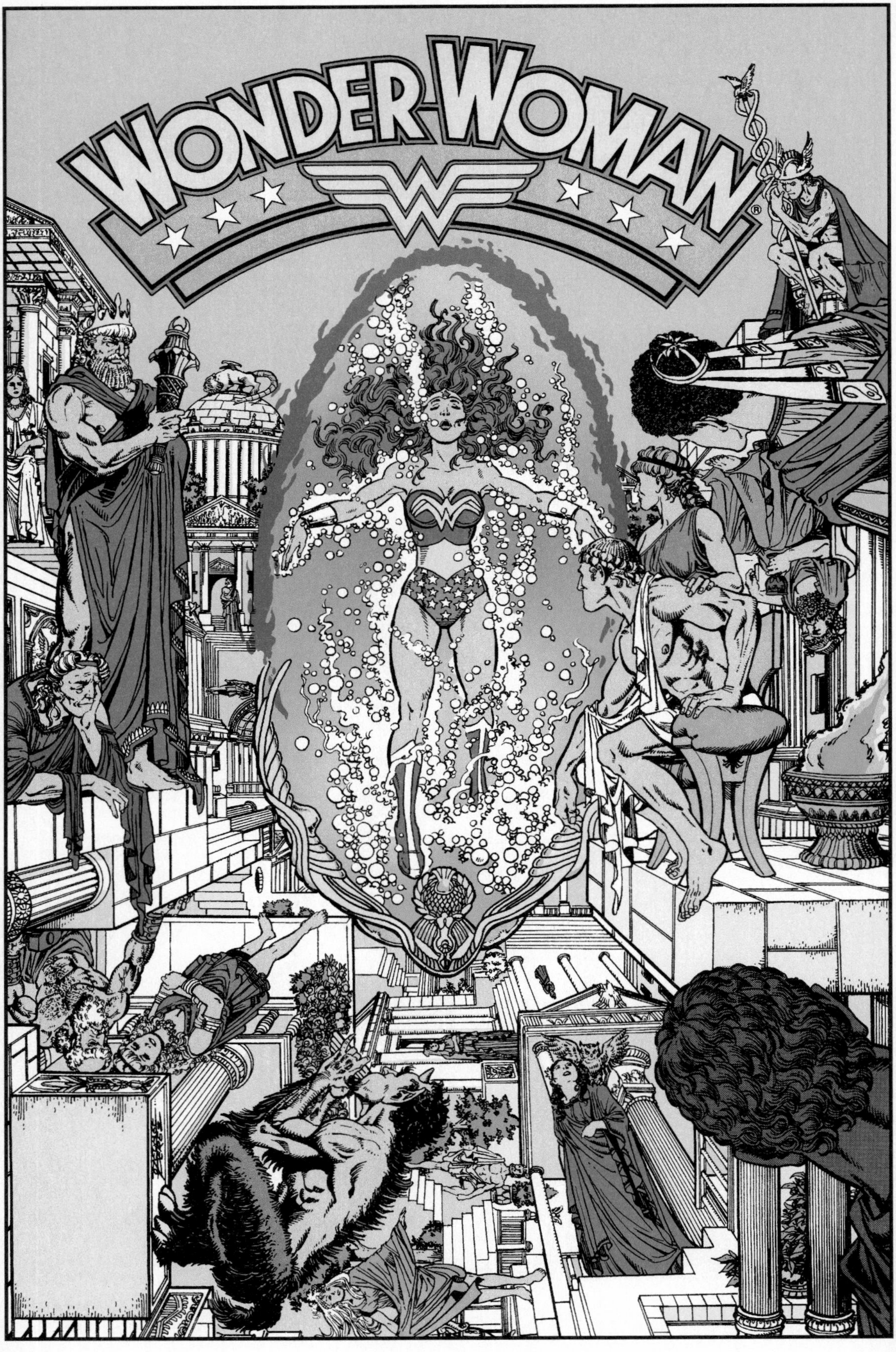
WONDER WOMAN

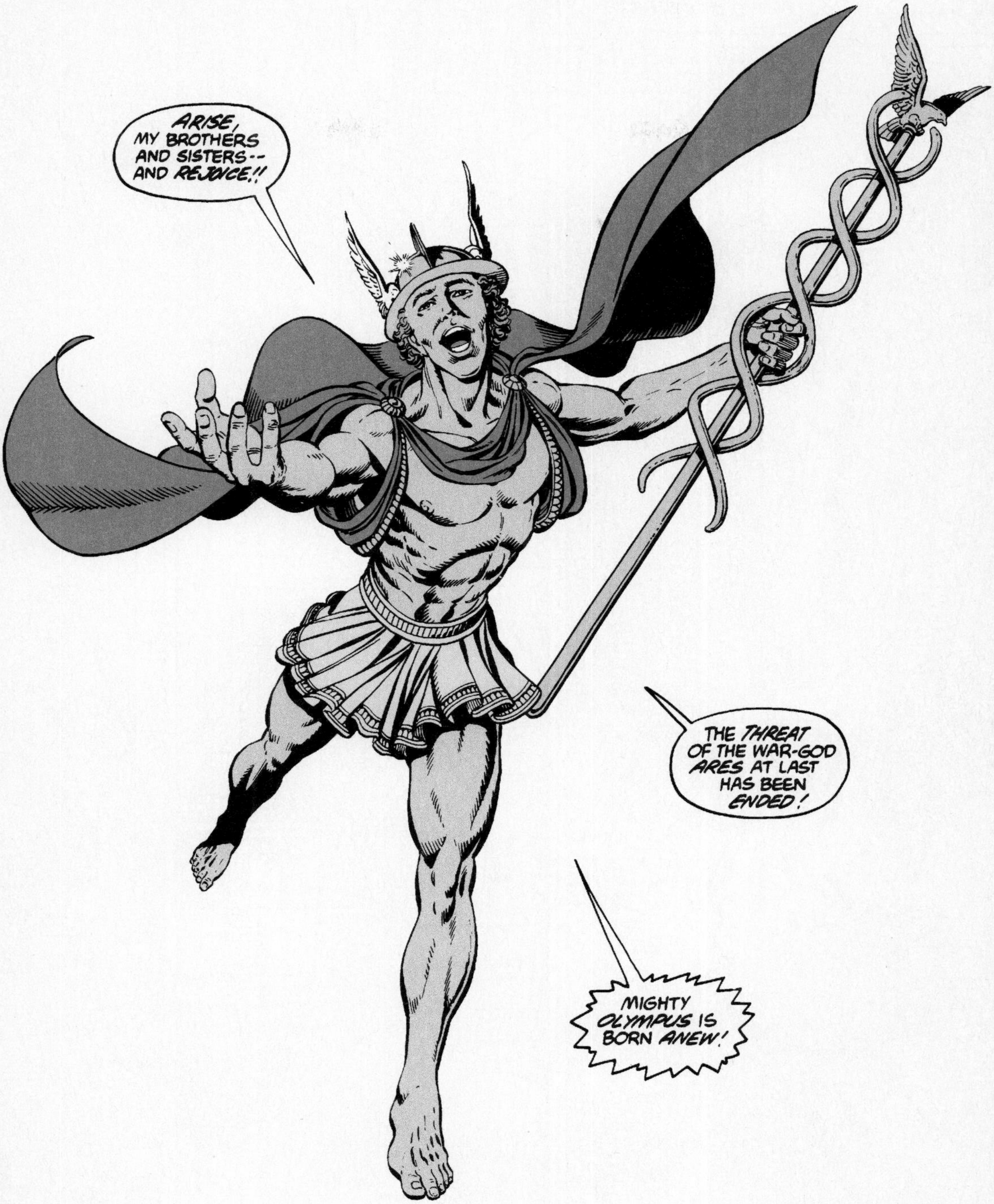
ARISE, MY BROTHERS AND SISTERS-- AND REJOICE!!
THE THREAT OF THE WAR-GOD ARES AT LAST HAS BEEN ENDED!
MIGHTY OLYMPUS IS BORN ANEW!

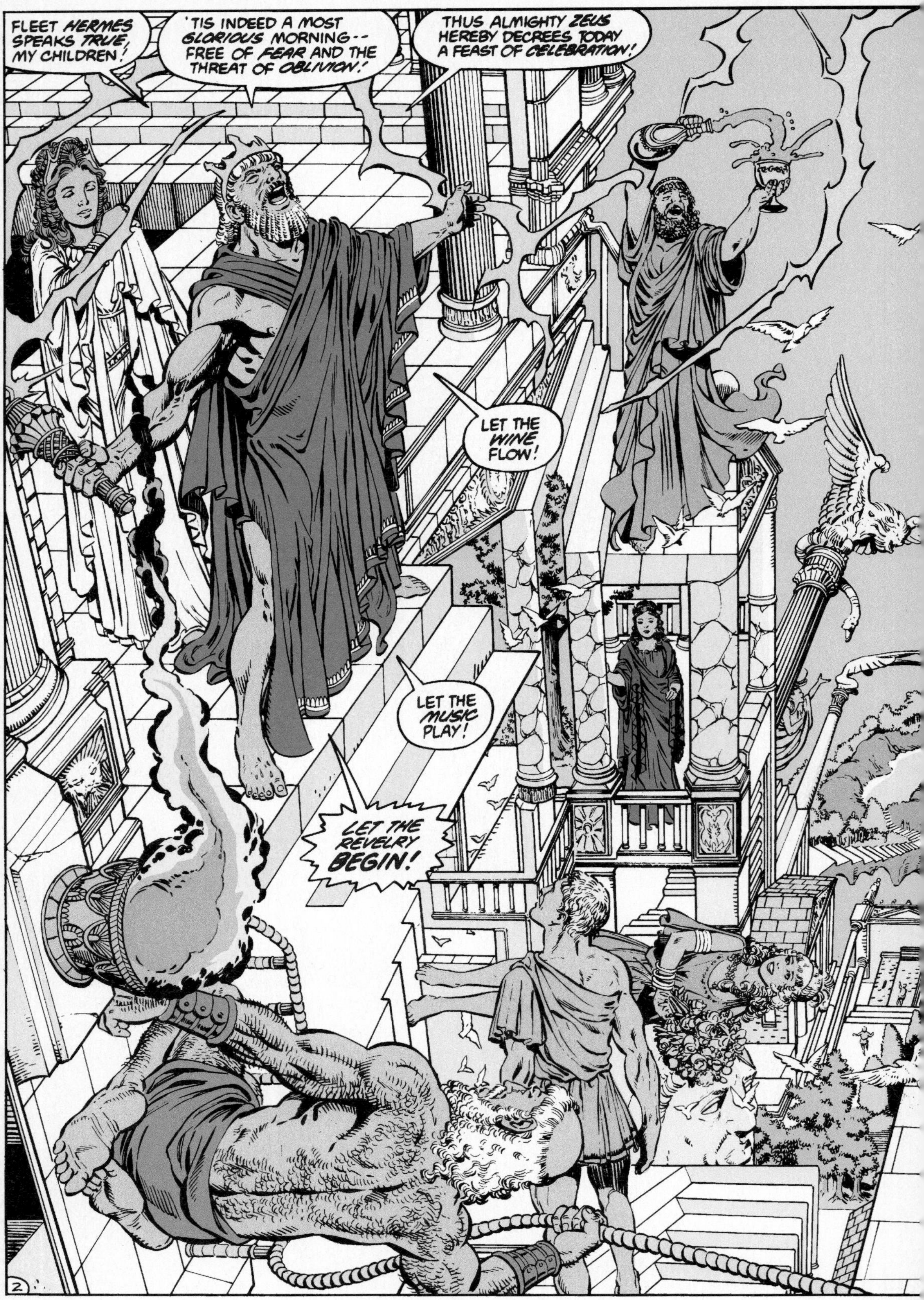

FLEET HERMES SPEAKS TRUE, MY CHILDREN!
'TIS INDEED A MOST GLORIOUS MORNING-- FREE OF FEAR AND THE THREAT OF OBLIVION!
THUS ALMIGHTY ZEUS HEREBY DECREES TODAY A FEAST OF CELEBRATION!
LET THE WINE FLOW!
LET THE MUSIC PLAY!
LET THE REVELRY BEGIN!
2

REBIRTH!

George Pérez . Len Wein . Bruce D. Patterson
plotter/penciller   scripter   inker

John Costanza . Tatjana Wood . Karen Berger
letterer   colorist   editor

THUS, AS THE MELODIES OF FLUTE AND LYRE FILL THE MARBLED HALLS OF FABLED MOUNT OLYMPUS--

--AND THE OTHER GODS MAKE MERRY TO THE MUSIC OF THE SPHERES...

'TIS INDEED A DAY OF REJOICING, MIGHTY ZEUS... NOBLE HERA...

AYE, ATHENA...

IT APPEARS THY BELOVED AMAZONS WERE MORE THAN EQUAL TO THE TASK YOU SET FOR THEM!

INDEED, M'LORD... WE CONTINUE TO THRIVE BECAUSE OF THEIR UNDYING FAITH IN US--!

AND YET THE PRINCESS DIANA-- SHE WHO BATTLED ARES TO SAVE US ALL-- NOW LIES AT DEATH'S THRESHOLD!

AYE, THEY ARE A MOST INTRIGUING RACE, THESE AMAZONS OF YOURS!

PERHAPS HENCE-FORTH I SHALL KEEP A CLOSER EYE ON THEM!

BUT PRAY, DEAR HUSBAND, 'TIS ONLY THINE EYE!

WHILE, OFF THE ROCKY SHORES OF THEMYSCIRA, KNOWN ALSO AS PARADISE ISLAND--

--THE MIST-SHROUDED HOME OF THE IMMORTAL AMAZONS--

-- THE ASSEMBLED SISTERHOOD STANDS UPON THE NEARBY ISLAND OF HEALING, WHILE THE MORTALLY WOUNDED PRINCESS DIANA UNDERGOES THE ANCIENT RITUAL OF REVIVAL...

ANY PROGRESS, SISTERS?

NONE, EPIONE.

IT SEEMS THE PRINCESS'S MANY WOUNDS HAVE DONE MORE THAN MERELY REND HER PRECIOUS FLESH.

AYE, HER VERY SPIRIT SEEMS TO BE DYING.

BEHOLD, MIGHTY ZEUS-- THE CHILD WHO *SAVED* US IS NOW *HERSELF* IN NEED OF *SALVATION!*

SHE WILL SURELY *PERISH*, M'LORD--UNLESS WE *INTERVENE!*

SUCH AN *APPEALING* PLACE, THIS *PARADISE ISLAND*, POPULATED SOLELY BY *WOMEN*--!

WHY, WHEN ONE CONSIDERS THE *POSSIBILITIES*--!

HOLD YOUR *SALACIOUS TONGUE*, PAN!

THOUGH YOU ARE MY *SON*, THESE WOMEN ARE A *SPECIAL BREED*-- AND NOT AT ALL THY *PLAYTHINGS!*

AS EVER, YOU SPEAK *TRUE*, HERMES-- A SPECIAL BREED *INDEED!*

WHY, ONCE DIANA'S *MOTHER*, THE FAIR *HIPPOLYTE*, EVEN HUMBLED MY *HALF-BREED* SON *HERACLES!*

I AM WELL *AWARE* OF THE SITUATION, BRAVE ARTEMIS.

AYE, THE *OFFSPRING* OF SUCH AS SHE INDEED DESERVES TO *LIVE!*

THUS, *HEAR* ME, POSEIDON! *ATTEND* ME, AEOLUS!

THY LORD HAS URGENT *NEED* OF THEE!

THAT *SOUND*--! THAT SUDDEN RUSH OF WIND--!

WHAT--?

LOOK TO THE *SKIES*, MY QUEEN!

IT SEEMS THE GODS AT LAST HAVE ANSWERED OUR *PRAYERS!*

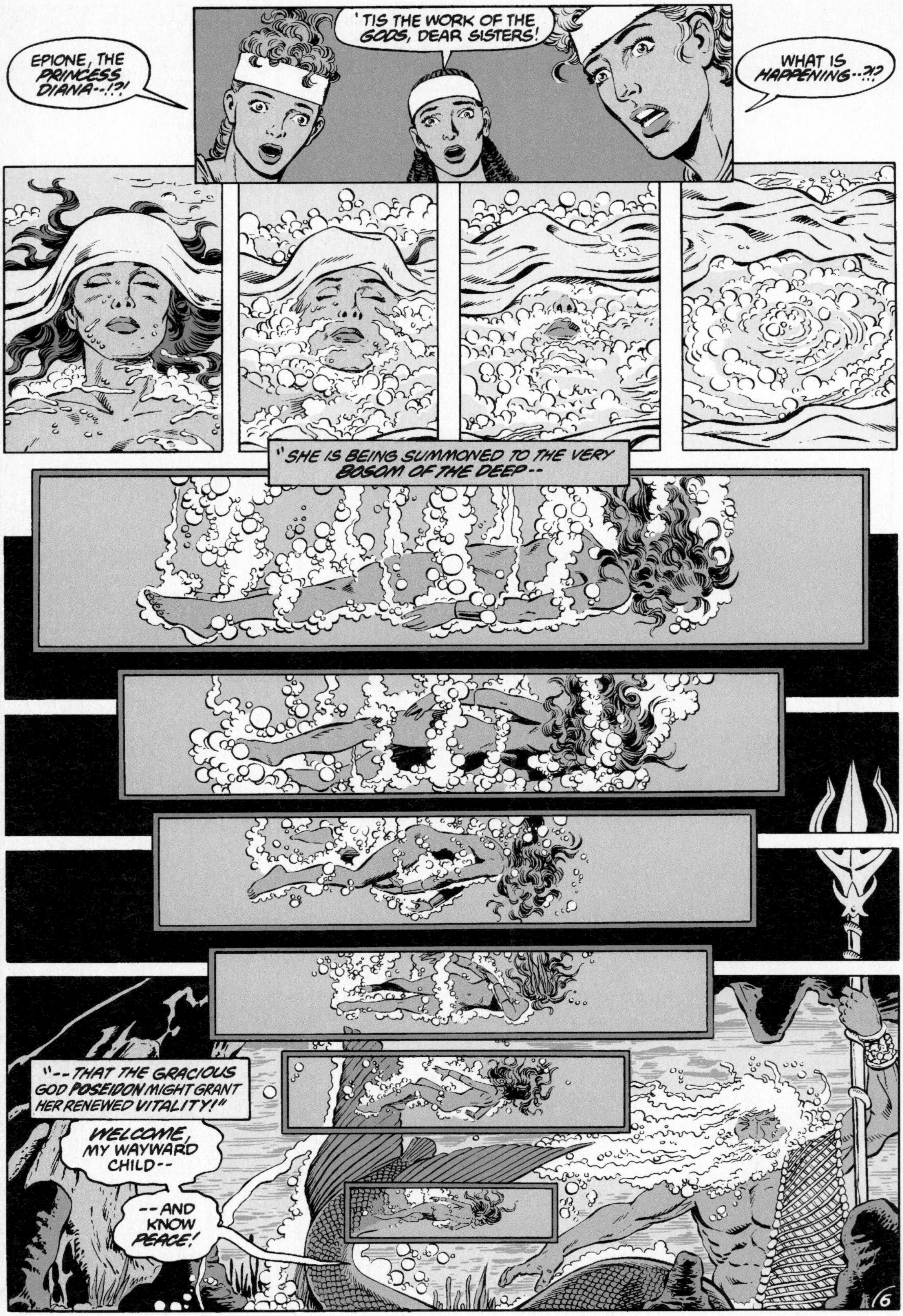
EPIONE, THE PRINCESS DIANA--!?!
'TIS THE WORK OF THE GODS, DEAR SISTERS!
WHAT IS HAPPENING--?!?
"SHE IS BEING SUMMONED TO THE VERY BOSOM OF THE DEEP--
"--THAT THE GRACIOUS GOD POSEIDON MIGHT GRANT HER RENEWED VITALITY!"
WELCOME, MY WAYWARD CHILD--
--AND KNOW PEACE!
6

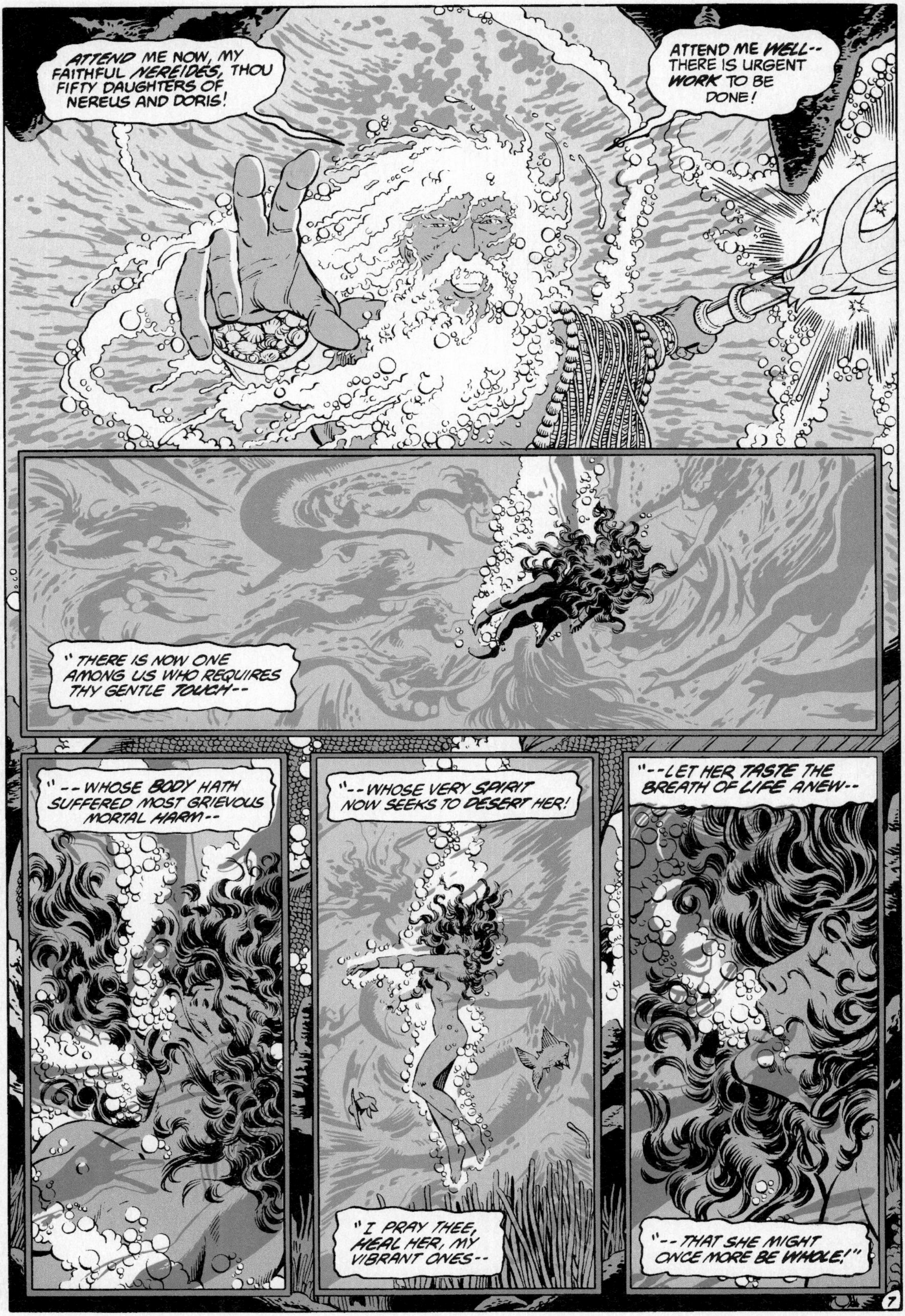
ATTEND ME NOW, MY FAITHFUL NEREIDES, THOU FIFTY DAUGHTERS OF NEREUS AND DORIS!
ATTEND ME WELL-- THERE IS URGENT WORK TO BE DONE!
"THERE IS NOW ONE AMONG US WHO REQUIRES THY GENTLE TOUCH--
"--WHOSE BODY HATH SUFFERED MOST GRIEVOUS MORTAL HARM--
"--WHOSE VERY SPIRIT NOW SEEKS TO DESERT HER!
"I PRAY THEE, HEAL HER, MY VIBRANT ONES--
"--LET HER TASTE THE BREATH OF LIFE ANEW--
"--THAT SHE MIGHT ONCE MORE BE WHOLE!"
7

DIANA HAS BEEN UNDER FOR *SO LONG*--! IF SOMETHING HAS GONE *WRONG*--!

HER *FATE* IS NOW IN THE HANDS OF THE *GODS*, QUEEN HIPPOLYTE.

WE MUST HAVE *FAITH*!

MY FAITH NEVER *WAVERS*, AND YET-- WHEN THE LIFE OF MY OWN *DAUGHTER* IS AT STAKE--!

BEHOLD, MY QUEEN--!

THY WAIT IS *OVER*!

THE *RITUAL OF REVIVAL* HAS REACHED ITS *END*--!

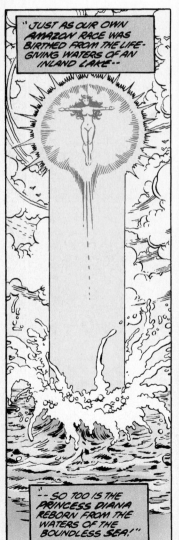

"JUST AS OUR OWN *AMAZON* RACE WAS BIRTHED FROM THE LIFE-GIVING WATERS OF AN INLAND LAKE--

--SO TOO IS THE *PRINCESS DIANA* REBORN FROM THE WATERS OF THE *BOUNDLESS SEA*!"

SHE *LIVES*! DIANA *LIVES*!!

PRAISE BE TO THE *GODS*!

YOU HAVE SERVED ME WELL, HIPPOLYTE--AND THUS I RETURN THY DAUGHTER TO YOU!

I LOOK FORWARD TO YOUR AMAZONS SERVING ME *FURTHER*-- AND SHARING IN THE *TRUE LOVE OF ZEUS*!

ALMIGHTY ZEUS HAS COMMENDED US. WE'VE REASON TO BE *PROUD*--!

SO *WHY* THEN DO HIS WORDS FILL ME WITH SUCH *FOREBODING*?

8

I TELL YOU, ATHENA--DESPITE HIS GRACIOUS *COMPLIMENTS*, I STILL DO NOT *TRUST* ZEUS!

WHY *SO*, ARTEMIS?

I FEAR HIS SUDDEN *INTEREST* IN THE AMAZONS WILL ULTIMATELY *UNDERMINE* THE VERY REASON FOR THEIR *EXISTENCE*!

INDEED, HUNTRESS. THE *OTHERS* ARE ALL DRUNK WITH THE *EXCITEMENT* OF OUR VICTORY OVER ARES--

--BUT CONNIVING *PAN* HAS ALREADY PLANTED SOME UNFORTUNATE *SEEDS* IN THE ALMIGHTY ONE'S *HEART*!

YOU ARE *WISE*, ATHENA--! WHAT CAN WE DO TO *STOP* HIM?

WORRY *NOT*, ARTEMIS-- THIS TIME YOU ARE NOT *ALONE*!

I DID NOT HAVE *FAITH* IN YOUR AMAZONS BEFORE, ARTEMIS--

--AND THUS I LET MY *LOVE* FOR ZEUS AFFECT MY *JUDGMENT*!

THAT HAS ALWAYS BEEN HIS *POWER* OVER ME...

I EITHER ACT BECAUSE OF MY *DEVOTION* TO HIM--

--OR BECAUSE HE HAS ONCE AGAIN *BETRAYED* THAT DEVOTION.

QUEEN *HERA*?! I-- I DO NOT *UNDERSTAND*--!

BUT PERHAPS IT IS TIME FOR A *CHANGE*!

AND, WHILE THE GODDESSES OF MOUNT OLYMPUS PONDER THE *PAST,* ON PARADISE, TWO OTHER WOMEN *URGENTLY* DISCUSS THE *FUTURE...*

BUT YOU *MUST* ALLOW ME TO RETURN TO *MAN'S WORLD,* MOTHER!

WHEN YOU HAVE SO *RECENTLY* BEEN *RETURNED* TO ME, DAUGHTER-- *BARELY ALIVE?*

I RATHER *DOUBT* IT!

MOTHER, *PLEASE--* MY *WORK* THERE IS NOT YET *FINISHED!*

ARES HAS CHARGED ME WITH *TEACHING* MAN THE *ERROR* OF HIS WAYS-- LEST THE WAR-GOD RETURN *ANEW!*

THE DARK ONE'S WORDS ARE SELDOM TO BE *TRUSTED,* DIANA. WHAT IF THIS IS BUT ANOTHER *TRICK?*

AND WHAT IF IT IS *NOT?*

BESIDES, I CANNOT *REST* UNTIL I KNOW THE FATE OF MY *COMPANIONS!* I OWE SUCH *BRAVE* SOULS AT LEAST *THAT* MUCH!

ALSO, THERE IS YOUNG *VANESSA* TO CONSIDER! HER VERY *LIFE* NOW HANGS BY A *THREAD!*

AS A *MOTHER,* YOU MUST *KNOW* THE FEAR OF LOSING A CHILD--!

AYE, DAUGHTER-- WHICH IS WHY I *HESITATE* TO LET YOU *LEAVE* ME ONCE AGAIN!

STILL, THERE IS *MERIT* IN WHAT YOU SAY! IF THE GODS WOULD BUT GIVE ME SOME *SIGN--!*

YOU NEED ONLY TO *ASK,* HIPPOLYTE!

WHAT--?!?

GREAT HERA!

NAY, DIANA-- NOT HERA!

'TIS *ATHENA* WHO NOW BRINGS THEE GREETINGS--

--AS WELL AS A *GIFT* FROM THE *GODS!*

10

166

'TIS A PRESENT FROM *FLEET-FOOTED HERMES!*

HE CLAIMS YOU WILL KNOW WHAT TO *DO* WITH IT!

I TRUST YOU WILL USE IT *WISELY!*

FOR *NOW*, MY *CHILDREN...*

...FAREWELL.

WELL, I *PRAYED* FOR A SIGN AND IT WAS *GIVEN--*

--BUT 'TWAS *NOT* THE SIGN I HAD *HOPED* FOR!

MOTHER-- LOOK!

NOBLE HERMES HAS GIVEN ME HIS *WINGED SANDALS--!*

WITH *THEM*, I CAN JOURNEY FROM PARADISE ISLAND TO MAN'S WORLD *AT WILL!*

THE SIGNS ARE *CLEAR*, MOTHER!

THE GODS THEM-SELVES SUPPORT MY *PLEA!*

THIS PUTS ME IN AN AWKWARD *POSITION*, DAUGHTER.

I CANNOT *QUESTION* THE WILL OF THE *GODS--*

--AND YET, AS YOUR *MOTHER*, I HAVE THE RIGHT TO REQUIRE CERTAIN *RESTRICTIONS* OF YOU!

IF YOU WILL AGREE TO *FOLLOW* THESE RESTRICTIONS--

--ONLY *THEN* SHALL I GRANT YOU LEAVE TO WALK ONCE MORE AMONG *MEN!*

11

MEREDITH MILITARY MEDICAL CENTER, IN BOSTON'S HISTORIC NORTH END:

HERE, SOME OF THE NATION'S GREATEST PHYSICIANS STRUGGLE DAILY TO SOLVE THE INFINITE MYSTERIES OF THE HUMAN BODY--

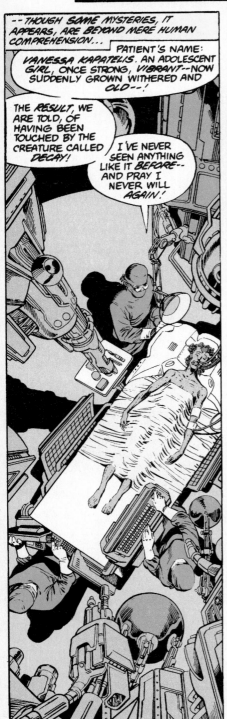

--THOUGH SOME MYSTERIES, IT APPEARS, ARE BEYOND MERE HUMAN COMPREHENSION...

PATIENT'S NAME: VANESSA KAPATELIS. AN ADOLESCENT GIRL, ONCE STRONG, VIBRANT--NOW SUDDENLY GROWN WITHERED AND OLD--!

THE RESULT, WE ARE TOLD, OF HAVING BEEN TOUCHED BY THE CREATURE CALLED DECAY!

I'VE NEVER SEEN ANYTHING LIKE IT BEFORE-- AND PRAY I NEVER WILL AGAIN!

HER CONDITION CONTINUES TO DETERIORATE WITH EVERY MINUTE --

--AND THERE'S NOT A DAMNED THING WE CAN DO TO STOP IT!

GENERAL HILLARY SIR, ARE YOU OKAY?

I'M FINE, LT. CANDY-- JUST A LITTLE FRUSTRATED!

I'VE NO IDEA WHAT'S GOING ON AROUND HERE --

HILLARY

--AND I CERTAINLY CAN'T GO TO THE BRASS WITH THAT GARBAGE YOU AND TREVOR TOLD ME!

IF ONLY THE GIRL IN THE STAR-SPANGLED SUIT HADN'T SUDDENLY DISAPPEARED LIKE THAT--!

NO ONE EVEN KNOWS HOW SHE DID IT! ONE SECOND SHE WAS THERE, THE NEXT SHE WASN'T!

I KNOW IT ALL SOUNDS INSANE, SIR--

--BUT HOW ELSE CAN YOU EXPLAIN WHAT HAPPENED?

I CAN'T! BUT THERE'S GOT TO BE A LOGICAL--

ARROOOARROO

CODE RED TO SURGERY THREE-- STAT!

WHAT--?!?! THAT'S VANESSA'S ROOM!

EASY, GENERAL-- IT'S *OKAY!* YOU NEEDN'T CALL MORE *GUARDS!* SHE ONLY ACTED IN *SELF-DEFENSE!*

SHE'S COME TO HELP THE *GIRL!*

SHE APPEARS TO BE USING A SPECIAL *SALVE* COMPOSED OF *ROOTS, HERBS,* AND THE SPECIAL *WATERS* SURROUNDING HER ISLAND HOME!

AS A *DOCTOR,* I HAVE TO SAY IT SOUNDS LIKE PURE *MUMBO-JUMBO--*

--BUT I CAN'T DENY IT'S *WORKING!*

WELL, I'LL BE A--!

SHE *WHO?*

IT'S *HER,* SIR! IT *HAS* TO BE!

AMAZING! THE DETERIORATION PROCESS IS *REVERSING* ITSELF!

HER *VITAL SIGNS* ARE GROWING *STRONGER!*

IT'S LIKE *MAGIC!*

NOT *LIKE MAGIC--* IT *IS* MAGIC!

GOOD TO SEE YOU AGAIN, DIANA. THANK GOD YOU'RE *ALIVE.*

AND *YOU,* LIEUTENANT CANDY.

BUT WHERE... ARE THE *OTHERS?*

COLONEL TREVOR IS ON ANOTHER *ASSIGNMENT*--AND COLONEL *MICHAELIS...*

COLONEL MICHAELIS IS *DEAD.*

THEN HE DIED...A *HERO.*

AND *JULIA...?*

BACK AT *HARVARD--WORRYING.*

I MUST *SPEAK* TO HER -- AND *QUICKLY!*

FINE. CALL HER!

I'LL HAVE A *CAR* SENT OVER TO THE *COLLEGE.*

13

HARVARD UNIVERSITY:

TAK
TAK
TAK TAK
TAK

NOK NOK

NOK

PROF. J. KAPATI 305 EY D

LIEUTENANT *CANDY?* THANK HEAVEN YOU'RE--

HEY, *YOU'RE NOT* ETTA CANDY!

PROF. J. KAP 30 ARCHAEOLOG

CERTAINLY *NOT*, PROFESSOR KAPATELIS.

I'M MERELY THE ANSWER TO ALL YOUR *PRAYERS*, SWEET THING--

--HERE TO MAKE YOU AN *OFFER* YOU'D BE CRAZY TO *REFUSE!*

BUT I...

MYNDI MAYER IS THE NAME!

PUBLICITY IS THE GAME!

I HEAR YOU'RE PALS WITH THIS *WONDER WOMAN* WHO SAVED BOSTON FROM BECOMING A *DUST BOWL* A FEW DAYS BACK!

JUST TELL ME WHERE I CAN *FIND* HER--AND I PROMISE I'LL MAKE IT *PROFITABLE* FOR YOU!

BUT I...

BRRINGG

AT LAST-- THE *PHONE*--!

I ♥ BONES

HELLO? ETTA?

IS IT *VANESSA?* IS SHE--?

OH, THANK GOD!

YES, I'LL BE WAITING DOWN-STAIRS!

AND, ETTA--? *THANK YOU.*

14

LOOK, I DON'T KNOW WHO THIS *VANESSA* PERSON IS-- BUT *WHATEVER* SHE'S OFFERING, I'LL *DOUBLE* IT!

C'MON, PROF-- WHAT ARE YOU *AFRAID* OF?

JUST *INTRODUCE* ME TO THIS *FRIEND* OF YOURS!

I'LL TAKE CARE OF IT FROM *THERE!*

LISTEN, LOUDMOUTH-- LET'S GET SOME- THING *STRAIGHT* HERE!

YOU COME WALTZING IN HERE *UNINVITED--*

--AND EXPECT ME TO *FEED* YOU A WOMAN WHO *MATTERS* TO ME?

FAT *CHANCE,* LADY!

FIRST, THIS IS A *NO SMOKING* ZONE-- SO GET THAT FOUL WEED OUT OF MY *FACE!*

HUH?

EVEN IF DIANA *WANTED* PUBLICITY-- WHICH SHE *DOESN'T*-- SHE WOULDN'T NEED A *CHEAP SHARK* LIKE *YOU* TO GET IT FOR HER!

NOW, IF YOU'LL *EXCUSE* ME--

SLAM!

--YOU CAN FIND YOUR *OWN* WAY OUT!

WELL, *SHE* CERTAINLY HAS A *TEMPER,* DOESN'T SHE?

BUT IF I WANT TO *INK* THIS *DIANA* DAME, I'LL HAVE TO GET ON THE PROFESSOR'S *GOOD SIDE--*

--ASSUMING, OF COURSE, I CAN *FIND* IT!

WHAT *NERVE*-- CALLING ME A *CHEAP SHARK!*

WHATEVER *ELSE* MYNDI MAYER MAY BE--

-- SHE CERTAINLY AIN'T *CHEAP!*

MEREDITH MEDICAL CENTER:

PROFESSOR *KAPATELIS?*

THANK HEAVEN YOU'RE *HERE!*

15

171

THE GENERAL'S *LIMO* BROKE MOST OF THE LOCAL TRAFFIC LAWS *GETTING* ME HERE, ETTA.

NOW WHAT'S HAPPENED TO *VANESSA?*

YOU'RE NOT GOING TO *BELIEVE* IT, PROFESSOR--!

DIANA IS BACK, *HEALTHIER* THAN EVER--!

RIGHT THIS WAY, LADIES!

AND WAIT'LL YOU *SEE* WHAT SHE'S DONE TO YOUR *DAUGHTER*--!

VANESSA--?!?

BABY?

HI, MOM.

LONG TIME, NO SEE.

OH, BABY, BABY--!

THANK GOD!

THANK YOUR FRIEND *DIANA!* SHE USED THIS WEIRD *STUFF* ON ME-- SAVED MY *LIFE*--!

OH, MOMMY-- I WAS SO *SCARED*--!

DIANA, THERE'S NO WAY I CAN EVER *REPAY* YOU!

YOUR DAUGHTER'S *SMILE*...IS PAYMENT *ENOUGH*...

THERE IS SO MUCH...I MUST *TELL* YOU...SO MUCH I MUST... TELL THE *WORLD*...

...BUT MY *MOTHER*...GAVE ME SO LITTLE *TIME*... BEFORE I MUST RETURN *HOME*...

WELL, I HATE TO DISAPPOINT A MOTHER, BUT YOU'RE NOT *GOING* HOME-- AT LEAST NOT *YET.*

THERE ARE STILL A LOT OF QUESTIONS TO WHICH THE TOP BRASS WANTS *ANSWERS!*

I'M SORRY, MISS--*DIANA,* IS IT?--BUT WE'RE GOING TO HAVE TO HOLD YOU OVER FOR *DEBRIEFING!*

DE...*BRIEFING*...? WHAT *IS* THIS... DEBRIEFING...?

THOUGH THE WAR-GOD IS *GONE,* IT APPEARS HIS *INFLUENCE* LIVES ON.

THESE *HUMANS* ARE STILL SO *STRANGE* TO ME!

16

IT'S NOTHING *COMPLICATED*, DIANA--WE JUST NEED *NAMES*, *DATES*, *PLACES*--!

THE *REASONS* GENERAL TOLLIVER WENT *MAD* AND TOOK OVER THAT *MISSILE BASE*--!

BUT THAT...IS WHAT I *AM* TRYING...TO *TELL* YOU...

...TO TELL *EVERYONE*...!

MOM, WHAT'S *WRONG*? WHY ARE THEY *PICKING* ON DIANA LIKE THAT?

-- SOME WAY TO GET HER *MESSAGE* ACROSS TO THE *GENERAL PUBLIC* BEFORE THE MILITARY SCREWS THINGS UP *COMPLETELY.*

SHE NEEDS *HELP*, BABY--

AND I'M AFRAID I KNOW *HOW*!

GENERAL, LET *ME* SPEAK TO *DIANA*--!

REMEMBER, SHE'S A *STRANGER* HERE-- AND OUR CUSTOMS MAY SEEM *ALIEN* TO HER.

I APPRECIATE YOUR *CONCERN*, PROFESSOR, BUT--

GENERAL, WHAT COULD IT *HURT*? I'M CERTAIN I CAN *EXPLAIN* YOUR PROBLEM TO HER--

--BUT I'VE GOT TO GET HER AWAY FROM ALL THIS *CONFUSION* FIRST!

WELL, IT'S AGAINST MY *BETTER JUDGMENT*, BUT--

OKAY, PRO-FESSOR--GIVE IT YOUR *BEST SHOT*!

THE HEART OF THE BOSTON BUSINESS DISTRICT, SEVERAL HOURS LATER:

YOU WERE *RIGHT*, MS. MAYER--THEY'RE *HERE*!

YES, MA'AM, SHE'S EVERYTHING YOU *THOUGHT* SHE'D BE--AND *MORE*!

I'LL SHOW THEM RIGHT IN.

I STILL DO NOT *UNDERSTAND*, JULIA...WHY I MUST WEAR THIS STRANGE GARMENT?

YOU'D BE JUST A TAD *CONSPICUOUS* IN YOUR *OTHER* OUTFIT, DIANA. VANESSA CLAIMS I KNOW *NOTHING* ABOUT TODAY'S FASHIONS--

--BUT I *DO* KNOW YOU LOOK *STUNNING*!

I SHOULD WARN YOU ABOUT THIS *WOMAN* WE'RE GOING TO SEE, THOUGH-- SHE'S A TRIFLE-- AH--*DIFFERENT* FROM WHAT YOU'RE *USED* TO.

MS. MAYER IS *READY* FOR YOU NOW.

17

173

MS. MAYER, PROFESSOR KAPATELIS AND HER FRIEND ARE HERE TO--

--SEE--

--YOU--?

WELL I'LL BE--!

SO KIND OF YOU BOTH TO COME!

PLEASE, SIT DOWN-- MAKE YOURSELF COMFORTABLE!

WE HAVE A GREAT DEAL TO DISCUSS!

SO YOU'RE DIANA, EH?

I AM.

SISTER, YOUR NEWS PHOTOS DON'T BEGIN TO DO YOU JUSTICE!

YOU'RE GOING TO BE A LOT EASIER TO SELL-- ER-- PROMOTE THAN I'D THOUGHT!

PROMOTE...?

IF YOU WANT TO AFFECT THE PUBLIC CONSCIOUSNESS, DIANA-- YOU MUST FIRST BECOME PART OF THAT CONSCIOUSNESS!

BEFORE THE PUBLIC WILL LISTEN TO YOU, YOU HAVE TO BE AS WELCOME IN THE AVERAGE AMERICAN HOME AS GOOD OLD GRANDMA!

FIRST, WE OUGHT TO CHANGE YOUR NAME-- SO THEY DON'T CONFUSE YOU WITH THAT OTHER PRINCESS DI!

SO HOW DOES DIANA PRINCE SOUND TO YOU?

I CAME TO MAN'S WORLD TO TEACH...BASED ON WHO I AM...HOW WILL THEY TRUST ONE... WHO HIDES BEHIND A FALSE NAME?

BESIDES...THIS OTHER DIANA... HAS NOT CHANGED HER NAME, HAS SHE?

WHY SHOULD I?

POINT TAKEN. OKAY, SCRATCH DIANA PRINCE!

Wonder Woman

Diana Prince

FORTUNATELY, THE MEDIA HAVE ALREADY COME UP WITH ANOTHER NICKNAME FOR YOU!

JUST LEAVE IT TO ME, LADIES-- AND DIANA'S TEACHINGS WILL BE HEARD AROUND THE WORLD!

JUST KEEP IT TASTEFUL AND SUBTLE, MYNDI. I DON'T WANT DIANA TO BECOME SOME MEDIA SIDE-SHOW!

TRUST ME, SWEET THING-- NOTHING BUT CLASS!

18

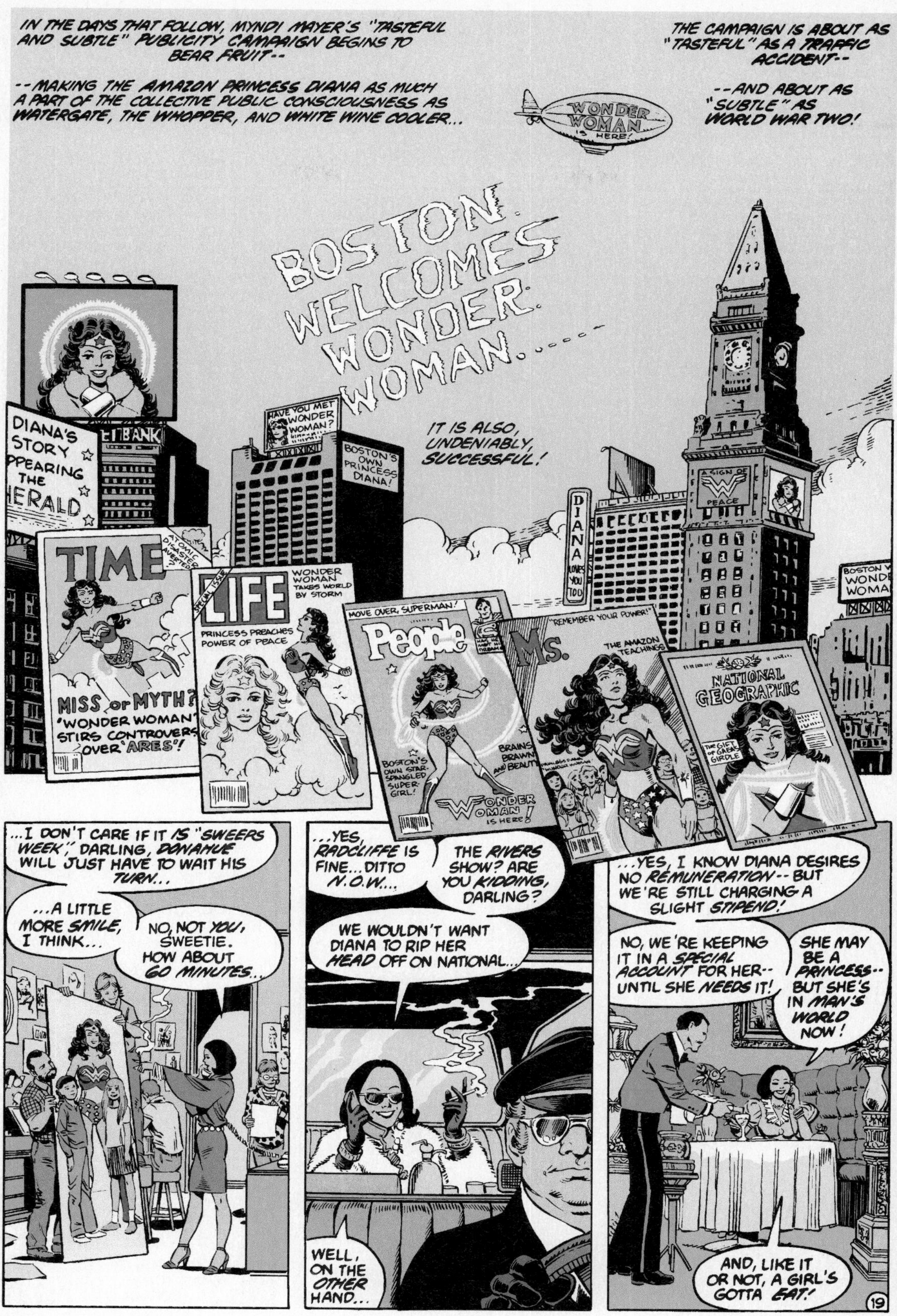
IN THE DAYS THAT FOLLOW, MYNDI MAYER'S "TASTEFUL AND SUBTLE" PUBLICITY CAMPAIGN BEGINS TO BEAR FRUIT--
--MAKING THE AMAZON PRINCESS DIANA AS MUCH A PART OF THE COLLECTIVE PUBLIC CONSCIOUSNESS AS WATERGATE, THE WHOPPER, AND WHITE WINE COOLER...
THE CAMPAIGN IS ABOUT AS "TASTEFUL" AS A TRAFFIC ACCIDENT--
--AND ABOUT AS "SUBTLE" AS WORLD WAR TWO!
WONDER WOMAN IS HERE!
BOSTON WELCOMES WONDER WOMAN......
IT IS ALSO, UNDENIABLY, SUCCESSFUL!
DIANA'S STORY PPEARING THE HERALD
HAVE YOU MET WONDER WOMAN?
BOSTON'S OWN PRINCESS DIANA!
DIANA LOVES YOU TOO
A SIGN OF PEACE
BOSTON WONDER WOMA
TIME
ATOMIC DISASTER AVERTED
MISS or MYTH? 'WONDER WOMAN' STIRS CONTROVERSY OVER 'ARES'!
SPECIAL ISSUE
LIFE
WONDER WOMAN TAKES WORLD BY STORM
PRINCESS PREACHES POWER OF PEACE
MOVE OVER, SUPERMAN!
People
BOSTON'S OWN STAR-SPANGLED SUPER-GIRL!
BRAINS BRAWN AND BEAUTY
WONDER WOMAN IS HERE!
Ms.
"REMEMBER YOUR POWER!"
THE AMAZON TEACHINGS
NATIONAL GEOGRAPHIC
THE GIFT OF GAEA'S GIRDLE
...I DON'T CARE IF IT IS "SWEERS WEEK," DARLING, DONAHUE WILL JUST HAVE TO WAIT HIS TURN...
...A LITTLE MORE SMILE, I THINK...
NO, NOT YOU, SWEETIE. HOW ABOUT 60 MINUTES...
...YES, RADCLIFFE IS FINE... DITTO N.O.W....
THE RIVERS SHOW? ARE YOU KIDDING, DARLING?
WE WOULDN'T WANT DIANA TO RIP HER HEAD OFF ON NATIONAL...
WELL, ON THE OTHER HAND...
...YES, I KNOW DIANA DESIRES NO REMUNERATION--BUT WE'RE STILL CHARGING A SLIGHT STIPEND!
NO, WE'RE KEEPING IT IN A SPECIAL ACCOUNT FOR HER--UNTIL SHE NEEDS IT!
SHE MAY BE A PRINCESS--BUT SHE'S IN MAN'S WORLD NOW!
AND, LIKE IT OR NOT, A GIRL'S GOTTA EAT!
19

GENERAL HILLARY, WE ARE *PERTURBED* BY ALL THE PUBLICITY THIS *WONDER WOMAN* HAS GENERATED REGARDING THE *ARES ASSAULT!*

STILL, THE DAMAGE HAS BEEN *DONE!* THE QUESTION NOW IS *SIMPLE:*

WHAT ARE WE GOING TO DO TO *FIX* IT?

WELL, SIR, I'VE ALREADY SENT BOTH *COLONEL STEVE TREVOR* AND *LIEUTENANT ETTA CANDY* ON SEPARATE *SPECIAL ASSIGN-MENTS*--

--AND ORDERED THEM BOTH TO MAINTAIN *COMPLETE SILENCE* REGARDING THE SITUATION UNTIL FURTHER *NOTICE!*

WELL, I'M GLAD THEY'RE AT LEAST BEING KEPT *BUSY.*

I DON'T *CARE* HOW GORGEOUS OR CONVINCING THIS WONDER WOMAN IS, I STILL CAN'T *BUY* ALL THIS *ARES* NONSENSE!

THERE'S SOMETHING *MORE* TO THE MATTER-- AND I INTEND TO FIND OUT *WHAT!*

ELSEWHERE:

WELL, IT'S *BEGUN.*

LOOKS LIKE *DIANA* HAS FINALLY GAINED THE PUBLIC *EAR*--!

LET'S HOPE SHE CAN TALK SOME *SENSE* INTO THOSE IDIOTS-- BEFORE IT'S *TOO LATE!*

AMAZON PRINCESS SET FOR UN TALK

AND I SEE THEY'VE FINALLY GOTTEN AROUND TO GIVING THE *MEDAL OF HONOR* TO MATT MICHAELIS' *WIDOW.*

FALLEN AIR FO HONORED AT

DIANA ARES WARPED MILITARY MINDS

IT ISN'T *MUCH* CONSOLATION-- BUT I GUESS IT'LL HAVE TO *DO.*

GOD, I *MISS* YOU, OLD BUDDY.

LET'S HOPE DIANA CAN FORCE THE BRASS TO *COME CLEAN*-- SO YOU WON'T HAVE DIED IN VAIN!

ONCE UPON A TIME, I *LOVED* THIS JOB--

--NOW THERE ARE DAYS WHEN I CAN'T *STAND* IT!

20

NOTTINGHAM, ENGLAND, THE ANCESTRAL HOME OF NOTED ARCHAEOLOGIST BARBARA MINERVA...

MADAM--?

IN MY CHAMBERS, CHUMA.

DE DAILY POST HAVE ARRIVED, MA'AM!

ALL DE ARTICLES YOU WANTED ON DIS NEW WONDER WOMAN--

--THOUGH DE GODS ONLY KNOW WHY YOU WANT DEM!

I HAVE MY REASONS, OLD MAN.

I ALWAYS HAVE MY REASONS.

AYE, MA'AM-- DAT YOU DO!

THIS PRINCESS DIANA IS A MOST FASCINATING SUBJECT, CHUMA--

--SUPPOSEDLY THE HEIR OF A RACE OF AMAZONS!

BOSTON HERALD
WONDER WOMAN REVEALS 'ARES PROJE...
TOP BRASS SILENT ABOUT C...
GODFRE CAMPAIGN GATHERS MOMENTUM

AND THIS LASSO OF HERS-- ACCORDING TO THIS KAPATELIS WOMAN, IT WAS FORGED FROM THE GOLDEN GIRDLE OF THE EARTH-GODDESS GAEA!

Gaea's Gift

IF SO, IT IS A PRIZE BEYOND PRICE!

21

177

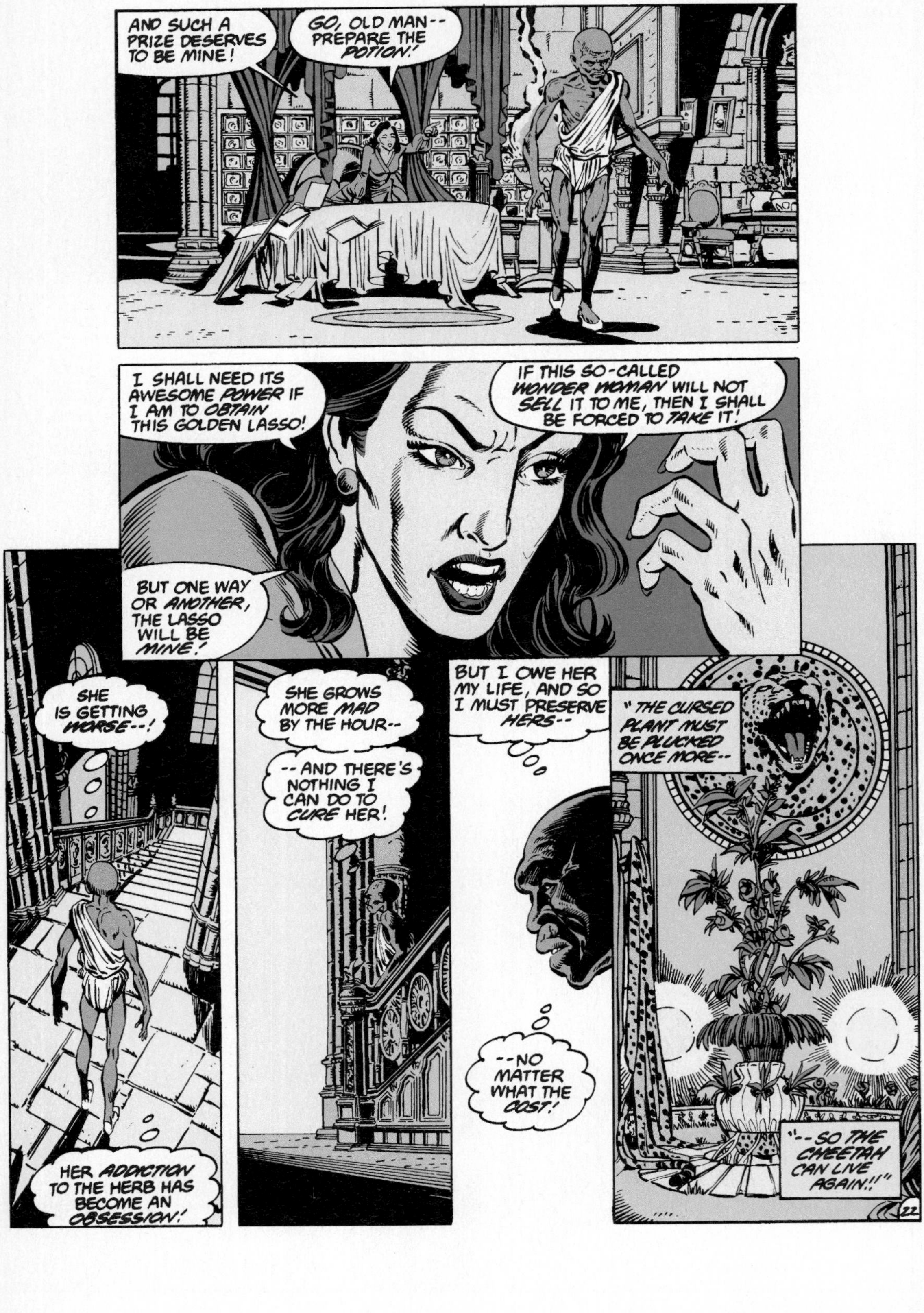
AND SUCH A PRIZE DESERVES TO BE MINE!
GO, OLD MAN--PREPARE THE POTION!
I SHALL NEED ITS AWESOME POWER IF I AM TO OBTAIN THIS GOLDEN LASSO!
IF THIS SO-CALLED WONDER WOMAN WILL NOT SELL IT TO ME, THEN I SHALL BE FORCED TO TAKE IT!
BUT ONE WAY OR ANOTHER, THE LASSO WILL BE MINE!
SHE IS GETTING WORSE--!
HER ADDICTION TO THE HERB HAS BECOME AN OBSESSION!
SHE GROWS MORE MAD BY THE HOUR--
--AND THERE'S NOTHING I CAN DO TO CURE HER!
BUT I OWE HER MY LIFE, AND SO I MUST PRESERVE HERS--
--NO MATTER WHAT THE COST!
"THE CURSED PLANT MUST BE PLUCKED ONCE MORE--
"--SO THE CHEETAH CAN LIVE AGAIN!!"
22

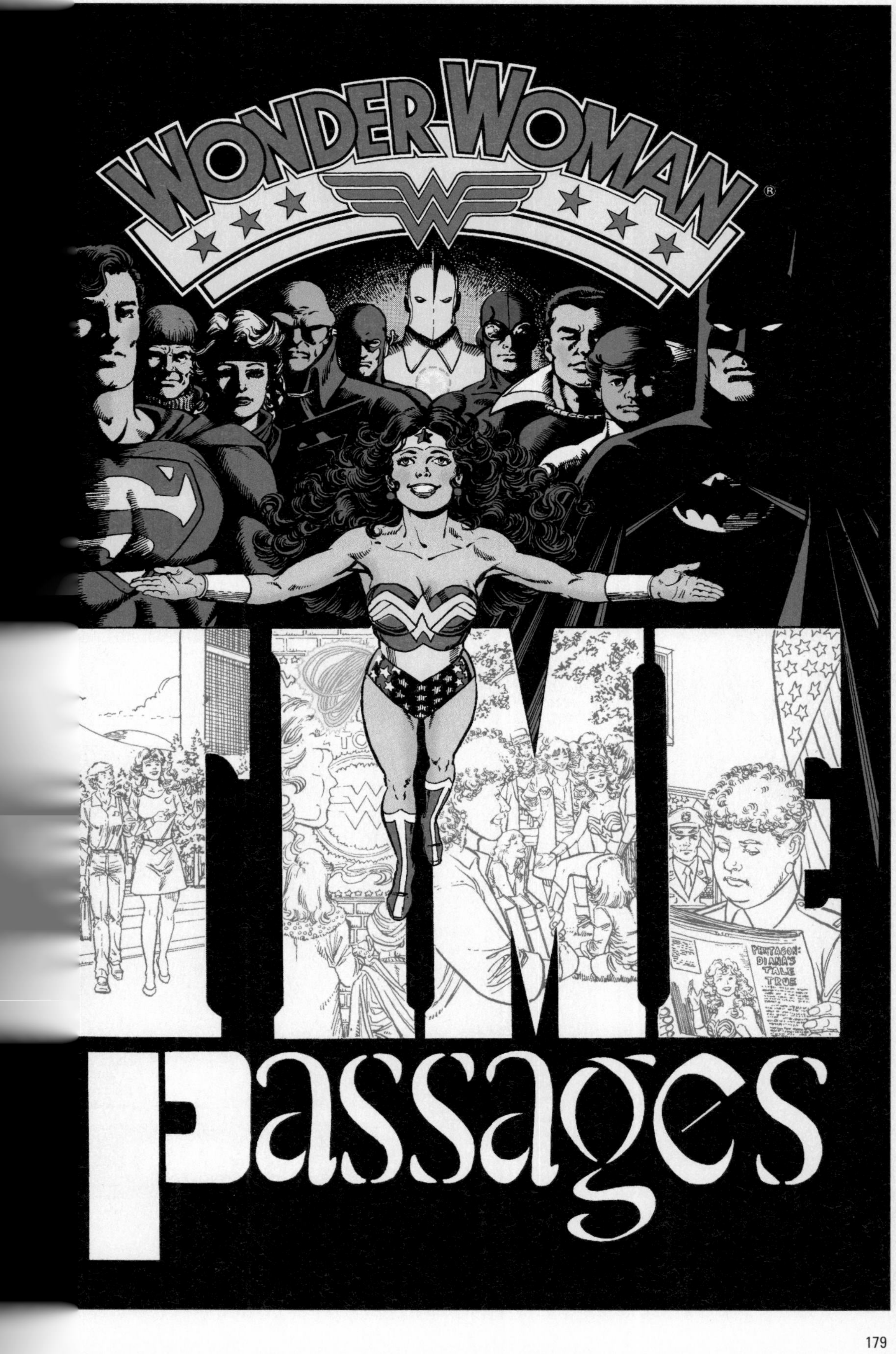
WONDER WOMAN
TIME
Passages
PENTAGON: DIANA'S TALE TRUE

DC Comics Proudly Presents

WONDER WOMAN

created by
William Moulton
Marston

BOSTON, MASSACHUSETTS

HARVARD UNIVERSITY

PROF. J. KAPATELIS
305
ARCHAEOLOGY·ANCIENT HISTORY
CLASSICAL GREEK·GEOLOGY

GEORGE PÉREZ
Plotter/Penciller

LEN WEIN/
GEORGE PÉREZ
scripters

BRUCE PATTERSON
inker

JOHN COSTANZA &
L.S. MacINTOSH
letterers

TATJANA WOOD
colorist

KAREN BERGER
editor

TIME PASSAGES

WELL, I'VE SHARPENED ALL THE PENCILS...PUT A NEW RIBBON IN THE OLD SMITH-CORONA... AND TURNED ON THE ANSWERING MACHINE SO I WON'T BE DISTURBED...

GUESS I CAN'T PUT IT OFF ANY LONGER...

IT'S TIME TO GET TO WORK...

JOURNAL

I have walked the sands of the Kalahari, inhaled the dust of Tutankhamon's tomb, published four definitive volumes of Greek history, borne a daughter, buried a husband, but nothing I've ever done before has been as difficult as this. There is so much to say about the Princess Diana, so little time to say it.

I sit here studying the stunning poster of Diana that her publicist, Myndi Mayer, commissioned for the Wonder Woman speaking tour. Despite my initial reservations about Ms. Mayer, I have to admit she has done an admirable job of promoting Diana's mission to Man's World (as the Amazons are wont to call it).

It has been a rather intense time for Diana, what with the untold hours we spent in my library to prepare the Princess for her appearance before the United Nations General Assembly. I would have preferred more hours of rehearsal, but the time limit imposed on Diana by her mother, Queen Hippolyte, made that practically impossible. Despite the pressure, I'm still astonished by Diana's ability to assimilate so much information so quickly.

At the UN, Diana insisted I act as her interpreter, since she spoke in her native Themysciran, the Amazon dialect derived from ancient Greek. Diana felt the English language was still too new to her, and she wanted no possible misinterpretation of her message of love and peace.

Unfortunately, Diana soon discovered that, in some backward countries of this supposedly "enlightened" world, the words of a woman, no matter how meaningful or true, simply will not be heard.

To make matters worse, the Russian delegate protested that Diana's star-spangled uniform belied her true political leanings and thus her involvement in the Ares Affair. He casually dismissed the mythological aspects of the Affair as patently absurd and denounced Diana as an American propagandist. This left the Princess more perplexed than ever regarding the strange political problems her costume seemed to generate in Man's World, and she was determined to discover the cause.

Thus, despite my protestations, Diana accepted an invitation from the military to prove that the Ares Assault had been much more than an attempted military coup. The Government requested I not attend this meeting, and I couldn't really blame them, considering how I'd ruined their plans to keep the matter quiet. Still, I accompanied Diana to the airfield to see her off.

It would be a week before I saw her again.

181

Something happened to Diana while she was away, something that changed her attitude completely. She returned to Boston quite subdued, determined to dedicate herself to quiet, contemplative study. Despite her little time remaining in our world, Diana asked me to call Myndi Mayer and cancel all further public appearances. It seemed the Princess was finally becoming aware of how different this new, troubled world was from her beloved Paradise Island.

In retrospect, I have begun to wonder if Diana has clairvoyant powers as well. For her self-imposed exile came at almost precisely the same moment that the self-styled savior of the Human Race, that fanatical Psychologist who called himself G. Gordon Godfrey, began his nationwide campaign to outlaw all of America's so-called "super-heroes."

Though his one-man campaign seemed almost ludicrous at first, it quickly picked up steam. Suddenly, some of America's foremost political figures were siding with Godfrey, as if all the collective good that these supremely gifted beings had accomplished over the years was being erased from the public consciousness by some form of mass hypnotism.

In my own classroom, I watched helplessly as my students divided themselves into opposing factions. Violent factions. Though the effects of Godfrey's tirades were not universal, it was obvious they were still painfully far-reaching.

Suddenly, because of my relationship with Diana, I found myself under public scrutiny. It reminded me all too much of the infamous Red Scare of the 1950s, an era I had absolutely no desire to relive. I was suddenly considered a subversive by some for harboring a supposed "super-hero" in my home, and they did not hesitate to make their displeasure known.

When the new house that I had rented was brutally attacked, it was more than Diana could tolerate. After weeks of self-imposed silence, the Amazon Princess known to our world as "Wonder Woman" decided the time had finally come for her to fight for her unalienable rights.

Before I could even begin to dissuade her, Diana was once again gone.

Despite her many public appearances, Diana was still very much an enigma to most of the world. Thus, Guy Gardner, the newest -- and, so Diana tells me, the most irritating -- member of the intergalactic Green Lantern Corps, had no idea what to make of the Amazon Princess when she first crossed his path in Washington, D.C., during the height of Gordon Godfrey's anti-heroic madness.

Finally though, G. Gordon Godfrey met his inevitable downfall. When his own arrogance caused him to lose control of the raging mobs he himself had created, Godfrey donned the gleaming golden helmet of the mysterious Doctor Fate -- a helmet purportedly possessed of incredible mystic power -- and, unable to endure such power, Godfrey was reduced to a gibbering mound of flesh.

Suddenly, Diana found herself standing among many of the other costumed heroes who had suffered because of Godfrey's madness, other super-powerful beings such as she. Now, for the first time, it seemed as if Diana might finally find some sense of belonging in Man's World. But, despite their warm welcome, Diana fled this company of heroes even as she was invited to join the newly re-formed Justice League.

Later, I asked Diana why she had refused such an incredible invitation. She told me she did not believe the point of her mission to Man's World was to become a costumed crimefighter. That, she said, implied violence condoned by society in the name of order. Apparently, crime is unknown on Paradise Island, and order there is a state of mutual respect and love. Diana believed her true destiny was to teach the world the Amazon way.

However, from that day forward, Diana was constantly discussing these unique beings. The Black Canary was the first female crimefighter the Princess had ever seen. On Paradise Island, Diana said, the Canary would have been hailed as a great gladiator. Then there was J'onn J'onzz, the Manhunter from Mars, the proud, emerald-skinned alien from that bright red planet named for a god who was Ares in all but name. Diana found the irony most amusing. And, of course, Diana was fascinated by the militarily named Captain Marvel, whose own powers were supposedly derived from the gods of various pantheons. Who were all these others who claimed to be gods, Diana wondered? Now, for the first time, it seemed Diana had begun to better understand the widespread skepticism regarding her own mythic origins.

Most interesting was the strange silence that would come over Diana whenever I mentioned Superman. She would not talk about him -- as if some unspoken secret existed between them.

Maybe some day she'll tell me about it.

It was a day or two after the official announcement by the Pentagon Chiefs, acknowledging the veracity of Diana's various claims regarding the Ares Affair, that we received a call from Colonel Matthew Michaelis' widow, Angelina.

Now that the whole insane Affair was finally a matter of public record, she sincerely needed to know the details of how fiercely her husband had fought to save the world, how bravely he had died. And, with both Colonel Steve Trevor and Lieutenant Etta Candy away on special assignment, I was the last person on earth who had seen her husband alive.

That brave woman, still wearing black, smiled proudly through her tears as Diana and I told her of her husband's unwavering loyalty and heroism. He had been gunned down while shielding Lt. Candy and myself from a withering hail of bullets. As Mrs. Michaelis and her young son, Andrew, took some small comfort from our words, I noticed Diana was weeping as well. She would later confide that she had never before experienced the loss of a loved one and that she now understood the terrible fear that must have gripped her mother's heart when Diana was called upon to face almost certain death in battle against Ares. As a widow myself, I knew exactly what she meant.

Some nights thereafter I would awaken to find Diana standing nude on the lawn behind the house, praying to her Amazon gods. I realized then what an amazing contradiction she is. On the one hand, nature's innocent, her very voice like a warm, comforting breeze. On the other hand, desperate energy, forever searching for proper outlets. She is, in short, the living seed of change.

However, despite all her determination and energy, even Diana must eventually face her own humanity. Some nights Vanessa and I have found her sprawled in my library amidst a mountain of books. I suppose even Amazons must sleep.

Diana's time here is growing short, and there is still so much to do. And, frankly, I have begun to despair. The Amazon Princess is the closest thing I will ever know to a Goddess; the woman Diana is the closest thing I will ever have to a true friend.

God, how I'm going to miss her.

BRITISH AIRWAYS FLIGHT #1236:

BOUND FOR BOSTON'S LOGAN INTERNATIONAL AIRPORT FROM LONDON'S HEATHROW...

I DISLIKE BEING FORCED TO *TRAVEL* -- BUT *TAM* IS EXPECTING US IN *BOSTON!*

AND THOUGH I DISLIKE *TAM* -- HE *IS* THE PERFECT *CANDIDATE!*

WELL, *CHUMA?* IS IT *SAFE?*

TELL ME THAT IT'S *SAFE!*

BE *CALM*, MADAM -- I HAVE CHECKED DE CARGO HOLD...

AH, WELL -- IN *THIS* LIFE, ONE DOES WHAT ONE *MUST!*

DE PLANT IS *UNTOUCHED*, MA'AM -- IT *SURVIVES!*

THANK THE *FATES!* IF ANYTHING WERE TO *HAPPEN* TO IT --!

WHEN DO WE *LAND*, OLD MAN? I JUST WANT TO PUT AN *END* TO THIS SICK BUSINESS!

SOON NOW... WE BE LANDIN' SOON!

BUT, AS THE SEEMINGLY *ENDLESS* FLIGHT CONTINUES...

STEWARDESS!

TAKE THIS -- THIS *ABOMINATION* AWAY AT ONCE!

IS THERE A *PROBLEM*, MISS?

I SPECIFICALLY *ORDERED* THIS STEAK RARE!

BUT, MISS -- IF IT WERE ANY *MORE* RARE, IT WOULD STILL BE *MOOING!*

DON'T *ARGUE* WITH ME! JUST TAKE IT *AWAY!*

CALM YOURSELF, MADAM -- TRY TO T'INK OF *OTHER* T'INGS!

DON'T DARE *LECTURE* ME, OLD MAN! MY BODY ACHES -- IT *BURNS!*

T'INK OF DE *MISSION* -- OF DE *AMAZON'S GOLDEN LARIAT!*

WHAT IF THE LASSO ISN'T *REAL?*

IN YOUR HEART, YOU *KNOW* DAT IT *REAL*, MA'AM -- DE *AMAZON* SPEAKS *TRUE!*

JUST BE *CALM* -- FOR TONIGHT YOU SHALL *FEED!*

CALL 1-800-555-9487

AYE -- AND DE *PLANT* SHALL FEED AS WELL!

DENVER, COLORADO

LOWRY AIR FORCE BASE

M.E.T.
RECORDS & FORMS
G218 LOWRY

LT. E. CANDY

TIME PASSAGES

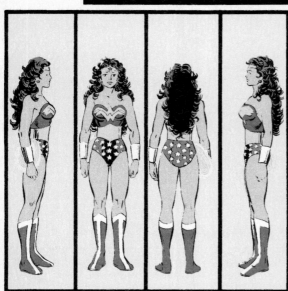

WHEN I WAS A LITTLE GIRL, I USED TO DREAM ABOUT HAVING A BODY LIKE HERS WHEN I FINALLY *GREW UP*...

UNFORTUNATELY, WHEN I GREW UP, I ALSO GREW OUT...

THERE'S SO MUCH ABOUT HER IN THE PAPERS THESE DAYS... SHE'S BECOME AN OVERNIGHT *CELEBRITY*...

...WHICH I GUESS IS AS IT SHOULD BE, WHEN YOU CONSIDER SHE SAVED THE WORLD...

PENTAGON: DIANA'S TALE TRUE

BUT, LIKE YOU ALWAYS SAY, STEVE...

"THEY ALSO SERVE WHO ONLY SIT AND TYPE."

Dispatch

186

Dear Colonel Trevor,

Enclosed with this personal dispatch you'll find the Tribunal's findings and recommendations regarding the so-called "Ares Project / Wonder Woman Affair." Though most of the enclosed information is already public knowledge, I thought you might be interested in my own opinions on the matter.

With your own current duties taking you so far away, I was ordered to serve as an official observer during the now-famous "Wonder Woman Maneuvers." Since the Brass was aware that Princess Diana both knew and trusted me, I guess it was only logical that I attend. Of course, it was under the stipulation that I not voice any personal opinions which might in any way affect Diana's decision to cooperate.

After they had completed taking all of her vital statistics and some photos (see enclosed), General Hillary delivered the Princess into the capable hands of Major Dennis Warren and his research team.

By this point, Diana's English was good enough for her to understand the meaning and necessity of the tests. Nevertheless, an interpreter, a MSgt. Lodicos, was assigned to the Princess in the event of any unforeseen problems. As you may or may not already be aware, the Brass wouldn't approve of Prof. Kapatelis being there because of, quote, the risks to civilian personnel, unquote.

Yeah. Sure.

At any rate, Diana was briefed as to the potential dangers of these tests, but the Amazon was determined to prove her claims in the hope that this would also prove and validate the respective reports you and I filed regarding the various events, natural and otherwise, that culminated at that Missile Base. She was also interested in perhaps learning whether the amazing similarities between our flag and her costume did indeed indicate that an alliance with the U.S. was part of Diana's destiny.

As the transport chopper carried us to the Arizona testing site, I noticed the Princess quietly composed in prayer. I later learned it was a prayer common to the Amazons when they were preparing for contest or battle.

Maybe it was just the intensity of the moment, but I could have sworn the sky suddenly opened then, as if somehow it was actually answering her.

When we got to the test site, preparations had already been made. At the Princess' request, the cameras had been set up in the observation building. Since the first test was going to be "The Flashing Thunder," as Diana called it (military code name: Bullets and Bracelets), she was afraid the equipment might be damaged by ricochets.

The volunteer marksmen were all wearing protective clothing and had been armed with specially modified Uzis. I couldn't believe it. I considered lodging a formal protest against Major Warren for putting the Princess in such danger, but Diana talked me out of it, assuring me she was at no risk.

(A curious aside here: while discussing the impending Bullets and Bracelets tests, Diana mentioned that a simpler version of "The Flashing Thunder" was a test she had faced on Themyscira when competing for the right to challenge Ares. From her description, it sounds like she was shot at with a .45 Magnum, though how such a weapon had come to be on Paradise Island, Diana either couldn't or wouldn't explain. In any case, the Princess said that this particular test had been given specifically to prepare her for possible combat with modern military weaponry. Still, I'd sure love to learn more about that gun.)

Suddenly, at a radioed command, the three marksmen opened fire on Diana -- point blank. I nearly screamed then, but I needn't have worried.

In a frantic flurry of motion even a frame-by-frame playback had difficulty catching, Diana deflected the barrage with her bracelets. I don't know what strange alloy those things are made of, but the bracelets weren't even scratched.

As the bullets flew, the Princess quickly, unexpectedly, charged the riflemen, and not only disarmed them, but also crushed their weapons with her bare hands.

It was at this point, I think, that Major Warren finally started to be impressed.

To be honest though, as impressive as the results of the Bullets and Bracelets test were, even I was stunned at the extent of Diana's abilities that were demonstrated in subsequent tests.

I mean, at one point she actually prevented a Grumman 14A Tomcat -- one they'd commissioned from the Navy specifically for these tests -- from taking off from its runway. She simply lassoed the plane's tail fin with that incredible glowing lariat of hers (the one she says is actually the reforged girdle of the Earth-goddess Gaea), planted her heels firmly against the tarmac, and held her ground. The powerful jet fighter didn't move an inch. In fact, Major Warren finally had to order the pilot to shut down the engine before the bird was damaged from the strain.

When the Princess actually lifted and toppled the Army's new M1 MBT Tank, I knew the Major was certifiably stunned. Interestingly enough, Diana later told me her first instinct was to destroy both the jet and the tank, until she realized they were manned by human crews. Diana's reservations against harming another human being seemed visibly to annoy the Major, who was growing progressively more and more dumbfounded by this enigmatic woman warrior.

For myself, I find I'm growing to respect her more and more.

When Diana outperformed that same jet in aerial maneuvers, she actually smiled. She told me this was what she preferred -- a contest of skill which endangered no one -- and besides, she said, she adored the sensation of flying.

With that final test over, Major Warren summoned the Princess to his office. Although he was finally convinced of the truth of Diana's claims, he thought the U.S. should be permitted to examine and, if possible, duplicate the materials used to form her bracelets and lariat.

To say she did not take kindly to that concept is to put it mildly. What were perceived as weapons by the Major were, to Diana, gifts from the Gods and her sister Amazons, and she would permit no one to take them from her.

Frankly, it took all of my composure and military training to keep from telling off the Major myself. Even though Diana had proven herself beyond a doubt, he still seemed strangely ambivalent -- perhaps even antagonistic -- towards her. Nevertheless, he had no choice but to allow Diana to return to Prof. Kapatelis.

Overall, the whole affair seemed to unnerve the Princess, and I felt somewhat ashamed of how she must perceive us. She had come to our world to help us, and here she was, being treated like some sort of subversive. Beyond various televised appearances and such, I haven't seen or spoken to Diana since that day.

In fact, she seemed to disappear for a while, until that strange anti-hero business generated by G. Gordon Godfrey boiled over.

At least Diana's acceptance by the other heroes, including that Martian Manhunter who saved President Reagan's life, opened the way for the announcement by General Hillary, exonerating us and clarifying the events at that Missile Base for the general public.

Steve, this is my last week at Lowry. I'll be back at Hanscom when you return. I opened this letter with a formal greeting, hoping to reaffirm my belief that the Military life is still for you.

I just hope that past problems won't harden you against the career you once loved so much.

I'm also enclosing some letters from your family, and I hope all is well. I miss you, Steve. More than I can say.

Looking forward to your return.

Respectfully,

Etta

BOSTON, MASSACHUSETTS:

LOGAN INTERNATIONAL AIRPORT, SEVERAL MINUTES AFTER THE ARRIVAL OF BRITISH AIR FLT. #1236...

WELL, THIS *SPECIAL MUSEUM PERMIT* APPEARS TO BE IN ORDER, MISS--!

THEN WHY DO YOU CONTINUE TO *DETAIN* US?

LET US TAKE OUR *PLANT*-- AND OUR *LEAVE*!

YOU WANT THIS *ANY* PLACE *SPECIAL*?

BE *GENTLE* WITH IT, IDIOT! THAT EXHIBIT IS *UNIQUE*!

HEY, *EASY*, LADY-- IT'S JUST A *PLANT*!

THAT PLANT IS *MORE* VALUABLE TO ME THAN YOUR MISERABLE *LIFE*!

HARM IT-- AND I PROMISE YOU WILL *PAY*!

WELL, *LA-DE-DAH*!

AMAZING THEY HAD *ROOM* ON THE PLANE FER BOTH *QUEEN GUINEVERE* THERE *AND* HER *HIGH HORSE*!

AYE, 'TIS GOOD T'*SEE* YE AGAIN, BARBARA!

CHARLES STREET, TWENTY MINUTES LATER:

AH TOLD YE THE DAY WOULD COME WHEN YE'D BE NEEDIN' OL' TAM'S *SPECIAL SERVICE* AGAIN!

SO WHAT'LL IT BE *THIS* TIME? *GUNS? MEN?* MAYBE ANOTHER *JUNKIE MUSEUM CURATOR*?

AH C'N GET YE *PURE GOLD* IF YE WANT IT!

WELL, TELL ME ABOUT THAT LITTLE *DARKIE* O'YURS THEN! LAD AIN'T ONE FER *TALKIN'*, IS HE?

AN' WHAT'S IN THAT *CRATE* HE'S HOLDIN', LASS?

WHAT'VE YE GONE AN' *STOLEN* *THIS* TIME?

C'MON, LASSIE-- *TALK* T'OL' TAM!

WHAT IN THE BLOODY *NEWS-PAPER* COULD BE SO INTERESTING?

DIANA'S FINAL U.S. APPEARANCE

THE WONDER WOMAN FAREWELL TOUR

CALL 1-800-555-8487 FOR TOUR DETAILS

WAKEFIELD, MASSACHUSETTS

THE KAPATELIS SUMMER HOME

NESSIE'S ROOM!

KNOCK TWICE-- THEN GO AWAY!

TIME PASSAGES

NOT A BAD PICTURE... I MEAN, HONESTLY, IT'S GREAT...

FOR A CHANGE, MY DUMB TEETH DON'T EVEN LOOK STUPID... AND YOU CAN'T SEE A SINGLE ZIT...

ON THE WHOLE, I'D GIVE LIFE AT THE MOMENT AN 82...

IT'S GOT A GOOD BEAT AND YOU CAN DANCE TO IT...

WONDER WHAT BARRY IS DOING RIGHT NOW?

Dear Diary...

Dear Diary,

Well, just got that picture Mom took of Diana and me the same day I got those special "Wonder Woman" bracelets and earrings from Myndi. The photo looks so excellent! Diana looks great! And so do I !

Y'know, Diary, I never did tell you all about that day. (I was so exhausted, since Mom made me do all my homework and stuff before she would take the picture -- YUK !)

Anyway, that was the day Diana and me finally had a lo-o-o-ong talk about things, and I found out how really terrific she is. Did I tell you she thinks I'm beautiful? Really! She told me I was the first young girl she'd ever seen, 'cause when she grew up (on Paradise Island), she was the only child and all the other Amazons were all adults. That must have been the pits!

Anyway, she kept telling me what a beautiful place her home is and how the air there is so clean and how you can go swimming there every day and all. (Too bad it was too cold to use the pool!) The not-so-cool part is that they also spend a lot of time doing schoolwork, sort of. Diana says that learning is "part of growing." See, they don't age on Paradise Island -- they grow. Isn't that weird? Diana said she'd like to take me there someday, but I don't know. I mean, some of it sounds really neat and all, but there's no movies, no MTV, no clothing stores -- NO BOYS !!

Though it DOES sound like an excellent place to get a TAN!

By the way, it seems Diana is also the only Amazon with her special powers. She said they were a gift from the Gods she wor-shipped (seems the Amazons are really heavy

into their religion). I told her we studied some about Zeus and the other Gods in school, but I never believed they REALLY existed. Now I do.

The saddest part was when Diana asked me about Daddy. She'd seen pictures of him around the house and wondered what it was like to have a father. Listening to her made me feel really lucky that I'd had him for even such a short time before he died.

I mean, we were really getting along, and it made me feel like a real DORK for the way I acted when we first met. Honest, I wouldn't have blamed her if she hadn't saved my life.

Anyway, suddenly, Diana got this most excellent urge, and she picked me up in her arms, and we went flying! Really FLYING !!

Okay, I'll admit I was scared at first -- just a LITTLE scared -- but after a while it was really awesome.

I guess Diana and I flew all over the place for hours, talking about anything that popped into our heads. Diana told me she was nervous about talking at my school (more about that later). She said the English language still confused her some of the time. (Honestly, she speaks it better than me!) I tried talking Greek to her for a while, but my Greek stinks! (Just ask Mom -- HA HA!)

Anyway, we came home really late 'cause we got so LOST! Diana said this world was so much bigger than her tiny island, and she thought I knew where we were. Boy, did we laugh. (Even Mom!)

*****

Well, today was the big day! I got to school super-early so I could talk to Joanne, Charlene, and the other girls. I told them all about me and Diana flying over the city and stuff. Boy, were they impressed

That's when HE walked in! BARRY LOCATELLI! Remember, Diary, how I told you about him? He is absolutely the cutest boy in the whole school! He actually came over to talk to me -- ME!! The other girls were so jealous! I just prayed I wouldn't do anything stupid -- like throw up or faint or anything. I mean, until this morning I thought flying was the biggest thrill of my life! GOD! I couldn't stand it! Barry leaned towards me, backing my trembling body against the cold lockers. He stared at me with those Rob Lowe eyes of his. Spoke to me with those Michael J. Fox lips. Smiled that Kirk Cameron smile. (I was going to DIE, I just knew it!) He said he had admired me from afar for ages. He said he thought I was cute! (Nope, I wasn't going to die. I was already dead and in Heaven!)

If you don't believe me, just ask the other girls. They all heard him. He said he wanted to sit next to ME at Diana's lecture.

I mean, I tried to be cool. I didn't drool or anything. I think I just nodded my head, because I couldn't say a word. But when he finally walked away, I let out such a SCREAM!

Well, anyway, Diana gave her lecture in the auditorium that afternoon. She was wearing that weird red-white-and-blue costume she wears most of the time. I really wish Mom would let me help buy her some normal clothes.

The speech was going just great and Diana had no problem with English like she was afraid she would. Of course, I'd heard it all before when we were flying, but that was okay since the lecture got me out of introductory physics class. All the other girls were really excited and started imitating Diana's Amazon salute (which is when you cross your arms like an X and have the bracelets touch each other). Boy, the local stores must have sold a lot of those bracelets just from our school alone.

A lot of boys listened too, except for the usual jerks like Johnny Meekins. He just kept bothering Lisa Choi by pretending to fall asleep while Diana was talking. Honestly, if I was an Amazon, I'd hit him where it hurts!

But then again, if I was an Amazon, I wouldn't have Barry. He was just so beautiful! He actually listened to Diana. I could tell how interested he was. He never took his attention off her for a second. I mean, he's just so different from the other boys.

Even though I only just turned 13, he made me feel mature, like I was his equal. (He's 15½, but I've always liked older men). Maybe --oh, PLEASE, God--, maybe he'll even ask me to next month's dance. (I know I'm going CRAZY, but isn't that what love is all about?)

Anyway, after school, Barry and I went to the yard, where Diana was still talking to some of the kids. Even some of the teachers, like Mr. Kettering from Algebra, were standing around listening.

I told Diana what a hit she'd been. Barry told her too. He's so gorgeous!

Around 3:30, Diana finally left and I was just kind of walking around with Barry when we saw Johnny Meekins, Louie Lucas, and Vinnie Capola acting like real goons behind a tree. They were looking at this picture and making all kinds of rude and disgusting noises.

Barry pushed Louie and Vinnie aside and took the picture from Johnny, who looked really scared that Barry was gonna hit him.

When we looked at the picture, I nearly wanted to barf. It was a shot of Diana that those morons had drawn all over to make it look really gross and disgusting. It reminded me of what Diana had said during the lecture, about how the Amazons had been treated by the Greek armies.

Well, I didn't get sick—! I just got fighting mad! And so did Barry! We really piled into those creeps like Sigourney Weaver in "Aliens"! While Barry beat on Johnny, I jumped on Vinnie and hit him in the head with my bracelets. I don't know how long we were fighting, but Mr. Nanko stopped us before we clobbered those idiots. Thankfully, Mom used her influence to keep us from getting suspended, but, boy, was she MAD! Mom never yells, y'know—she just looks at you. I swear, you can positively feel her eyes blistering your skin! Mom made me apologize to Johnny and the others. She said that Diana wouldn't have acted that way, and she was right. Diana never uses violence except as a last resort. Mom also grounded me for a whole MONTH!!

Well, at least I'll still see Barry in school. He thought I was really cool during the fight and he even gave me a picture of him. He said I was his "Wonder Woman"!
Wow, grounded for a whole MONTH!
Y'know something, Dear Diary? It was WORTH it!

BOSTON AFTER MIDNIGHT:

BLAST IT, LAD--YE CAN'T *DO* THIS T'OL' *TAM!*

AH WANT T'SPEAK T'YUIR *MISTRESS--* AN' AH MEAN *NOW!*

IT TOOK SOMETHIN' *BIG* T'BRING BARBARA MINERVA HALFWAY 'ROUND THE WORLD FROM HER PRECIOUS *IVORY TOWER--*

--AN' I MEAN T'KNOW WHAT IT *IS!*

I HAVE *TOLD* YOU, SIR-- DE MISTRESS WILL CONTACT YOU *SHORTLY!*

NOT BLOODY *GOOD ENOUGH!*

NOW *STEP ASIDE*, LAD-- AH DON'T WANNA *HURT* YE!

WHUMP

WHUUFF!!

CURSE YE BOTH-- WHO D'YE THINK YUIR *DEALIN'* WITH HERE ?!? AH KNOW ENOUGH T'GO T' THE *FEDS--* T'*FARADAY* HIMSELF!

AH WANT MUH *CUT*, LASSIE-- OR AH'LL *BURY* YE!

BOSTON BEFORE DAWN:

CHUMA, IS IT *READY?*

AYE, MA'AM-- DE FINAL CYCLE IS *BEGUN!*

ARE YOU CERTAIN THE LETTER HAS BEEN *RECEIVED?*

ABSOLUTELY! I SENT DE TING RETURN RECEIPT REQUESTED!

BY DE WAY, MA'AM-- I APPROVE OF YOU 'CHOICE OF *MISTER TAM--!*

JUST STIR, OLD MAN! IT WAS NOT *MY* CHOICE!

THE CURSED *PLANT* IS FAR MORE *IMPARTIAL* THAN I !

BUT I WILL NEED ALL MY *STRENGTH*, SHOULD THE AMAZON PRINCESS PROVE *DIFFICULT!*

ALL SHE HAS TO DO NOW IS *BELIEVE* MY *CLAIM!*

BOSTON, MASSACHUSETTS

DOWNTOWN BUSINESS DISTRICT

MYNDI MAYER
PUBLICITY MANAGER

TIME PASSAGES

DIANA'S FINAL U.S. APPEARANCE
THE WONDER WOMAN
FAREWELL TOUR

CALL 1-800-555-8487
FOR TOUR DETAILS

NOT BAD, IF I DO SAY SO MYSELF...

IF THERE'S ANYONE LEFT IN AMERICA WHO HASN'T HEARD HER MESSAGE BY THE TIME THIS IS OVER, I'LL EAT MY HAT...

WELL, MAYBE NOT MY HAT...

I LIKE THAT HAT...

STILL, LIFE CERTAINLY HAS BEEN INTERESTING SINCE THE PRINCESS DIANA WALKED THROUGH MY DOOR...

AND THE COMMISSION HASN'T BEEN HALF-BAD NEITHER...

"TOUR UPDATE"

Darling Julia,

Just to bring you up to date...

With that horrid G. Gordon Godfrey problem finally dealt with, and the military's public acknowledgement of Diana's claims regarding the "Ares Affair," our Wonder Woman Tour couldn't have been better-timed. Especially since the princess' brief period of seclusion had whetted everyone's appetite to learn more about her.

Being all too well-aware of the time limits imposed upon us by Diana's mother, I knew the only way to accomplish Diana's goals was with a juggernaut media blitz.

The press coverage I arranged of Boston's Mayor Flynn presenting the princess with the key to the city was an overwhelmingly positive and her subsequent appearance on the Carson show was a ratings blockbuster. The audience reaction to Diana lifting the entire Tonight Show set, complete with Johnny, Ed, Doc, and even -- God help us -- Tommy Newsome still sitting on it, was nothing short of spectacular.

Of course, arranging Diana's meeting with the President was the crowning touch. Because of her hectic schedule, Diana was the only super-hero who had not yet been honored by the Big Man for her participation in the Godfrey affair. By arranging a separate audience for Diana, we assured she wouldn't have to share the spotlight with anyone else.

On the merchandising front, it seems that stores nationwide can't seem to stock enough Wonder Woman material. Add to that the licensing of Diana's own monthly comic book to be published by DC Comics, Inc., as well as licensing her likeness to various Wonder Woman clothing and notions lines, huge profits are being projected across the board for the final two fiscal quarters of this year.

Since Diana claims she'll no longer be with us by year's end, her share of the profits will be channeled toward a "Wonder Woman Foundation" whose principal aim will be to publicize, promote, and encourage the contribution of various women over 40 years old toward equality and advancement.

ZOWIE!
DIANA SIGNS DEAL FOR 'WONDER WOMAN' COMIC BOOK

WONDER WOMAN

DIANA'S FINAL U.S. APPEARANCE
THE WONDER WOMAN FAREWELL TOUR

CALL 1-800-555-8487
FOR TOUR DETAILS

Though I'll miss her, it may be just as well that Diana's stay here on "Man's World" is temporary. There has been increasing pressure from various religious spokespeople over the past few weeks, demanding they be allowed to question the Princess regarding her religious beliefs. In a round-table discussion with prominent Christian and Judaic leaders, great concern was expressed regarding the "Pagan" aspects of the Mythic Greek philosophy Diana expounds. While meetings such as these have generally been civil, a growing number of Fundamentalists and even Atheists have called me at all hours of the day to lodge formal complaints.

As you remember that day up at your summer place, I finally had no choice but to tell the Princess about the problem, and it became obvious that the strain of the tour was finally beginning to take its toll. Though I tried to emphasize the potential positive responses we could make, Diana seemed lost in thoughts of male chauvinism, political polarization, anti-heroic prejudice, and now religious persecution, all still so new to her.

Though the tour is finally drawing to a close, the fan mail just keeps pouring in. One letter in particular caught my eye, and I thought I should forward it to you.

It's from a Doctor Barbara Minerva, and it strikes me as just the tonic Diana needs right now.

Besides, if Minerva's claims are valid, we've got a nifty new piece of publicity here.

Take care of our Princess, Professor.

Myndi Mayer

**FROM THE DESK OF
DR. BARBARA MINERVA**

To: Princess Diana
c/o Mayer Publicists, Inc.
Boston, MA 02112

Dear Princess Diana,

As a student of History and Archaeology, I have followed all reports of you with great interest.

As a result of my years of extensive research and travel, I have managed to procure many items of historical value. Thus, your claims regarding your golden lasso have particularly fascinated me.

GOD, WHAT A *MESS!*

ANY IDEA WHO *DID* HIM?

HE HAD ENOUGH *ENEMIES!*

TAKE YOUR *PICK!*

SO? WHAT IS IT *THIS* TIME?

BETTER SEE FOR *YOURSELF,* DOC.

MY *GOD!* THIS MAN'S BEEN *TORN APART!*

SO TELL US SOMETHING WE *DON'T* KNOW.

You see, I have in my possession an ancient forged relic that I have been unable to identify, until I read your account of your lasso and its supposed origins.

WOUNDS WERE DEFINITELY MADE BY *CLAWS* OF SOME SORT--AND THE BODY WAS THEN *GUTTED!*

NOT MUCH *BLOOD,* THOUGH! IT'S AS IF SOME ANIMAL *KILLED,* THEN BEGAN TO *EAT* HIM!

ANY *I.D.?*

I now believe that I possess the second girdle of Gaea, the prize once given your mother by the Goddesses themselves. I am so certain of its authenticity that I felt obliged to inform you before I make this information public.

NAME WAS *TAMSYN McCONNELL,* SMALL-TIME *SMUGGLER* AND *GUNRUNNER!*

TWELVE *ARRESTS...* NO *CONVICTIONS...*

With this new discovery, I am certain new insights as to the true fate of your Aunt Antiope and the Amazons she led can finally be learned. I firmly believe that several of them survive to this day. Perhaps this can also help explain your true destiny in this world.

GUESS THAT WON'T BE A *PROBLEM* ANYMORE.

WELL, LET'S JUST SAY HE WON'T BE *MISSED.*

As a woman myself, I am excited by these possibilities and hope you will agree to contact me at the above address.

Very truly yours,
Dr. Barbara Minerva

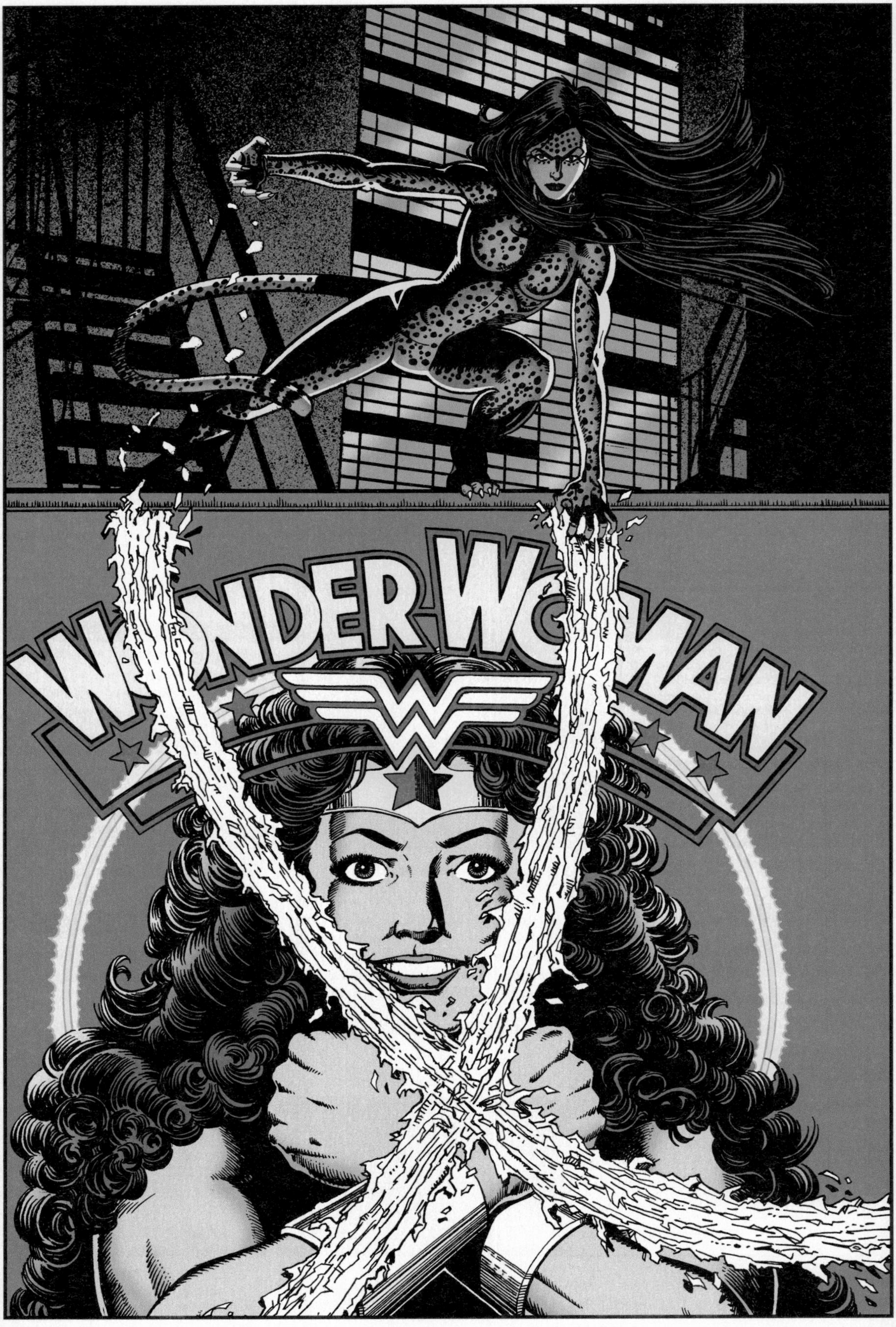
WONDER WOMAN

LISTEN! CAN YOU HEAR IT?

ABOVE THE RUMBLE OF THE TRAFFIC AND THE NEON'S CRACKLING HUM?

THERE ARE DRUMS IN THE NIGHT!

AND, TO THE RHYTHM OF THE DRUMS, THERE IS CHANTING!

THE OLD MAN STANDS ON THE BALCONY, HIS WEATHERED FACE AWASH WITH MOONLIGHT--

--AND RAZORED DEATH GLEAMS BRIGHTLY IN HIS HAND!

HE TURNS, AND THE DRUMS GROW LOUDER--

--AS IF KNOWING WHAT IS NEXT TO COME...

MORE OFTEN THAN HE CARES TO REMEMBER, THE OLD MAN HAS PERFORMED THE SACRED RITUAL--

--AND HE PRAYS EACH TIME WILL BE THE LAST!

TONIGHT WAS THE NIGHT OF THE KILL--

-- THE NIGHT OF THE HUNGER--

--THE NIGHT WHEN THE DRUMS ARE ONE WITH HER HEART--

-- AND HER HEART BEATS QUICK AND STRONG...

TONIGHT IS THE NIGHT OF THE BLOODFEAST!

1

GENTLY, THE OLD MAN TAPES UP HER WOUND...

IN THE MORNING, THERE WILL BE NO SCAR...

SUCH IS THE GOD'S GIFT OF HEALING...

SUCH IS ITS CURSE...

BUT NOW THE GOD GROWS HUNGRY...

NOW MUST THE GOD BE FED...

...THE JEALOUS GOD...

...THE PLANT-GOD...

...THE FRAIL GOD GIVEN LIFE BY THE WOMAN, THAT SHE MIGHT LIVE AS WELL...

TO THE REST OF THE SACRED POTION, THE OLD MAN ADDS THE PRECIOUS BLOOD--

--AND THE DRUMS GROW LOUDER STILL!

DC COMICS presents

WONDER WOMAN

BLOOD
OF THE
CHEETAH

Plot and layouts **GEORGE PÉREZ** · *script* **LEN WEIN** · *finishes* **BRUCE D. PATTERSON** · *letters* **J. COSTANZA** · *colors* **T. WOOD** · *editor* **KAREN BERGER** · *thanks to* **BOB SMITH**

SATED NOW, THE PLANT-GOD SIGHS IN CONTENTMENT--

--AND THE OLD MAN PREPARES TO RETURN HIS MISTRESS--AND ITS SLAVE--TO HER BED...

FOR MOST OF THE APPROACHING DAY, BARBARA MINERVA WILL SLEEP--

--FOR THE ECHO OF THE DRUMS HAS FINALLY CEASED!

2

WAKEFIELD, MASSACHUSETTS, ONE WEEK LATER:

FOR THE PRINCESS DIANA, CHOSEN OF THE AMAZONS, THERE IS NO GREATER EXHILARATION THAN THE SHEER JOY OF FLYING--

--THE INVIGORATING FEELING OF THE BRISK BREEZE WHIPPING WILDLY PAST HER FACE--

--THE INCOMPARABLE SENSATION OF PURE UNBRIDLED FREEDOM!

3

AND FOR PUBLICIST MYNDI MAYER, WATCHING FROM THE WOODS NEARBY, THE THRILL, THOUGH VICARIOUS, IS NO LESS REAL...

THIS IS GOING TO BE *SENSATIONAL!*

IF SHE REALLY *DOES* HAVE THE *SECOND* GIRDLE OF GAEA, IT COULD CHANGE DIANA'S WHOLE *PERCEPTION* OF HER *AMAZON HISTORY*--!

AND IT WOULDN'T EXACTLY BE A BAD *PUBLICITY COUP* EITHER!

YOU'D *MERCHANDISE* MOTHER TERESA IF YOU COULD MANAGE IT, WOULDN'T YOU?

THE THOUGHT *HAS* CROSSED MY MIND, PROFESSOR.

HI, MS. MAYER!

HI, YOURSELF, CUTIE.

THAT LETTER FROM *DR. MINERVA* COULDN'T HAVE COME AT A BETTER *TIME.*

SORRY IF I *SNAPPED* AT YOU, MYNDI--

--BUT I'M *WORRIED* ABOUT *DIANA!*

JUST *LOOK* AT HER!

WELL, I CAN'T IMAGINE *WHY,* JULIA!

"I HAVEN'T SEEN HER THIS *HAPPY* SINCE I'VE KNOWN HER!"

"*BARBARA MINERVA'S* LETTER WAS LIKE A TONIC!"

IF THE LETTER'S *TRUE,* ARE YOU GONNA HAVE A PARTY TO *CELEBRATE?*

CAN *I* COME?

CAN I BRING A *FRIEND?*

GOT SOMEBODY *SPECIAL* IN MIND, SWEET THING?

LET'S JUST *SAVE* THE CELEBRATION TILL IT'S APPROPRIATE, OKAY?

I'VE DONE A BIT OF *CHECKING* INTO THIS DR. BARBARA MINERVA'S *REPUTATION*--

--AND SHE'S ABOUT AS *SHADY* AS YOUR AVERAGE *WEEPING WILLOW!*

SO SHE'S NOT A *SAINT*--! SO *WHAT?*

YOU AND DIANA HAVE ALREADY *DISCUSSED* THIS--AND YOU KNOW SHE WANTS TO AT LEAST *TALK* TO THE LADY.

BESIDES, I'LL BE *WITH* DIANA FOR THE MEETING WHILE YOU AND VANESSA ARE IN *SCHOOL!*

"*LIKE IT OR NOT,* PROFESSOR, DIANA IS A *RESPONSIBLE ADULT*--

"--AND SHE *DOESN'T NEED* A *SECOND MOTHER!*"

4

MIDTOWN BOSTON, LATER THAT SAME MORNING:

C'MON, HONEY-- RELAX!

HOW *CAN* I, MYNDI-- WHEN SO MUCH *DEPENDS* UPON THIS MEETING?

I MEAN, WHAT'S THE *WORST* THAT COULD HAPPEN?

SHE ISN'T GOING TO *BITE*, YOU KNOW.

YOU DON'T *UNDERSTAND*, MYNDI--

IF WHAT BARBARA MINERVA SAYS IS *TRUE*, IT COULD CHANGE MY ULTIMATE *PURPOSE* HERE IN MAN'S WORLD--

--AND AFFECT THE VERY *DESTINY* OF THE AMAZONS!

YOU'RE NOT HELPING MY *CASE* AT--

PENTHOUSE FLOOR-- WE'RE *HERE*!

MAY HERA *HELP* US.

DING

UH... HI.

MYNDI MAYER AND THE PRINCESS DIANA TO SEE *DOCTOR MINERVA*?

AYE--DE MADAM IS *EXPECTING* YOU.

PLEASE, CHUMA-- BRING OUR GUESTS SOME *REFRESHMENT*!

I'LL TAKE A *KAHLUA* AND CREAM.

I AM NOT *THIRSTY*, THANK YOU.

YOU ARE...?

THE WOMAN WHO *WROTE* YOU, PRINCESS.

I AM *BARBARA MINERVA*.

SHALL WE *SIT DOWN*?

YOU DO UNDERSTAND WE HAVE *THINGS* TO DISCUSS--*PUBLICITY* AND *PROMOTION*-- BEFORE WE GET DOWN TO *BUSINESS*?!

ALL IN *GOOD TIME*, MS. MAYER.

I HAVE LOOKED FORWARD TO THIS *MEETING*, PRINCESS.

DID YOU BRING THE *LASSO* AS I ASKED?

DIANA?

DO NOT *WORRY*. IT IS *ALWAYS* WITH ME--

--AS *BEFITS* A GIFT FROM THE GODS!

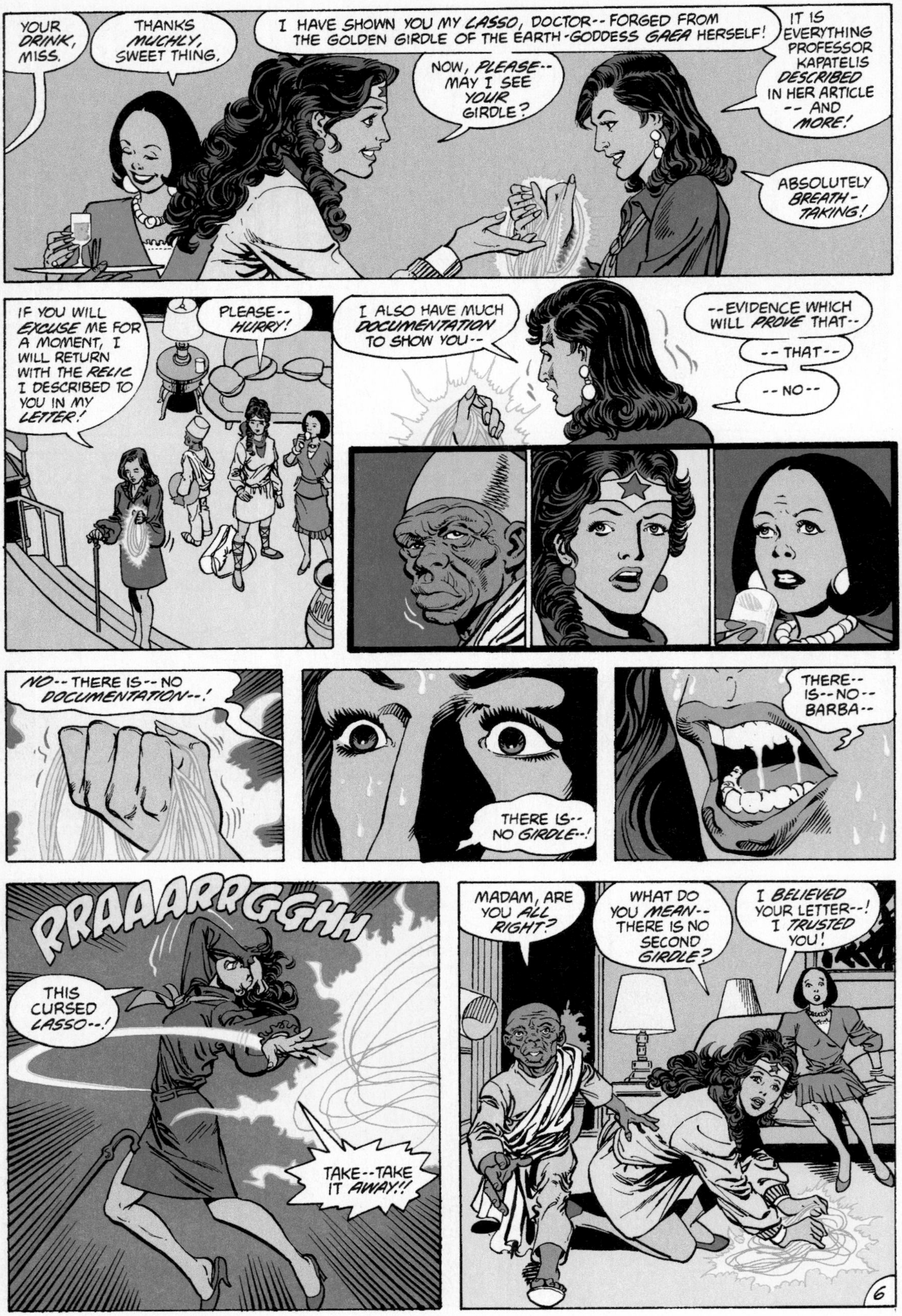
YOUR DRINK, MISS.
THANKS MUCHLY, SWEET THING.
I HAVE SHOWN YOU MY LASSO, DOCTOR--FORGED FROM THE GOLDEN GIRDLE OF THE EARTH-GODDESS GAEA HERSELF!
NOW, PLEASE--MAY I SEE YOUR GIRDLE?
IT IS EVERYTHING PROFESSOR KAPATELIS DESCRIBED IN HER ARTICLE--AND MORE!
ABSOLUTELY BREATH-TAKING!
IF YOU WILL EXCUSE ME FOR A MOMENT, I WILL RETURN WITH THE RELIC I DESCRIBED TO YOU IN MY LETTER!
PLEASE--HURRY!
I ALSO HAVE MUCH DOCUMENTATION TO SHOW YOU--
--EVIDENCE WHICH WILL PROVE THAT--
--THAT--
--NO--
NO--THERE IS--NO DOCUMENTATION--!
THERE IS--NO GIRDLE--!
THERE--IS--NO--BARBA--
RRAAARRGGHH
THIS CURSED LASSO--!
TAKE--TAKE IT AWAY!!
MADAM, ARE YOU ALL RIGHT?
WHAT DO YOU MEAN--THERE IS NO SECOND GIRDLE?
I BELIEVED YOUR LETTER--! I TRUSTED YOU!
6

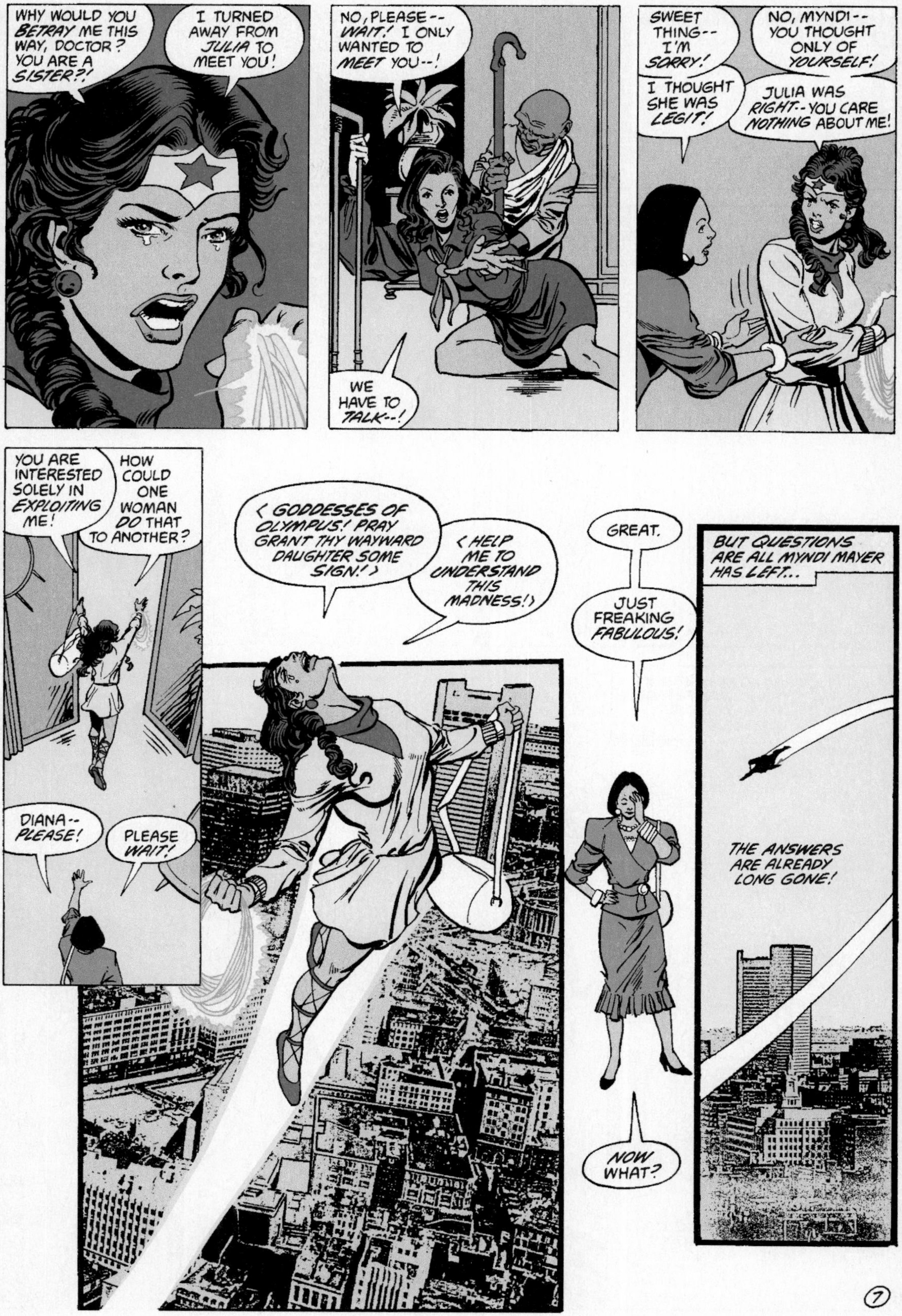
WHY WOULD YOU BETRAY ME THIS WAY, DOCTOR? YOU ARE A SISTER?!
I TURNED AWAY FROM JULIA TO MEET YOU!
NO, PLEASE-- WAIT! I ONLY WANTED TO MEET YOU--!
WE HAVE TO TALK--!
SWEET THING-- I'M SORRY!
I THOUGHT SHE WAS LEGIT!
NO, MYNDI-- YOU THOUGHT ONLY OF YOURSELF!
JULIA WAS RIGHT--YOU CARE NOTHING ABOUT ME!
YOU ARE INTERESTED SOLELY IN EXPLOITING ME!
HOW COULD ONE WOMAN DO THAT TO ANOTHER?
DIANA-- PLEASE!
PLEASE WAIT!
< GODDESSES OF OLYMPUS! PRAY GRANT THY WAYWARD DAUGHTER SOME SIGN! >
< HELP ME TO UNDERSTAND THIS MADNESS! >
GREAT.
JUST FREAKING FABULOUS!
NOW WHAT?
BUT QUESTIONS ARE ALL MYNDI MAYER HAS LEFT...
THE ANSWERS ARE ALREADY LONG GONE!
7

THE KAPATELIS SUMMER HOME, LATER THAT SAME AFTERNOON:

YEAH... UH-HUH... I UNDERSTAND...

I'LL TELL HER, MIZ MAYER.

SHE WON'T LISTEN--BUT I'LL TELL HER.

BUT SHE HAS TO LISTEN, SWEET THING!

SHE HAS TO LET ME APOLOGIZE!

WE'VE GOT TOUR DATES TO TALK ABOUT--A CAMPAIGN TO RUN!

SHE CAN'T JUST CUT ME OFF LIKE THIS!

WELL, NOW ISN'T REALLY THE BEST TIME TO TALK TO DIANA, MIZ MAYER.

MOM IS STILL OUTSIDE WITH HER, TRYIN' TO CALM HER DOWN!

I'LL LET YOU KNOW HOW IT GOES. YEAH... BYE.

SO MUCH HAS HAPPENED SINCE WE BEGAN THIS WONDER WOMAN TOUR, JULIA-- SO MUCH HAS CHANGED!

I HAVE SO MANY QUESTIONS... I FEEL SO LOST...

WILL I LEAVE MAN'S WORLD HAVING TAUGHT PEOPLE NOTHING MORE THAN MY NAME?

EVERYTHING SEEMED SO SIMPLE ON PARADISE ISLAND-- YET NOW I REALIZE I AM NO LONGER LIKE MY SISTER AMAZONS!

MY LIFE IS PART OF SOME GREATER DESIGN -- AND STOPPING ARES WAS BUT ONE SMALL PART OF IT!

MY NAME... MY COSTUME ... MY MISSION...

THEY ARE ALL TATTERS OF SOME VAST TAPESTRY-- LACKING THE THREAD TO MAKE THEM WHOLE!

DIANA, DON'T-- YOU'VE ACCOMPLISHED MUCH IN YOUR TIME HERE!

AND TIME IS SOMETHING THIS OLD WORLD NEEDS-- TO LEARN FROM YOU!

UNFORTUNATELY, JULIA--

-- TIME IS THE ONE COMMODITY I CANNOT AFFORD TO SPARE!

8

THE RENTED PENTHOUSE OF BARBARA MINERVA, THAT SAME NIGHT:

--DELICATELY PLUCKING THE RIPENED BERRIES FROM THE GOD-PLANT, AND CRUSHING THEM TO PASTE--

IN THE RITUAL CHAMBER, THE OLD MAN NAMED CHUMA PREPARES THE SACRED ELIXIR--

--ALL THE WHILE CHANTING, AS IF TO THE SOUND OF DISTANT DRUMS!

IN HER PRIVATE QUARTERS, BARBARA MINERVA READIES HERSELF FOR THE ORDEAL YET TO COME--

--PAINTING HER FACE IN THE ANCIENT MANNER--

--PREPARING HERSELF FOR WAR!

DID YOU SEE HOW THE LASSO WORKED, CHUMA? HOW IT FORCED ME TO SPEAK THE TRUTH?

IT IS EVERYTHING I COULD HAVE HOPED FOR! IT MUST BE MINE!

IS THE ELIXIR READY, OLD MAN?

AYE, MA'AM.

YOU MUST DRINK IT NOW--

--RAW--

--WHILE DE BREW STILL BURNS!

IT SMELLS LIKE FIRE, OLD MAN!

IT SMELLS LIKE--LIFE!

9

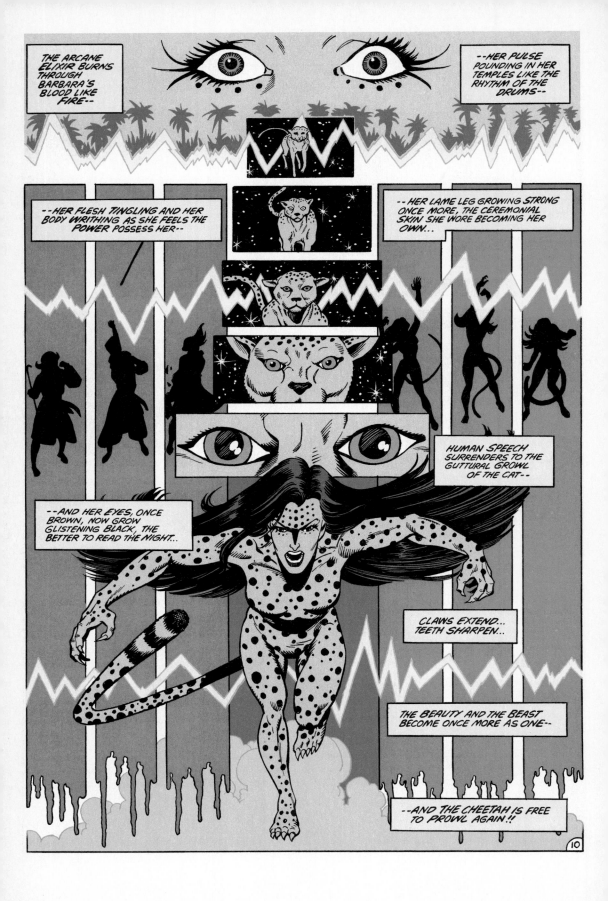

THE ARCANE ELIXIR BURNS THROUGH BARBARA'S BLOOD LIKE FIRE--

--HER PULSE POUNDING IN HER TEMPLES LIKE THE RHYTHM OF THE DRUMS--

--HER FLESH TINGLING AND HER BODY WRITHING AS SHE FEELS THE POWER POSSESS HER--

--HER LAME LEG GROWING STRONG ONCE MORE, THE CEREMONIAL SKIN SHE WORE BECOMING HER OWN...

HUMAN SPEECH SURRENDERS TO THE GUTTURAL GROWL OF THE CAT--

--AND HER EYES, ONCE BROWN, NOW GROW GLISTENING BLACK, THE BETTER TO READ THE NIGHT...

CLAWS EXTEND... TEETH SHARPEN...

THE BEAUTY AND THE BEAST BECOME ONCE MORE AS ONE--

--AND THE CHEETAH IS FREE TO PROWL AGAIN !!

10

HER CLAWS GOUGING HANDHOLDS IN THE BUILDING'S SHEER FACE, THE CHEETAH DESCENDS INTO THE DARKNESS--

--INTO THE CONCRETE JUNGLE THAT IS HER HUNTING GROUND--

LEAVING THE OLD MAN BEHIND TO *WAIT*--

--AND TO PONDER...

SHE BE THE *LAST* OF HER *KIND*, DAT ONE--

--AS HER *GOD* BE DE LAST OF *ITS* KIND--

--YET HER *SURVIVAL* BE IN DE HANDS OF A *FICKLE* GOD INDEED!

TANK YOU, ANCIENT ONE, FOR BRINGING DE CHEETAH *BACK* TO ME!

I PRAY YOU-- *KEEP* HER *SAFE*!

AND IN THE DARKNESS, THE CHEETAH *STALKS* THROUGH THE SHADOWS OF BOSTON--

--DRAWN BY SCENT AND INSTINCT UNERRINGLY TO HER PREY!

LISTEN! CAN YOU HEAR IT?

THERE ARE *DRUMS* IN THE NIGHT!

THE LONG HUNT HAS *BEGUN*...

BRINNNG BRINNNG

HELLO? LT. ETTA CANDY SPEAKING.

WHO--?

STEVE? STEVE TREVOR?

OH, COLONEL --IT'S SO GOOD TO HEAR YOUR *VOICE*!

...AND THE INVESTIGATION CONTINUES INTO THE MYSTERIOUS *DEATH* OF LOCAL CRIMINAL TAMSYN MCCONNELL...

ANIMAL ATTACK

...WHO WAS *SLAIN* LAST WEEK, APPARENTLY BY SOME *WILD* ANIMAL...

11

ETTA, I'M AFRAID I WON'T BE COMING BACK TO *BOSTON* TOMORROW AS INTENDED.

JUST GOT A *LETTER* FROM HOME AND I HAVE TO RETURN TO *OKLAHOMA* AS QUICKLY AS POSSIBLE...

... MY *FATHER* IS DYING.

OH, STEVE... I'M SO SORRY. LOOK, I'VE GOT SOME *LEAVE* TIME COMING.

AND YOU SOUND LIKE YOU COULD USE SOME *COMPANY.*

THAT'S *GREAT,* ETTA--I APPRECI-ATE THE *OFFER.*

LET ME CHECK WITH MY *AUNT EDNA* AND WORK OUT THE *ARRANGEMENTS.*

GOD, IT FEELS STRANGE TO BE GOING *HOME* AGAIN.

SO MUCH HAS *CHANGED* SINCE I WAS A *KID!*

THE OUTSKIRTS OF BOSTON, SEVERAL MINUTES LATER:

SHE MOVES THROUGH THE NIGHT AS THOUGH PART OF IT--

--COVERING GROUND WITH ALMOST *SUPERHUMAN SPEED* --

--NOSTRILS FLARED AND SEARCHING--

--KNOWING HER PREY IS SOMEWHERE *NEAR* --

--ALMOST NEAR ENOUGH NOW TO *TASTE...*

ABRASIVE TONGUE LICKING LEATHERY LIPS, THE CHEETAH RACES ON--

--FEELING HER HUNGER *GROWING,* KNOWING IT MUST BE *APPEASED...*

SOON IT WILL BE TIME FOR THE *BLOODFEAST!*

12

THE KAPATELIS SUMMER HOME, SEVERAL MINUTES LATER:

DIANA?

DIANA, YOU HERE?

MOM, HAVE YOU SEEN DIANA AROUND?

I THINK SHE'S STILL OUT IN THE WOODS, HONEY.

SO LATE?

IS SHE OKAY?

SHE OFTEN STAYS OUT THERE, BABY -- TO COMMUNE WITH NATURE!

CONSIDERING WHAT A DISASTER TODAY TURNED OUT TO BE --

-- I THINK SHE NEEDS ALL THE MEDITATION TIME SHE CAN GET!

TRUST ME -- SHE'LL COME BACK IN WHEN SHE'S READY.

BESIDES, THAT'S ONE WOMAN WHO CAN TAKE CARE OF HER--

PRRRRR

--EH?

MOMMY...

...WH-WHAT WAS THAT?

I'M NOT SURE, BABY...

...SOUNDED LIKE IT MIGHT HAVE BEEN SOME SORT OF ANIMAL!

"BUT WHATEVER, I'M SURE IT'S NOTHING TO WORRY ABOUT!"

BY THE SHORE OF THE LAKE, THE AMAZON SLUMBERS, ALONE SAVE FOR A DARING RACCOON WHO HAS SHUFFLED CLOSE TO SHARE HER WARMTH...

13

NOW, IN THE TANGLED BRUSH ABOVE HER, SOMETHING *STIRS*--

-- SOMETHING *SILENT* AS THE MOONLIGHT YET *QUICK* AS A TWITCH--

--SOMETHING THAT CROUCHES UNMOVING, STUDYING ITS PREY--

--OBSERVING THE STEADY RISE AND FALL OF HER CHEST, LISTENING TO THE EVEN RHYTHM OF HER HEARTBEAT--

--DARK EYES NARROWED AS IT SEARCHES FOR THE SLEEPING PREY'S PULSE--

--ANTICIPATING THE WARM GUSH OF BLOOD WHEN RAZORED CLAWS SLASH TENDER FLESH...

THE HUNTER TENSES, SLEEK MUSCLES BUNCHED BENEATH ITS FUR--

--PREPARING ITSELF FOR THE *MOMENT*--

EH?

--THE EXULTANT MOMENT WHEN IT FINALLY STRIKES.!!

WHAT IN--

UURRKK!!

14

216

THIS ONE IS STRONG, THE HUNTER SENSES INSTANTLY, STRONGER BY FAR THAN THE REST--

--AND THUS THE PREY MUST BE FINISHED SWIFTLY--

--BEFORE IT CAN RALLY ITS RESOURCES TO STRIKE BACK!

WH-WHAT STRUCK ME--?

SEEMED LIKE SOME GREAT CAT--

LIKE A CHEETAH OR AN--

--AARRGHH!!

RRRAARRRR

THOSE CLAWS-- SO SHARP--!

GREAT HERMES, GRANT ME SPEED--

--OR HER NEXT BLOW MAY SLAY ME!

BLOOD--?!?

BY THE GODS, SHE ACTUALLY DREW BLOOD!

WHAT MANNER OF MONSTER IS SHE?

15

WHATEVER THE *REASON* FOR HER UNWARRANTED ATTACK--

-- IT IS TIME FOR THE *HUNTER* TO BECOME THE *HUNTED*--!

STILL, SHE CANNOT LONG *ELUDE* ONE WHO POSSESSES THE GOD-GIVEN POWER OF *FLIGHT*!

UUNNHH!!

RRRAARRR

IMPOSSIBLE! NOTHING *HUMAN* CAN MOVE SO *SWIFTLY*--!

SHE CONTINUES TO *ATTACK* WHEN *ANY SANER* MIND WOULD *FLEE*!

THIS CHEETAH IS *CONSTANT AGGRESSION* IN HUMAN FORM--

--AND SHE HAS CHOSEN *ME* AS HER *TARGET*!

HER *CLAWS* WILL SCRATCH OUT *MY EYES* IF THEY REACH ME--!

HER *FANGS* WILL RIP OUT MY *THROAT*--!

SHE WILL QUICKLY TEAR ME TO PIECES--

--UNLESS I STRIKE *NOW*--

--AND STRIKE *HARD*!!

16

FOR AN INSTANT, THE SHE-BEAST HOLDS HER GROUND, CROUCHES ONCE MORE TO SPRING--

--AND THEN, AS IF SUDDENLY THINKING BETTER OF IT, SHE HURLS HERSELF INTO THE BUSH...

SHE'S STILL CLOSE AT HAND, STALKING ME--!

I CAN FEEL IT--!

YET STILL AM I THE SPIRITUAL DAUGHTER OF THE GODDESS ARTEMIS!

MINE ARE THE HEIGHTENED INSTINCTS OF THE HUNTRESS!

MUST CONCENTRATE--

--INCREASE MY STATE OF AWARENESS--!

LISTEN, DIANA...

HEAR YOUR OWN HEART-BEAT...

RECOGNIZE ITS RHYTHMS...

NOW SEARCH THE BRUSH FOR A SECOND PULSE...

FIND THE HEAVING HEART OF THE BEAST...

THERE!

RRRAAARRGH??

THE HUNT IS ENDED, CHEETAH!

YOU ARE MINE!!

17

219

BOUND BY THE GLEAMING GOLDEN LARIAT, THE CHEETAH SUDDENLY HESITATES--

--AS IF AT LAST SUCCUMBING TO THE LASSO'S AWESOME ARCANE POWER--

--BUT THEN, IMPOSSIBLY...

GREAT HERA! THE LASSO HAS NO EFFECT ON HER!

THE SHE-BEAST IS PULLING ME TOWARD HER--!

DIGGING IN HER HEELS, THE PRINCESS DIANA HOLDS HER OWN GROUND--

--AND THE STRAIN OF THE RESULTANT STALEMATE CAN QUICKLY BE SEEN ON THE TORTURED FACES OF THE TWO COMBATANTS...

THE CHEETAH HISSES IN INARTICULATE RAGE, SPITTLE FLYING FROM HER LEATHERY LIPS IN A FINE SPRAY--

--WHILE THE AMAZON MERELY CLENCHES HER TEETH IN GRIM DETERMINATION, ATTEMPTING TO STUDY THE FACE OF HER FOE--

--AND THUS GIVING THE SHE-BEAST THE INFINITESIMAL OPENING SHE NEEDS...

UUNNHH!!

RRAARR

FALLEN TREE TRUNK HAS ME PINNED--!

CAN'T MOVE--!

THE CHEETAH HAS WON!

18

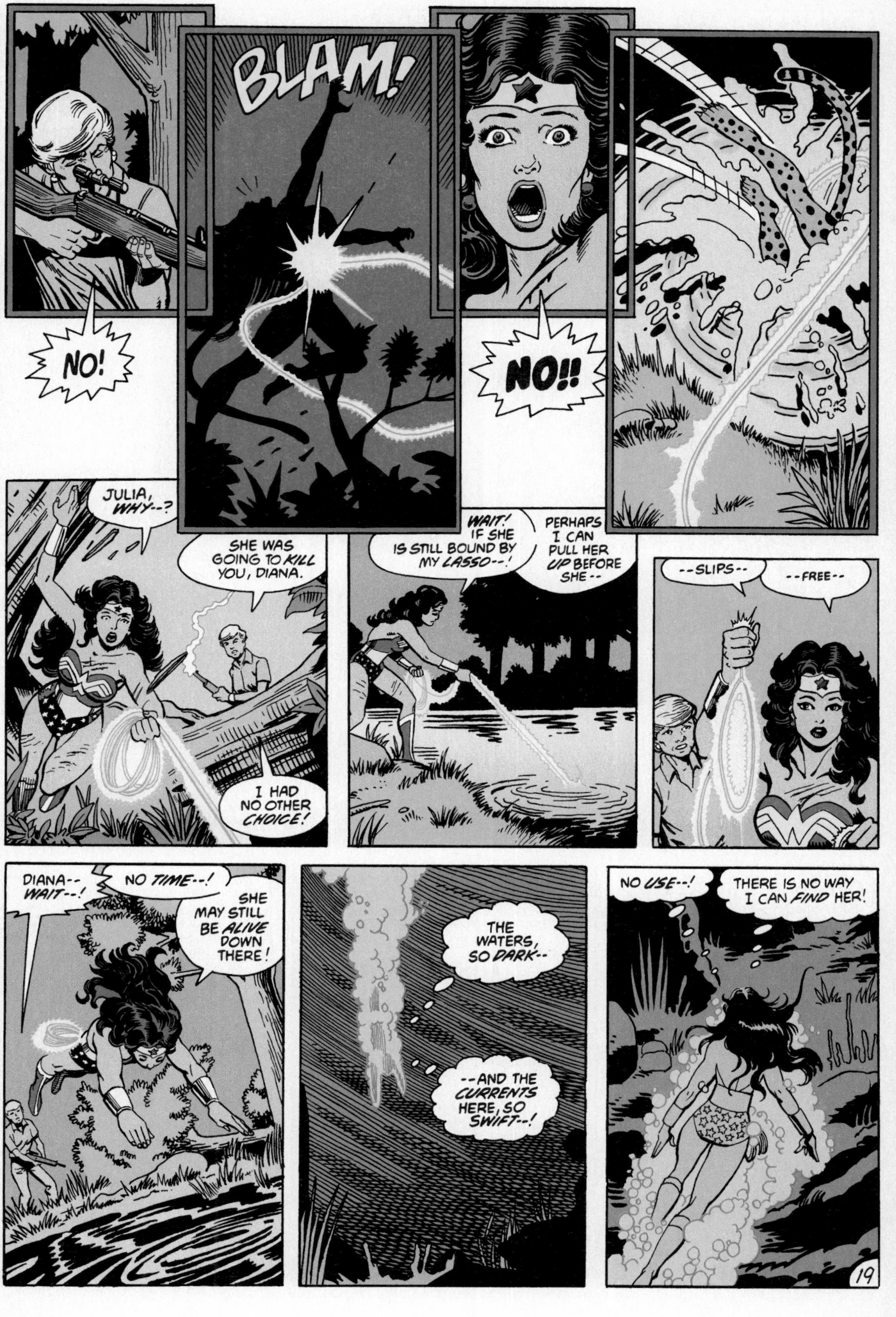
NO!
BLAM!
NO!!
JULIA, WHY--?
SHE WAS GOING TO KILL YOU, DIANA.
I HAD NO OTHER CHOICE!
WAIT! IF SHE IS STILL BOUND BY MY LASSO--!
PERHAPS I CAN PULL HER UP BEFORE SHE--
--SLIPS--
--FREE--
DIANA-- WAIT--!
NO TIME--!
SHE MAY STILL BE ALIVE DOWN THERE!
THE WATERS, SO DARK--
--AND THE CURRENTS HERE, SO SWIFT--!
NO USE--!
THERE IS NO WAY I CAN FIND HER!
19

MOM, WHAT'S *HAPPENING* OUT HERE? I HEARD THE *SHOT* AND--!

HEY--WHERE'S *DIANA*?

VANESSA, I THOUGHT I TOLD YOU TO STAY *HOME*!

WHILE THERE'S TROUBLE OUT *HERE*?!

NO *WAY*, JOSE!

:*GASP*:

DIANA, IS SHE--?

I COULD FIND NO *TRACE* OF THE SHE-BEAST IN THAT EBONY DEEP, JULIA.

WHATEVER SHE *WAS*... WHATEVER SHE *WANTED* FROM ME...

THE CHEETAH IS--

--GONE--

LISTEN! CAN YOU *HEAR* IT?

THE SUDDEN, ALL-OPPRESSIVE *SILENCE*?

THE SOUND OF THE *DRUMMING* HAS FINALLY *STOPPED*!

THE HEART OF BOSTON:

SEVERAL DAYS LATER...

MYNDI MAYER SPEAKING!

IT'S *YOUR* QUARTER, SWEET THING-- DON'T *WASTE* IT!

OH-- IT'S ONLY *YOU*, CHRISSIE. SOME PROBLEM AT THE *OFFICE*?

WORST *KIND*, MIZ MAYER. I JUST GOT A MESSAGE FROM *JULIA KAPATELIS*--!

EVEN AS WE *SPEAK*, YOUR PRINCESS DIANA IS HEADING *HOME*!

SHE'S *WHAT*--?!?

BUT WHAT ABOUT ALL MY *PUBLICITY* PLANS?!

WE'VE GOT A *CONTRACT*, BLAST IT!

SHE CAN'T *DO* THIS TO ME!!

20

GAYHEAD CLIFFS, MARTHA'S VINEYARD:

IT SEEMS SOMEHOW *FITTING* THAT I SHOULD *DEPART* FROM MAN'S WORLD AT THIS PARTICULAR PLACE...

THESE *CLIFFS* ARE SO LIKE THOSE OF MY BELOVED *PARADISE ISLAND.*

ONE CAN TRULY BE AT *PEACE* HERE.

AND YET, DESPITE MY GREAT *NEED* TO BE AMONG MY *OWN* AGAIN, I CANNOT HELP *REGRETTING* THAT I MUST LEAVE.

TRULY, THIS HAS BECOME A SECOND *HOME* TO ME...

THEN *STAY*, DIANA-- *PLEASE* DON'T GO!

YOU'RE LIKE THE BIG *SISTER* I NEVER *HAD* BEFORE!

WHAT'LL I DO *WITHOUT* YOU?

YOU WILL WATCH OVER YOUR *MOTHER*, LITTLE ONE-- AND YOU WILL BE *STRONG!*

BUT I *TOO* HAVE A MOTHER THAT I LOVE-- AND THE TIME HAS COME TO *RETURN* TO HER.

I WILL *MISS* YOU, VANESSA--

--FOR YOU HAVE SHOWN ME A *YOUNG* WORLD FULL OF BRIGHT *PROMISE!*

REMEMBER YOUR *POWER,* LITTLE SISTER--

--AND KNOW I WILL ALWAYS *LOVE* YOU.

OH, *DIANA*--!

21

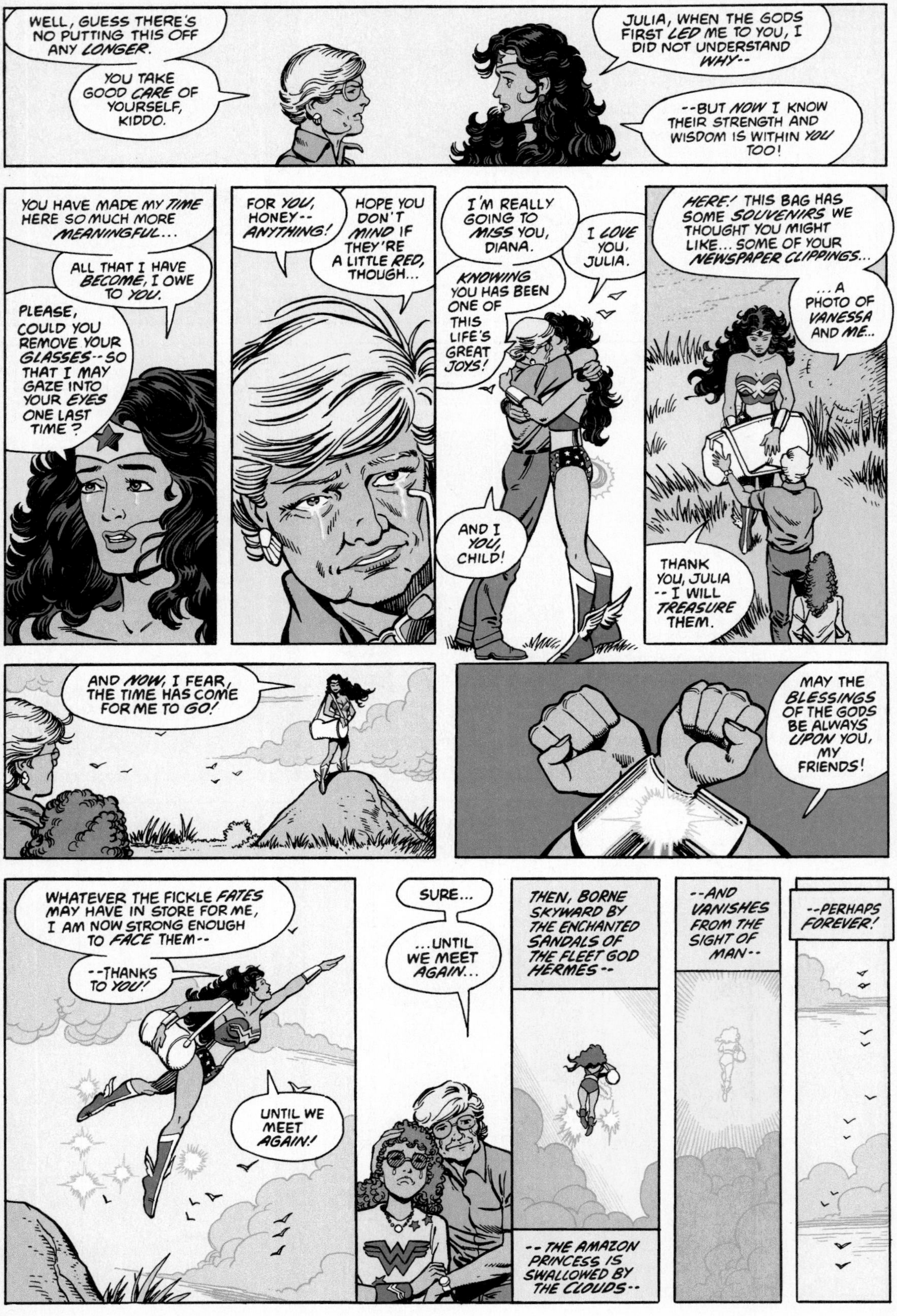

WELL, GUESS THERE'S NO PUTTING THIS OFF ANY *LONGER*.
YOU TAKE GOOD *CARE* OF YOURSELF, KIDDO.
JULIA, WHEN THE GODS FIRST *LED* ME TO YOU, I DID NOT UNDERSTAND *WHY*--
--BUT *NOW* I KNOW THEIR STRENGTH AND WISDOM IS WITHIN *YOU* TOO!
YOU HAVE MADE MY *TIME* HERE SO MUCH MORE *MEANINGFUL*...
ALL THAT I HAVE *BECOME*, I OWE TO *YOU*.
PLEASE, COULD YOU REMOVE YOUR *GLASSES*-- SO THAT I MAY GAZE INTO YOUR *EYES* ONE LAST TIME?
FOR *YOU*, HONEY-- *ANYTHING!*
HOPE YOU DON'T MIND IF THEY'RE A LITTLE *RED*, THOUGH...
I'M REALLY GOING TO *MISS* YOU, DIANA.
KNOWING YOU HAS BEEN ONE OF THIS LIFE'S GREAT JOYS!
I *LOVE* YOU, JULIA.
AND I *YOU*, CHILD!
HERE! THIS BAG HAS SOME *SOUVENIRS* WE THOUGHT YOU MIGHT LIKE... SOME OF YOUR *NEWSPAPER CLIPPINGS*...
...A PHOTO OF *VANESSA* AND *ME*...
THANK YOU, JULIA -- I WILL *TREASURE* THEM.
AND *NOW*, I FEAR, THE TIME HAS COME FOR ME TO *GO!*
MAY THE *BLESSINGS* OF THE GODS BE ALWAYS *UPON* YOU, MY FRIENDS!
WHATEVER THE FICKLE *FATES* MAY HAVE IN STORE FOR ME, I AM NOW STRONG ENOUGH TO *FACE* THEM--
--THANKS TO *YOU!*
UNTIL WE MEET *AGAIN!*
SURE...
...UNTIL WE MEET *AGAIN*...
THEN, BORNE SKYWARD BY THE ENCHANTED SANDALS OF THE FLEET GOD HERMES--
--THE AMAZON PRINCESS IS SWALLOWED BY THE CLOUDS--
--AND VANISHES FROM THE SIGHT OF MAN--
--PERHAPS FOREVER!

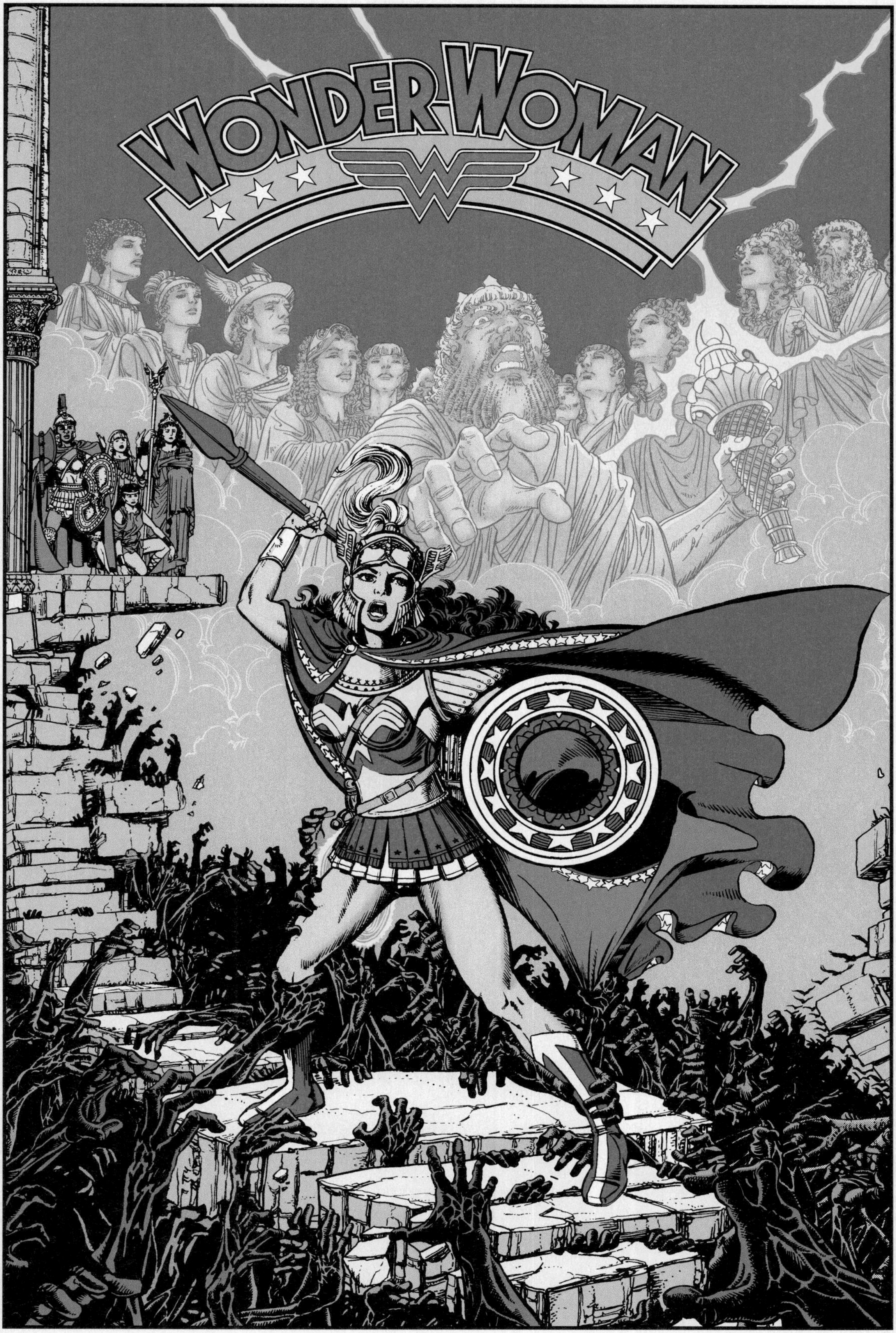
WONDER WOMAN

ONCE THEY WERE MERELY COMMON REEDS, PLUCKED FRESH FROM THE GENEROUS EARTH, AND TRANSFORMED BY CLEVER HANDS...

NOW THEY ARE THE SYRINX, THE LEGENDARY PIPES OF PAN--

-- AND, IN ALL THE REALMS OF GODS AND MAN, NO INSTRUMENT HAS EVER PLAYED MORE SWEET...

IS IT MERELY MY *IMAGINATION,* DIONYSUS--

--OR DOES SLY PAN SEEM UNCOMMONLY *JOYFUL* OF LATE ?

INDEED, DEAR EOS...

HE HAS *BEEN* THUS EVER SINCE THE FAIR PRINCESS DIANA *THWARTED* ARES' MAD SCHEME TO *DESTROY* US ALL !

"METHINKS THE HOOVED ONE SEEKS TO BECOME UNSOLICITED ADVISOR TO MY ALMIGHTY FATHER ZEUS ON ALL MATTERS AMAZON...

"...AND *THAT,* DEAR EOS, IS A MOST *CHILLING* THOUGHT INDEED !"

PARDON THE *INTRUSION,* EXALTED ONE--!

I MERELY WONDER IF YOU HAVE GIVEN ANY *THOUGHT* TO OUR *EARLIER* CONVERSATION--?

INDEED, LITTLE GOAT-- A GREAT *DEAL* OF THOUGHT !

IN TRUTH, I PONDER *STILL* !

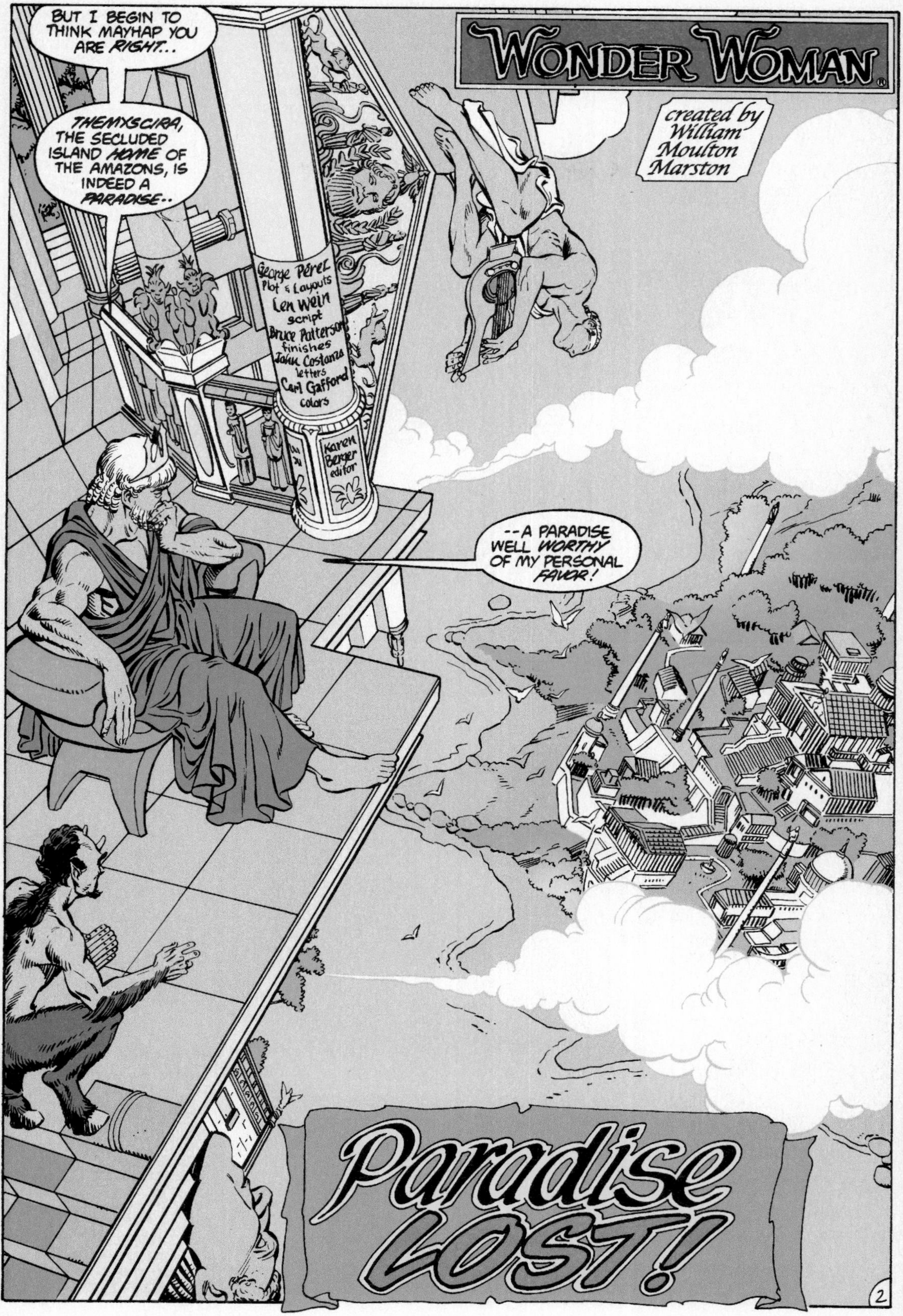

BUT I BEGIN TO THINK MAYHAP YOU ARE RIGHT...
WONDER WOMAN®
created by William Moulton Marston
THEMYSCIRA, THE SECLUDED ISLAND HOME OF THE AMAZONS, IS INDEED A PARADISE..
George Pérez Plot & Layouts
Len Wein script
Bruce Patterson finishes
John Costanza letters
Carl Gafford colors
Karen Berger editor
--A PARADISE WELL WORTHY OF MY PERSONAL FAVOR!
Paradise LOST!
2

BEHOLD THE *PRINCESS DIANA*, FOR EXAMPLE, OUT FOR AN AFTERNOON *GALLOP...*

SHE IS A MOST *SPECIAL* BREED, THIS YOUNG AMAZON--

--FOR SHE *ALONE* HAS FACED THE AWESOME POWER OF THE WAR-GOD *ARES*, AND *BESTED* HIM!

AYE, SUCH AS SHE DESERVES MY *SPECIAL* FAVOR!

INDEED, MILORD--AS YOUR OWN SON *HERACLES* ONCE FAVORED HER PROUD *MOTHER!*

'TIS ONLY FITTING THAT THE *DAUGHTER* SHOULD BE THE *FIRST* OF THE AMAZONS TO EXPERIENCE THY MANLY *GRACE*--

--BEFORE YOU TURN YOUR ATTENTION TO THE *OTHERS!*

WHILE THAT MAY WELL BE A *TEMPTING* THOUGHT, ALMIGHTY ONE--

--QUEEN HERA AND THE GODDESSES STILL HAVE *PLANS* FOR THEIR PRECIOUS AMAZONS!

I DOUBT THEY WILL TAKE *KINDLY* TO YOUR AMOROUS INTENTIONS!

THE APPOINTED *MISSION* OF THE AMAZONS WAS TO PUT AN END TO ARES' *INSANITY*, APOLLO--AND THAT HAS BEEN *DONE!*

NOW 'TIS TIME THEY WERE WELCOMED AT LAST TO MY *BOSOM*.

PLAY ON, LITTLE GOAT, THY LORD *COMMANDS* YOU--

--AND MAKE YOUR TUNE A *LOVE SONG!*

'TIS AS WE *FEARED*, ARTEMIS-- ALMIGHTY ZEUS SEEKS TO MAKE THE AMAZONS HIS *PLAYTHINGS!*

NEVER, HESTIA!

I WILL NOT ALLOW HIM TO *BETRAY* US THUS!

AND JUST HOW DO YOU INTEND TO *STOP* HIM, HUNTRESS?

WITH THE AID OF *QUEEN HERA* AND WISE *ATHENA!*

FOR I SWEAR TO YOU *THIS*, GOOD HESTIA--

--*PARADISE ISLAND* WILL BE NO ONE'S *BROTHEL!*

③

I TELL YOU, EUBOEA, THERE IS NO OTHER *WATER* IN ALL THE WORLD AS BLUE AND BRIGHT AS *THIS*...

IT IS GOOD TO BE *HOME!*

AND YET YOU'VE SEEN SO MANY *MIRACLES* IN YOUR TIME *AWAY* FROM US, PRINCESS...

PLEASE *TELL* ME ABOUT IT, DIANA-- ABOUT THE WORLD *BEYOND* THE SEA.

IS THERE MUCH YOU *MISS* OF IT?

MY NEW *FRIENDS*, MOSTLY.

THE YOUNG ONE, *VANESSA*, EVEN LEFT ME HER PRECIOUS *NECKLACE* IN THE BAG THEY PACKED--!

THEY ARE SO *DIFFERENT* FROM US, EUBOEA--AND YET SO MUCH THE *SAME!*

THERE IS MUCH WE ALL COULD *LEARN* FROM ONE ANOTHER...

IT SOUNDS MOST *WONDROUS*, PRINCESS--AND YET SO *TERRIFYING!*

EVEN NOW, THE *COUNCIL OF JUSTICE* PONDERS THE *GIFTS* AND *RECORDS* YOU BROUGHT BACK WITH YOU FROM *MAN'S WORLD!*

AYE, THERE ARE THOSE WHOSE HEARTS AND MINDS LIVE ONLY IN THE *PAST*--

--BUT WHAT I'VE SEEN OF *MAN* HIMSELF SEEMS TO SHOW MUCH *PROMISE!*

STILL, THAT IS ALL IN MY *PAST* NOW.

WHATEVER QUESTIONS REMAIN *UNANSWERED*, I'M SURE THE *GODS* WILL REVEAL THE *TRUTH* IN THEIR OWN GOOD TIME.

YOU HAVE SEEN THE *EVIDENCE*, SISTERS...

NOW THE TIME HAS COME TO RENDER YOUR *DECISION*...

YOU HAVE STUDIED ALL THESE *ITEMS* WHICH THE PRINCESS DIANA BROUGHT BACK FROM HER LONG *JOURNEY*--

--ALL THE *TREASURES* MAN'S WORLD HAS TO *OFFER!*

DO WE NOW *SHARE* THIS KNOWLEDGE WITH OUR SISTER AMAZONS?

WELL, *I* FOR ONE SAY *NO*, MNEMOSYNE!

4

AS I ASSUMED YOU *WOULD*, PHILIPPUS--BEING A *WARRIOR!*

BUT, AS A *TEACHER*, AS THE MOTHER OF *MEMORY*, I KNOW THE INESTIMABLE *VALUE* OF KNOWLEDGE!

FROM THE TRANSLATIONS OF THESE *BOOKS* DIANA BROUGHT US, IT SEEMS MAN HAS CHANGED *LITTLE* OVER THE YEARS--!

STILL, IF WHAT THEY TELL US OF THE *FATE* OF OUR CENTURIES-LOST *SISTER* AMAZONS IS *TRUE...*

MISERABLE *LIES*, ACANTHA--AS MAN HAS *ALWAYS* LIED TO US!

I WISH NOTHING TO *DO* WITH MAN OR HIS WORLD! HIS WEAPONS ALMOST *DESTROYED* US ONCE!

I'VE NO URGE TO GIVE THEM A *SECOND* CHANCE!

AND YET WHAT IF THESE THINGS ARE PART OF PRINCESS DIANA'S *DESTINY?*

TWICE BEFORE HAVE WE SEEN THIS *BANNER--*

--ONCE AT A MOMENT OF *SALVATION*, THE NEXT AT A MOMENT OF NEAR *CATASTROPHE!*

ARE WE SOMEHOW *TIED* TO THIS COAT OF ARMS THROUGH THE *PRINCESS?*

BECAUSE SHE WORE THESE COLORS AS HER *CLOAK* WHEN SHE BATTLED *ARES?*

I THINK *NOT.*

WHATEVER ITS IMPORTANCE IN THE *PAST*, ACANTHA--THIS *BANNER* HOLDS NO MEANING FOR US *NOW!*

MY *DAUGHTER* IS HOME TO *STAY!*

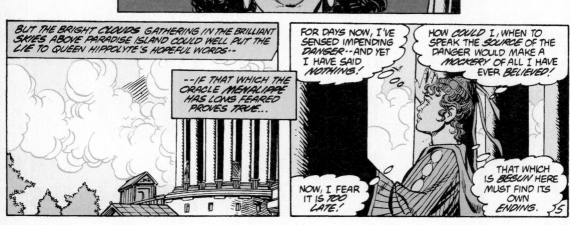

BUT THE BRIGHT *CLOUDS* GATHERING IN THE BRILLIANT SKIES ABOVE PARADISE ISLAND COULD WELL PUT THE *LIE* TO QUEEN HIPPOLYTE'S HOPEFUL WORDS--

--IF THAT WHICH THE ORACLE *MENALIPPE* HAS LONG FEARED PROVES *TRUE...*

FOR DAYS NOW, I'VE SENSED IMPENDING *DANGER*--AND YET I HAVE SAID *NOTHING!*

NOW, I FEAR IT IS *TOO* LATE!

HOW *COULD* I, WHEN TO SPEAK THE *SOURCE* OF THE DANGER WOULD MAKE A *MOCKERY* OF ALL I HAVE EVER *BELIEVED!*

THAT WHICH IS *BEGUN* HERE MUST FIND ITS *OWN* ENDING.

DIANA... DIANA... HEED THY MASTER'S VOICE...

THE *WIND*-- CALLING MY *NAME*?!?

'TIS *SORCERY*, PRINCESS!

NO, EUBOEA--IT IS THE WORK OF THE *GODS*!

'TIS THE VOICE OF ALMIGHTY *ZEUS* HIMSELF!

BUT WHAT DOES HE *WANT* FROM US?

DO YOU NOT *RECOGNIZE* THOSE STENTORIAN TONES?

BE NOT ALARMED, MY CHILDREN... BE JOYFUL... FOR THOU ART BELOVED IN MY SIGHT...

THE ALMIGHTY ONE *PRAISES* US, MY QUEEN-- AND YET I FEEL *UNEASY*--!

I, *TOO,* PHILIPPUS --FOR THERE IS SOMETHING PAINFULLY *FAMILIAR* IN HIS *TONE*--!

FOR HER *TRIUMPH* OVER ARES, THE PRINCESS DIANA HAS EARNED A *SPECIAL* GIFT... ...ONE WHICH I ALONE AM ABLE TO BESTOW...

THUS COME WITH ME, DIANA... COME INTO THE PRESENCE OF THY MASTER...

AS YOU *COMMAND,* ALMIGHTY ONE--

--SO DO I *LEAP* TO *OBEY*!

PRINCESS-- *NO!!*

YOU KNOW *NOT* ZEUS' INTENTIONS!

'TIS THE *WILL* OF THE GODS THAT HAS MADE ME ALL I *AM,* EUBOEA.

THUS HOW COULD I THINK TO *DEFY* THEIR WISHES?

WORRY *NOT,* SISTER-- I PROMISE YOU ALL WILL BE *WELL*!

6

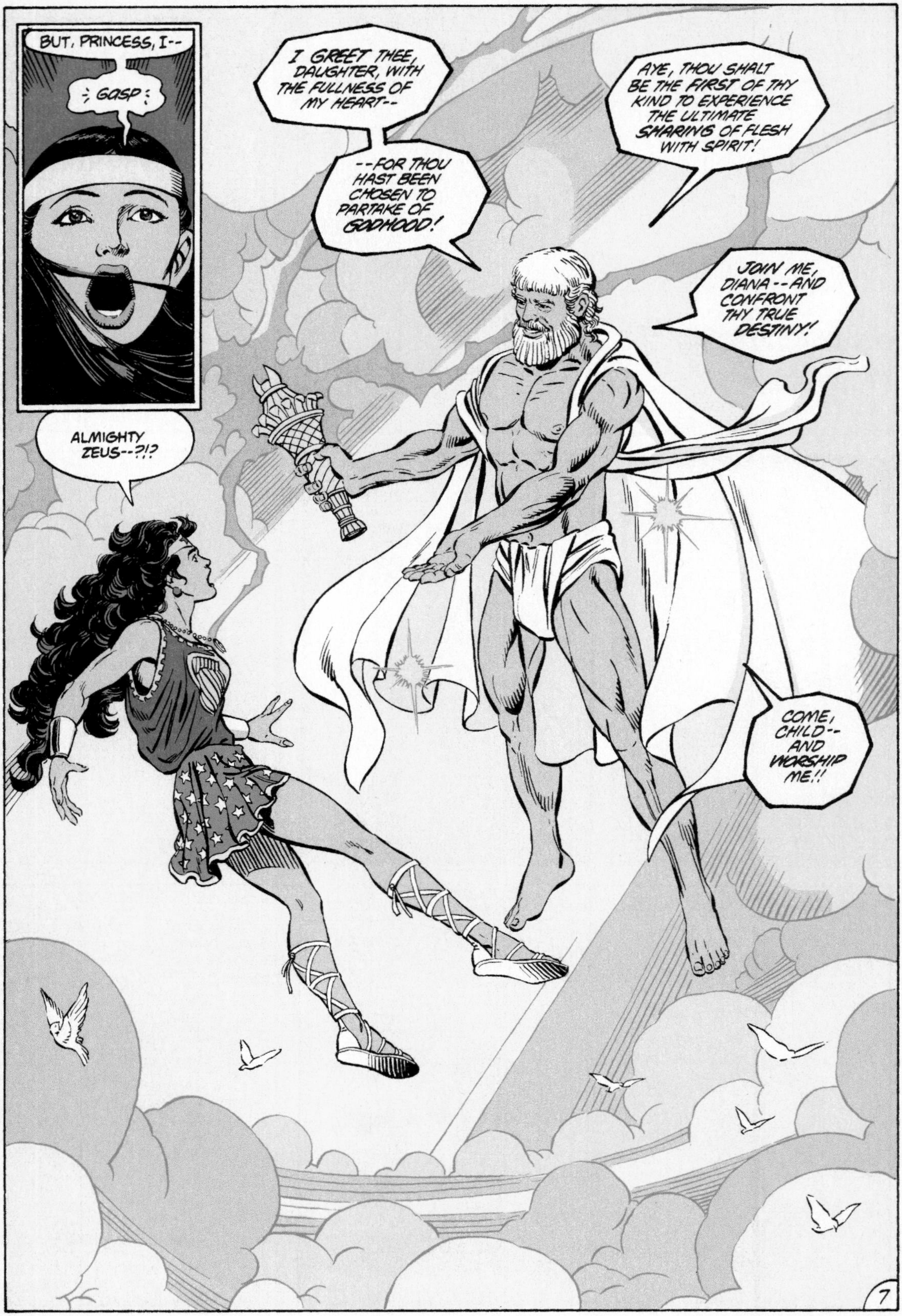
BUT, PRINCESS, I--
GASP
ALMIGHTY ZEUS--?!?
I GREET THEE, DAUGHTER, WITH THE FULLNESS OF MY HEART--
--FOR THOU HAST BEEN CHOSEN TO PARTAKE OF GODHOOD!
AYE, THOU SHALT BE THE FIRST OF THY KIND TO EXPERIENCE THE ULTIMATE SHARING OF FLESH WITH SPIRIT!
JOIN ME, DIANA--AND CONFRONT THY TRUE DESTINY!
COME, CHILD--AND WORSHIP ME!!
7

IT CANNOT BE--!

ALMIGHTY ZEUS HIMSELF--?!?

AYE, SISTERS!

I'VE HEARD SUCH BEGUILING WORDS *BEFORE*--

--FROM THE SNEERING MOUTH OF HIS TREACHEROUS SON *HERACLES*!

QUICKLY, SISTERS-- FETCH ME MY *STEED*!

IF WHAT I FEAR IS *TRUE*, MY DAUGHTER HAS DESPERATE *NEED* OF ME!

ALMIGHTY ONE, I DO NOT *UNDERSTAND*--!

DO I NOT *ALREADY* WORSHIP YOU?

IN SPIRIT, AYE--

--BUT I SEEK NOW COMMUNION OF THE FLESH!

DURING MY TIME IN *MAN'S WORLD*, GREAT ZEUS, I LEARNED THAT SUCH DECISIONS MUST BE *MUTUAL*!

I CANNOT *SURRENDER* THAT WHICH IS MINE ALONE TO *GIVE* WITHOUT A TRUE FEELING OF DESIRE AND *COMMITMENT*!

PLEASE, ALMIGHTY ONE, TRY TO *UNDERSTAND*--!

PRINCESS ?!?

NOOOOOO!!

UNDERSTAND, CHILD?

I UNDERSTAND ONLY THAT THOU HAST DARED *DEFY* ME--

--AND, FOR THAT, THOU MUST BE *PROPERLY PUNISHED*!

ZEUS?

8

HOW DAREST THOU THINK TO *REJECT* THY LORD AND MASTER?

BEFORE I AM *THROUGH,* CHILD, THOU WILT *BEG* TO GIVE THYSELF TO ME!

PLEASE, LORD ZEUS -- DO NOT *FORCE* YOURSELF UPON ME!

THOUGH I LIVE TO *SERVE* YOU, I AM NOT YOUR... *TOY!*

NO, CHILD? WE SHALL *SEE ABOUT--*

--*EH?*

NO!!

I *PRAY* YOU, ALMIGHTY ONE, *RELEASE* MY DAUGHTER -- *NOW!*

IF YOU WOULD DEAL WITH *ANYONE* THIS DAY -- DEAL WITH *ME!*

SEEK NOT TO *INTERFERE,* HIPPOLYTE! THINE OWN *TIME* SHALL COME SOON ENOUGH!

I SHALL SHOW THEE THE *RESPECT* ONLY A *GOD* CAN SHOW!

YOUR CRUEL SON *HERACLES* SHOWED ME SUCH "*RESPECT*" CENTURIES AGO, ZEUS!

THAT WHICH WOULD *NOT* BE FREELY GIVEN, HE *STOLE!*

THOU... DOST... *DARE...?!?*

AND I SHALL *NOT* ALLOW HIS FATHER TO TRIFLE THUS WITH MY ONLY *DAUGHTER!*

9

234

THOU DOST FORGET THY *PLACE,* HIPPOLYTE!

MAYHAP 'TIS TIME I *REMINDED* THEE!

PLEASE, MOTHER --FLEE FOR YOUR *LIFE!*

IN HIS *RAGE,* THE ALMIGHTY ONE WILL NOT HESITATE TO *SLAY* YOU!

INDEED, CHILD! I SHALL-- *NO!!*

WH-WHAT IS *HAPPENING?!?* WHO DARES TO *INTERFERE NOW?!?*

HERA?

HERAAAAA!!

WHEN THOU SHALT PAY FOR THISSSSS!

DIANA, ARE YOU *ALL RIGHT?*

SPEAK TO ME, DAUGHTER!

THE PRINCESS SEEMS *UNHARMED,* YOUR MAJESTY-- MERELY *SHAKEN!*

I CANNOT BELIEVE WHAT I HAVE *SEEN* HERE--THAT YOU SHOULD SPEAK THUS TO A *GOD--?!?*

A MOTHER DOES WHAT A MOTHER *MUST,* EUBOEA!

DIANA...?

HE DID NOT *HURT* ME, MOTHER.

IN FACT, I BELIEVE !N HIS *HEART,* THE ALMIGHTY ONE THOUGHT HE WAS *REWARDING* ME.

TO SUCH AS *ZEUS,* WE ARE MERELY *PETS--*

--AND, BY DARING TO *SNAP* AT HIM, I MAY WELL HAVE DOOMED US *ALL!*

10

THE *TEMPLE OF THE ORACLE,* LATER THAT SAME AFTERNOON:

IS THERE ANY *SIGN,* MENALIPPE?

NONE, QUEEN HIPPOLYTE--

--WHICH, AT *THIS* POINT, IS PROBABLY A *GOOD* SIGN.

THIS IS ALL SO *CONFUSING,* MOTHER...

AFTER ALL, THE GODS *MADE* ME.

PERHAPS IT IS *MY DESTINY* TO BE WITH THEM...TO *GIVE* MYSELF TO THEM...

NEVER! YOU WERE MINE *BEFORE* THE GODS BREATHED *LIFE* INTO THAT CLAY, DIANA...

THE GODDESSES PROMISED US *GREAT-NESS* IF WE SERVED THEM, BUT I CANNOT SEE *THIS* AS OUR DESTINY--OR *YOURS!*

IT GOES *AGAINST* EVERY-THING WE HAVE BEEN *TAUGHT!*

WELL, WE SHALL KNOW THE *TRUTH* SOON ENOUGH, YOUR HIGHNESS.

THE CAULDRON *BOILS...*

THE GODS MAKE READY TO *REPLY...*

MOTHER, I--I CAN *HEAR* THEM IN MY MIND, *CALLING* TO ME!

WHAT--?!?

IT IS INDEED *ME* THEY WANT--

--AND I MUST *GO* TO THEM!

IN THAT WAY *ALONE* WILL OUR TRUE *PURPOSE* AT LAST BECOME CLEAR!

THEN, SUDDENLY, A *VOICE*--

--AS IF FROM THE HEAVENS THEMSELVES--

--CALLING--

--*BECKONING*--

--MAKING SOMETHING HAPPEN--

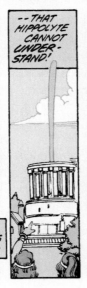

--THAT HIPPOLYTE CANNOT UNDER-STAND!

AND IT MAKES HER WANT TO--

--*SCREAM!*

11

236

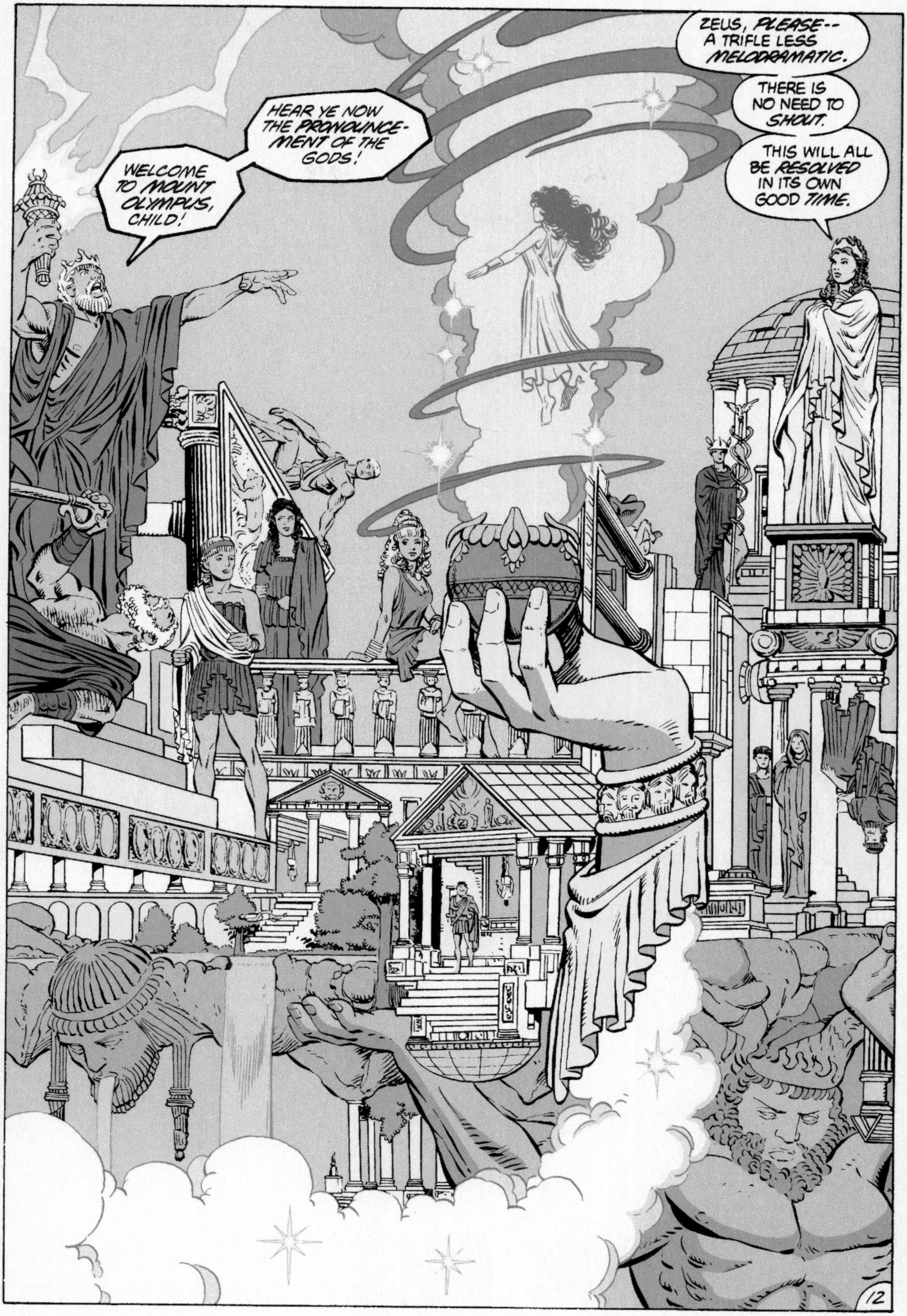
WELCOME TO MOUNT OLYMPUS, CHILD!
HEAR YE NOW THE PRONOUNCEMENT OF THE GODS!
ZEUS, PLEASE-- A TRIFLE LESS MELODRAMATIC.
THERE IS NO NEED TO SHOUT.
THIS WILL ALL BE RESOLVED IN ITS OWN GOOD TIME.
12

QUEEN HERA...?

AYE, CHILD--AND *THOU* ART THE SPIRIT OF THE *WARRIOR-PRINCESS* WHO BESTED MY SON *ARES.*

THE OTHER GODDESSES HAVE SPOKEN TRULY OF *THEE*... THOU ART A *UNIQUE* CREATION INDEED.

'TIS EASY TO SEE WHY ZEUS' *EYE* DID ROAM... *AGAIN.*

ENOUGH! THE GIRL IS HERE TO HEAR MY *JUDGMENT!*

SHE DID *SPIT* UPON US WITH HER *PRIDE*--AND SUCH ARROGANCE CANNOT BE *TOLERATED* IF WE ARE TO ONCE MORE RULE *SUPREME!*

REMEMBER, LORD ZEUS-- YOU AGREED TO ALLOW THE AMAZONS TO *PROVE* THEIR WORTH.

THEY ARE NOT AS *ORDINARY* MORTALS.

PERHAPS *NOT,* ARTEMIS--

--BUT NEITHER DOES *IMMORTALITY* MAKE THEM *GODS!*

PLEASE, ALMIGHTY ONE-- I MEANT NO *DISRESPECT!*

DO NOT *FEAR,* CHILD.

THOU ART MERELY BEING CALLED UPON ONCE MORE TO PROVE OUR *FAITH* IN THEE IS *JUSTIFIED.*

IF THOU DOST *SUCCEED,* THEN THOU SHALT KNOW AT LAST *WHO* THOU TRULY ART--

-- AND THE NATURE OF THY TRUE *DESTINY!*

IF THOU DOST *FAIL* HOWEVER, MY HUSBAND *HADES* SHALL MEET THEE AT THE SHORE OF THE *RIVER STYX*--

--AND ESCORT THEE TO *ELYSIUM.*

HUSH, PERSEPHONE-- YOU'LL *UN-SETTLE* HER!

I SAY THEE-- *ENOUGH!*

'TIS TIME TO *REVEAL* TO THIS UPSTART THE *NATURE* OF HER CHALLENGE!

...NO...

BEHOLD, CHILD-- AND *DESPAIR!*

13

238

"*IT IS THE GATEWAY TO THE DEMON LAIR BENEATH PARADISE ISLAND!*"

"*MY SISTER AMAZONS HAVE PERISHED OVER THE CENTURIES GUARDING THAT CURSED PORTAL!* "

AYE, HUSBAND, SUCH A TEST WOULD *PROVE* THE YOUNG ONE'S *METTLE.*

IF SHE CAN OVERCOME THE *MONSTERS* THAT LURK WITHIN, THEN TRULY IS SHE *WORTHY* TO BE CONSIDERED *EQUAL* TO THE *GODS.*

STILL, MILORD, IT DOES SEEM A DREADFUL *WASTE* OF GOOD WARM *FLESH!*

I'LL NOT REMIND YOU AGAIN TO HOLD YOUR *TONGUE*, MY SON!

LORD ZEUS, SHOULD YOU NOT MORE FULLY *EXPLAIN* THE CHALLENGE TO OUR YOUNG GUEST...?

ALL WILL BE MADE *CLEAR* TO THE AMAZON AS SHE *GOES*, HERMES.

WHEN--AND *IF*-- SHE *SURVIVES* EACH LABOR, ANOTHER GOD SHALL ADD A *NEW* CHALLENGE--

--UNTIL ALL *OLYMPUS* SHALL HAVE PROOF OF HER *WORTH!*

AT THE *END* OF THY TASK, CHILD, MY GREATEST *TREASURE* AWAITS THEE-- AND THOU SHALT *RETRIEVE* IT!

IF IT IS *LOST,* SO TOO SHALL BE ALL THE *AMAZONS!*

BUT SHOULDST THOU *SUCCEED,* THY BELOVED *THEMYSCIRA* SHALL KNOW FREEDOM AND *PROSPERITY*--

-- AND *THOU* SHALT KNOW AT LAST WHAT THE *PROPHECIES* INTEND FOR THEE!

I *ACCEPT* YOUR CHALLENGE, ALMIGHTY ONE--AND *GLADLY!*

TO FINALLY *UNDERSTAND* MY PAST AND FUTURE, I WOULD RISK *ANY* FATE--

-- AND *DEATH* NOT LEAST AMONG THEM!

THEN *BEGONE,* YOUNG AMAZON!

EITHER *DESTINY* OR *DESTRUCTION* AWAITS THEE NOW!

14.

239

PARADISE ISLAND:

AN AUDIENCE IN THE ROYAL CHAMBERS OF THE NOBLE HIPPOLYTE...

IT ISN'T *FAIR*, I TELL YOU!

I AM QUEEN OF THE AMAZONS, NOT MY *DAUGHTER*!

IF THERE IS A *CHALLENGE* TO BE MET, THEN *I* SHOULD BE THE ONE TO *MEET* IT!

WE *RETREATED* TO THIS ISLAND BECAUSE I ONCE ALLOWED A BRUTISH DEMIGOD TO TREAT ME LIKE A *DOG*!

MUST WE ALL NOW *SUFFER* FOR REFUSING TO ALLOW IT *AGAIN*?!

PLEASE, MOTHER--IT IS *MORE* THAN THAT! THIS IS AN OPPORTUNITY TO FINALLY LEARN MY TRUE *DESTINY*!

DEFEATING *ARES* WAS BUT THE FIRST *STEP* IN MY ULTIMATE AWAKENING!

ONLY BY *ANSWERING* THIS CHALLENGE SHALL I EVER FEEL TRULY *WHOLE*!

AND TO COMPLETE YOUR SPIRITUAL *BIRTH*, YOU MUST RISK PROBABLE *DEATH* ONCE MORE--WITHOUT *QUESTION*?

IT IS THE WILL OF THE *GODS*, MOTHER!

THEN HOW CAN I BELIEVE WE WILL EVER TRULY BE *FREE*-- WHEN THE GODDESSES WHO BORE US *SURRENDER* TO ZEUS' EVERY *WHIM*!

SOMETIMES I BELIEVE THAT WE ARE ALL MERELY *PAWNS* IN SOME INCOMPRE- HENSIBLE CELESTIAL *GAME*--

-- AND *FRANKLY*, DAUGHTER, I HAVE BEGUN TO *TIRE* OF IT!

MOTHER...?

DO NOT FRET, DIANA-- YOUR MOTHER'S BITTERNESS WILL *PASS*.

WE OWE OUR VERY *EXIST- ENCE* TO THE WILL OF THE *GODS*-- AND WE MUST SERVE THEM *NOBLY*.

YOU HAVE BEEN CHOSEN FOR A GREAT AND AWE- SOME *MISSION*, PRINCESS.

DO NOT *SHIRK* YOUR RESPONSI- BILITY, DIANA...

...AND YOU MAY WELL BECOME OUR *SAVIOR*! //15

MIDNIGHT:

AND A COLD *FULL MOON* LOOKS DOWN DISAPPROV-INGLY--

--AS THREE CIRCUM-SPECT RIDERS MOVE SILENTLY THROUGH THE DARKENED STREETS OF THEMYSCIRA--

--AND OUT INTO THE SHADOW-STREWN *WOODS*--

--TO THE BENIGHTED CAVERN AT THE ISLAND'S EDGE--

-- WHERE THE IMAGE OF THE WAR-GOD *ARES* STANDS ETERNAL *WATCH*-- OVER A LONG-CAPTIVE *NIGHTMARE!*

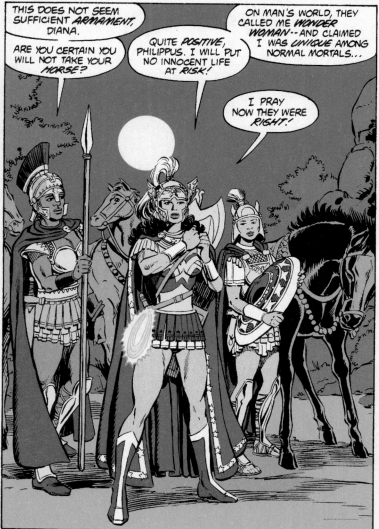

THIS DOES NOT SEEM SUFFICIENT *ARMAMENT,* DIANA.

ARE YOU CERTAIN YOU WILL NOT TAKE YOUR *HORSE?*

QUITE *POSITIVE,* PHILIPPUS. I WILL PUT NO INNOCENT LIFE AT *RISK!*

ON MAN'S WORLD, THEY CALLED ME *WONDER WOMAN*-- AND CLAIMED I WAS *UNIQUE* AMONG NORMAL MORTALS...

I PRAY NOW THEY WERE *RIGHT!*

I ONLY WISH MY *MOTHER* HAD DEIGNED TO *ACCOMPANY* ME HERE.

I PRAY OUR LAST *PARTING* WILL NOT BE OUR FINAL *MEMORY* OF ONE ANOTHER.

THANK YOU, DEAR SISTERS, FOR BEING MY *ESCORTS* THIS NIGHT.

BUT WHERE I JOURNEY *NOW,* I MUST JOURNEY *ALONE!*

16

241

THIS IS THE *FIRST* TIME I HAVE ACTUALLY *COME* TO THIS CURSED PLACE.

MOTHER WOULD NEVER ALLOW ME TO SERVE *GUARD DUTY* HERE LIKE MY *SISTER* AMAZONS.

HOW *IRONIC* THAT I MUST NOW FACE THE INFINITE DANGERS LURKING WITHIN *ALONE!*

SINCE THERE IS NO *MECHANISM* TO OPEN THE GATE, I WILL HAVE TO USE *BRUTE FORCE*--

-- AND IT-- WILL NOT-- BE EASY--!

THE *SEAL* OF THIS PORTAL HAS NOT BEEN *VIOLATED* SINCE THE TRAGIC *DEATH* OF HER WHOSE *NAME* I BEAR!

I REALIZE NOW THAT EVEN *THAT* IS JUST PART OF THE INTRICATE *TAPESTRY*--

--WOVEN BY CAPRICIOUS *GODS!*

STILL, LIVE OR DIE, THIS IS WHERE MY *DESTINY* LIES--

--AND I MUST NOT KEEP IT *WAITING!*

THE *WIND*-- SO *FIERCE*-- SO *COLD*--!

THE *LOCKING BOLT* SEEKS TO *SHUT* THE PORTAL--

-- AND, IN TRUTH, I CANNOT *BLAME* IT!

I MUST *ENTER* WITH THE SPEED OF *HERMES*--

--BEFORE THE UNSPEAKABLE *EVIL* THAT DWELLS WITHIN CAN *ESCAPE*--!

MY DAGGER WILL WEDGE THE PORTAL *OPEN*--

17

--LONG ENOUGH TO GRAB MY PRECIOUS *WEAPONS*--

--AND DESCEND INTO *PANDORA'S BOX!*

THE PRINCESS GONE, HER DAGGER SNAPS--

--*AND THE PORTAL SLAMS OMINOUSLY SHUT!*

THAT FAINT *LIGHT*, FROM *NOWHERE* AND YET FROM *EVERYWHERE*--!

AND A SLOW, STEADY *THUMPING* SOUND ECHOES FROM THE DARKENED WALLS LIKE *THUNDER*--

-- OR SOMETHING FAR *WORSE!*

STILL, THE WAY AHEAD IS *CLEAR* TO ME--

--MARKED BY *STAIRS* AS WHITE AS *CHALK*--!

SOMETHING *GLEAMING* ON THE STAIRWAY--?!?

EH?

IT SEEMS *FAMILIAR* SOMEHOW, LIKE--

GREAT *HERA!*

A *CARTRIDGE SHELL*--!

I SAW *ENOUGH* OF ITS LIKE IN *MAN'S WORLD*--!

BUT HOW DID IT COME TO BE HERE?

WHY WAS IT USED--?

18

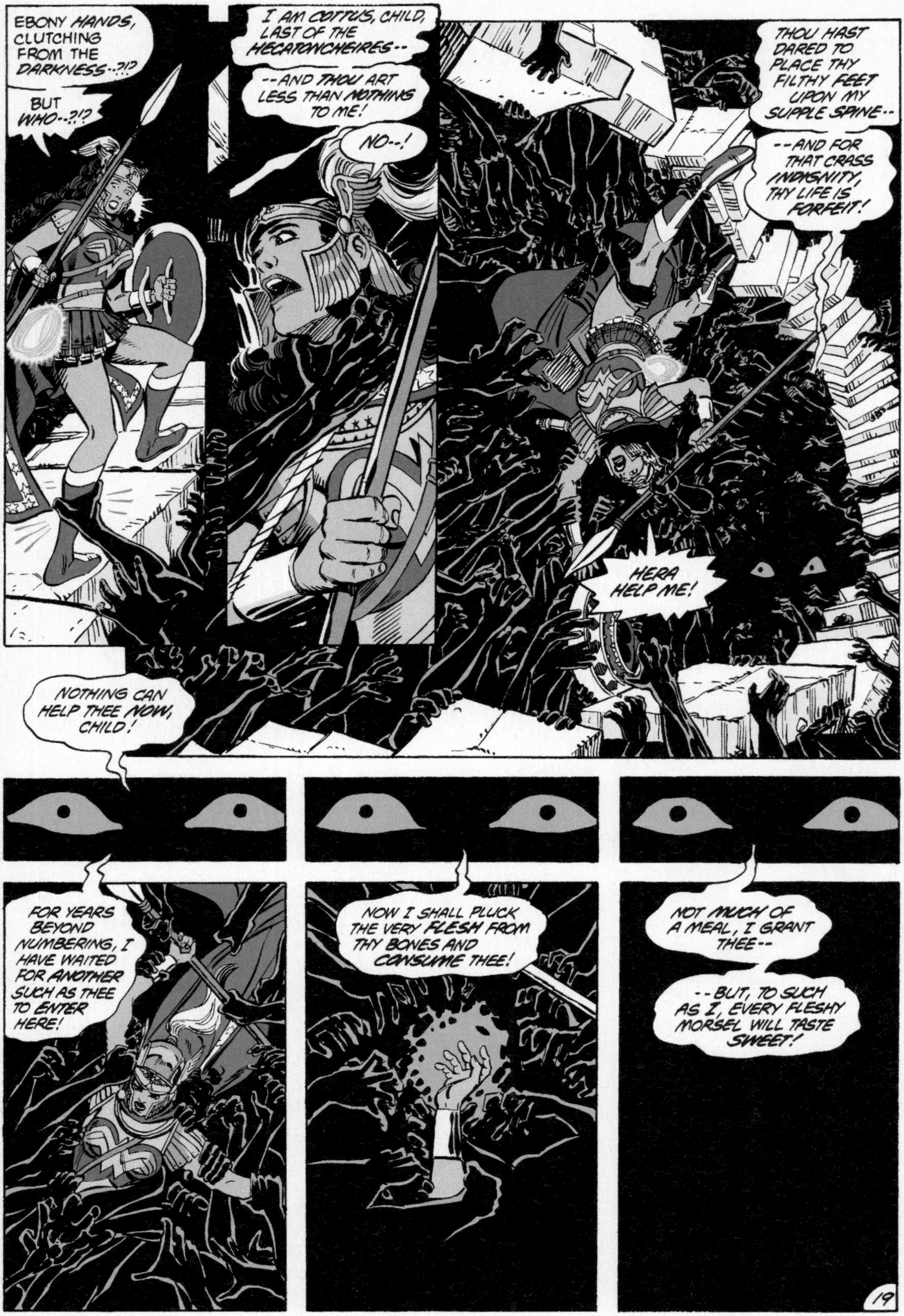
EBONY HANDS, CLUTCHING FROM THE DARKNESS--?!?
BUT WHO--?!?
I AM COTTUS, CHILD, LAST OF THE HECATONCHEIRES--
--AND THOU ART LESS THAN NOTHING TO ME!
NO--!
THOU HAST DARED TO PLACE THY FILTHY FEET UPON MY SUPPLE SPINE--
--AND FOR THAT CRASS INDIGNITY, THY LIFE IS FORFEIT!
HERA HELP ME!
NOTHING CAN HELP THEE NOW, CHILD!
FOR YEARS BEYOND NUMBERING, I HAVE WAITED FOR ANOTHER SUCH AS THEE TO ENTER HERE!
NOW I SHALL PLUCK THE VERY FLESH FROM THY BONES AND CONSUME THEE!
NOT MUCH OF A MEAL, I GRANT THEE--
--BUT, TO SUCH AS I, EVERY FLESHY MORSEL WILL TASTE SWEET!
19

AND EVEN AS I *CONSUME* THEE, I SHALL MAKE MY WAY TO THE *OUTSIDE* WORLD ONCE MORE--

--FOR THY FORCED *ENTRANCE* HATH AT LAST WEAKENED THE *CURSED SEAL!*

AYE, SOON SHALL I--

NOOOOOOOO!!

BUT I AM *NOT* MERELY MORTAL, MONSTER!

I AM AN *AMAZON* BORN--

--AND I WILL ALLOW *NOTHING* TO THWART MY SACRED *QUEST!*

NOR WILL I ALLOW SUCH AS *YOU* TO ESCAPE BACK INTO THE *LIGHT!*

THEN, CHILD, THOU MUST *DIE!!*

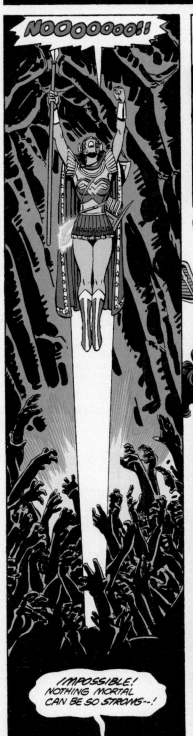

IMPOSSIBLE! NOTHING MORTAL CAN BE SO *STRONG--!*

THAT CONSTANT *THUMPING* HAS GROWN *LOUDER, MORE QUICK--!*

I REALIZE NOW IT CAN BE ONLY *ONE THING--*

"-- THE BEATING OF HIS HIDEOUS *HEART!*"

ARRR...GGHHH

20

PRAISE *ARTEMIS* AND MY HUNTER'S *INSTINCTS!*

MY HUNGRY *LANCE* STRUCK STRAIGHT TO THE MONSTER'S *HEART!*

CHILD, THOU SHALT PAY FOR THIS!!

NO, BEHEMOTH-- I THINK *NOT!*

I HAVE WASTED *ENOUGH* PRECIOUS TIME ON THIS *SENSELESS BATTLE!*

AAARRGGHHH

'*TIS TIME* TO PUT AN END TO IT!!

ITS SPINE SHATTERED, THE REST OF THE CREATURE CALLED *COTTUS* SWIFTLY FOLLOWS *SUIT*--

--PLUNGING THE *AMAZON PRINCESS* DEEPER INTO THE ALL-OPPRESSIVE *BLACKNESS*--

-- AND WHEN SHE AT LAST REGAINS HER *FEET*...

TOO MANY OF MY *SISTERS* HAVE BEEN *SLAIN* BY THE LIKES OF YOU, *COTTUS!*

PERHAPS MY *LANCE* JUTTING FROM YOUR HEART SHALL SERVE AS THEIR *MEMORIAL!*

THE CONSTANT *THUMPING* OF *COTTUS'* HEART NOW FOREVER STILLED, DIANA MOVES ON IN *SILENCE*--

--FOLLOWING THE STENCH OF *BRIMSTONE*--

21

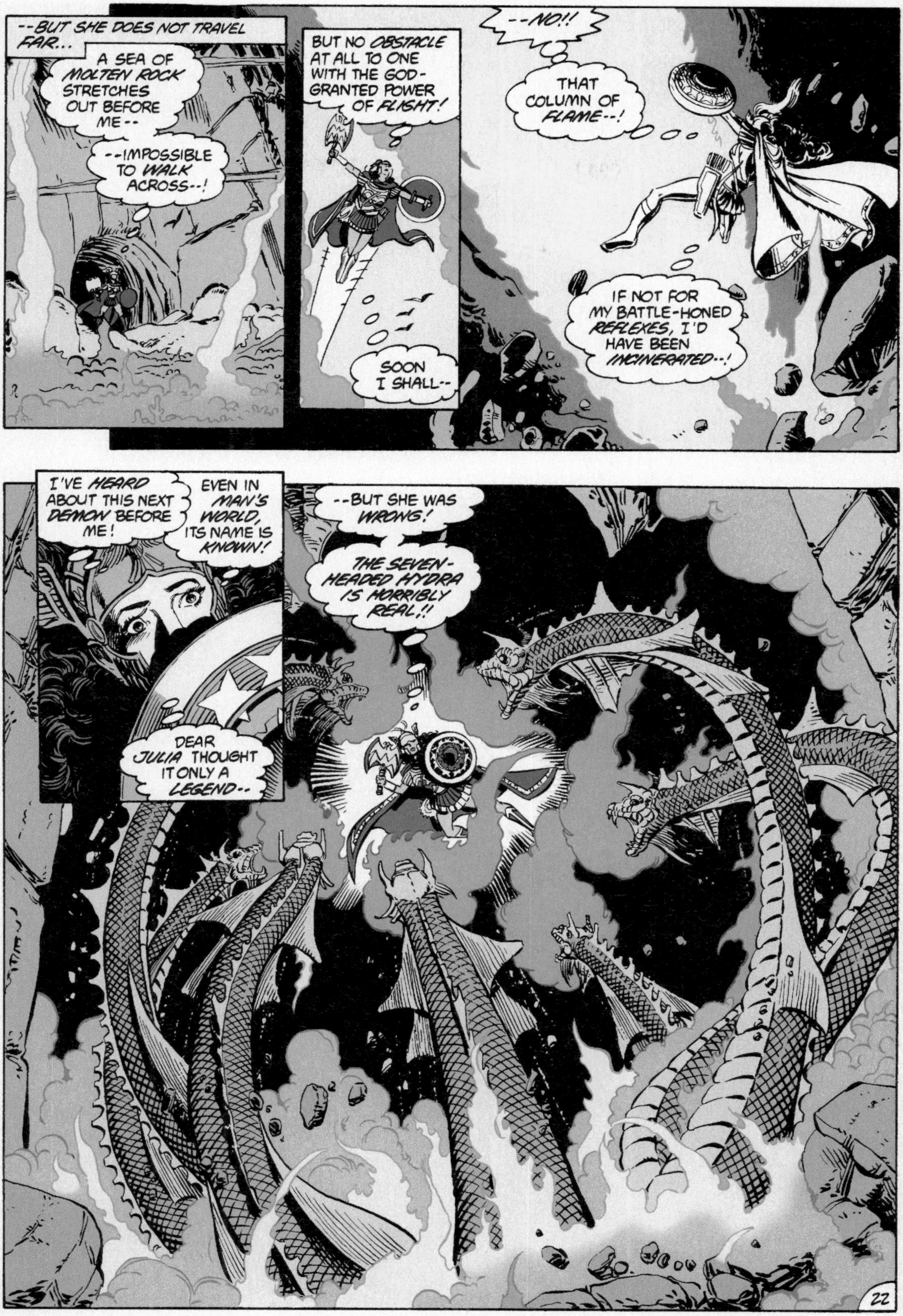
--BUT SHE DOES NOT TRAVEL FAR...
A SEA OF MOLTEN ROCK STRETCHES OUT BEFORE ME--
--IMPOSSIBLE TO WALK ACROSS--!
BUT NO OBSTACLE AT ALL TO ONE WITH THE GOD-GRANTED POWER OF FLIGHT!
SOON I SHALL--
--NO!!
THAT COLUMN OF FLAME--!
IF NOT FOR MY BATTLE-HONED REFLEXES, I'D HAVE BEEN INCINERATED--!
I'VE HEARD ABOUT THIS NEXT DEMON BEFORE ME!
EVEN IN MAN'S WORLD, ITS NAME IS KNOWN!
DEAR JULIA THOUGHT IT ONLY A LEGEND--
--BUT SHE WAS WRONG!
THE SEVEN-HEADED HYDRA IS HORRIBLY REAL!!
22

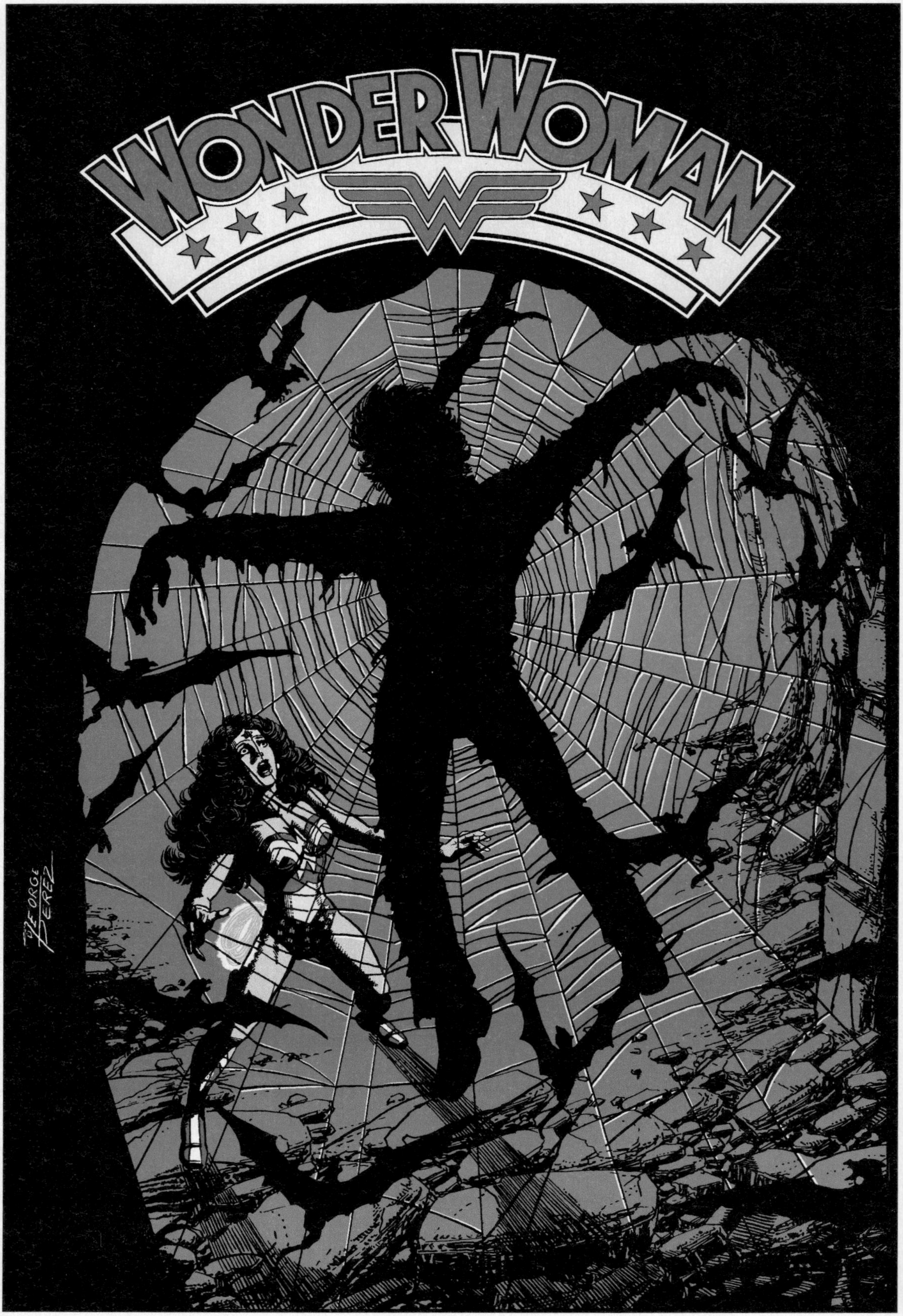
WONDER WOMAN
GEORGE PEREZ

ABOVE THE FROTHING *CLOUDS* AND THE INCONSEQUENTIAL WORKS OF MAN, IN THE CALIGARIAN CORRIDORS OF MOUNT OLYMPUS, ALMIGHTY ZEUS AND HIS COMPANY LOOK DOWN IN MILD *AMUSEMENT*--

--WHILE, BENEATH *PARADISE ISLAND*, BEYOND THE IMPENETRABLE *DOORWAY OF DOOM*, THE DARING *PRINCESS DIANA*, MIGHTIEST OF ALL THE AMAZONS, BATTLES A SEVEN-HEADED *NIGHTMARE* TO PRESERVE HER *IMMORTAL* RACE...

IT IS NOT THE FIRST OF THE *GOD-CHOSEN* CHALLENGES SHE MUST FACE THIS DAY--:

-- NOR WILL IT BE THE *LAST!*

METHINKS YOUR PRECIOUS DIANA WILL NOT *SURVIVE* HER ENCOUNTER WITH THE *HYDRA,* HERA.

WOULD YOU CARE TO WAGER *OTHERWISE?*

IS THERE NOT ALREADY *ENOUGH* AT STAKE, ALMIGHTY ONE?

THE *DESTRUCTION* OF THE AMAZON WILL SURELY MAKE HER SISTERS MORE... *COMPLIANT* TO YOUR WISHES.

I WILL NOT WARN YOU AGAIN TO KEEP *SILENT,* PAN.

I UNDERSTAND YOUR *CONCERN,* HERMES...

YOU MUST TRUST SHE WILL NOT *FAIL.*

I GAVE DIANA GREAT *BEAUTY* AND THE *LOVE* OF SAME, ATHENA--

--BUT OF WHAT *GOOD* IS THAT *NOW?*

BEAUTY OF THE *SOUL* CAN BE A GREAT *WEAPON,* APHRODITE--

--IF IT CAN REMAIN *UNCORRUPTED.*

GEORGE PÉREZ · plotter/layouts
LEN WEIN · scripter
BRUCE D. PATTERSON · finisher
JOHN COSTANZA · letterer
CARL GAFFORD · colorist
KAREN BERGER · editor

Challenge of the Gods
Book Two

2

INDEED, ATHENA. SHOULD SHE *SURVIVE* THIS FIERY CHALLENGE, THEN I *TOO* SHALL SIDE WITH YOU AND *HESTIA.*

IF SHE CAN BEST THE *FLAMES* I FORGE, THEN SHE IS A MOST *SINGULAR* CREATURE INDEED.

I *FEAR* FOR THE DAUGHTER OF GAEA'S WOMB WHOM I HELPED *BIRTH,* APOLLO.

SHOULD DIANA *FAIL,* WHAT WILL BECOME OF THE *OTHER* AMAZONS?

MY HEART *RAGES* THAT ZEUS MIGHT *HEED* PAN'S VILE SUGGESTIONS-- AND *DEFILE* THAT GLORIOUS RACE!

'TIS NOT ONLY THE *ALMIGHTY ONE* WHO CAN TIP THE SCALES OF FATE, SISTER ARTEMIS.

SHOULD SHE PROVE *WORTHY,* THE FATE OF YOUR DAUGHTER'S DAUGHTER RESTS WITH *ALL* OF US.

I AM *AWARE,* BROTHER--

--BUT I WORRY MOST THAT *WE* MAY NOT PROVE WORTHY OF *HER!*

AND *TORMENT*

3

BEHEADING THE BEAST WILL SERVE NO *PURPOSE!* IF THE *LEGENDS* I LEARNED FROM JULIA ARE *TRUE*, IT WILL MERELY GROW *ANOTHER!*

AND ONLY THE *SPEED* GRANTED ME AT BIRTH BY *HERMES* HAS THUS FAR PREVENTED MY *INCINERATION!*

YET NOT EVEN GOD-GIVEN *SWIFTNESS* IS SUFFICIENT TO EVADE A SIMULTANEOUS ATTACK FROM SO MANY DIRECTIONS...

SUDDENLY, THE AMAZON IS STRUCK...

SHE FALLS...

AND IT IS ONLY THE *VOLCANIC ASH* INTO WHICH SHE PLUMMETS THAT EXTINGUISHES THE FLAMES THAT WOULD *CONSUME* HER...

IT SEEMS *OBVIOUS*...

...I MUST *RETHINK* MY STRATEGY.

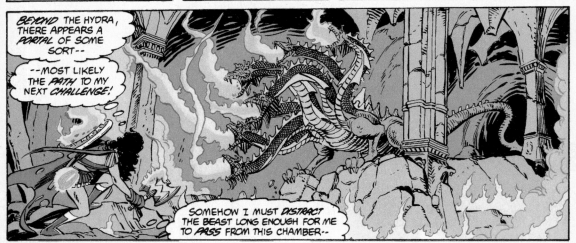

BEYOND THE HYDRA, THERE APPEARS A *PORTAL* OF SOME SORT--

--MOST LIKELY THE *PATH* TO MY NEXT *CHALLENGE!*

SOMEHOW I MUST *DISTRACT* THE BEAST LONG ENOUGH FOR ME TO *PASS* FROM THIS CHAMBER--

-- AND THESE *COLUMNS* WHICH SUPPORT THE CAVERN'S *CEILING* SEEM MY ONLY *ANSWER*--!

WITH A BLOW SO POWERFUL IT *SHATTERS* THE VERY *AXE* SHE WIELDS, THE AMAZON *DEMOLISHES* THE ANCIENT STONE *STRUTS*--

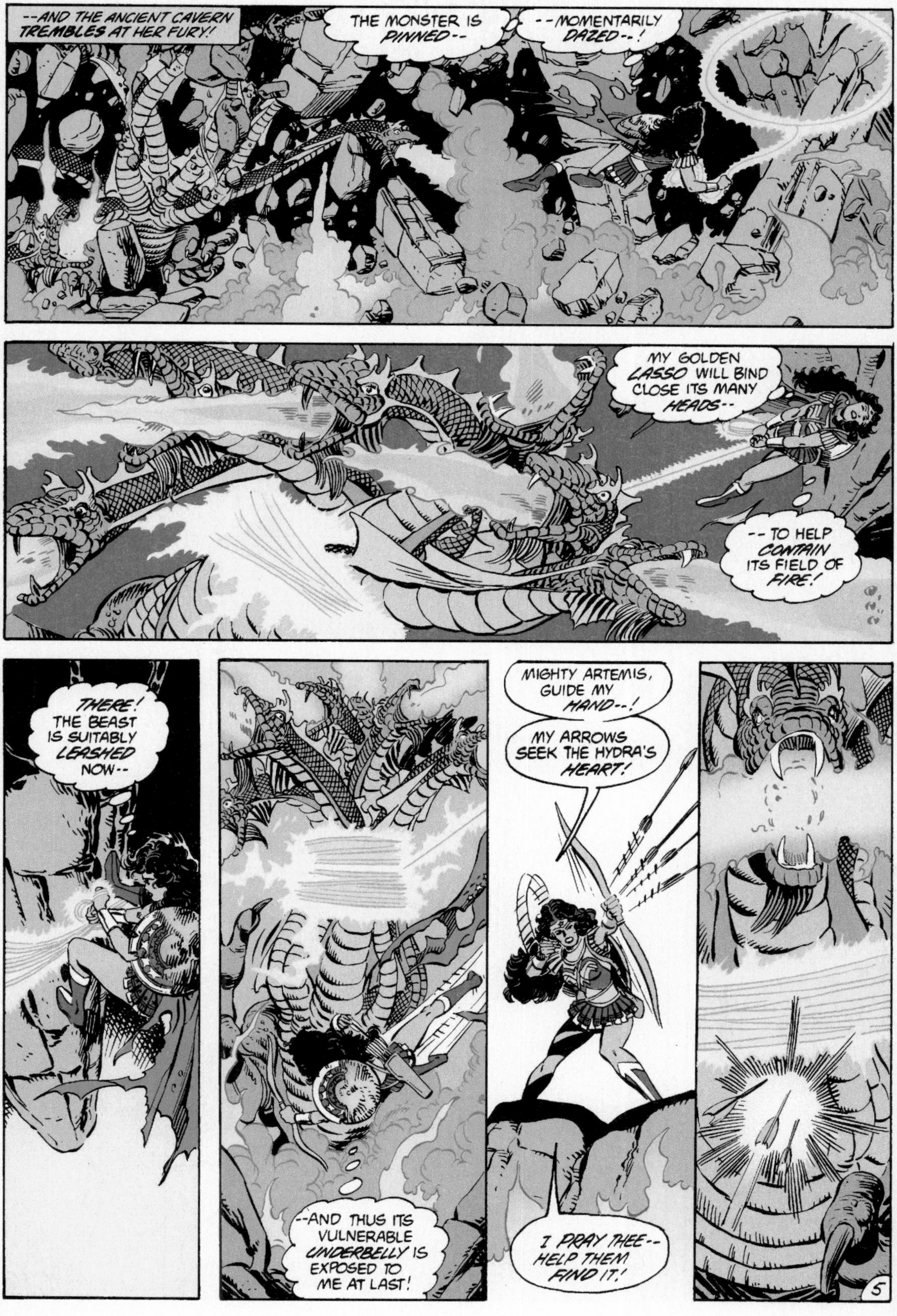
--AND THE ANCIENT CAVERN TREMBLES AT HER FURY!
THE MONSTER IS PINNED--
--MOMENTARILY DAZED--!
MY GOLDEN LASSO WILL BIND CLOSE ITS MANY HEADS--
--TO HELP CONTAIN ITS FIELD OF FIRE!
THERE! THE BEAST IS SUITABLY LEASHED NOW--
--AND THUS ITS VULNERABLE UNDERBELLY IS EXPOSED TO ME AT LAST!
MIGHTY ARTEMIS, GUIDE MY HAND--!
MY ARROWS SEEK THE HYDRA'S HEART!
I PRAY THEE--HELP THEM FIND IT!
5

THE DEATHSONG OF THE HYDRA IS A TERRIBLE THING TO HEAR, FILLED WITH FRUSTRATION AND FURY--

MY LASSO--! MUST RETRIEVE IT BEFORE IT'S TOO LATE--!

SUCH AN IRREPLACEABLE GIFT FROM THE GODS THEMSELVES--

--CANNOT BE ABANDONED--!

--AS THE FLAMES THAT HAD BIRTHED IT NOW RECLAIM THEIR WAYWARD CHILD...

FOR THE NEXT SEVERAL SECONDS, THE AMAZON PRINCESS STRUGGLES TO FREE HER PRECIOUS LARIAT--

--AS THE HYDRA SINKS FOREVER BENEATH THE MOLTEN MAGMA--

--ITS VIOLENT DEATH-THROES CHURNING THE RUINED CAVERN INTO A FRENZY--

--BELCHING FIRE THAT SENDS THE STUNNED AMAZON HURTLING UNCONTROLLABLY THROUGH THE SUPER-HEATED AIR--

--TO SLAM WITH STARTLING FINALITY AGAINST THE HEAVING CAVERN FLOOR--

--WHERE SHE LIES STILL--

--DEATHLY STILL--

YOU ALLOW THE AMAZON TO SLEEP, MORPHEUS?

AYE, EROS --HER BODY HAS EXPERIENCED GREAT PAIN.

SLEEP WILL HELP TO HEAL HER.

BUT SLEEP IS ONLY A TEMPORARY FRIEND TOO MUCH WILL QUICKLY DESTROY HER.

THUS I CHALLENGE HER TO FREE HERSELF FROM THE TEMPTATION OF MORPHEUS' "BLISS"..

...IF SHE CAN!

6

BENEATH THE
HEAVENS:

THE
EARTH:

OKLAHOMA:

ENID WOODRING MUNICIPAL AIRPORT:
AS A COMMERCIAL JETLINER TAXIS IN
FOR A LANDING--

-- CARRYING *TWO PASSENGERS* WHO WOULD BE FAR MORE AT HOME IN A *MILITARY AIRCRAFT...*

FEELS SO *STRANGE* BEING HERE, ETTA.

HAVEN'T BEEN *BACK* SINCE I DID A TOUR AT NEARBY *VANCE AIR FORCE BASE.*

DAD AND I USED TO SPEND OUR WEEKENDS IN THE NEARBY *MOUNTAINS,* SOAKING UP *NATURE--!*

AH-- SEEMS THE LOCAL *WELCOMING PARTY* HAS ARRIVED TO *GREET* US.

STEVE! THANK GOD YOU'RE FINALLY *HERE!*

LT. ETTA CANDY, I'D LIKE YOU TO MEET MY COUSIN, *DOUG AARONSON.*

PARDON MY *RUDENESS,* LT. CANDY-- BUT THIS IS *IMPORTANT.*

WHAT IS ?

WE COULDN'T *CONTACT* YOU ON THE *PLANE.* IT'S... IT'S YOUR *DAD...*

STEVE, I'M *SORRY.*

HE... HE *DIED* ABOUT AN HOUR AGO.

C'MON-- I'LL GET YOUR *BAGS.* MY FOLKS SAY THE *LIEUTENANT* CAN STAY WITH *THEM* UNTIL THE *FUNERAL.*

STEVE, IF IT *HELPS* --HIS LAST WORDS WERE ABOUT *YOU.*

STEVE, ARE YOU *ALL RIGHT?*

I DIDN'T EVEN GET A CHANCE TO SAY *GOOD-BYE.*

FIRST, *MATT MICHAELIS,* THE CLOSEST THING I EVER HAD TO A *BROTHER...*

...AND NOW MY *DAD...*

I'M *GLAD* YOU CAME *WITH ME,* ETTA.

RIGHT NOW, I FEEL SO TERRIBLY... *ALONE.*

⑦

PARADISE ISLAND: AS THE BRIGHT GOLDEN FINGERS OF DAWN CARESS HER IVORY TEMPLES--

--AND THE SOUND OF IMPATIENT FOOTSTEPS ECHOES THROUGH THE PALACE ROYAL...

I'VE SPENT MY ENTIRE LIFE HONORING THE GODS, PLACING MY FAITH IN THEIR JUDGMENT--

--BUT NOW I FEAR THE WEIGHT OF SUCH BLIND TRUST MAY BE MORE THAN I CAN BEAR!

WHY DID THE GODDESSES BLESS ME WITH A DAUGHTER IF THEY INTENDED TO CONTINUALLY TAKE HER FROM ME?

AND IF THE GODDESSES ARE OBEDIENT TO ZEUS, THEN WHOM DO WE SERVE?

IT'S BEEN SAID HERACLES WAS IN A MAD FEVER INDUCED BY HERA WHEN HE DID RAVISH ME AND MY SISTERS AND RAVAGED OUR CITY...

COULD SUCH MADNESS NOW BE CONTROLLING ZEUS? I MUST DO SOMETHING--

--AND YET HOW CAN I DISOBEY THE GODS WITHOUT RISKING THE RUIN OF ALL I HOLD DEAR?

BUT QUEEN HIPPOLYTE'S THOUGHT GOES UNFINISHED--

--AS A SHARP CHILL, DEEPER THAN ANY GRAVE, SUDDENLY CLUTCHES HER HEART...

THAT BIRD-- A VULTURE--!

BUT THERE ARE NO VULTURES ON PARADISE ISLAND--!

"AND ITS EYES--THE WAY IT'S STARING AT ME--

--STARING THROUGH ME--!"

ITS DARK EYES BURNING, THE CARRION BIRD SOMEHOW TOUCHES HIPPOLYTE'S MIND AND SOUL--

--AND THE ANSWER TO HER SILENT PRAYERS AT LAST BECOMES CLEAR...

"IT IS TIME...

...FOR THE QUEEN TO SURRENDER...

...TO THE MOTHER!"

8

ELSEWHERE IN THE CAPITAL CITY:

MENALIPPE!

COME QUICKLY, ORACLE!

WHAT *IS* IT, SISTER?

THAT ARMORED *WARRIOR*--RACING TOWARD THE *CAVERN OF DOOM*--!

COULD IT *BE*--?

"AYE, SISTER--HER STANDARD IS *CLEAR!*"

"IT IS AS I HAVE *FEARED*...

"QUEEN HIPPOLYTE HAS GONE *MAD!*"

OBVIOUSLY, THE DANGER TO HER DAUGHTER WAS *TOO MUCH* FOR HER TO *BEAR!*

QUICKLY, SISTER--! CALL *PHILIPPUS!* HIPPOLYTE MUST BE *STOPPED!*

BUT SHE--SHE IS OUR *QUEEN!*

"AND YET, IN HER *MADNESS*, SHE MAY WELL DESTROY US ALL!

"THOUGH MY HEART ACHES FOR HER, SHE MUST *NOT* BE PERMITTED TO ENTER THE CAVERN!"

DOOM'S DOORWAY:

IT *SMOLDERS* NOW AT THE EDGES WITH WISPS OF *ESCAPING EVIL*--

--WHILE THE AMAZON WHO *BROKE* ITS AGES-OLD *SEAL* SEEKS ESCAPE IN HER OWN WAY...

SO HURT... SO TIRED... JUST WANT TO SLEEP..

...BUT I MUST CONTINUE THE *QUEST* ZEUS HAS *SET* FOR ME...

9

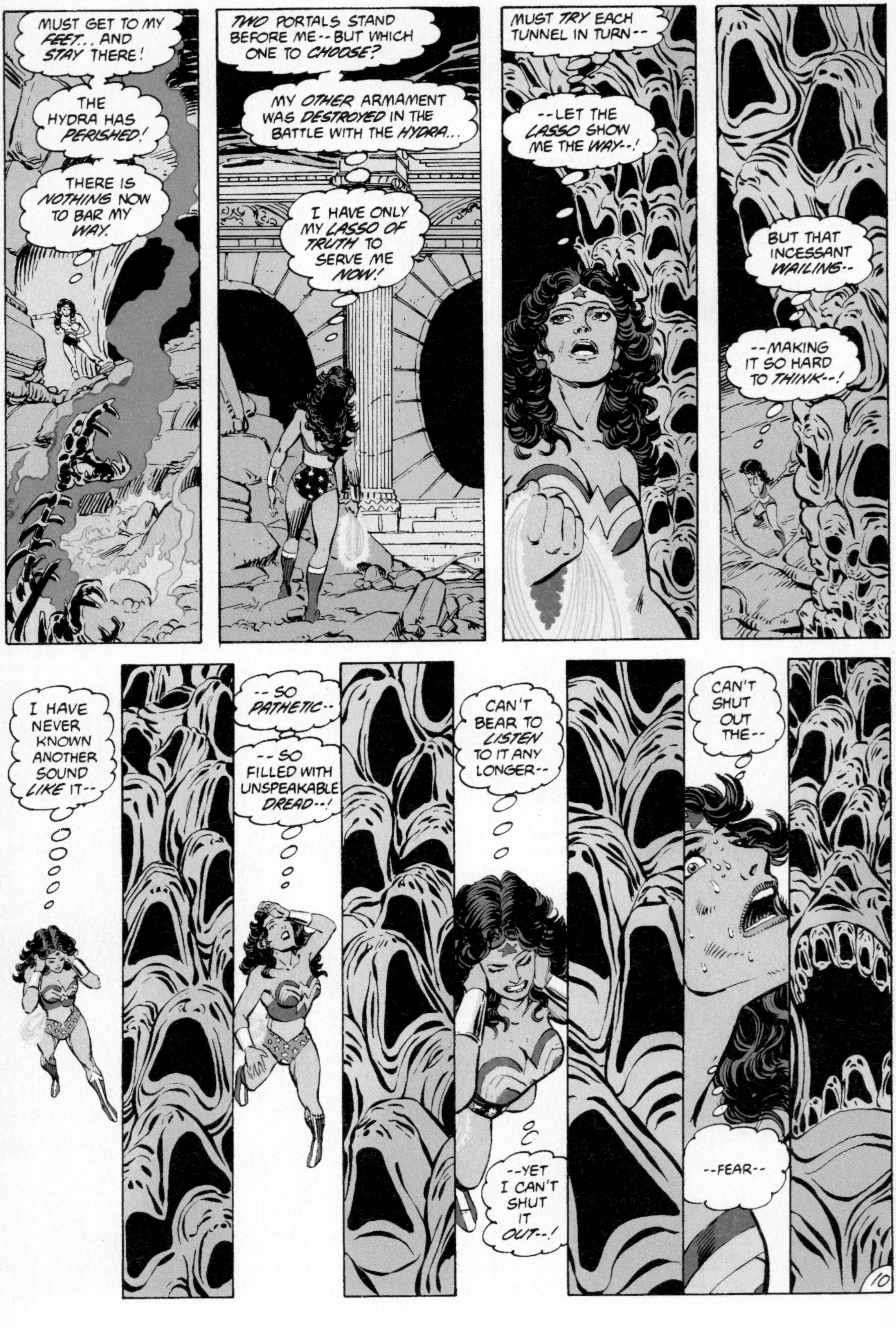
MUST GET TO MY FEET... AND STAY THERE!
THE HYDRA HAS PERISHED!
THERE IS NOTHING NOW TO BAR MY WAY.
TWO PORTALS STAND BEFORE ME--BUT WHICH ONE TO CHOOSE?
MY OTHER ARMAMENT WAS DESTROYED IN THE BATTLE WITH THE HYDRA...
I HAVE ONLY MY LASSO OF TRUTH TO SERVE ME NOW!
MUST TRY EACH TUNNEL IN TURN--
--LET THE LASSO SHOW ME THE WAY--!
BUT THAT INCESSANT WAILING--
--MAKING IT SO HARD TO THINK--!
I HAVE NEVER KNOWN ANOTHER SOUND LIKE IT--
--SO PATHETIC--
--SO FILLED WITH UNSPEAKABLE DREAD--!
CAN'T BEAR TO LISTEN TO IT ANY LONGER--
--YET I CAN'T SHUT IT OUT--!
CAN'T SHUT OUT THE--
--FEAR--
10

FEAR, IRRATIONAL, UNCON-
TROLLABLE, SWEEPS OVER
THE AMAZON LIKE A TIDE--

--AS HER WIDENED BLUE EYES
BEHOLD WITH HORROR--

--THE SWIRLING STUFF OF NIGHTMARE!

THAT *PORTAL*-- SUDDENLY FILLED WITH WRITHING FEMALE *SHAPES*--?!?

BUT *WHO*--?!?

HELP US, DIANA... HELP YOUR FALLEN SISTERS...

COULD IT *BE*...? THEY APPEAR TO BE *AMAZONS*... AND *YET*...

I DON'T *UNDERSTAND*... THIS MAKES NO *SENSE*...

WE ARE THOSE WHO WERE *SLAIN* WHILE DEFENDING DOOM'S DOORWAY...

FOR AGES, OUR SOULS HAVE BEEN *TRAPPED* HERE...

...AWAITING OUR *SAVIOR!*

SAVE US, PRINCESS... BEFORE WE ARE *SWEPT AWAY*--

HELP US... HELP US...

IN MERCY'S NAME... HELLLLPPPP..

CANNOT JUDGE IF THIS IS *REAL*....YET NEITHER CAN I STAND IDLY BY AND WATCH THEIR SOULS *BURN*...

ATHENA, *HELP* ME! SHOW ME WHAT TO *DO!*

DIANA... PLEASE HELP ME...

11

NO...IT CANNOT BE...!

'TIS SHE WHO, AMONG *MORTALS,* WAS MOST LIKE A *MOTHER* TO ME...

...*JULIA!*

...IT HURTS, DIANA...HURTS SO TERRIBLY...

DON'T... DON'T *LEAVE* ME HERE...

...*RELEASE* ME...

PLEASE... I'M *DYING...*

IF YOU *LOVE* ME, DAUGHTER...

...*SET...ME... FREE...*

HAVE *FAITH,* JULIA--

--I AM *COMING* FOR YOU!

THANK YOU, DIANA...

...*THANK* YOU...

...*YOU* LITTLE *FOOL!!*

WHAT--?!?

WHO--?!?

I AM *ECHIDNA,* LITTLE ONE--

--AND I SHALL BE THE *DEATH* OF THEE!

12

JUST BEYOND DOOM'S DOORWAY, YET A UNIVERSE AWAY...

AS THE GODS HAVE COMMANDED, THE *ENTRANCE* TO THE CAVERN IS *UNGUARDED* FOR THE FIRST TIME IN *CENTURIES*--

--WHICH MEANS I WILL BE *UNOPPOSED* AS I PENETRATE THE BARRIER--

...TO REACH MY *DAUGHTER* AND THE--

--UUNNFF!!

PHILIPPUS?!?

PLEASE, HIPPOLYTE-- RETURN WITH ME TO *THEMYSCIRA!*

YOU ARE IN GREAT *DANGER* HERE!

I *BEG* YOU, MY QUEEN--

--DO NOT FORCE ME TO RAISE *ARMS* AGAINST ONE I SO DEARLY *LOVE!*

NO, MY CAPTAIN-- YOU MUSTN'T *STOP* ME!

THOUGH I CANNOT YET *EXPLAIN,* I TELL YOU THE GODS HAVE MADE AN *ERROR!*

YOU MUST LET ME *PASS!*

IF INDEED THE GODS *ARE* WRONG, THEN THE *PROOF* SHALL BE MY *DEATH*--

--FOR I *CANNOT* ALLOW YOU TO ENTER THAT *CAVERN!*

13

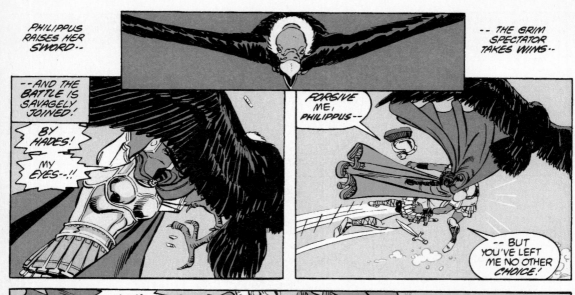

PHILIPPUS RAISES HER SWORD--

-- THE GRIM SPECTATOR TAKES WING--

--AND THE BATTLE IS SAVAGELY JOINED!

BY HADES!

MY EYES--!!

FORGIVE ME, PHILIPPUS--

-- BUT YOU'VE LEFT ME NO OTHER CHOICE!

NO!!

UUNNHH!!

I LOVE YOUR DAUGHTER TOO, MY QUEEN...

...BUT...WOULD YOU SACRIFICE...YOUR ENTIRE RACE...TO SAVE HER?

I FEAR, MY QUEEN--

I DO ONLY WHAT A MOTHER MUST!

NOW SURRENDER, PHILIPPUS--

--BEFORE I AM FORCED TO HURT YOU!

"--'TIS ALREADY FAR TOO LATE FOR THAT!"

UUNNHH!!

14

AND SO THE BATTLE *RAGES*, BETWEEN TWO *SPIRITUAL SISTERS* WHOSE HEARTS *BREAK* ANEW WITH EACH *BLOW* LANDED--

--THOUGH NO QUARTER IS EVER ASKED OR GIVEN...

FOR THEY ARE BOTH *WARRIORS* BORN, THESE TWO *IMMORTALS*, AND FOR THEM SUCH COMBAT CAN *END* ONLY ONE OF TWO WAYS:

IN *VICTORY*--

--OR IN *DEATH!*

THUS, AS THE *BLEAK BIRD* BEARS SILENT WITNESS...

PHILIPPUS IS *DOWN*, BUT I MUST MAKE CERTAIN SHE IS LEFT *SENSELESS* BEFORE I ARISE--

--ELSE SHE WILL NOT *REST* TILL SHE HAS *SLAIN* ME!

YOU ARE FAR TOO HONORABLE TO *LIVE* WITH SUCH *GUILT*, PHILIPPUS.....

--THUS I *FREE* YOU FROM THAT *RESPONSIBILITY!*

FORGIVE ME, DEAR SISTER--

--IF YOU *CAN!*

SOON, AS THE GREAT BIRD CIRCLES 'ROUND PAST THE EVER-VIGILANT STATUE OF ARES...

YOU CAN RETURN TO THEMYSCIRA *UNASHAMED,* DEAR PHILIPPUS.

NO WARRIOR HAS EVER FOUGHT MORE *VALIANTLY*--

--NOR KNOWN A MORE HONORABLE *DEFEAT!*

I PRAY YOU AND YOUR SISTERS WILL FIND IT IN YOUR HEARTS TO *FORGIVE* ME SOMEHOW--

--FOR I DO ONLY WHAT I *MUST!*

FAREWELL, DEAR SISTER. WHEN YOU *REMEMBER* ME, REMEMBER THAT I *LOVED* YOU...

...THAT I LOVED YOU *ALL.*

NOW *RUN,* BRAVE STEEDS! *RUN!*

CARRY YOUR MISTRESS SAFE *HOME!*

FOR *ME,* I GO NOW TO FACE MY *DESTINY,* IN A LAND NO NOBLE HEART HAS *EVER* CALLED HOME--

--AND FROM WHICH NONE HAS EVER *RETURNED!*

CURSE THE AMAZON QUEEN FOR *INTERFERING!*

I HAD NOT *COUNTED* ON THIS!

THOUGH I KNOW NOT *HOW*--

THUS I MUST TAKE STEPS TO DEAL WITH THE DISOBEDIENT *HIPPOLYTE*--

--BEFORE THE TERRIBLE *TRUTH* ABOUT PAN IS UN-WITTINGLY *REVEALED!*

--I FEAR MY TRUE *PURPOSE* HERE HAS BECOME *SUSPECT!*

16

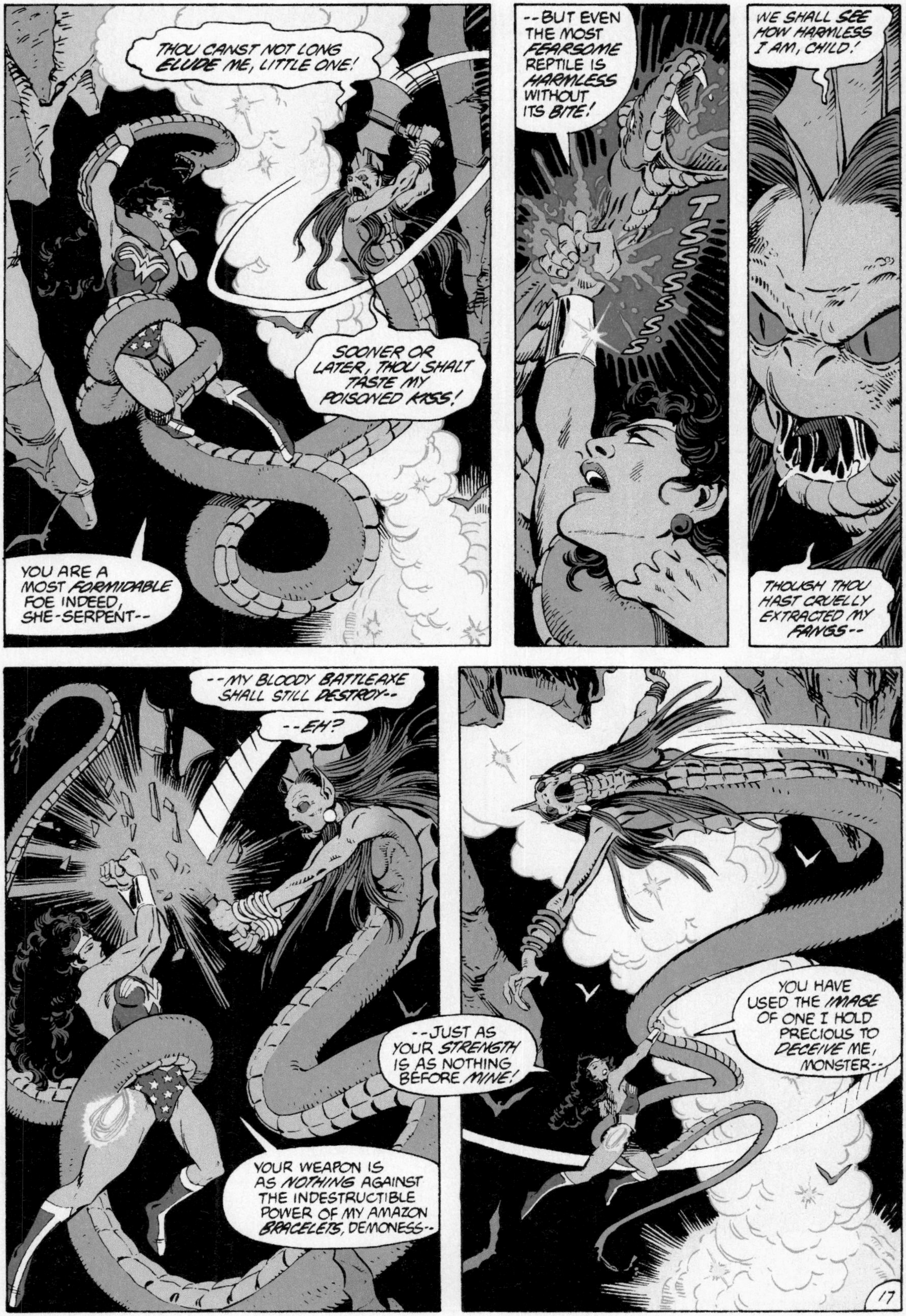
THOU CANST NOT LONG ELUDE ME, LITTLE ONE!
SOONER OR LATER, THOU SHALT TASTE MY POISONED KISS!
YOU ARE A MOST FORMIDABLE FOE INDEED, SHE-SERPENT--
--BUT EVEN THE MOST FEARSOME REPTILE IS HARMLESS WITHOUT ITS BITE!
TSSSSSSS
WE SHALL SEE HOW HARMLESS I AM, CHILD!
THOUGH THOU HAST CRUELLY EXTRACTED MY FANGS--
--MY BLOODY BATTLEAXE SHALL STILL DESTROY--
--EH?
YOUR WEAPON IS AS NOTHING AGAINST THE INDESTRUCTIBLE POWER OF MY AMAZON BRACELETS, DEMONESS--
--JUST AS YOUR STRENGTH IS AS NOTHING BEFORE MINE!
YOU HAVE USED THE IMAGE OF ONE I HOLD PRECIOUS TO DECEIVE ME, MONSTER--
17

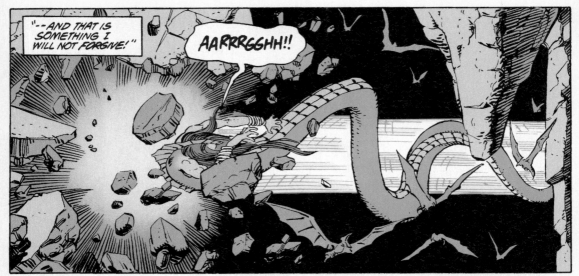

"--AND THAT IS SOMETHING I WILL NOT FORGIVE!"

AARRRGGHH!!

HER SNAPPING *DEMONS* SEEK TO *DISTRACT* ME-- TO KEEP ME FROM MY *GOAL*--!

BUT JUST WHERE *IS* MY GOAL?

THAT POOL OF *LIQUID LIGHT* BELOW SEEMS TO BE CALLING ME--

--BUT IS IT A *TRUE* SUMMONS OR MERELY ANOTHER *TRAP*?

NO! *IGNORE* THE LIGHT! IT IS *NOT* FOR SUCH AS *THEE*!

IF YOU WOULD KEEP ME *FROM* IT, SHE-SERPENT -- THEN *THAT* IS WHERE I MUST *GO*!

ALMIGHTY ZEUS HAS CHARGED ME WITH A MOST SACRED *MISSION*, ECHIDNA--

--AND NEITHER *YOU* NOR ALL THE HORDES OF *HADES* SHALL BAR MY *WAY*!

18

IF THIS POOL IS INDEED THE *TRUE EXIT* FROM THIS CAVERN, I SHALL *KNOW* IT SOON ENOUGH! IF *NOT...*

...THEN I PRAY MY AMAZON SISTERS WILL *FORGIVE* ME FOR MY *FAILURE!*

BUT NO MATTER THE *CONSEQUENCES* NOW, THERE CAN BE NO THOUGHT OF *TURNING BACK!*

MY FUTURE LIES *AHEAD* OF ME--

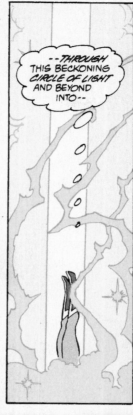

--THROUGH THIS BECKONING *CIRCLE OF LIGHT* AND BEYOND INTO--

-- *WHAT--?!?*

THE *LIQUID LIGHT* HAS BECOME A *STORM-TOSSED SKY!*

BY *HERA!* THAT *PLANE--?!?*

HAVE THE GODS RETURNED ME TO THAT FATEFUL MOMENT WHEN *STEVE TREVOR* ALMOST DESTROYED *PARADISE ISLAND?*

IT WOULD SEEM *SO--* AND YET THE PLANE LOOKS SOMEHOW *DIFFERENT!*

WELCOME, *DIANA!* BOREAS GREETS THEE--

-- AS MY OBEDIENT WINDS SWEEP AWAY THE GREAT MYSTERY THAT IMPEDES THY QUEST FOR *FULFILLMENT!*

I--I DON'T *UNDERSTAND--!*

I CANNOT CONTROL MY *FLIGHT--!*

PLUNGING STILL *DEEPER--* INTO AN UNKNOWN *SEA--!*

19

267

IT SEEMS *IMPOSSIBLE*-- BUT I CAN STLL *BREATHE!*

IS THIS MERELY ANOTHER *ILLUSION* OR--

--*NO!* IT IS THE *WRECKAGE* OF THAT SAME *PLANE* I SAW *ABOVE*--!

TOO DAMAGED TO *IDENTIFY*-- BUT WHAT *ELSE* COULD IT BE BUT COLONEL TREVOR'S *PHANTOM JET?*

POSEIDON WELCOMES THEE, *DAUGHTER!*

THOU HAST ENTERED INTO A PORTION OF THINE OWN *ESSENCE,* CHILD-- AND THOU MUST HAVE *FAITH!*

FOR, AS THE *SEA* WASHES AWAY THE *MYSTERY* THOU HAST FOR SO LONG PONDERED--

--SO SHALT THOU MEET WHO THOU TRULY *ART!*

20

SUDDENLY I REST UPON THE *OCEAN BOTTOM*-- AS IF IT WERE *DRY LAND?!?*

MY BODY IS NOT EVEN *WET!*

IF MIGHTY POSEIDON KNOWS THE *REASON* FOR THIS MADNESS, HE DOES NOT *SAY*-- NOR WOULD I TRULY *EXPECT* HIM TO!

THERE IS THE RUINED *PLANE*-- YET GLEAMING AS IF IT WERE *NEW?!?*

STILL, IT SEEMS SOMEHOW *SMALLER* THAN I REMEMBER IT--!

THOUGH I HAVE FELT A SPECIAL *BOND* WITH COL. TREVOR, I HAVE NEVER UNDERSTOOD WHY...

...COULD THIS BE THE GODS' WAY OF *EXPLAINING* THAT BOND?

AND YET I SEE NOW THIS IS *NOT* THE SAME PLANE--!

IT SEEMS AN *OLDER* MODEL--LESS *SOPHISTICATED*--!

THEN *WHY*--?!?

HELLO, PRINCESS!

I'VE BEEN WAITING A LONG *TIME* FOR YOUR *ARRIVAL!*

WHO--?!?

YOU--YOU SPEAK *AMERICAN?!*

FOR AS LONG AS I CAN *REMEMBER.*

YOU'RE PRETTY *FLUENT* IN IT YOURSELF.

THAT BLINDING *LIGHT*--! I CANNOT *SEE* YOU--!

SORRY--GUESS I'VE GROWN *ACCUSTOMED* TO IT OVER THE YEARS.

THERE! IN A FEW SECONDS, YOU'LL BE ABLE TO SEE *CLEARLY*...

NO--IT CANNOT *BE*--!

THAT *ARMOR*-- THE *COAT-OF-ARMS* YOU WEAR--!

21

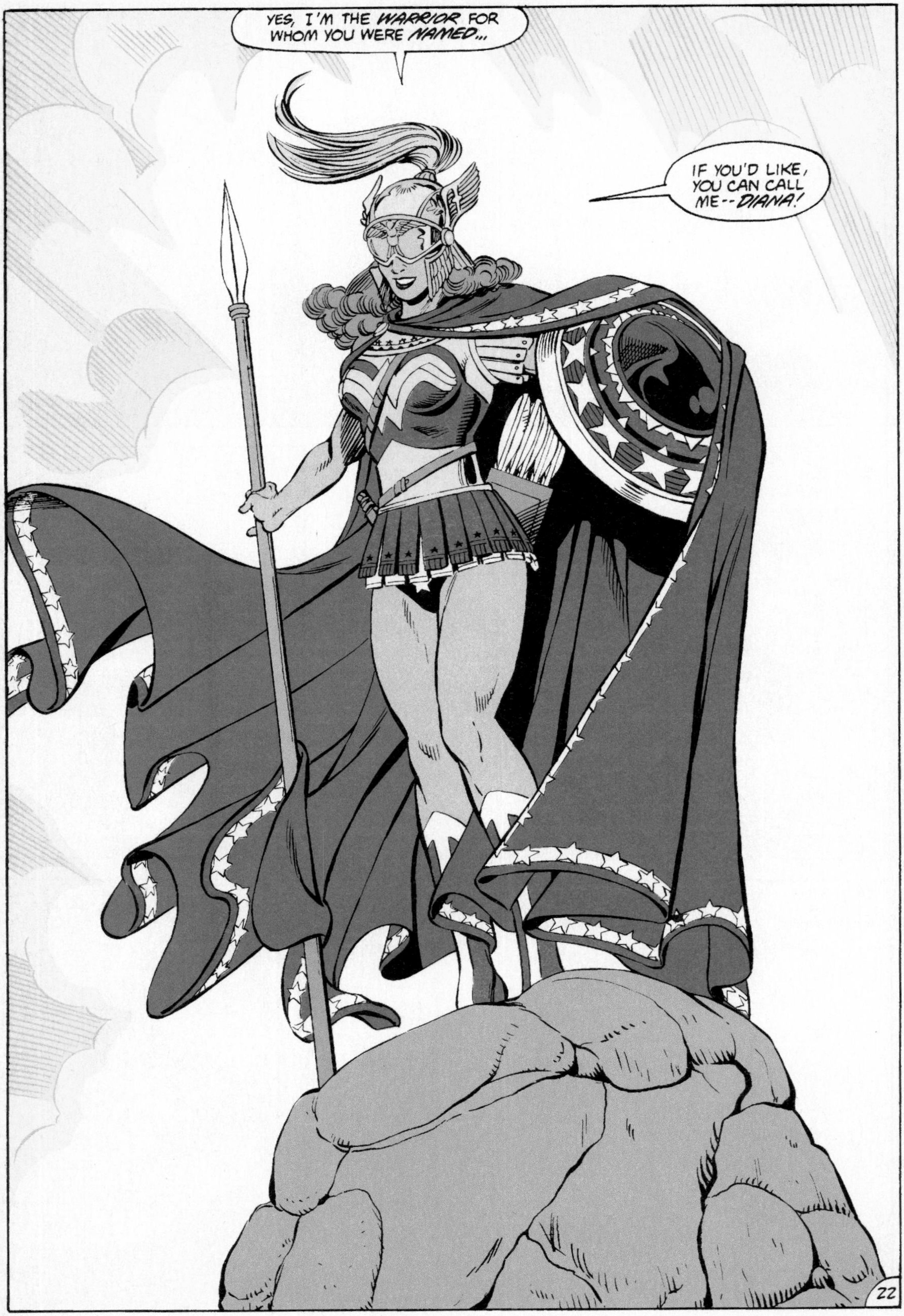
YES, I'M THE WARRIOR FOR WHOM YOU WERE NAMED...
IF YOU'D LIKE, YOU CAN CALL ME--DIANA!
22

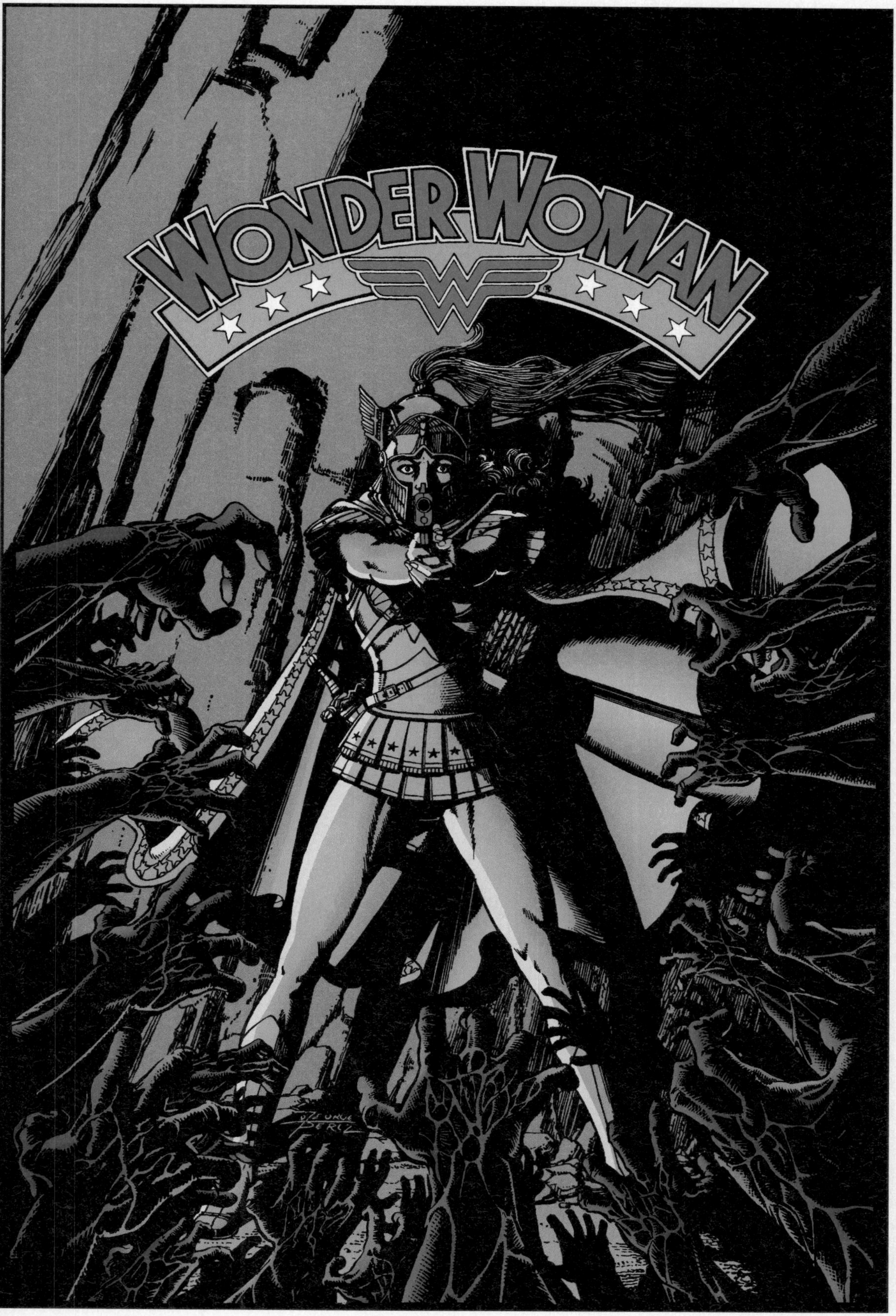
WONDER WOMAN

DOOM'S DOORWAY:

HERE IN THE DANK BOWELS OF PARADISE ISLAND, THERE IS ONLY *DARKNESS*--

THE *HILT* OF A *SHATTERED DAGGER* --

-- AND THE HASTY IMPRINT OF SANDALED FEET...

AN INSTANT AGO, AN ETERNITY AGO, THE AMAZON PRINCESS *DIANA* PASSED THROUGH THIS SEETHING PORTAL TO MEET THE *CHALLENGE* OF THE GODS...

NOW HER MOTHER, THE *WARRIOR-QUEEN HIPPOLYTE,* FOLLOWS...

IT APPEARS MY FEATHERED COMPANION HAS GREAT *INFLUENCE* IN THIS UNHOLY REALM...

DOOM'S DOORWAY CRACKED JUST WIDE ENOUGH TO *ADMIT* ME-- THEN SLAMMED *SHUT* ONCE MORE BEHIND!

STILL, I WONDER WHAT HAS HAPPENED TO *COTTUS,* HE WHO IS SAID TO DWELL AT THE *ENTRANCE* TO--

--EH?

THAT *SOUND*-- LIKE THE GROWING RUSTLE OF LEAVES IN A *STORM*--!?!

"FROM *THE* DARKNESS, *DEMONS*--

"--THE ROAR OF THEIR WINGS ALMOST *DEAFENING*--!"

IS THIS WHAT MY WANDERING *DAUGHTER* FACED WHEN SHE PASSED THIS WAY *BEFORE* ME?

IF *SO,* THESE VILE CREATURES SHALL NOT FIND HER MOTHER *WANTING!*

I AM HOPELESSLY *OUTNUMBERED*--YET THE VULTURE THAT *LED* ME HERE MAKES NO MOVE TO *HELP!*

OBVIOUSLY, IT IS HERE MERELY AS A *GUIDE*, NOT AS AN *ALLY!*

THUS IT REMAINS FOR *ME* TO STAND OR FALL ALONE!

HAVE TO GAIN *LEVEL GROUND*-- WIDEN THE FIELD OF *BATTLE*--!

IT SEEMS THE STRENGTH OF MY *SWORD-ARM* ALONE WILL NOT WIN THE DAY HERE--

--BUT I CAME PREPARED FOR *MORE* THAN BATTLE!

I BROUGHT *OIL* TO MAKE *TORCHES*, IF NECESSARY--

--ENOUGH OIL TO ALMOST *FILL* THE BOWL OF MY SHIELD--

--AS WELL AS STONE AND *FLINT*--

-- TO STRIKE THE NECESSARY *SPARK!*

AS I EXPECTED, DEMONS BORN OF DARKNESS *FEAR* THE BRIGHT FLAMES!

WELL, THEY SHALL LEARN TO FEAR THEM *MORE!*

AND THE BLAZING DEMONS SPIRAL *SCREAMING* DOWN INTO THE HUNGRY DEPTHS...

2

273

ENID, OKLAHOMA:

THE MODEST HOME OF EVERETT AND EDNA AANONSON, ELDERLY AUNT AND UNCLE OF AIR FORCE COLONEL STEPHEN TREVOR--

--WHO HAS FINALLY COME HOME AFTER ALL THESE YEARS--

--JUST IN TIME FOR HIS FATHER'S FUNERAL...

I'M SORRY I DIDN'T GET HERE SOONER, DAD--

--BUT BETWEEN THE ARES PROJECT AND MY MISSION WITH CAPT. SCOTT, I DIDN'T GET THE WORD TILL IT WAS TOO LATE.

THERE'S SO MUCH I WANTED TO TELL YOU... ONE LAST TIME.

YOU WERE ALWAYS THERE FOR ME, DAD...

AFTER MOM DIED, YOU WERE EVERY-THING TO ME...

...FATHER...MOTHER ...AND THE BEST DAMN SOLDIER I EVER KNEW!

"THOSE SUMMERS TOGETHER ON THE LAKE WILL ALWAYS BE SPECIAL TO ME--

"--AS YOU WERE SPECIAL!"

EVEN WHEN YOU WEREN'T THERE, I NEVER FELT ALONE.

YOU AND MOM HAVE ALWAYS BEEN A PART OF ME--

--AND ALWAYS WILL BE.

"I ALWAYS WANTED YOU TO BE PROUD OF ME--

"--THAT LOOK IN YOUR EYES WHEN I GRADUATED FROM THE ACADEMY MEANT MORE TO ME THAN ANY MEDAL--"

--SO I HOPE YOU'LL UNDERSTAND MY DECISION!

I JUST WISH I COULD HAVE TOLD YOU ONE LAST TIME, DAD...

THANK YOU FOR BEING MY FATHER!

WAS THIS REALLY STEVE'S MOTHER, MRS. AANONSON?

THE NAME IS EDNA -- AND YES, IT WAS! WE LOST HER NEARLY 90 YEARS AGO. PERTY NEAR BROKE ULYSSES STEPHEN'S HEART.

WE TOOK YOUNG STEVIE IN FER A SPELL TILL U.S. COULD LOOK AFTER HIM PROPER.

BOY COULDN'T HAVE ASKED FOR A BETTER FATHER.

S'FUNNY. I'VE KNOWN STEVE FOR YEARS, BUT HE'S NEVER REALLY TALKED MUCH ABOUT HIS MOTHER.

WHAT WAS HER NAME?

IT WAS... DIANA!

3

DIANA?!?

THEN *YOU*--?

ARE THE ONE FOR WHOM YOU'RE *NAMED?*

THAT'S *ME*, DIANA-- THAT SAME MYSTERIOUS *WARRIOR* YOUR MOTHER AND SISTERS WOULD NEVER *DISCUSS* WITH YOU!

I'VE *AWAITED* THIS DAY FAR *LONGER* THAN YOU COULD *IMAGINE*--

--BUT IF THERE'S ANYTHING I'VE *LEARNED* HERE, IT'S THAT LIFE ON THE *MORTAL COIL* FOLLOWS A GRAND DESIGN!

WE WERE *FATED* TO MEET, CHILD-- FROM THE DAY YOU WERE *BORN!*

IT'S *TIME* YOU LEARNED OF YOUR TRUE *HERITAGE!*

BUT THE *CHALLENGE OF THE GODS*--?!?

CHALLENGES COME IN *MANY* FORMS, PRINCESS...

THE CHALLENGE TO ACCEPT YOUR OWN *SIGNIFICANCE* IS IN MANY WAYS MORE *DIFFICULT* THAN BATTLING ANY *HYDRA!*

BETTER *SIT DOWN*, DIANA-- WE HAVE A LOT TO *TALK* ABOUT.

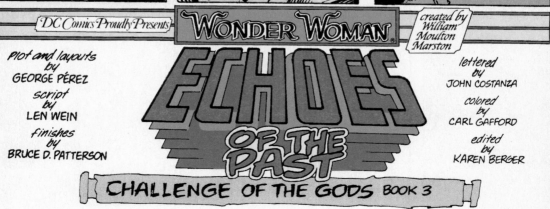

DC Comics Proudly Presents

WONDER WOMAN

created by William Moulton Marston

ECHOES OF THE PAST

plot and layouts by GEORGE PÉREZ

script by LEN WEIN

finishes by BRUCE D. PATTERSON

lettered by JOHN COSTANZA

colored by CARL GAFFORD

edited by KAREN BERGER

CHALLENGE OF THE GODS BOOK 3

FOR STARTERS, I WAS BORN *DIANA ROCKWELL*, IN A PLACE CALLED *OMAHA, NEBRASKA*, AND WE HAVE A LOT IN COMMON, YOU AND I--

--BOTH OF US ARE FIERCELY *INDEPENDENT*, DOWNRIGHT *MULE-HEADED* THEY'D CALL US BACK HOME--

--AND WE WERE BOTH BORN WITH A LOVE OF *FLYING!*

WHILE *OTHER* GIRLS MY AGE WANTED TO BE WIVES AND MOTHERS, I WANTED TO BE *AIRBORNE!*

EVER SINCE I SAW THE MOVIE *"WINGS"* WHEN I WAS SEVEN, I KNEW THAT WAS MY *DESTINY.*

"SO, WHILE STILL A TEEN-AGER, I BECAME WHAT WAS THEN CALLED A BARN-STORMER"--

"--AND PUTTING A *PT-19* THROUGH ITS PACES BECAME THE BIGGEST THRILL OF MY LIFE!"

"ONLY ONE THING EVER MATCHED THAT EXCITEMENT-- THE DAY A YOUNG *LIEUTENANT* ARRIVED TO ASK ABOUT PURCHASING MY PLANES..."

"GUESS THE POOR GUY GOT MORE THAN HE BARGAINED FOR--

"--BECAUSE, ON *NOVEMBER 8, 1940,* I BECAME MRS. LT. ULYSSES STEPHEN TREVOR!"

TREVOR?

STEPHEN TREVOR IS...

"ABOUT A YEAR LATER, EVERY-THING WENT *CRAZY* FOR U.S. AND ME--

EXTRA

OMAHA OBSERVER 2¢

JAPS BOMB PEARL HARBOR

WAR FEARED!

EXTRA OMAHA

DEC 7, 1941

"--WHEN AMERICA SUDDENLY FOUND ITSELF SMACK IN THE MIDDLE OF THE *SECOND WORLD WAR...*"

"HOWEVER, MY OWN ENTRY INTO THE FRAY WAS DELAYED BY A WELCOME ARRIVAL...

"JUST WEEKS AFTER THE SNEAK ATTACK ON *PEARL HARBOR,* I GAVE BIRTH TO OUR SON *STEPHEN...*"

...YOUR SON?!?

5

DO YOU MEAN TO TELL ME THAT YOUR *SON* IS THE SAME MAN WHO ALMOST *DESTROYED* PARADISE ISLAND--

--THEN FOUGHT *BESIDE* ME AGAINST THE MINIONS OF *ARES?*

ARES ALWAYS *DID* HAVE AN ACUTE SENSE OF *IRONY!* GUESS USING MY SON AS A *PAWN* WAS TOO MUCH OF A *TEMPTATION* FOR HIM!

STILL, ARES HIMSELF WAS ONLY A PAWN OF THE *FATES!*

BY *USING* STEVE, HE MERELY RE-AFFIRMED THE SPECIAL *BOND* BETWEEN YOU AND MY SON.

NOW, IF I MIGHT *CONTINUE...?*

"THOUGH I'D BEEN ASKED TO TRAIN OTHER PILOTS, IN LATE '42, I JOINED THE *WOMEN'S AUXILIARY FERRYING SQUADRON...*"

"OF COURSE, THE ENEMY COULDN'T *TELL*--AND PROBABLY DIDN'T *CARE*--IF IT WAS A *WOMAN* FLYING THOSE PLANES..."

"...SO WE WERE FREQUENTLY USED FOR *TARGET PRACTICE*..."

"WITH *BOTH* OF HIS PARENTS IN THE *SERVICE,* YOUNG STEPHEN STAYED WITH U.S.'S SISTER'S FAMILY--"

"--THOUGH I MADE A *POINT* OF WRITING TO THEM BOTH EVERY *DAY*.."

"THOSE WERE THE *LONGEST* DAYS OF MY LIFE, BUT THEY ALL CAME TO AN *EXPLOSIVE END* IN EARLY AUGUST OF 1945--"

"--WHEN AMERICA DROPPED THE FIRST *ATOMIC BOMBS* ON THE JAPANESE CITIES OF *HIROSHIMA* AND *NAGASAKI!*..."

"HOWEVER, THE FATE OF THOSE 120,000 DEAD MEANT *LITTLE* TO US THEN..."

"ALL WE KNEW WAS THAT WE WERE ALL *TOGETHER* AGAIN-- FINALLY A *FAMILY*..."

I HONESTLY INTENDED TO BECOME THE KIND OF WIFE AND MOTHER U.S. *WANTED* ME TO BE--BUT IT JUST WASN'T *ENOUGH!*

THAT'S WHEN I MADE MY *FATEFUL DECISION*...

6

IN THE BOWELS OF PARADISE ISLAND, SOMEWHERE BETWEEN DIANA AND THE QUESTING HIPPOLYTE...

THE AMAZON PRINCESS FARED FAR *BETTER* THAN I WOULD HAVE *EXPECTED*...

'TWAS NO *EASY* TASK TO DESTROY SUCH AS THE *HYDRA*--

--BUT, EVEN IN *DEATH*, THE SEVEN-HEADED SERPENT MAY YET KNOW THE SWEET TASTE OF *VENGEANCE!*

I HAVE *PLUCKED* ITS STILL-SMOLDERING *TEETH*--

--AND THEY, IF PROPERLY *PLANTED*, SHALL MAKE CERTAIN THE UNSPOKEN SECRET OF *PAN* IS KEPT ETERNALLY *SAFE!*

WHAT DEMONS WERE NOT *INCINERATED* BY MY FLAMES HAVE FLED FROM ITS *LIGHT*--

--THUS I'M *FREE* TO FOLLOW MY SILENT GUIDE IN SEARCH OF MY *DAUGHTER!*

THE VULTURE PASSES THROUGH THAT ANCIENT *PORTAL* AHEAD--

--AND WHEREVER IT *GOES*, I MUST *FOLLOW!*

IT SEEMS A *BATTLE* WAS RECENTLY FOUGHT HERE--!

THE SIGNS OF CARNAGE ARE *FRESH*--!

AND *THERE*, HALF-SUNK IN THE MOLTEN MIASMA, THE SKULL OF SOME HIDEOUS SERPENT--!

WHERE I *TREAD* FROM THIS STEP FORWARD, I MUST TREAD *CARE-FULLY*--!!

7

278

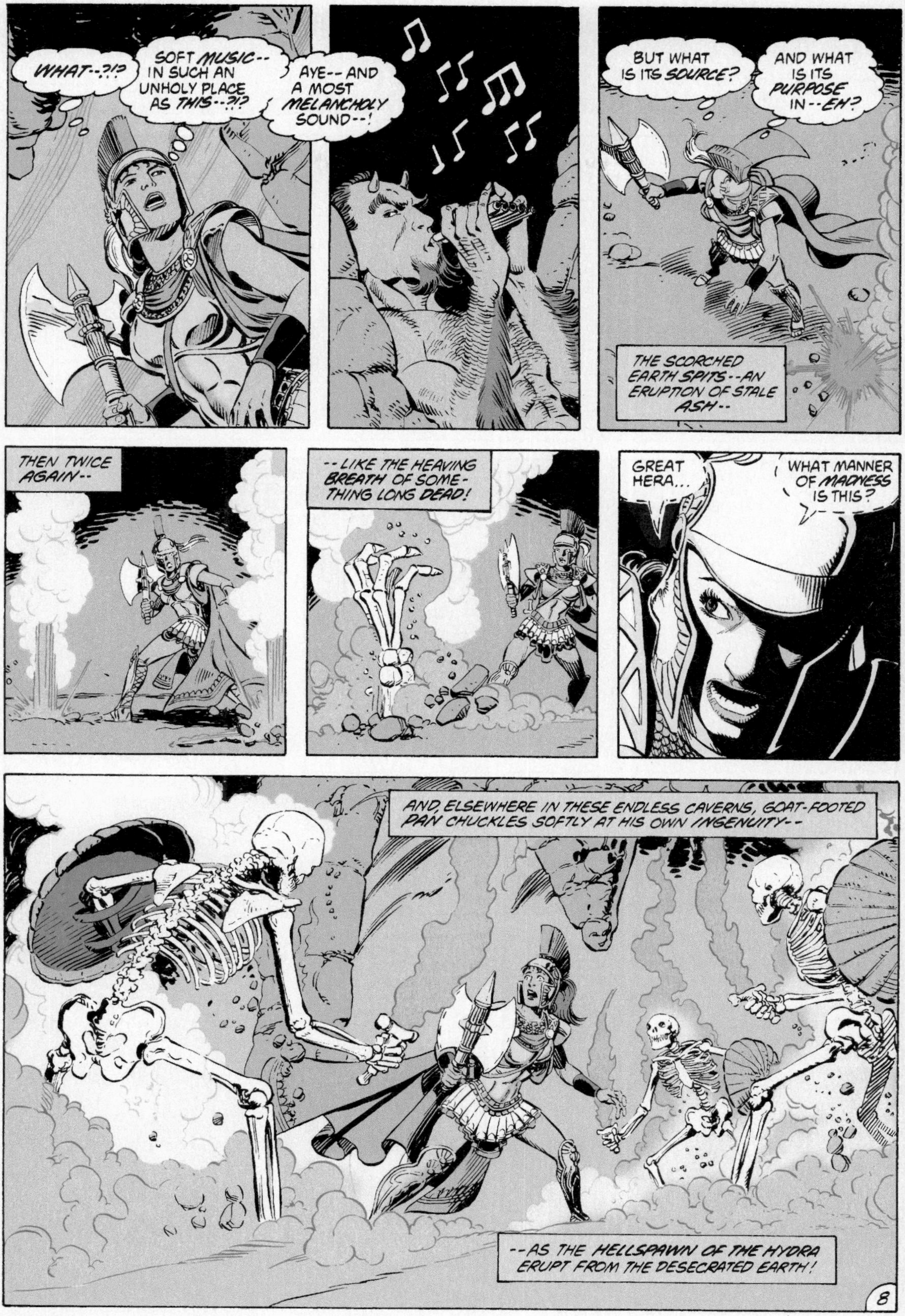

WHAT--?!?
SOFT MUSIC-- IN SUCH AN UNHOLY PLACE AS THIS--?!?
AYE-- AND A MOST MELANCHOLY SOUND--!
BUT WHAT IS ITS SOURCE?
AND WHAT IS ITS PURPOSE IN--EH?
THE SCORCHED EARTH SPITS--AN ERUPTION OF STALE ASH--
THEN TWICE AGAIN--
--LIKE THE HEAVING BREATH OF SOMETHING LONG DEAD!
GREAT HERA...
WHAT MANNER OF MADNESS IS THIS?
AND, ELSEWHERE IN THESE ENDLESS CAVERNS, GOAT-FOOTED PAN CHUCKLES SOFTLY AT HIS OWN INGENUITY--
--AS THE HELLSPAWN OF THE HYDRA ERUPT FROM THE DESECRATED EARTH!
8

AT THE AANONSON HOME, PREPARATIONS FOR THE FUNERAL HAVE ALL BEEN MADE...

THE MILITARY CHAPLAIN HAS COME AND GONE--

--AND THE NIGHT IS FILLED WITH *MEMORIES*...

MY *GOD,* STEVE -- YOU WERE SUCH A CUTE *BABY!*

SO I'M *TOLD,* ETTA...

SORT OF MAKES YOU WONDER WHERE I WENT *WRONG!*

GEE, WHEN WAS *THIS* ONE TAKEN?

THANKSGIVING OF '48, I THINK--! I REMEMBER THE FOLKS TALKING ABOUT HOW *GREAT* IT WOULD BE TO FINALLY CELEBRATE A *CHRISTMAS* TOGETHER.

SEE THAT *JACKET,* ETTA?

MOM PUT IT TOGETHER FROM VARIOUS *PATCHES* AND HER *WAFS INSIGNIA* WHEN SHE BECAME A *TRANSPORT PILOT...*

IT WAS THE *LAST* THING I EVER *SAW* HER IN.

BEING A *PILOT* MEANT MAKING *SACRIFICES,* PRINCESS--

--THOUGH I THINK MY POOR SON MADE FAR *MORE* OF THEM!

"I TRIED TO EXPLAIN TO STEVIE THAT I MIGHT MISS HIS *BIRTHDAY,* BUT WOULD DEFINITELY BE HOME FOR CHRISTMAS...

"SEE, THE MILITARY WAS WAITING FOR THE NEW *SABRE JET*-- AND I REALLY WANTED TO *FLY* THAT BABY...

"BUT WHEN I KISSED STEVIE GOOD-BYE, HE DIDN'T KISS ME *BACK...*

"...GUESS HE DIDN'T REALLY *BELIEVE* HE'D SEE ME FOR CHRISTMAS..

"POOR BABY... I STILL WONDER HOW HE KNEW..."

9

"I TRIED TO FORGET STEVIE'S TEARS BY BURYING MYSELF IN MY WORK -- SPECIFICALLY, IN THE COCKPIT OF THE PROTOTYPE SABRE JET..."

"JETS WERE STILL *NEW* TO ME -- AND THE *THRILL* MADE ME FORGET EVERYTHING EXCEPT THE SHEER *JOY* OF FLYING..."

"I'M STILL NOT SURE EXACTLY WHEN IT *STARTED* --"

"-- BUT I SUDDENLY FOUND MYSELF IN THE THICK OF THE WORST *LIGHTNING* STORM I'D EVER ENCOUNTERED..."

"MY INSTRUMENTS WENT COMPLETELY *WILD...* SUDDENLY, NOTHING MADE SENSE ANYMORE..."

"THEN, A LIGHTNING-BOLT SHATTERED MY *LEFT* WING!"

"EVERYTHING HAPPENED PRETTY *QUICKLY* AFTER THAT..."

"I MANAGED TO *EJECT* IN TIME -- BUT THE BUFFETING WINDS SWEPT ME BACK TOWARDS THE PLUMMETING PLANE..."

"THEN, BY WHAT I THOUGHT WAS A ONE-IN-A-MILLION FLUKE, THE SHEARED WING RIPPED MY *PARACHUTE* --"

"-- AND THE SABRE JET AND I PLUNGED LIKE ROCKS INTO THE CHURNING SEA..."

"THE IMPACT OF MY FALL KNOCKED ME SENSELESS --"

"-- BUT EVEN AS I LOST *CONSCIOUSNESS* --"

"-- I COULD SWEAR THE WATER CAME *ALIVE!*"

SUDDENLY...

...MY *LIFE* WAS IN THE HANDS OF THE *GODS!*

10

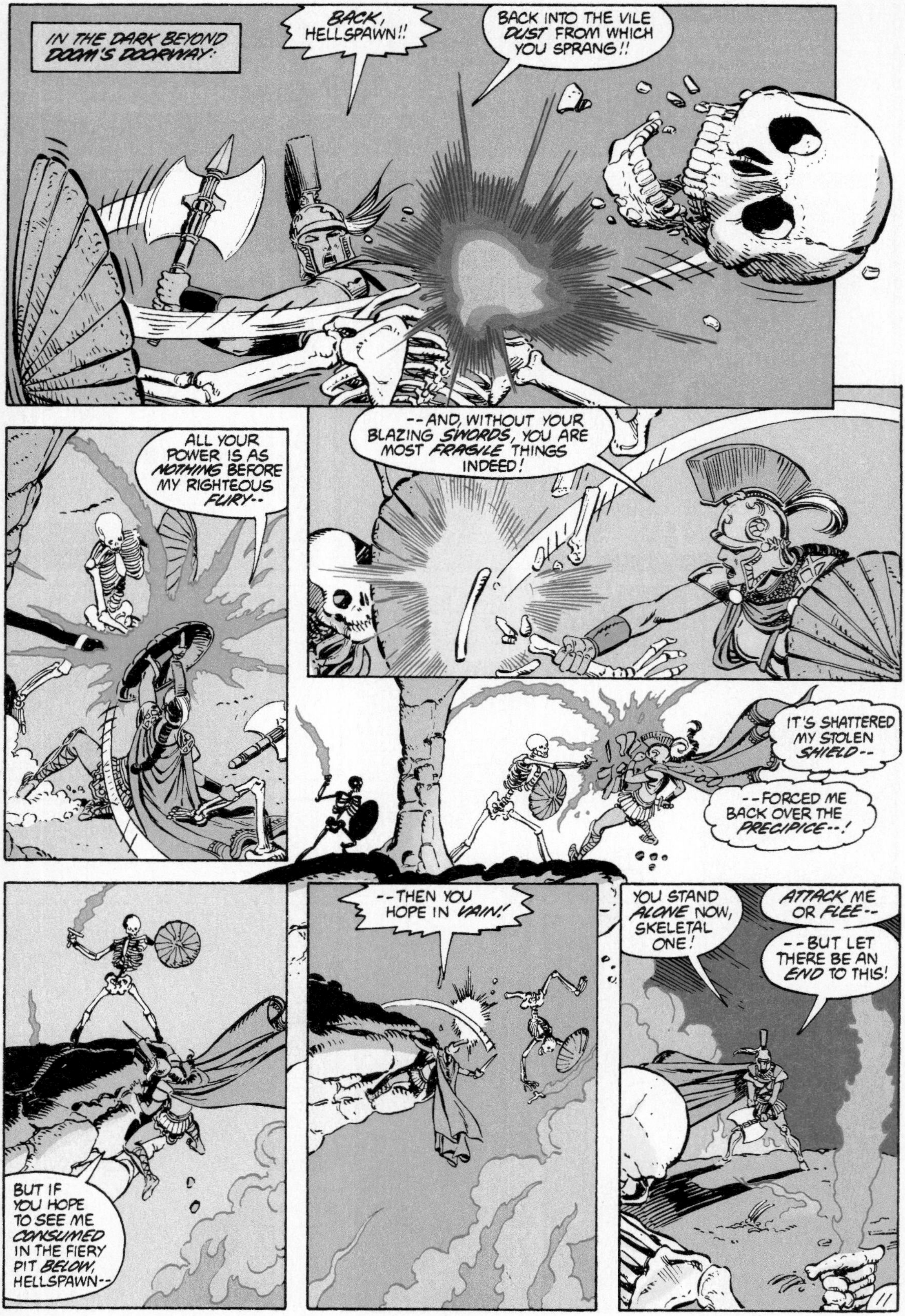
IN THE DARK BEYOND DOOM'S DOORWAY:
BACK, HELLSPAWN!!
BACK INTO THE VILE DUST FROM WHICH YOU SPRANG!!
ALL YOUR POWER IS AS NOTHING BEFORE MY RIGHTEOUS FURY--
--AND, WITHOUT YOUR BLAZING SWORDS, YOU ARE MOST FRAGILE THINGS INDEED!
IT'S SHATTERED MY STOLEN SHIELD--
--FORCED ME BACK OVER THE PRECIPICE--!
BUT IF YOU HOPE TO SEE ME CONSUMED IN THE FIERY PIT BELOW, HELLSPAWN--
--THEN YOU HOPE IN VAIN!
YOU STAND ALONE NOW, SKELETAL ONE!
ATTACK ME OR FLEE--
--BUT LET THERE BE AN END TO THIS!

VERY *WELL*--

--YOU HAVE MADE YOUR *CHOICE!*

NOW SUFFER THE *CONSEQUENCES!!*

IN HADES' *NAME,* I SEND YOU *BACK* TO HIM!!

MY BATTLEAXE CLEFT THE CREATURE IN *TWAIN*-- AND ITS FLAMING SWORD STRUCK MY *LEFT* SHOULDER!

STILL, THE WOUND WILL *HEAL* --ASSUMING I MANAGE TO *SURVIVE* THIS!

AHEAD STAND THE TWIN *PORTALS* TO WHICH THE VULTURE LED ME--

--BUT *WHICH* IS THE ONE THROUGH WHICH MY *DAUGHTER* PASSED?

TO MAKE THE *WRONG* CHOICE NOW COULD PROVE *FATAL* TO US *BOTH*--!

. . . .

THAT CURSED *WAILING*-- SO UNBEARABLY *LOUD*--!

WHY WON'T IT *STOP?!?*

BECOMING DIFFICULT TO *THINK*--!

YET, DESPITE HIPPOLYTE'S *PROTESTS,* THE ETERNAL MOANING OF THE PILLAR OF PALLOR GROWS EVER LOUDER...

2

--UNTIL THE BLEAK BIRD WHO HAS BEEN HER CONSTANT COMPANION IN THIS DARK REALM SWOOPS SILENTLY FORWARD--

--ITS DARK EYES SPEAKING TO THE WAILING PILLAR IN A LANGUAGE BEYOND WORDS--

--AS IF IT SOMEHOW UNDERSTANDS THE CREATURE'S PAIN...

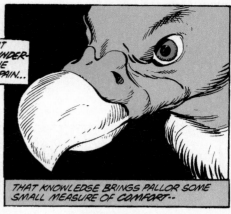

THAT KNOWLEDGE BRINGS PALLOR SOME SMALL MEASURE OF COMFORT--

--AND WITH COMFORT, FOR THE FIRST TIME IN THE MOURNFUL PILLAR'S ENDLESS EXISTENCE, THERE COMES PEACE...

THE PILLAR HAS GROWN SILENT-- AND THUS MY MIND GROWS CLEAR ONCE MORE.

THIS WAS SOMEHOW THE VULTURE'S DOING...

OBVIOUSLY, MY FEATHERED FRIEND INTENDS TO SEE ME SAFE TO MY DESTINATION--

--WHEREVER THAT MAY BE!

THE VULTURE TOOK THE LEFT PORTAL-- AND THUS DO I FOLLOW!

AND MAY HERA HELP ME ALONG MY WAY!

SO...THE CURSED AMAZON CHOSE THE PROPER PORTAL!

NO MATTER!

IN THE END, PAN SHALL STILL STAND TRIUMPHANT!

FOR, WITHOUT HER DAUGHTER HERE TO HELP HER--

--HIPPOLYTE SHALL MOST CERTAINLY PERISH!

13

"WHEN I FINALLY REGAINED *CONSCIOUSNESS*, I FOUND MYSELF ON AN ALIEN *SHORE*--

"-- THE COOL *SAND* PRESSED AGAINST MY CHEEK, WARM *WAVES* LAPPING AT MY FEET--

"--AND, IN THE DISTANCE, A SUDDEN, SAVAGE *ROARING* THAT COULD HAVE AWAKENED THE *DEAD*...

"AS I STAGGERED TO MY FEET, I COULD SEE IN THE DISTANCE AN AWESOME DISPLAY OF *ENERGY.*

"--AND I HEARD *VOICES* SHOUTING-- *FEMALE* VOICES...

"I CHECKED MY *SIDEARM*-- SAW IT HADN'T BEEN *DAMAGED*-- AND HEADED TOWARDS THE *DISTURBANCE*...

"I GUESS *BRIGHT* WAS NEVER MY *LONG SUIT*...

"SEVERAL HUNDRED YARDS IN, I ENTERED AN OPEN AREA MARKED BY A CLASSICALLY-DESIGNED COLUMN...

"BEYOND THE COLUMN STOOD THE ENTRANCE TO A *CAVERN*--

"-- THE *SOURCE*, IT SEEMED, OF THOSE INCREDIBLE ENERGIES...

"HEART POUNDING, I STEPPED INTO THE DARKNESS--

"--AND IMMEDI-ATELY WISHED I HADN'T!

"BEFORE ME, A SQUAD OF *WOMAN WARRIORS* STRUGGLED AGAINST THE MULTI-HANDED *MONSTER* WHO SOUGHT TO ESCAPE THROUGH THE CRACKS IN *DOOM'S DOORWAY*...

"I LATER LEARNED THE MONSTER'S NAME WAS *COTTUS*...

14

APPARENTLY, COTTUS HAD BROKEN THROUGH DURING A *PRAYER RITUAL* CONDUCTED BY THE ORACLE MENALIPPE, WHO WAS NOW IN THE CREATURE'S CLUTCHES...

"I WATCHED IN HORROR AS THE AMAZON CAPTAIN CALLED PHILIPPUS WAS STRUCK DOWN BY THE FLAILING ARMS...

"I DIDN'T NEED TO UNDERSTAND ANCIENT *GREEK* TO RECOGNIZE PHILIPPUS' CRIES OF PAIN AS COTTUS TRIED TO TEAR HER APART--

"--AND, WITHOUT HESITATION, I *OPENED FIRE!*

"LORD ONLY KNOWS WHAT POOR PHILIPPUS *THOUGHT* AS SHE TURNED--

"--TO SEE A *MADWOMAN* STANDING THERE, BLASTING AWAY AT HER TORMENTOR...

"COTTUS, MEANWHILE, DECIDED COWARDICE WAS THE BETTER PART OF *SURVIVAL,* AND DUCKED BACK BEYOND THE PORTAL--

"-- TAKING MENALIPPE WITH HIM!

"ORDERING HER SOLDIERS TO PREPARE TO TIGHTEN THE *SEAL* ONCE MORE, PHILIPPUS CHARGED AFTER COTTUS--

"--AND, LIKE A TRUE *MADWOMAN,* I WENT AFTER HER!

"EVEN AS I REACHED PHILIPPUS, COTTUS SWATTED HER ASIDE LIKE A TOY--

"--BUT YOUR CAPTAIN SPRANG BACK TO HER FEET, BATTLEAXE RAISED AND READY--

"--WHILE I EMPTIED HALF AN AMMO CLIP INTO THE MONSTER...

"STILL, THE HANDS OF COTTUS SEEMED TO BE EVERYWHERE, GRABBING, CLUTCHING...

"I FELT MY SKULL BEING CRUSHED, OTHER PARTS OF ME TORN AWAY...

"AND THROUGH MY OVER-WHELMING PAIN, AS MENA-LIPPE WAS DRAGGED DOWN AND PHILIPPUS STRUGGLED VALIANTLY BUT IN VAIN--

"--I COULD SEE TWO BALEFUL CRIMSON EYES GLOWERING AT ME FROM THE SHADOWS...

"WITH WHAT LITTLE STRENGTH REMAINED IN ME, I AIMED DIRECTLY BETWEEN THOSE TWO COLD EYES--

"--AND SQUEEZED THE TRIGGER!

"THE LAST THING I SAW BEFORE OBLIVION OVERTOOK ME WAS THE BLINDING MUZZLE FLASH...

"THE LAST THING I HEARD WAS THUNDER..."

IT WAS THE DAY BEFORE CHRISTMAS...

"I'LL NEVER FORGET THE LOOK ON MY DAD'S FACE AS HE CAME INTO THE ROOM, HOLDING A TELEGRAM--

"HIS EYES SAID IT ALL..."

I WOULD NEVER SEE MY MOTHER AGAIN.

16

EVERYTHING WAS PRETTY MUCH A *BLUR* FOR A WHILE AFTER THAT.

I CAN VAGUELY REMEMBER WHISPERING MY *NAME* TO SOMEBODY WHO *HELD* ME...

...AND THEN I *DIED*.

YOU... *WHAT?!?*

SHE *DIED*, CHILD--

--SO THAT HER *NEW* LIFE COULD FINALLY *BEGIN!*

WHO--?!?

FEAR *NOT*, CHILD, FOR THOU DOST NOT FACE AN *ENEMY*. I AM *HADES*-- MOST *INEVITABLE* OF THE GODS.

ONLY THOSE WHO HAVE *WASTED* LIFE NEED FEAR ME-- FOR THE *UNDERWORLD* HOLDS NO TERROR FOR THE INNOCENT, WISE, AND BRAVE.

I AM HERE TO *COMPLETE* THE NARRATIVE OF THE *LIVING*--

--AND BEGIN THE NARRATIVE OF THE *DEAD!*

"SINCE DIANA TREVOR PERISHED IN SERVICE TO THE AMAZON RACE, HIPPOLYTE VOWED SHE WOULD BE GIVEN A *WARRIOR'S* FUNERAL..."

"BATTLE ARMOR AND A COAT-OF-ARMS WERE *FORGED*, THE TATTERED REMAINS OF DIANA'S CLOTHING PROVIDING THE STANDARD...

"TWO SUCH SUITS OF ARMOR WERE FASHIONED...

"*ONE* WAS WORN BY DIANA TREVOR ON HER *FIERY* JOURNEY TO THE *UNDERWORLD*...

"THE *SECOND* SUIT-- AS WELL AS THE MYSTERIOUS *WEAPON* DIANA HAD WIELDED-- WAS SEALED AWAY IN A PLACE OF *HONOR*--

"--UNTIL THE WEAPON COULD ULTIMATELY BE USED TO HELP DETERMINE ONE WORTHY TO WEAR DIANA'S MANTLE--"

-- THE MANTLE *THOU* DOST NOW WEAR, PRINCESS--

-- THE MANTLE OF THE *WARRIOR!*

IT IS TIME TO GO NOW, DIANA TREVOR.

I'VE BEEN *WAITING* FOR THIS MOMENT, HADES.

THEN THY LONG WAIT AT LAST IS *OVER.*

"COME, DIANA -- A LOVED ONE SHALL BE *WAITING* FOR THEE IN THE ELYSIAN FIELDS..."

GUESS I HAVE TO *LEAVE* YOU NOW, CHILD...

I JUST HOPE THE *KNOWLEDGE* YOU'VE GAINED WILL HELP *GUIDE* YOU.

I'VE PLACED ALL MY *HOPES* IN YOU WHO BEARS MY *FIRST* NAME--

--AND IN HIM WHO BEARS MY *OTHER* NAMES...

STEPHEN ROCKWELL TREVOR.

I JUST *REMEMBERED* SOMETHING, ETTA--

--SOMETHING I ONCE *TOLD* DAD...

OH DEAR GOD...

STEVE...?

"IT WAS A NIGHT SOON AFTER MOM *DISAPPEARED...*

"AT THE TIME, I THOUGHT IT WAS A *DREAM*--

"--BUT IT SEEMED SO *REAL...*

"I SAW MY *MOTHER* STANDING OVER ME, *COMFORTING* ME...

"DAD SAID MOM WOULD *ALWAYS* WATCH OVER ME...*"

GUESS NOW THEY *BOTH* WILL.

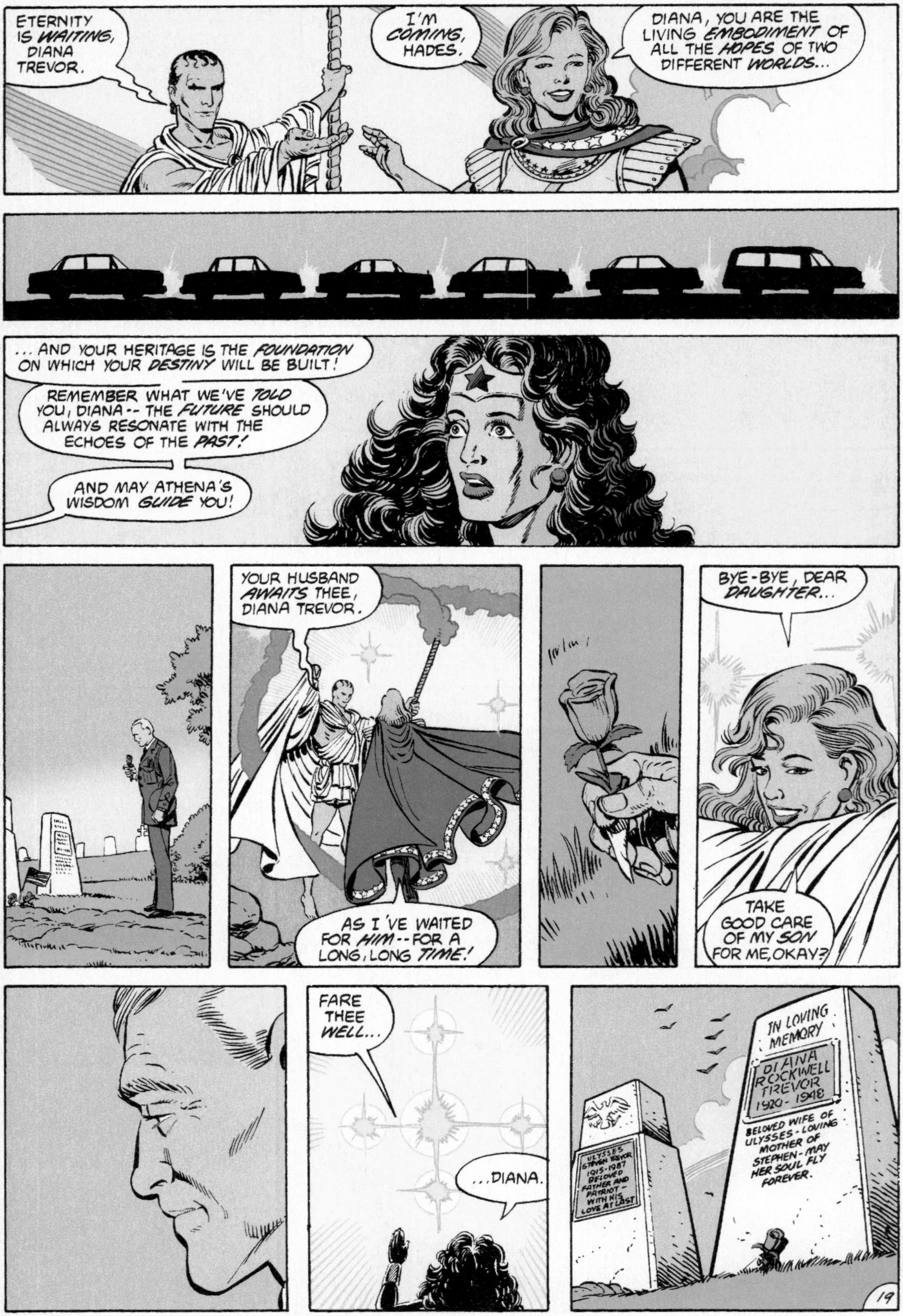
ETERNITY IS WAITING, DIANA TREVOR.
I'M COMING, HADES.
DIANA, YOU ARE THE LIVING EMBODIMENT OF ALL THE HOPES OF TWO DIFFERENT WORLDS...
... AND YOUR HERITAGE IS THE FOUNDATION ON WHICH YOUR DESTINY WILL BE BUILT!
REMEMBER WHAT WE'VE TOLD YOU, DIANA -- THE FUTURE SHOULD ALWAYS RESONATE WITH THE ECHOES OF THE PAST!
AND MAY ATHENA'S WISDOM GUIDE YOU!
YOUR HUSBAND AWAITS THEE, DIANA TREVOR.
AS I'VE WAITED FOR HIM -- FOR A LONG, LONG TIME!
BYE-BYE, DEAR DAUGHTER...
TAKE GOOD CARE OF MY SON FOR ME, OKAY?
FARE THEE WELL...
...DIANA.
ULYSSES STEVEN TREVOR 1915-1987 BELOVED FATHER AND PATRIOT - WITH HIS LOVE AT LAST
IN LOVING MEMORY
DIANA ROCKWELL TREVOR 1920 - 1948
BELOVED WIFE OF ULYSSES - LOVING MOTHER OF STEPHEN - MAY HER SOUL FLY FOREVER.
19

SO MUCH IS *DIFFERENT* NOW-- SO MUCH HAS *CHANGED*--!

I FINALLY UNDERSTAND NOW MY SPECIAL *BOND* WITH STEVE TREVOR--

--BUT I STILL DO *NOT* KNOW ZEUS' ULTIMATE *PLAN* FOR ME!

I SUPPOSE I SHOULD JUST KEEP GOING *DEEPER* UNTIL I SEE SOME *SIGN* OF-- EH?

THAT *SOUND*--?

SUCH *COMPELLING* MUSIC-- *HERE*?!?

GREAT HERA! THERE SITS THE GOAT-GOD *PAN*!

COULD *HE* BE RESPONSIBLE FOR MY NEXT CHALLENGE?

HORNED ONE, ARE YOU--?

INDEED I *AM*, MY BEAUTIFUL YOUNG FAWN.

THY *NEXT* CHALLENGE SHALL PUT THEE IN CONFLICT WITH POWERS TO EQUAL THOSE OF THE GODS!

THOU SHALT JOURNEY TO THE CITADEL OF THE GREEN LANTERNS-- TO CONFER WITH THE LEGENDARY GUARDIANS OF THE UNIVERSE.

THERE THOU SHALT UNDERTAKE THY *NEXT* CHALLENGE-- TO ASSIST IN THE *BIRTHING* OF IMMORTAL *MAN*!

BUT, *BEWARE*, CHILD, FOR *DANGER* LURKS THERE THAT *THREATENS* ALL THAT IS--

--AND *THEY* ARE AT THE *HEART* OF IT!

WHO--?

"THEY ARE CALLED *MANHUNTERS*, DIANA--"

--AND *NO* MAN--

--OR *WOMAN*--

--ESCAPES THE *MANHUNTERS*!

WELL, CHILD-- WHAT *SAY* THEE?

20

IF THIS IS WHAT THE GODS *WISH* OF ME, THEN THIS IS WHAT I SHALL *DO!* FOR I KNOW NOW THAT *MY* WORLD IS *TWO* WORLDS...

IN *ONE,* I AM *DIANA,* PRINCESS OF *THEMYSCIRA!*

BUT IN THE *OTHER,* I AM CALLED--

--*WONDER WOMAN!*

FAREWELL... LITTLE *FOOL!*

MY PINIONED GUIDE *LED* ME TO THIS RUINED *TEMPLE*--THEN FLEW ON OUT OF *SIGHT!*

IT SEEMS I MUST FIND MY *OWN* WAY FROM *HERE!*

THAT STRANGE *ROCK FORMATION* BELOW ME--!

IT SEEMS A *PATH* TO THE *LOWER DEPTHS*--!

SHALL I *FOLLOW* THE PATH TO--

EH? I HEAR *WINGS!*

HAS MY GUIDE *RETURNED* OR--

--*NO!!*

I AM SET UPON BY-- *HARPIES!!*

21

I AM *CORNERED* --
HOPLESSLY
OUTNUMBERED --

-- BUT I STILL
MUST *FIGHT
ON* --!

AND THUS
HIPPOLYTE *DOES,*
BRAVELY,
HEROICALLY --

-- BUT
ULTIMATELY
IN *VAIN!*

SKRAAAWW

NO!

HARPIES
PUSHED ME
OVER THE
PRECIPICE --!

I MAY FALL
THROUGH
DARKNESS
FOREVER --

-- UNLESS MY
BATTLEAXE CAN
GAIN ME
PURCHASE!

AARRGGHH

THE STONE *CRIED?!?*

BUT *HOW,*
UNLESS --

BY THE
GODS -- I *KNOW*
THAT VOICE!

IT CANNOT
BE, YET IT *IS* --!

IT IS --
HERACLES!!

293

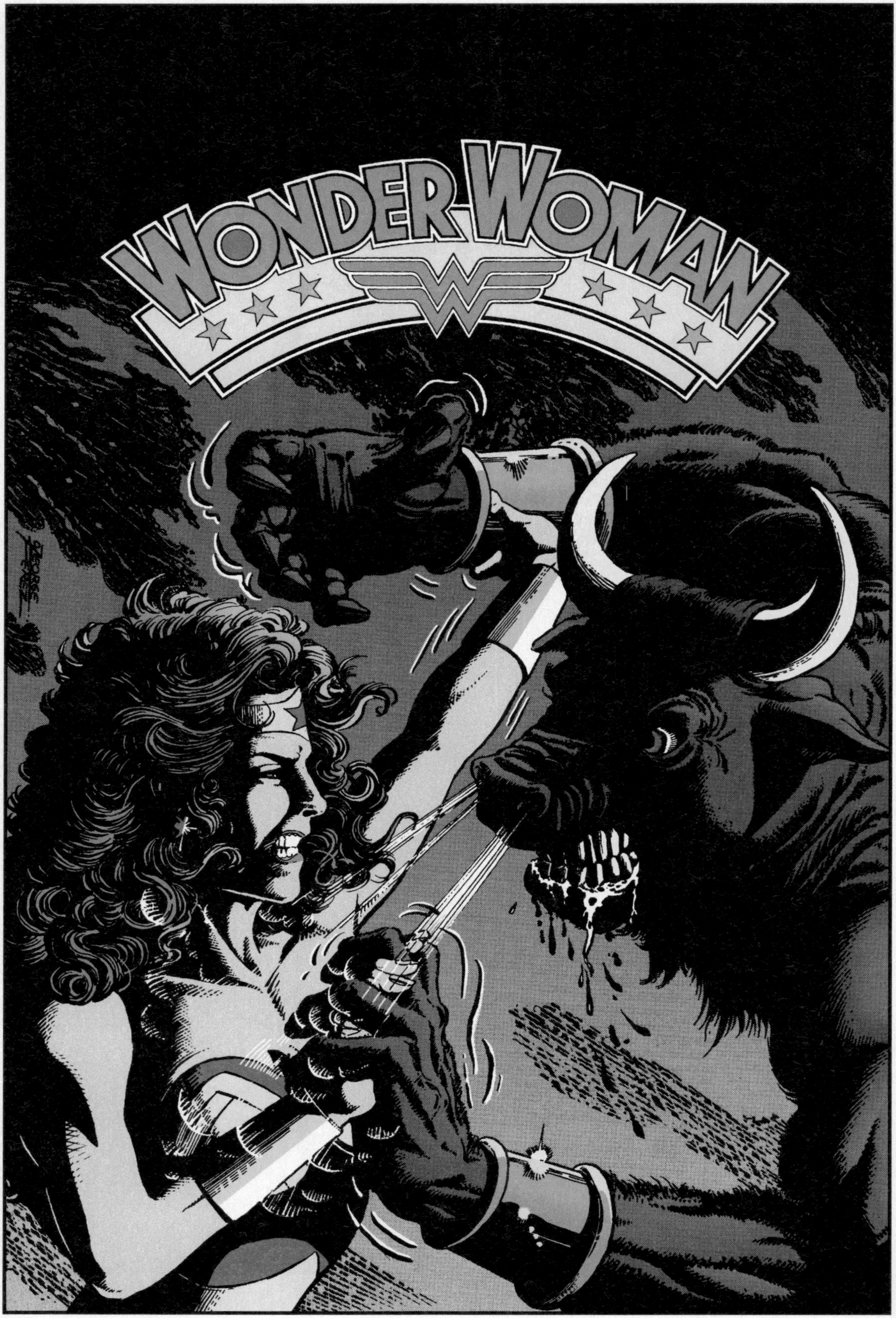
WONDER WOMAN

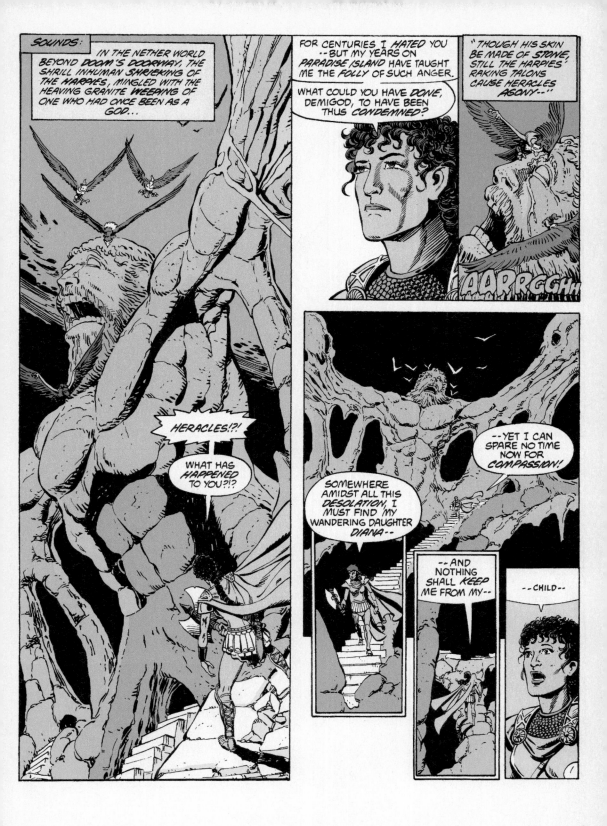

SOUNDS: IN THE NETHER WORLD BEYOND **DOOM'S DOORWAY**, THE SHRILL INHUMAN **SHRIEKING** OF THE **HARPIES**, MINGLED WITH THE HEAVING GRANITE **WEEPING** OF ONE WHO HAD ONCE BEEN AS A **GOD**...

FOR CENTURIES I **HATED** YOU --BUT MY YEARS ON **PARADISE ISLAND** HAVE TAUGHT ME THE **FOLLY** OF SUCH ANGER.

WHAT COULD YOU HAVE **DONE,** DEMIGOD, TO HAVE BEEN THUS **CONDEMNED?**

"*THOUGH HIS SKIN BE MADE OF **STONE,** STILL THE HARPIES' RAKING TALONS CAUSE HERACLES AGONY--*"

LAARRGGHH

HERACLES!?!

WHAT HAS **HAPPENED** TO YOU?!?

--YET I CAN SPARE NO TIME NOW FOR **COMPASSION!**

SOMEWHERE AMIDST ALL THIS **DESOLATION,** I MUST FIND **MY** WANDERING DAUGHTER **DIANA**--

--AND NOTHING SHALL **KEEP** ME FROM MY--

--CHILD--

GREAT HERA! I HAVE STUMBLED UPON THE *CAVERN OF THE CYCLOPS!*

YET THIS ONE SLUMBERS SO *SOUNDLY,* HIS SNORING FAIRLY SHAKES THE CAVERN *WALLS--!*

THE *TUNNEL* BEHIND HIM MAY WELL BE THE PATH *DIANA* TOOK--

--BUT I MUST TREAD *LIGHTLY* TOWARDS IT--

"--LEST I WAKE THE SLEEPING *GIANT!*"

HIS SEEMS SUCH AN *UN-COMFORTABLE* SLUMBER. BUT THANK *MORPHEUS* HE SLEEPS.

WITH MY SWORDARM *INJURED* IN BATTLE WITH THOSE *SKELETAL WARRIORS,* I'VE LITTLE DESIRE FOR *FRESH* COMBAT--!

"*POOR HERACLES!* HIS MOURNFUL MOANING GROWS LOUDER--

"--AS IF HE WERE SOMEHOW CALLING TO ME!"

PERHAPS I WILL *RETURN* TO HIM ONCE I'VE RESCUED MY *DAUGHTER!*

AMONG THE *BONES,* A HUMAN SKULL--

"--OR *IS IT* HUMAN?

"THOSE HORNS--"

"BY ZEUS, I KNOW WHOSE SKULL THIS IS--!"

2

SOUNDS:

IN THE TWISTING HALLS OF *MOUNT OLYMPUS*, THE FEARSOME, FRENZIED *BELLOWINGS* OF A GOD ENRAGED --

-- AS ALMIGHTY *ZEUS* UNCOVERS A DARK *DECEPTION...*

BY MY POWER!

HERMES, THOSE SKELETAL REMAINS ARE THOSE OF YOUR SATYR SON --

-- THE *GOAT-GOD PAN!*

BUT IF PAN IS LONG *DEAD,* THEN *WHO* --?!?

AN EXCELLENT *QUESTION,* HERMES --

-- AND ONE I SHALL SOON SEE *ANSWERED!*

THAT INSIDIOUS *IMPOSTOR* SHALL BE *FOUND* --

-- AND PAY WITH HIS *LIFE* FOR THIS *DECEPTION!*

A DECEPTION TO WHICH YOU WERE A *PARTY,* HUSBAND -- WITH YOUR ENORMOUS *PRIDE!* FOR CENTURIES NOW, YOUR *ARROGANCE* HAS BROUGHT US NAUGHT BUT *TROUBLE* --

HERA, YOU *DARE* --?!?

-- AND I, FOR ONE, HAVE HAD ABOUT *ENOUGH* OF IT!

FROM PROMETHEUS THROUGH HERACLES THROUGH ARES WE HAVE LET THE MADNESS ESCALATE --

-- BUT *NO LONGER!*

I KNOW NOW THAT GAEA'S DESTINY IS TO BE FINALLY *FULFILLED* THROUGH THE AMAZONS --

-- AND I WILL NOT ALLOW YOU TO *ABUSE* THEM!

THE IMPOSTOR HAS LED DIANA TO BELIEVE THAT TO SAVE HER RACE --

-- SHE MUST COMPLETE HIS CHALLENGE --!

AYE, HERMES -- YOU MUST *RETRIEVE* THE AMAZON PRINCESS!

THE *FATES* HAVE DECREED THAT SHE MUST *COMPLETE* THAT LABOR WHICH EVEN A *MAN-GOD* COULD NOT --!

AT YOUR *COMMAND,* MY QUEEN -- *I FLY!*

MY SON HAS BEEN *SLAIN*-- BUT BY *WHOM*?

SUCH *POWER*-- ENOUGH TO *MURDER* A *GOD* AND THEN *IMPERSONATE* HIM-- IS ALMOST TOO AWESOME TO *CONTEMPLATE!*

DEMONPLAGUE

Challenge of the Gods —— BOOK 4

plot & layouts: **GEORGE PÉREZ**

letters: **JOHN COSTANZA**

script: **LEN WEIN**

colors: **CARL GAFFORD**

finishes: **BRUCE D. PATTERSON**

editor: **KAREN BERGER**

SOUNDS:

IN THE *CALIFORNIA* CITADEL OF THE *GREEN LANTERN CORPS*, THE WHISTLING RUSH OF WIND THAT HERALDS THE IMMINENT ARRIVAL OF A *GOD*--

--A CACOPHONY OF CONCERNED VOICES, AS THE WORLD'S GREATEST HEROES DISCUSS THE PROMISED *MILLENNIUM*...

--AND, FOR THE *PRINCESS DIANA*, KNOWN AMONG THIS COMPANY AS *WONDER WOMAN*, A WHISPER THAT IS MORE THAN A *SHOUT*...

DIANA, I HAVE COME FOR YOU!

FLEET *HERMES*--?!?

BUT WHAT OF PAN'S *CHALLENGE?*

4

YOU HAVE BEEN *DECEIVED,* CHILD! HE WHOM YOU THOUGHT WAS PAN WAS *NOT* MY SON AT ALL--

--BUT RATHER, IT SEEMS, AN AGENT OF THE *MANHUNTERS* BENT ON DESTROYING YOUR CHANCE FOR *VICTORY!*

AND, IN SO DOING, HE HAS PLACED *MANKIND* IN FURTHER *JEOPARDY!*

EVEN AS WE SPEAK, YOUR MOTHER FIGHTS VALIANTLY AT THEMYSCIRA'S *CORE*-- BUT SHE CANNOT COMPLETE THE ULTIMATE *LABOR!*

YOU MUST *RETURN* WITH ME, DIANA--OR ALL YOU LOVE SHALL *PERISH!*

BUT MY *COMRADES* HERE--?!

MUST FIND THEIR WAY *WITHOUT* YOU!

GIVE ME YOUR *HAND,* DAUGHTER--

--AND LET US *BEGONE!*

WONDER WOMAN, WHAT DO *YOU* THINK ABOUT--*HUH?!?*

SHE'S *DISAPPEARED*-- JUST WHEN WE NEEDED HER *MOST!*

I'M SURE SHE HAS HER *REASONS,* ARISIA--!

WE'LL JUST HAVE TO TRUST THEY'RE *GOOD* ONES!

"AYE, I CAN *SEE* IT NOW, IN HER POSTURE, IN HER EYES...

"SHE IS INDEED THE ONE DESTINED TO END THIS MADNESS--

"--THE MADNESS I MYSELF *BEGAN!*"

PAN *KNEW*--AND PAN *USED* ME!

I CAN ONLY HOPE MY *VANITY* HAS NOT DOOMED US *ALL!*

THE IMPOSTOR FOOLED ALL OF *OLYMPUS,* LORD ZEUS-- WHICH IS AS IT WAS *MEANT* TO BE.

EVEN SUCH AS *WE* ARE SLAVES TO *FATE!*

SOUNDS: IN THE CAVERN OF THE CYCLOPS, A DEEP, INHUMAN *BELLOWING*--

--AND A HEAVY WOODEN *IMPACT* LIKE THE GROWLING BARK OF THUNDER...

I...SMELL... *FOOD!!*

CURSE YOU, MONSTER-- *UNHAND* ME!

THOU DOST YET *LIVE?!?* DAMN MY *BLIND EYE!*

THEN I SHALL SIMPLY *CONSUME* THEE AS THOU DOST *SCREAM*--

--AND PRAY THOU PROVEST NOT SO *INDIGESTIBLE* AS MY *LAST* MEAL!

BLIND *EYE*--?!? THEN YOU MUST BE *POLYPHEMUS!*

I AM *HIPPOLYTE*, AMAZON QUEEN OF THEMYSCIRA!

I COMMAND YOU TO *RELEASE* ME!

THOU ART *ROYALTY*, AY? THEN MAYHAP *THOU* SHALT NOT SOUR MY *STOMACH* AS DID THAT HAIRY-HOOVED MEAL OF YEARS *PAST!*

NO! YOU CANNOT--!!

AND HE *SHALL* NOT, MOTHER--

--NOT SO LONG AS YOUR DAUGHTER STILL *LIVES!!*

AARRGGHH!!

6

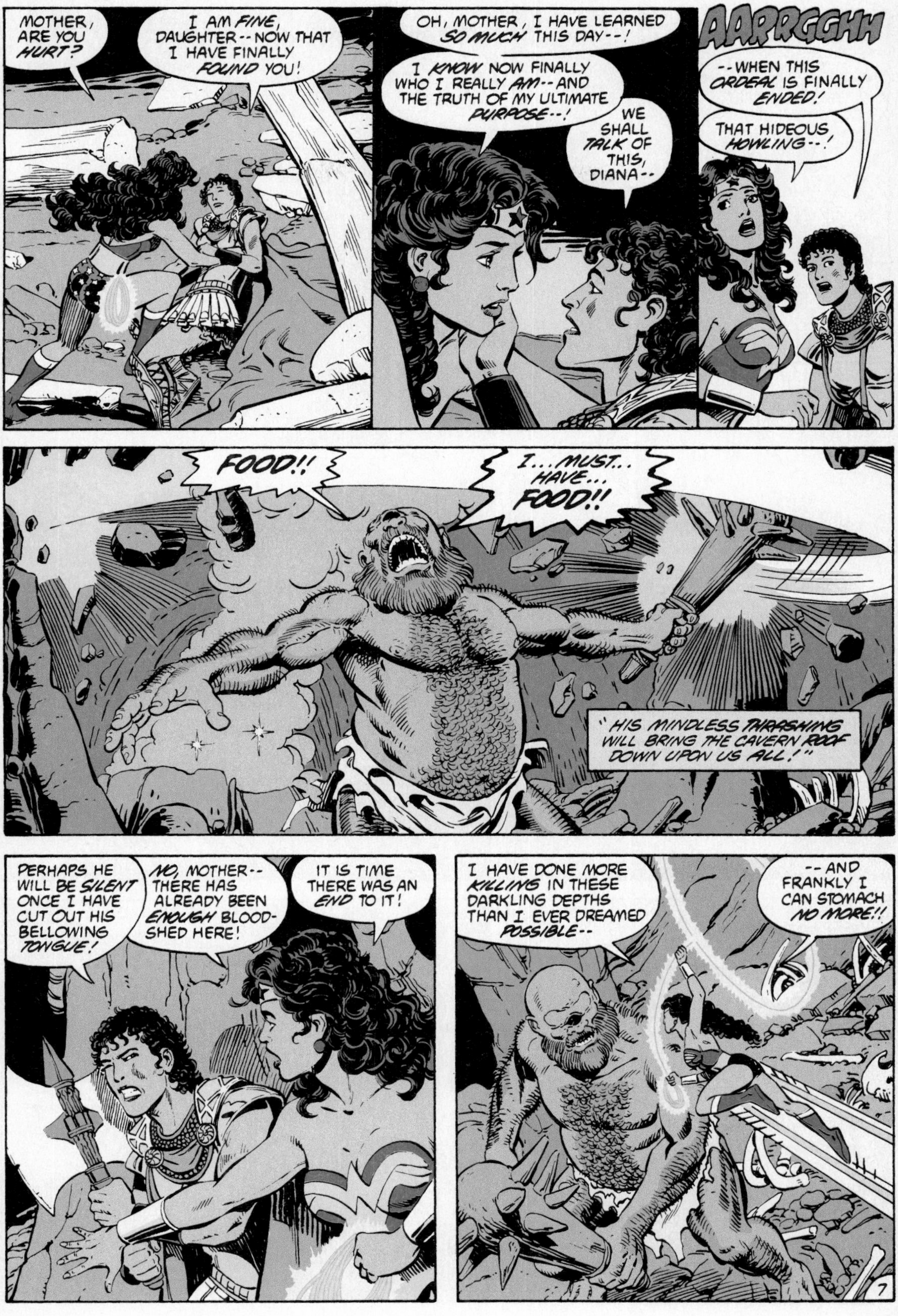
MOTHER, ARE YOU HURT?
I AM FINE, DAUGHTER -- NOW THAT I HAVE FINALLY FOUND YOU!
OH, MOTHER, I HAVE LEARNED SO MUCH THIS DAY--!
I KNOW NOW FINALLY WHO I REALLY AM -- AND THE TRUTH OF MY ULTIMATE PURPOSE--!
WE SHALL TALK OF THIS, DIANA--
AARRGGHH
--WHEN THIS ORDEAL IS FINALLY ENDED!
THAT HIDEOUS, HOWLING--!
FOOD!!
I... MUST... HAVE... FOOD!!
"HIS MINDLESS THRASHING WILL BRING THE CAVERN ROOF DOWN UPON US ALL!"
PERHAPS HE WILL BE SILENT ONCE I HAVE CUT OUT HIS BELLOWING TONGUE!
NO, MOTHER -- THERE HAS ALREADY BEEN ENOUGH BLOODSHED HERE!
IT IS TIME THERE WAS AN END TO IT!
I HAVE DONE MORE KILLING IN THESE DARKLING DEPTHS THAN I EVER DREAMED POSSIBLE--
--AND FRANKLY I CAN STOMACH NO MORE!!
7

THUS, MY INDESTRUCTIBLE *GOLDEN LARIAT* WILL HOLD *FAST* THE GIANT TO THIS STONE COLUMN--

--WHILE WE MAKE GOOD OUR *ESCAPE!*

NOOOOOOO!!

BY HERA! THE BLIND BEHEMOTH WAILS MORE LIKE A *WOUNDED CHILD* THAN A *RAVENOUS BEAST!*

NO.!! THOU CANST NOT *LEAVE* ME TO SUFFER THE AGES LIKE *THIS!*

PLEASE-- I *PRAY* THEE-- *SLAY* ME INSTEAD!

WHEN WE WERE BANISHED TO THE BOWELS OF THIS ISLAND, WE CYCLORS FOUGHT AND *CONSUMED* ONE ANOTHER-- UNTIL ONLY I *REMAINED!*

AND *THAT* WAS THE GODS' *CRUELEST JOKE!*

BLIND AS I AM, I CANNOT *HUNT!* THUS I MUST *WAIT* FOR FOOD-- AT TIMES FOR UNTOLD *AGES!*

ONLY *ONCE*, WHEN THE ALREADY-DEAD BODY OF A *MAN-GOAT* WAS DROPPED AT MY FEET, DID I FINALLY *EAT*--

--AND THAT MEAL HAS GIVEN ME ETERNAL *INDIGESTION!*

IN THIS CAVERN, NO ONE CAN *DIE* SAVE AT THE HAND OF *ANOTHER!*

THUS, I SHALL KNOW STARVATION AND INDIGESTION FOR ALL *ETERNITY!*

PLEASE, IF THOU HAST ANY *COMPASSION*, I BEG THEE...

...*SLAY* ME!

MOTHER, WHAT SHALL WE *DO?* WE *TOO* HAVE KNOWN *HUNGER*--

--YET WE CANNOT COLD-BLOODEDLY *SLAY* ONE SO *HELP-LESS*--!

AYE, DIANA...

PERHAPS WE SHOULD--

--EH?

MOTHER--?

8

CAN YOU NOT *HEAR* IT, CHILD?

HE *CALLS* TO ME--!

I HEAR *NOTHING*, MOTHER.

I KNOW ONLY THAT THE *EXIT* STILL STANDS BEFORE US--!

NO! I CANNOT ALLOW *ANYONE* TO SUFFER LIKE THAT-- NOT EVEN HE WHO SO HORRIBLY *WRONGED* ME THOSE LONG CENTURIES PAST...

IT IS NOT THE *AMAZON* WAY--!

FORGIVE ME, DIANA-- BUT I MUST TRY TO FREE *HERACLES!*

IT IS ALMOST AS IF I WAS *BROUGHT* HERE TO PERFORM THIS TASK--!

AND I MUST *DO* WHAT I BELIEVE TO BE--

--WHAT?!?

MOTHER!?!

HER BATTLE-AXE DEFLECTED *MUCH* OF THE FLAME--

--BUT NOT NEARLY *ENOUGH!*

SHE ROLLS IN THE DIRT TO *EXTINGUISH* THE FLAMES BEFORE THEY CAN *CONSUME* HER--!

COURAGE, MOTHER! I AM COMING TO *SAVE*--

9

--YUUNNHH!!

D-DIANA--?

THY DAUGHTER CAN NO LONGER *HEAR* THEE, HIPPOLYTE!

THOU HAST REACHED AT LAST THE *HEART OF DARKNESS,* AMAZON--

--AND HERE THOU SHALT *PAY* FOR THY TENACITY--WITH THY LIVES!

10

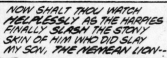

NOW SHALT THOU WATCH *HELPLESSLY* AS THE *HARPIES* FINALLY SLASH THE *STONY* SKIN OF HIM WHO DID SLAY MY SON, *THE NEMEAN LION*--

-- THEN *TOGETHER* SHALT THOU *DIE!*

AYE, WHEN THE *FLESH* OF *ZEUS'* TREASURED *SON* AT LAST IS *PIERCED*--

--THEN SHALL THE *TRUE HORRORS* OF THIS *CRYPT* BENEATH THINE *ISLAND* BE FINALLY *REVEALED!*

IS *THIS* THEN ZEUS' GREATEST *TREASURE* --?!?

EH--?!?

AARRGGHH!!

COULD IT BE *HERACLES* HIMSELF?

I KNOW NOT HOW THE *DEMI-GOD* CAME TO *BE* IN THIS DREADFUL PREDICAMENT--

--BUT I CANNOT PERMIT HIM TO SUFFER MORE *HARM!*

THOU HAST *LITTLE CHOICE,* AMAZON!

NONE CAN *DEFY* THE *MINOTAUR!!*

NO, HORNED ONE!

I *DEFY* YOU!! UNTO MY *FINAL BREATH!!*

305

THAT *HEAT* AT MY *BACK*--! THE *CHIMERA*--!

THE AMAZON MOVES *SWIFTLY,* MY SON!

THY FIERY *BLAST* BARELY SINGED HER!

BUT *MAYHAP* MY *SERPENTINE* COILS WILL SERVE WHERE THY FLAMING *BREATH* COULD NOT!

...CAN... NOT... BREATHE...

STOP, DEMONESS!

YOU HAVE COMMITTED SINS BEYOND *IMAGINING*--

"--AND 'TIS TIME THERE WAS AN *END* TO IT!"

AS THOU HAST SLAIN ECHIDNA, AMAZON--

--SO NOW SHALL THE *MINOTAUR* SLAY THEE!

UUNNHH!

ENOUGH, MINOTAUR!

WHEN WILL THIS SENSELESS *VIOLENCE* FINALLY BE *OVER?*

WHEN THOU ART *DEAD,* AMAZON--

--AND *ONLY* THEN!

HERA *HELP* ME!

THIS IS *NOT* THE WAY IT WAS MEANT TO BE!

12

FOR ONE WHO PROFESSES TO SEEK ONLY PEACE, AMAZON--

--THOU ART MOST PROFICIENT IN THE WAYS OF WAR!

NOT EVEN THESEUS, WHO THOUGHT HE HAD SLAIN ME, COULD MATCH THY SKILL AND POWER, CHILD--

--BUT THE MINOTAUR IS POWER INCARN--

--AARRGGHH!!

PRAISE ZEUS! FOOD!

'TIS ANOTHER HORNED ONE--

--BUT MY HUNGER HATH GROWN TOO GREAT TO BE DISCOURAGED--!

THE CYCLOPS HAS ESCAPED--!?!

IT MATTERS LITTLE, AMAZON--

--SINCE THE BEHEMOTH WILL SOON BE BUT A MEMORY!

BUT HOW--?!?

THE MINOTAUR BUTTS HARD, SHATTERING THE BLIND CYCLOPS' JAW--

--AND THE ENTIRE CAVERN SHUDDERS WITH THE WRITHING GIANT'S PAIN!

THE FRAGILE ROCK BRIDGE WHICH HAS BECOME THE MONSTERS' BATTLEGROUND BEGINS TO TREMBLE--

--THEN QUAKE--

--THEN COLLAPSES INTO RUBBLE--

--PLUNGING THE TWO GROTESQUE COMBATANTS INTO ETERNAL DARKNESS--

--DARKNESS WITHOUT END!

13

THE CYCLOPS AND THE MINOTAUR... *GONE!*

IT SEEMS THE *CAPRICIOUS* FATES HAVE GRANTED POOR POLYPHEMUS *BOTH* HIS WISHES!

BUT THE *TOLL* TAKEN BY THIS BATTLE HAS BEEN *TERRIBLE* INDEED--!

MOTHER'S *BREATHING--* SO *RAGGED--* SO *SHALLOW--!*

FORGIVE ME, DAUGHTER... FOR *RUINING* EVERYTHING...

NO, MOTHER-- YOU WERE *RIGHT!* I *FOUND* HERE WHAT I WAS *MEANT* TO FIND.

JUST WISH I KNEW HOW THE CYCLOPS *FREED* HIMSELF FROM MY ENCHANTED *LASSO--!*

WHY, WITH MY *ASSISTANCE,* OF COURSE--!

WHO--?!?

I AM SHE THOU DIDST KNOW AS A *MADWOMAN,* DIANA-- AND THY *MOTHER,* AS THE *VULTURE* WHO GUIDED HER!

I AM *HARMONIA,* RESTORED AT LAST TO THE *BEAUTY* THAT IS MY *BIRTHRIGHT!*

MY FATHER HATH *KNOWN* OF THIS PLACE SINCE ITS *CREATION--*

-- BUT IN HIS PAST MADNESS HE SAW NO REASON TO INTERFERE WITH PAN'S PLAN.

BUT THOU HAST CALMED THE *MADNESS* WITHIN HIM, DIANA--

-- AND, IN SO DOING, HATH PREPARED HIM TO *RECEIVE* THAT WHICH IS RIGHTFULLY *HIS!*

WITH THIS *TALISMAN,* ONLY SHE WHO IS *PURE OF ESSENCE* CAN CAPTURE THE *DEMONS* WITHIN THIS CRYPT--

-- AND DELIVER THEM UNTO THEIR *NEW* HOST--

-- THE *GOD OF DESTRUCTION--*

-- MY *FATHER ARES!*

14

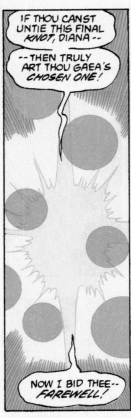

IF THOU CANST UNTIE THIS FINAL *KNOT*, DIANA --

-- THEN TRULY ART THOU GAEA'S *CHOSEN* ONE!

NOW I BID THEE -- *FAREWELL!*

SHE LEFT BEHIND HER *TALISMAN* AS WELL AS MY *LASSO*--!

SOMEHOW THE *SECRET* LIES IN THE *RESCUE* OF *HERACLES*--

--BUT HOW CAN ONE *RELEASE* THE *DEMONS* WITHIN HIM WITHOUT ALSO *DESTROYING* ZEUS' *SON*?

WE HAVE BEEN TOLD THAT IT WAS OUR *LOVE* FOR OUR FELLOW BEINGS THAT LED US TO THE *TRUTH*, DIANA...

AYE, MOTHER -- EVEN *HERACLES*, WHO ONCE SO GRIEVOUSLY *WRONGED* YOU, STILL ELICITS YOUR *COMPASSION.*

THEN PERHAPS HERACLES CAN ONLY BE SAVED BY OUR *FORGIVENESS*-- OUR ULTIMATE *UNDERSTANDING*--!

I *SEE* NOW WHY ARES HAD HARMONIA *BRING* YOU HERE--!

THE *CHIMERA* HAS CHASED AWAY THE *HARPIES*, MOTHER--!

THE REST REMAINS FOR *US* TO DO!

BY MY FORGE! ARES MUST HAVE *KNOWN* ABOUT THE FALSE *PAN* ALL ALONG!

OH, THE GLORIOUS COSMIC *IRONY* OF IT ALL! THAT YOU GODDESSES SHOULD *CREATE* THIS DIANA FROM COMMON *CLAY*--

--EVEN AS ZEUS HAD ME FORM THE MORTAL *PANDORA*, WHO FIRST SET LOOSE THE *DEMONPLAGUE!*

BUT HOW CAN THE AMAZON *CHALLENGE* THESE DEMONS *UNAIDED*?

ONLY BY ANSWERING *YOUR* CHALLENGE, APHRODITE--!

BY ALLOWING THE *PURE BEAUTY* OF HER SOUL TO BE HER *SHIELD!*

AYE, SHE SHALL *SURVIVE* ONLY IF THIS CLAY STATUE GIVEN LIFE IS INDEED ONE WITH THE *EARTH-GODDESS*--

15

"--ONLY IF SHE IS TRULY THE *LIVING EMBODI-MENT* OF ALL THAT IS *WOMAN!*"

HERACLES' PITIFUL *WAILING*-- SO *LOUD* IT IS *INTOLERABLE*--!

COURAGE, MOTHER--!

OBVIOUSLY SOME GREAT *BOND* STILL EXISTS BETWEEN YOU AND HERACLES-- ELSE WHY WOULD HIS VOICE *TORMENT* YOU SO?

WHY ARE *YOU* THE ONLY ONE LIVING WHO CAN *HEAR* HIM?

I... DO... NOT... KNOW...

THEN PERHAPS IT IS TIME YOU AND HERACLES SAW EACH OTHER THROUGH THE EYES OF *TRUTH*, MOTHER--

--THE TRUTH ONLY MY GOLDEN *LASSO* CAN REVEAL!

HIS *SCREAMING*-- SO *UN-BEARABLE*--!

ARE YOU *CERTAIN* ABOUT THIS, DAUGHTER?

NOT AT *ALL*, MOTHER-- I ONLY KNOW IT *FEELS* RIGHT!

PLEASE-- FOR ALL OUR SAKES -- DO NOT *FIGHT* IT!

THEN HESTIA'S FLAMES OF REVELATION ENVELOP THEM *BOTH*, SO THAT EACH MAY SEE AND KNOW WHAT THE *OTHER* HAS ALWAYS KNOWN...

NEW KNOWLEDGE, NEW *INSIGHTS*, SUDDENLY SURGE THROUGH HIPPOLYTE'S MIND, AND SHE *SUFFERS* FOR THE SON OF ZEUS--

--AS HE NOW SUFFERS FOR HER--

--AND BY THIS *INTIMATE UNION*, FOR THE FIRST TIME IN TOO MANY CENTURIES, TWO TORMENTED SOULS ABRUPTLY FIND *RELEASE!*

ANTIOPE...

16

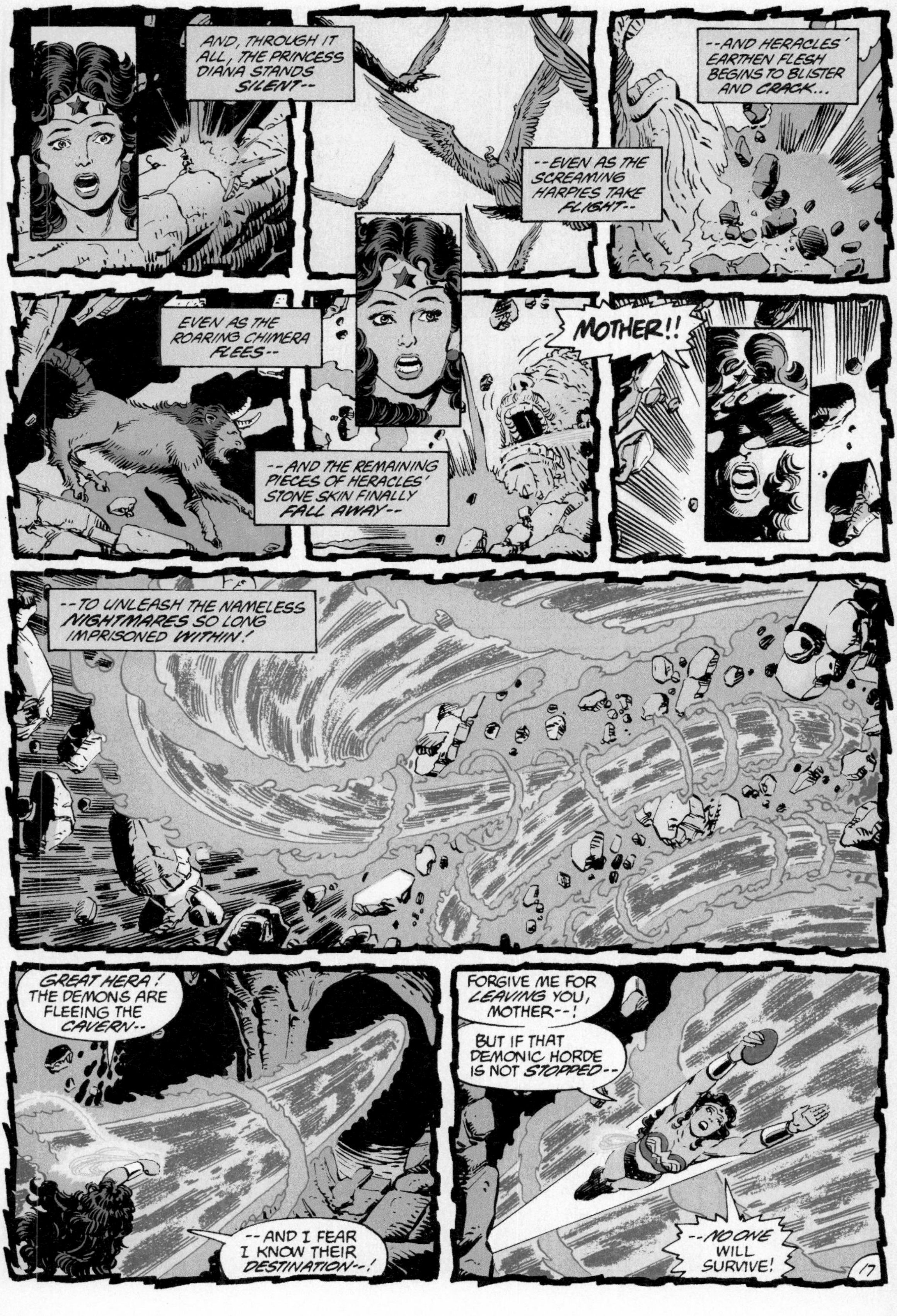
AND, THROUGH IT ALL, THE PRINCESS DIANA STANDS SILENT--
--EVEN AS THE SCREAMING HARPIES TAKE FLIGHT--
--AND HERACLES' EARTHEN FLESH BEGINS TO BLISTER AND CRACK...
EVEN AS THE ROARING CHIMERA FLEES--
--AND THE REMAINING PIECES OF HERACLES' STONE SKIN FINALLY FALL AWAY--
MOTHER!!
--TO UNLEASH THE NAMELESS NIGHTMARES SO LONG IMPRISONED WITHIN!
GREAT HERA! THE DEMONS ARE FLEEING THE CAVERN--
--AND I FEAR I KNOW THEIR DESTINATION--!
FORGIVE ME FOR LEAVING YOU, MOTHER--!
BUT IF THAT DEMONIC HORDE IS NOT STOPPED--
--NO ONE WILL SURVIVE!
17

I WAS *RIGHT!* THE DEMONS ARE *RETRACING* THE PATH I FIRST TOOK TO *REACH* THEM--!

I PRAY TO ATHENA I'VE PIECED THIS PUZZLE TOGETHER *PROPERLY*--

--ELSE I MAY HAVE *SLAIN* MY MOTHER AND DOOMED *MANKIND!*

FLEET *HERMES,* GRANT ME YOUR *SPEED*--

--FOR I HAVE *NEED* OF IT NOW AS NEVER *BEFORE!*

BEFORE ME LOOMS *DOOM'S* DOOR-WAY--

--CRACKED *OPEN* AS I'D FEARED, TO UNLEASH THE *DEMON-PLAGUE!*

ONLY HARMONIA'S *AMULET* CAN POSSIBLY *STOP* THEM NOW--

--IF IT IS STRONG ENOUGH TO *WITHSTAND* THE DEMONIC ONSLAUGHT--!

IF *I* AM STRONG ENOUGH--!!

18

BEHIND DIANA, DOOM'S DOORWAY STARTS TO CRACK AND *CRUMBLE*--

--WHILE THE PRINCESS STRUGGLES TO *HOLD HER GROUND* AGAINST POWERS BEYOND THE *IMAGINATION!*

VIOLENT *TREMORS* SUDDENLY SHAKE *PARADISE ISLAND*--

--AND THE STRICKEN AMAZONS WONDER IF PERHAPS THEIR IMMORTALITY IS AT LAST AT AN *END*--

--BUT STILL DIANA STANDS FIRM, HER AMULET SWIFTLY *ABSORBING* THE ONCOMING *EVIL*--

--THUS GROWING SO *HOT* AS TO BLISTER HER FINGERTIPS!

IN *SEISMOGRAPHIC* STATIONS ACROSS THE WORLD, SENSITIVE *NEEDLES* LEAP SCREAMING OFF THE CHARTS --

--AND *SCIENTISTS* FEAR THE COMING OF THE *APOCALYPSE*--

--BUT NEVER *ONCE* DOES THE STRUGGLING DIANA *SUCCUMB* TO HER IMPOSSIBLE *PAIN!*

SEISMOGRAPHIC INSTITUTION

19

UNTIL, AT LAST, THE TORRENT OF DEMONS IS GONE--

THE PAIN...IS INCREDIBLE... ...BUT I DARE NOT... LET GO...

--LOCKED AWAY IN HARMONIA'S AMULET, WHICH NOW BURNS WITH UNSPEAKABLE POWER...

NO! SOME OTHER FORCE... PULLING AT THE AMULET...

A SURGE OF SUPERNAL POWER --

-- A BLINDING BURST OF LIGHT --

-- AND THE PRINCESS DIANA PLUNGES THROUGH DARKNESS --

--INTO ANOTHER REALM!

WELCOME, CHILD! YOU HAVE DONE WELL!

YOU--?!?

AYE, CHILD--WHO ELSE BUT ARES!?

THE POWER YOU HOLD IS MINE!

BEFORE I WOULD HAVE DESTROYED MYSELF HAD I POSSESSED IT!

NOW, BECAUSE OF YOU, I AM AT LAST READY TO RECEIVE IT!

RELEASE THE AMULET!

NO-- I CANNOT--!

SUCH POWER IS NOT FOR SUCH AS YOU--!

YOU ARE SAID TO POSSESS GREAT WISDOM, CHILD!

USE ATHENA'S GIFT AND YOU SHALL KNOW 'TIS THE ONLY WAY!

HAND ME THE AMULET!

20

DESPITE ALL, MY HEART TELLS ME THE WAR-GOD SPEAKS *TRUE*--

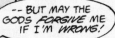

--BUT MAY THE GODS *FORGIVE* ME IF I'M *WRONG!*

COME TO ME, DENIZENS OF PANDORA'S BOX!

AS CLAY-MADE-FLESH DID LONG AGO FREE THE FIRST OF YOUR ILK--

--SO NOW HAS NEW CLAY-MADE-FLESH FREED YOUR FINAL NUMBER--

--TO INHABIT THE WORLD AND BODY OF ARES!

NOW, AT LAST, THE ULTIMATE POWER OF DESTRUCTION IS FINALLY MINE.!!

CONSUMED NOW BY THE VERY POWER HE HAD SO LONG SOUGHT, THE WAR-GOD HURTLES *SKYWARD*--

--HIS *TRIUMPHANT LAUGHTER* ECHOING THROUGH THE DECAYING CORRIDORS OF *AREOPAGUS*--

--UNTIL, IN A FLASH, HE IS GONE!

BY ALL THAT IS *HOLY*, WHAT HAVE I *DONE?*

THOU HAST RESTORED THE *BALANCE OF POWER*, PRINCESS.

THY MISSION FOR THE GODS IS AT LAST AT AN *END*--

--AND THOU HAST PROVEN THYSELF THE *GREATEST* OF WARRIORS!

IT IS *FINALLY OVER?*

'TIS NEVER *TRULY OVER*, CHILD! NOW *NEW* CHALLENGES AWAIT THEE--

--AND THE *CONSEQUENCES* OF WHAT TRANSPIRED HERE TODAY SHALL FOREVER SHAPE THY *FUTURE!*

21

BUT THOU DOST *KNOW* NOW THAT THY CREATION WAS *NOT* AN ACCIDENT OR IDLE *WHIM...*

THY *DESTINY* AWAITS THEE IN *TWO* WORLDS--

--AND *BOTH* SHALL KNOW GREAT CHANGE *BECAUSE* OF THEE!

THE *BLESSINGS OF THE GODS--* AYE, AND THEIR *GRATITUDE--* SHALL EVER BE *THINE*, CHILD...

...FARE THEE *WELL...*

HARMONIA...?

WOULD THAT I *COULD,* SWEET CHILD--BUT I *CANNOT!*

I FEAR ONE *FINAL CHALLENGE* AWAITS YOU--

--AND IT IS *MINE!*

GONE-- LIKE HER *FATHER*--!

I AM *ALONE* IN THIS DESOLATE PLACE--!

I DO NOT *UNDERSTAND,* HERMES-- HARMONIA TOLD ME ALL WAS *WELL!*

ONLY BECAUSE THE TREACHERY WHICH *MISLED* ALMIGHTY ZEUS WAS *DISCOVERED* IN TIME!

NAY, DAUGHTER-- *NEVER* ALONE!

HERMES --?!?

PLEASE, MY LORD-- RETURN ME TO MY *MOTHER!*

SHE IS IN *TERRIBLE DANGER*--!

YOUR *NEXT* CHALLENGE IS TO RETURN TO *MAN'S WORLD,* DIANA-- TO *AVENGE* THE MURDER OF MY *SON!*

YOU MUST SEEK OUT THE *MANHUNTER* WHO IMPERSONATED *PAN*--

--AND YOU MUST *SLAY HIM!*

22

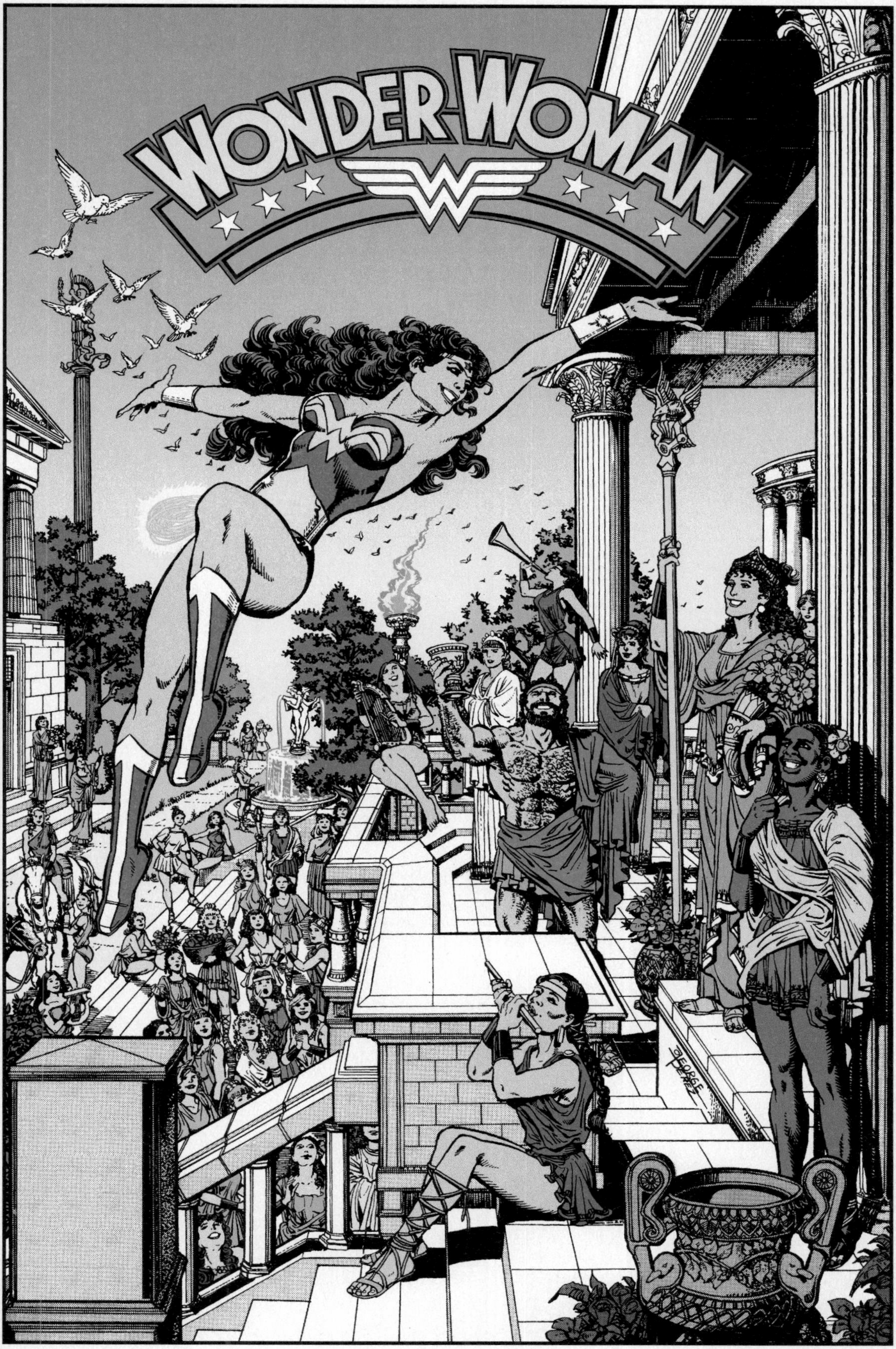
WONDER WOMAN
GEORGE PEREZ

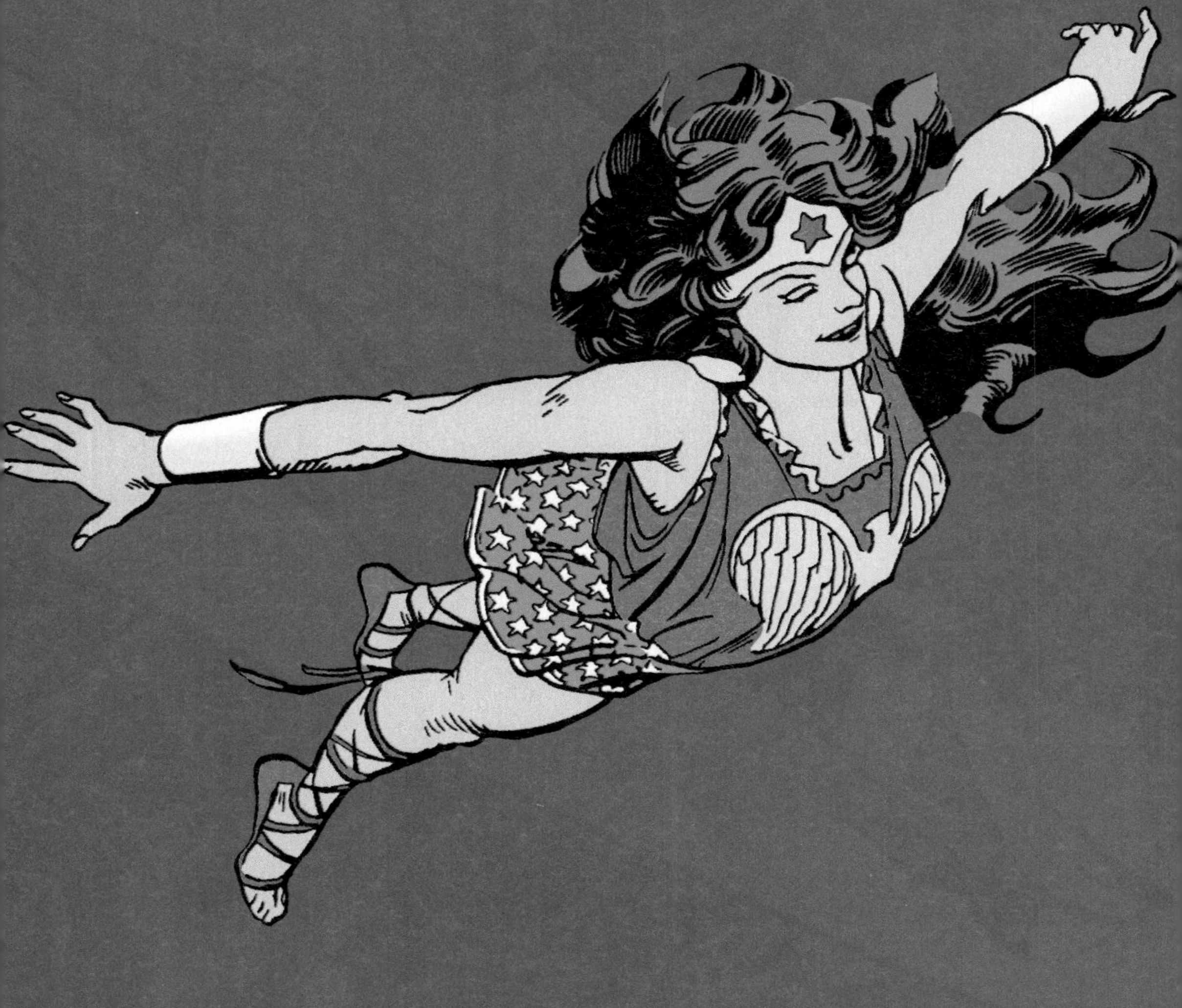

FOR THE AMAZON *PRINCESS DIANA*, RETURNING AT LAST FROM THE EVENTS OF THE *MILLENNIUM*, THE ROUTE BACK TO THE NETHERWORLD BENEATH PARADISE ISLAND IS OPPRESSIVELY *DARK*--

--BUT NOT NEARLY SO DARK AS HER OWN SWIRLING THOUGHTS...

THE *CHALLENGE* OF THE FLEET GOD HERMES HAS BEEN *MET*--AND REGRETTABLY *RESOLVED!*

THE *MANHUNTER* WHO MURDERED-- THEN *IMPERSONATED*-- THE GOAT-GOD *PAN* HAS CAUSED HIS OWN *DESTRUCTION!*

JUSTICE HAS BEEN *SERVED*--BUT WHY MUST SO *MANY* BATTLES END IN SENSELESS *SLAUGHTER?*

TO *OBEY* THE GRIEVING HERMES, I LEFT MY OWN *MOTHER* BEHIND ME, GRAVELY *WOUNDED* FROM HER BATTLE WITH THE *MINOTAUR*--!

I ONLY PRAY MY *SERVICE* TO HERMES HAS NOT COST *HER* DEAR LIFE AS--

GREAT GODS OF OLYMPUS!!

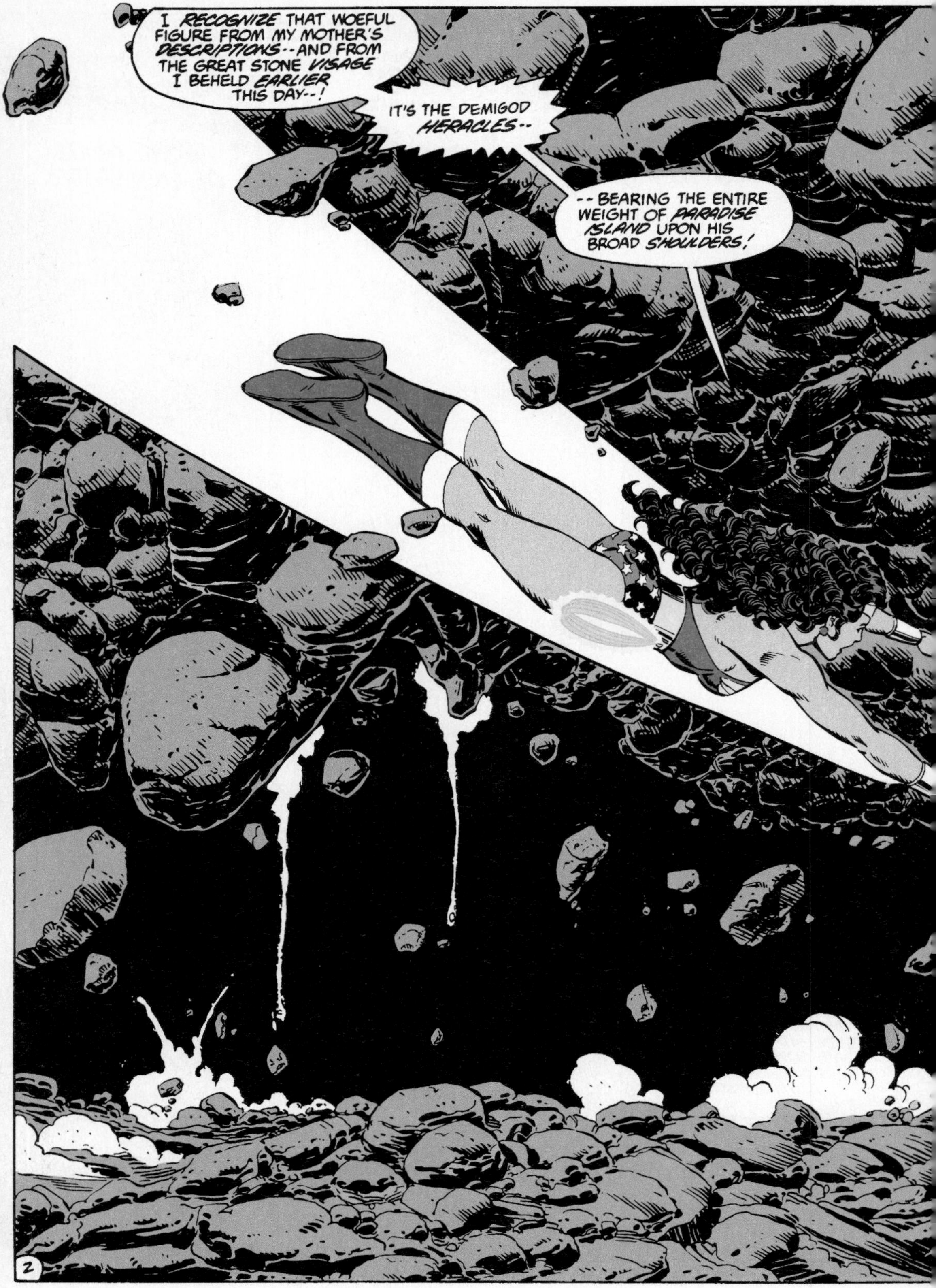
I RECOGNIZE THAT WOEFUL FIGURE FROM MY MOTHER'S DESCRIPTIONS--AND FROM THE GREAT STONE VISAGE I BEHELD EARLIER THIS DAY--!
IT'S THE DEMIGOD HERACLES--
--BEARING THE ENTIRE WEIGHT OF PARADISE ISLAND UPON HIS BROAD SHOULDERS!
2

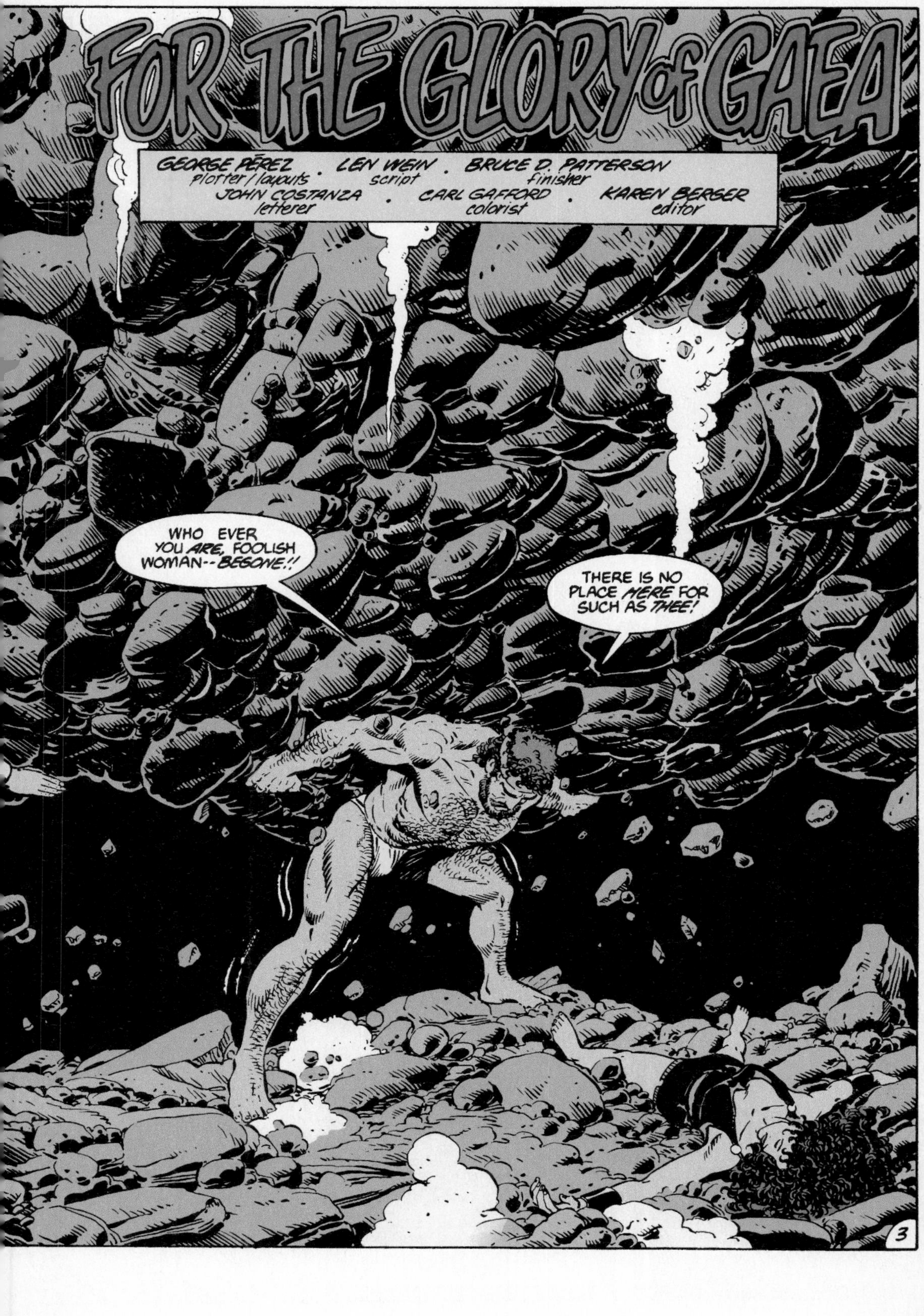
FOR THE GLORY of GAEA
GEORGE PÉREZ plotter/layouts . LEN WEIN script . BRUCE D. PATTERSON finisher
JOHN COSTANZA letterer . CARL GAFFORD colorist . KAREN BERGER editor
WHO EVER YOU ARE, FOOLISH WOMAN-- BEGONE!!
THERE IS NO PLACE HERE FOR SUCH AS THEE!
3

WRONG, DEMI-GOD -- MY PLACE IS EVER AT MY MOTHER'S SIDE!

THANK THE FATES SHE IS MERELY UNCONSCIOUS --!

THE QUEEN IS YOUR *MOTHER?!?* THEN TAKE HER *SWIFTLY,* CHILD -- *ABOVE GROUND!* THIS *ISLAND* IS UNIMAGINABLY *HEAVY!!*

OH? I ONCE READ YOU WERE *STRONG* ENOUGH TO SUPPORT THE *HEAVENS* THEMSELVES!

I FEAR THE LEGENDS TEND TO *EXAGGERATE --!*

NOW *GO!* TAKE YOUR MOTHER AND *FLEE --* WHILE YOU STILL *CAN!*

GO, CURSE YE -- *GO!!*

DESPITE HERACLES' *PROTESTS,* I SEE NOW THE TALES I READ OF HIM IN MAN'S WORLD SPOKE *TRUE --!*

BEYOND THE *BARBARISM* THAT ALLOWED HIM TO *IMPRISON* AND *HUMILIATE* MY AMAZON SISTERS THOSE LONG *CENTURIES* AGO --

-- THERE IS ALSO *HEROISM* AND A GREAT *NOBILITY* IN HERACLES!

IS IT TRULY *OVER* THEN, SISTERS?

IT WOULD SEEM *SO,* EUBOEA...

"*DOOM'S DOORWAY,* WHICH WE HAVE SO LONG BEEN CHARGED TO *GUARD* WITH OUR VERY LIVES, LIES IN *RUINS --*

"-- THE MONSTROUS *TERRORS* IT ONCE CONTAINED NOW *GONE!*"

IT APPEARS THE PRINCESS DIANA *SUCCEEDED* IN HER QUEST -- BUT AT WHAT *COST?*

AND WHAT OF QUEEN *HIPPOLYTE --?!?*

SISTERS -- *LOOK!*

AMIDST THE *RUINS --* SOMETHING *MOVES --!*

4

"PRAISE THE GODS-- 'TIS HIPPOLYTE!"

"THE QUEEN OF THEMYSCIRA HAS BEEN RETURNED TO US!"

BUT DOES SHE LIVE?

HER WOUNDS ARE MOST GRIEVOUS!

AYE, SISTER-- JUST BARELY!

SISTERS, SOMETHING GLISTENS IN HER HAND--!

IT'S PRINCESS DIANA'S TIARA--!

DID THE QUEEN TAKE IT FROM HER DAUGHTER'S DEAD BODY--?

OR DID DIANA LEAVE IT HERE AS SOME SORT OF MESSAGE?

WHAT HAS BECOME OF HER?

HAVE FAITH, HERACLES-- HELP IS HERE!

CURSE YE, CHILD-- I ORDERED YOU TO HIE YOUR MOTHER TO SAFETY!

AND THIS I HAVE DONE--!

BUT I CANNOT SIMPLY LEAVE YOU HERE TO SUFFER THIS FATE ALONE!

THIS IS MY ISLAND--AND I HAVE BEEN BLESSED WITH GREAT STRENGTH!

PLEASE, MILORD--LET ME BEAR THE BURDEN.

THIS IS NO PLACE FOR A GOD!

NO, CHILD-- I HAVE FAILED IN MY LABORS HERE AND ANGERED MY FATHER ZEUS!

THUS THIS IS THE FATE HE HAS CHOSEN FOR ME!

AFTER ALL I HAVE DONE TO YOUR KIND, IS THIS PUNISHMENT NOT JUST?

NO, HERACLES--I WILL NOT LEAVE YOU. SUCH SUFFERING MUST STOP.

IF ZEUS HAS PUNISHED YOU THUS, THEN I WILL SHARE YOUR PENANCE.

YOU HOLD THE LIVES OF MY SISTERS ON YOUR BACK-- BUT YOU SHAN'T BEAR THE BURDEN ALONE!

NOR SHALT THOU HAVE TO, MY CHILDREN!

I CAN BEAR THIS NO LONGER!

FATHER!

5

AYE, MY SON! I AM *AWAKENED* AT LAST FROM MY SLEEP OF *IGNORANCE*-- AND I AM DULY *HUMBLED*!

DESPITE *EVERYTHING*, THE AMAZONS CONTINUE TO BELIEVE IN US... AND MORE, HAVE EVEN *FORGIVEN* THOSE WHO ONCE ABUSED THEM...

THROUGH *THEM*, THE GLORY OF GAEA HAS TRULY BEEN *RESTORED*--

--AND IT IS TIME FOR THE GODS TO FINALLY *EARN* THE FAITH THE AMAZONS HAVE SO WILLINGLY *GIVEN* US!

THOU AND THY MOTHER HATH SHOWN *MERCY* TO MY SON-- AS WELL AS *STRENGTH* AND *COURAGE*!

IF THOU ART REPRESENTATIVE OF *ALL* AMAZONS, THEN TRULY IS THINE THE *NOBLEST* RACE EVER TO WALK THROUGH GAEA'S GARDEN!

THUS I *RELEASE* THEE FROM ANY *FURTHER* LABORS!

AND WE GODDESSES WHO *SHAPED* THEE RELEASE YE FROM THE *PENANCE* WE VISITED UPON THEE THESE LONG *CENTURIES* PAST!

THY *FUTURE* COURSE IS THINE *ALONE* TO MAP.

WE *KNOW* NOW THAT OUR *DESTINY* IS IN THY *CAPABLE* HANDS--

--AND WE HAVE *FAITH* IN THEE!

NOW THOU MUST *LEAVE* THIS PLACE-- FOR THOU SHALT HAVE NO CAUSE TO ENTER HERE *AGAIN*!

HENCEFORTH THE POWER OF *GAEA* SHALL BEAR THIS ISLAND'S *WEIGHT*!

WHAT--?!?

HERACLES-- *QUICKLY*--!

HAVE TO GET *OUT* OF HERE!

THOUGH WHY ALMIGHTY ZEUS DID NOT SIMPLY *TRANSPORT* YOU TO OLYMPUS I DO NOT *KNOW*!!

BECAUSE THERE IS ONE MORE *TASK* TO BE ACCOMPLISHED, AMAZON-- ONE *CENTURIES* IN COMING!

6

BACK, SISTERS!!

THE GROUND *QUAKES*--! THE *PORTAL* SURROUNDING DOOM'S DOORWAY *COLLAPSES*--!

WHAT IN HERA'S NAME IS *HAPPENING* HERE?!?

THE CAVERN IS *EXPLODING!* THE DEMONS ARE *FREE!!*

NO, EUBOEA-- THE LIGHT IS *PURE!*

IT IS THE DOING OF THE *GODS!*

SISTERS-- *BEHOLD!*

BATHED IN THAT HOLY *LIGHT*--

"--SOMEONE *APPROACHES!*"

GREETINGS, SISTERS-- I BRING YOU A GODLY *GUEST!*

HEAR ME, AMAZONS--

--FOR *HERACLES,* SON OF ZEUS, MUST SPEAK TO YE ALL!

AFTER ALL THESE CENTURIES... IT'S *HE*--!

HAS HE NOW BEEN SENT TO *DESTROY* US?

THE ONE WHO ABUSED AND *IMPRISONED* US!

NO, SISTERS-- THE AGE OF *DESTRUCTION* IS FINALLY ENDED.

PLEASE, YOU MUST *LISTEN* TO HERACLES--!

7

SISTERS, MY DAUGHTER SPEAKS *TRUE*--!

WE MUST NOT ALLOW OUR FEAR AND ANGER TO *UNDO* ALL WE HAVE *LEARNED*--

--ALL THAT MAKES US *AMAZONS*--!

WE ARE NOT THE *ONLY* ONES WHO'VE BEEN FORCED TO SUFFER *PENANCE*--!

I HAVE LEARNED *MUCH* THIS DAY--

--AND AS YOUR *QUEEN*, I ASK HERACLES TO ADDRESS THE *AMAZON NATION*!

THE ASSEMBLED AMAZONS STAND FEARFULLY *ENTRANCED* AS THE *SON OF ZEUS* IS LOWERED TO THE GROUND--

--AND HE WHO WAS ONCE THE *CAUSE* OF THEIR INITIAL RUINATION AND SUBSEQUENT EXILE--

--NOW BECOMES THE *FIRST* MAN TO SET FOOT ON *PARADISE ISLAND!*

AMAZONS, I HAVE GIVEN YE MUCH CAUSE TO *REVILE* ME!

IN A WORLD OF IGNORANCE AND BELLIGERENCE, I STOOD *TALL*--

--AS I BELIEVED WAS MY *RIGHT* AS A *MAN*!

I *BETRAYED* YOUR *TRUST* AND MADE MOCKERY OF YOUR *KINDNESS*!

I COULD NOT *ADMIT* THAT THE AMAZONS WERE NOT PREACHING *DOMINATION* OVER MAN, BUT RATHER *EQUAL MERIT*--!

THUS I ALLOWED *MADNESS* TO CLOUD MY HEART, AND THUS DID I ABUSE YE *ALL*--

--MOST ESPECIALLY YOUR LOVING *QUEEN*!

I *BETRAYED* YE-- AND THAT IS *UN-FORGIVABLE*!

NONETHELESS, I DO NOW BEG YOUR *FORGIVENESS*!

FOR AN INTERMINABLE *MOMENT*, THERE IS *SILENCE*--

--AS HERACLES WAITS HUMBLY FOR A *REPLY*...

THIS DAY, AT LAST, THE MIGHTY *DEMIGOD* HAS TRULY PROVEN HIMSELF ALSO A *MAN*--

B

-- AND THE GRATEFUL AMAZONS DO NOT HESITATE TO SHOW THEIR APPROVAL...

ALL HAIL HERACLES!!

FOR THE GLORY OF GAEA!!

HERACLES, WE BID YOU WELCOME!

FROM THIS DAY FORTH, OUR HOME IS ALSO YOURS!

I AM WELL PLEASED, MY SISTERS--

--AND MOST GRATEFUL!

AND THUS, AT LAST, IS PARADISE STRENGTHENED AND RESTORED--

THE TIME OF CONTRITION IS AT LONG LAST ENDED!

PRAISE THE GODS!

IT IS FINALLY OVER MOTHER!

PARADISE ISLAND ENDURES!

--BATHED IN THE SUNLIT SMILE OF THE GODS...

BEHOLD HOW HERACLES NOW CARRIES THE WOUNDED HIPPOLYTE!

TRULY THIS EXPERIENCE HAS CHANGED YOUR HEADSTRONG SON, ZEUS!

AS WE MUST ALL CHANGE, HERA-- TO FULFILL THE GREAT DESTINY THAT GAEA HAS ORDAINED FOR US!

I APPRECIATE THE PATIENCE YOU HAVE SHOWN ME, MY QUEEN.

AS I APPRECIATE THE LOVE THIS EXPERIENCE HAS AWAKENED IN YOU, ZEUS!

PERHAPS THERE IS TIME FOR LOVE TO GRACE ALL OLYMPUS NOW, HERA.

THEN I TAKE YOU, ZEUS, MY HUSBAND-- MY EQUAL --TO BE MY ONE TRUE LOVE AGAIN!

AND THUS DO I GIVE MYSELF TO YOU-- GLADLY!

9

WE HAVE *DONE* IT, SISTERS!

THE AMAZONS HAVE FINALLY *PROVEN* THEMSELVES TO ZEUS--

--AND *LOVE* AND *JOY* NOW REIGN ONCE MORE ON *OLYMPUS!*

IT HAS BEEN *AGES* SINCE I FELT SO *ALIVE!*

NOW IS TRULY THE TIME FOR *UNADULTERATED* *LOVEMAKING!*

INDEED, APHRODITE--BUT WE MUST ALSO *USE* THIS NEW AWAKENING *WISELY!*

NEVER AGAIN MUST WE ALLOW OURSELVES TO GROW SO *WEAK!*

AYE, ATHENA--BUT *THAT* IS A WORRY FOR *TOMORROW!*

LET THE WINE POUR *FREELY*, DIONYSUS! THIS IS A DAY FOR *CELEBRATION!*

WINE AND SONG ARE FINE IN THEIR PLACE, ARTEMIS--

--BUT WE MUST *ALSO* SPARE A MOMENT TO MOURN OUR *LOSS!*

"ONLY *NOW* HAS THE TRUE *MAGNITUDE* OF HERMES' LOSS BECOME CLEAR TO HIM--!"

"DESPITE THEIR VAST *DIFFERENCES*, STILL WAS PAN HIS *SON!*"

OH, MY POOR, DEAR *HERMES*--! I HAD ALL BUT *FORGOTTEN*--!

WE MUST *NEVER* FORGET THE LESSONS LEARNED THIS DAY, APHRODITE!

AYE, ATHENA--AS *GODS*, WE MUST EVER BE VIGILANT TO *DESERVE* OUR EXALTED STATUS!

"*TRUE*, DEMETER! WE REVEL NOW IN GAEA'S POWER *RESTORED*, BUT THERE WILL BE MANY *CHALLENGES* TO FACE IN THE AGES TO COME--

"--AND OUR PLACE IN THE *COSMIC* *BALANCE* MAY NECESSITATE GREAT *CHANGES* IN OLYMPUS ITSELF!"

10

ENID, OKLAHOMA:

THE MODEST RURAL HOME OF EDNA AND EVERETT AARONSON--

--WHERE AIR FORCE COLONEL STEVE TREVOR NOW RUMMAGES THROUGH THE DUSTY ATTIC--

--IN SEARCH OF MEMORIES...

QUE PASA, ETTA?

YOUR AUNT EDNA SAYS SUPPER WILL BE READY IN FIVE MINUTES, STEVE.

SHE'S EVEN MADE A SPECIAL DIET PLATE FOR ME.

YOU OKAY UP HERE?

JUST THINKING ABOUT MY DAD AGAIN. I ALWAYS WANTED HIM TO BE SO PROUD OF ME, ETTA.

WHEN THOSE CONGRESSIONAL HEARINGS ALMOST RUINED MY CAREER, I FELT I HAD SOMEHOW BETRAYED HIM--!

BUT THERE WAS ALWAYS A LOT OF MY MOTHER'S TENACIOUSNESS IN ME--AT LEAST THAT'S WHAT HE SAID!

GUESS I STAYED IN THE AIR FORCE THIS LONG SO I WOULDN'T BE A FAILURE IN HIS EYES--!

MOM AND DAD NEVER QUIT ANYTHING!

STEPHEN R. TREVOR, YOU LISTEN TO ME!

YOU ARE CERTAINLY NOT A FAILURE! I'VE NEVER KNOWN A MAN MORE COMMITTED TO HIS IDEALS!

SO MAYBE THE AIR FORCE ISN'T FOR YOU ANYMORE--BUT THAT DOESN'T MAKE YOU A QUITTER!

I KNOW I'VE TRIED TO CONVINCE YOU TO STAY--BUT THAT'S BECAUSE I DO LOVE THE AIR FORCE!

I WOULDN'T BE ON THIS DIET AND EXERCISE PLAN OTHERWISE!

BUT I KNOW NOW I WAS BEING SELFISH. YOU'VE GOT TO DO WHAT'S RIGHT FOR YOU!

BUT WHATEVER YOU DECIDE, STEVE, YOU'VE GOT TO KNOW THIS...

IF YOU GO, I WILL MISS YOU--MORE THAN I CAN SAY!

I HAVE LOVED YOU, STEPHEN TREVOR--FOR A VERY LONG TIME!

OH, ETTA--

--I LOVE YOU TOO!

AND SUDDENLY THE PAST ISN'T TERRIBLY IMPORTANT ANYMORE...

ALL THAT REALLY MATTERS NOW IS THE FUTURE...

11

THE ISLAND OF HEALING, OFF THE COAST OF *PARADISE ISLAND*--

--WHERE QUEEN HIPPOLYTE RESTS EASY NOW, HER WOUNDS SOOTHED AND SALVED...

PHILIPPUS?

I AM HERE AS YOU *REQUESTED*, MY QUEEN.

WHAT IS IT YOU *WISH* OF ME?

YOU LOOK *WELL*, MY CAPTAIN-- I AM JOYFUL OUR BATTLE DID NOT SERIOUSLY *INJURE* YOU!

THE ONLY TRULY *DEEP* WOUND WAS THE ONE IN MY *HEART*.

WHEN I SWORE TO CAPTAIN OUR *ARMIES*, I SWORE ALSO NEVER TO CAUSE YOU *SHAME*.

I ONLY PRAY YOU CAN *FORGIVE* ME FOR RAISING MY *SWORD* AGAINST ONE I SO DEARLY *LOVE*!

THERE IS NO NEED FOR SUCH *CONTRITION*, PHILIPPUS. YOU ACTED SOLELY FOR THE GOOD OF OUR *PEOPLE*.

I COULD HAVE ASKED FOR NO ONE *BETTER* TO ENTRUST WITH PROTECTING OUR *NATION*!

NOW THAT DOOM'S *DOORWAY* IS *NO MORE*, WE NEED NO LONGER FEAR LOSING ANOTHER *SISTER* TO IT--!

AYE, PHILIPPUS, ALL OUR *EFFORT*-- ALL OUR *SACRIFICE*--HAS AT LAST BORNE *FRUIT*!

MAY *JOY* FINALLY FILL THIS ISLAND--

-- SO WE MAY NEVER AGAIN NEED RAISE OUR *HANDS* TO ONE ANOTHER--

-- EXCEPT TO EXPRESS OUR *LOVE*!

NOW YOU MUST *REST*, MY QUEEN!

GREAT *FESTIVALS* AWAIT YOUR *RECOVERY*!

AYE, PHILIPPUS, I WILL *REST*--

-- SO THAT *PARADISE* MAY ONCE AGAIN GROW *STRONG*!

12

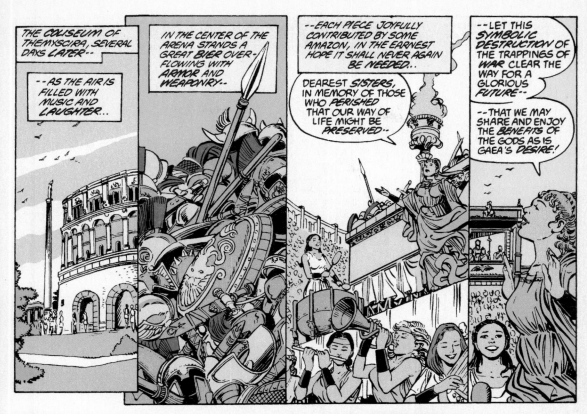

THE COLISEUM OF THEMYSCIRA, SEVERAL DAYS LATER--

--AS THE AIR IS FILLED WITH MUSIC AND LAUGHTER...

IN THE CENTER OF THE ARENA STANDS A GREAT BIER OVER-FLOWING WITH ARMOR AND WEAPONRY--

--EACH PIECE JOYFULLY CONTRIBUTED BY SOME AMAZON, IN THE EARNEST HOPE IT SHALL NEVER AGAIN BE NEEDED...

DEAREST SISTERS, IN MEMORY OF THOSE WHO PERISHED THAT OUR WAY OF LIFE MIGHT BE PRESERVED--

--LET THIS SYMBOLIC DESTRUCTION OF THE TRAPPINGS OF WAR CLEAR THE WAY FOR A GLORIOUS FUTURE--

--THAT WE MAY SHARE AND ENJOY THE BENEFITS OF THE GODS AS IS GAEA'S DESIRE!

ARE YOU ENJOYING THE FESTIVITIES, HERACLES?

A MOST IMPRESSIVE SPECTACLE, DIANA--

--THOUGH I CANNOT UNDERSTAND HOW YOU EXPECT TO SURVIVE WITHOUT AN ARMY!

ON THIS ISLAND, THERE IS NO NEED FOR ONE...

MAY THESE BRACELETS SERVE ONLY AS A REMINDER OF ALL WE STILL MUST ACCOMPLISH--

--NOT BITTERNESS OVER THINGS LONG PAST!

"LET THE FLAMES CONSUME THAT OIL-SOAKED WEAPONRY--

"--AND THE RESULTING LIGHT ILLUMINATE OUR FUTURE!"

13

BY *NOON* THE FOLLOWING DAY, APOLLO HAS BALANCED THE SUN AT *ZENITH*--

--SPRAYING ITS BRIGHT *RAYS* ACROSS THE THEMYSCIRAN LAKES LIKE GLITTERING JEWELS--

--SEEMING IN ITS GENTLE WAY TO *REAFFIRM* THE AMAZONS' *NEW COMMITMENT* TO *PEACE*--

--AND TO THE *SHEER JOY* OF *LIVING!*

AS *ONE* WITH HER FEATHERED COMPANIONS, THE PRINCESS DIANA SOARS JOYFULLY THROUGH THE CLOUDLESS SKIES--

--CAPTURING THE ATTENTION AND APPRECIATION OF ONE AND ALL!

THY *DAUGHTER* IS INDEED A MOST *WONDROUS* CREATURE, HIPPOLYTE! I CAN WELL UNDERSTAND YOUR *PRIDE* IN HER!

AYE, HERACLES-- THOUGH *I* CANNOT UNDERSTAND HER *RESTLESSNESS* AT TIMES.

BUT THEN, NEITHER COULD I UNDERSTAND SUCH FEELINGS IN *MYSELF.*

14

AYE, I CAN INDEED SEE THE SPIRIT OF HER *MOTHER* IN HER.

AND MAYHAP *MY SEED* AS WELL--?

NAY, HERACLES...

THE GODS TOLD ME HER *EGG* WAS WITHIN ME FROM A LIFE LONG *PAST.*

IT SEEMS IT WAS *FATED* I SHOULD BECOME MOTHER TO OUR NATION'S *SAVIOR.*

I AM *GLAD,* HIPPOLYTE-- *TRULY!*

'TWOULD HAVE BEEN A *MOCKERY* FOR SUCH A *BEAUTIFUL* CHILD TO BE BORN FROM SO *UGLY* AN ACT AS MY *VIOLATION* OF YOU!

THOUGH TIME HAS DONE NOTHING TO *DIMINISH* MY APPRECIATION OF THY GREAT *BEAUTY,* O QUEEN--

--IT HAS DONE *MUCH* TO ENHANCE MY *RESPECT* FOR YOU AS A *TRUE EQUAL!*

WHEN *FIRST* YOU SAID THAT, YOUR WORDS WERE DIPPED IN *VENOM*--

--BUT NOW I SENSE ONLY *SINCER-ITY.*

AND *NOW,* HIPPOLYTE, I AM CALLED *HOME!*

MAY A HUMBLED GOD HAVE ONE FINAL *KISS,* YOUR MAJESTY?

A KISS OF *FORGIVENESS?*

AYE, YOU HAVE *EARNED* THAT, HERACLES-- AND *MORE!*

I PRAY THAT MY SINS OF MADNESS CAN SOMEDAY BE *ERASED* FROM THY MEMORY, HIPPOLYTE--

--THAT YOU MIGHT TRULY SEE THE DEPTHS OF MY FEELINGS TOWARDS YOU!

COULD IT BE THAT *YOU*..?

I AM STILL A *WOMAN,* AFTER ALL--

--AND IT *HAS* BEEN A VERY LONG *TIME!*

BUT STILL AM I *QUEEN OF THEMY-SCIRA*-- AND THERE IS MUCH FOR ME TO *DO!*

GO NOW, HERACLES...

"--AND KNOW THAT THE LOVE OF *HIPPOLYTE* GOES WITH YOU!"

15

333

FATHER *ZEUS,* LORD OF THE *HEAVENS*--

-- THY SON AWAITS THY *SUMMONS!*

TAKE ME, I PRAY THEE, UNTO THE LOVING BOSOM OF *OLYMPUS* ONCE MORE--

-- FOR THIS DAY I FINALLY FEEL *WORTHY!*

I HAVE AT LAST BEEN *FORGIVEN* MY SINS BY THOSE I SINNED *AGAINST*--!

THE SLATE IS *CLEAN,* THE FUTURE *LIMITLESS!*

THE GLORY OF GAEA BE *WITH* YE, AMAZONS! MAY IT GUIDE AND *PROTECT* YE IN YOUR *MISSION* ON THIS PLANE!

AND *KNOW,* SHOULD THERE EVER COME A TIME WHEN IT IS *NEEDED*--

-- THE POWER OF *HERACLES* IS YOURS TO *COMMAND!*

FARE THEE *WELL,* MY PRECIOUS ONES...

...FARE THEE WELL...

16

THE AMAZON SENATE, SEVERAL DAYS LATER--

--WHERE A GREAT MEETING IS ABOUT TO COMMENCE THAT MAY WELL DETERMINE THE FUTURE OF PARADISE ISLAND...

SISTERS, FOR THE FIRST TIME WITHIN MEMORY, MAN HAS BEEN ALLOWED TO SET FOOT ON OUR ISLAND-- AND I, FOR ONE, AM FEARFUL!

BUT NOW THAT HAND IS OFFERED IN FRIENDSHIP, HELLENE--!

WHAT HAS MAN EVER GIVEN US SAVE THE BACK OF HIS HAND?

IS IT? MORE LIKELY THEY WILL COME TO US WITH WEAPONS IN HAND--

--SUCH AS THOSE WE HAVE SEEN IN DIANA'S BOOKS--!

PERHAPS, SISTER-- --BUT IF WE INTEND TO PREACH PEACE AND EQUALITY, WE CANNOT ISOLATE OURSELVES FROM THOSE WHO NEED US MOST!

THERE IS MUCH LOGIC IN WHAT YOU SAY, PRINCESS!

THOUGH I LONG FOR NEW STUDENTS TO TEACH-- STILL I FEAR WE TREAD ON DANGEROUS GROUND!

DIANA, WE HAVE LEARNED MUCH ABOUT MAN'S WORLD FROM YOU--

--BUT I FEAR WE MUST LEARN MORE!

ANY VOTE AMONG OUR SISTERHOOD MUST BE MADE WISELY!

THUS I CHARGE YOU TO RETURN TO MAN'S WORLD ONCE MORE--

--TO TEACH THEM AND TO LEARN!

ARE YOU CERTAIN, MOTHER?

QUITE SO! IF WE ARE EVER TO ACCOMPLISH A TRUE EXCHANGE OF CULTURES--

--WHO BETTER THAN MY DAUGHTER TO BE OUR AMBASSADOR?

WELL SAID!

17

THE TEMPLE OF HADES, THE FOLLOWING MORNING --

-- WHERE THE AMAZON SISTERHOOD HAS GATHERED TO ONCE MORE BID THEIR PRINCESS *FAREWELL*...

WITHIN, AMIDST THE ANCIENT STATUES OF LONG-FALLEN WARRIORS, QUEEN HIPPOLYTE WAITS *PATIENTLY* --

-- STARING IN SILENCE AT THE CLOSED *DOOR* TO THE HONORED SHRINE OF THE *FINAL* WARRIOR TO PERISH ON PARADISE ISLAND --

-- SHE WHO WAS ALSO THE NAME-SAKE OF HIPPOLYTE'S DAUGHTER --

-- *DIANA TREVOR!*

WHEN FIRST I *DONNED* YOUR *ARMOR,* DIANA --

-- I DID NOT UNDERSTAND ITS *SIGNIFICANCE* OR THE GREAT *RESPONSIBILITY* IT IMPLIED!

I SWEAR I SHALL CARRY YOUR STANDARD WITH *HONOR* --

-- AND THE SUIT OF *ARMOR* WHICH I NOW WEAR SHALL BE MY *TRIBUTE* TO YOU IN YOUR *WORLD!*

I WILL MAKE YOUR SON *PROUD* OF YOUR GREAT *SACRIFICE* FOR US --

-- AS I PRAY MY *DEEDS* WILL MAKE YOU PROUD OF *ME!*

THERE IS SO MUCH OUR PEOPLE CAN *LEARN* FROM ONE ANOTHER!

AND THOUGH I WEAR *ARMOR,* I COME TO YOUR WORLD NOT AS A *WARRIOR* --

-- FOR THIS STANDARD IS TO BE A *UNIVERSAL* SYMBOL OF *PEACE!*

ANY WORLD THAT CAN CREATE BEINGS SUCH AS *YOU* AND *JULIA* AND *VANESSA* -- AND YOUR SON *STEPHEN,* -- IS ONE WELL WORTH *PRESERVING!*

I ONLY PRAY I HAVE THE STRENGTH TO BE *WORTHY!*

ARE YOU *READY* THEN, DAUGHTER?

I AM *PREPARED*, MOTHER--

--BUT I WORRY ABOUT *YOU!*

YOU *NEEDN'T*, CHILD...

I *KNOW* NOW THAT YOU ARE NOT JUST *MY* DAUGHTER--YOU ARE A CHILD OF THE *WORLD!*

A GREAT *TRUST* HAS BEEN PLACED IN YOU.

THE GODS *PROVED* THAT WHEN THEY BEQUEATHED YOU *HERMES'* *WINGED SANDALS--*

--WHICH ALLOW YOU EFFORTLESS *PASSAGE* BETWEEN WORLDS!

JUST REMEMBER THEY ALSO ALLOW YOU TO *RETURN* TO ME.

I WILL RETURN HOME AS OFTEN AS I CAN, MOTHER--

--AND YOU WILL *ALWAYS* BE WITH ME IN MY *HEART*.

LOOK TO THE *SKY*, MNEMOSYNE--!

THE PRINCESS *DEPARTS!*

"SHE LOOKS SO *HAPPY*... SO *HOPEFUL!*"

"SHE CARRIES THE *WEIGHT* OF HER *MONUMENTAL BURDEN* WITH HEART *UPLIFTED!*"

YOU DID NOT *SPEAK* IN THE SENATE, MENALIPPE.

WHAT IS *YOUR* FEELING REGARDING THIS MOVEMENT TO ALLOW *MEN* ON OUR ISLAND?

"I BELIEVE THAT THE GODS *SPEAK* THROUGH DIANA, MNEMOSYNE.

WHATEVER DIANA DECIDES, I AM CERTAIN IT WILL ONLY FURTHER GAEA'S *GLORY!*

19

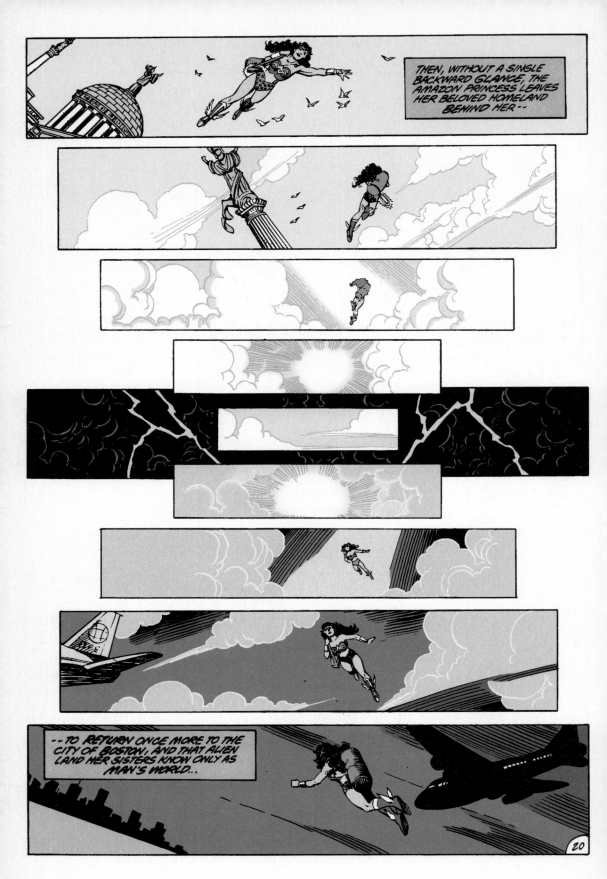

THEN, WITHOUT A SINGLE BACKWARD GLANCE, THE AMAZON PRINCESS LEAVES HER BELOVED HOMELAND BEHIND HER --

-- TO RETURN ONCE MORE TO THE CITY OF BOSTON, AND THAT ALIEN LAND HER SISTERS KNOW ONLY AS MAN'S WORLD...

20

"The Captain has turned on the NO SMOKING sign in preparation for our landing at Boston's LOGAN INTERNATIONAL AIRPORT."

"Please extinguish all smoking materials and return your seats to their UPRIGHT POSITION..."

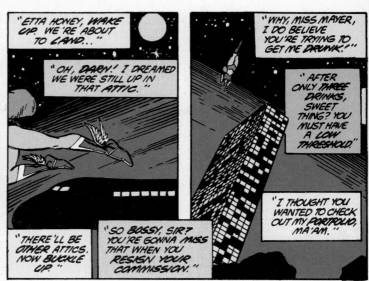

"ETTA HONEY, WAKE UP. WE'RE ABOUT TO LAND..."

"OH, DARN! I DREAMED WE WERE STILL UP IN THAT ATTIC."

"THERE'LL BE OTHER ATTICS. NOW BUCKLE UP."

"SO BOSSY, SIR? YOU'RE GONNA MISS THAT WHEN YOU RESIGN YOUR COMMISSION."

"WHY, MISS MAYER, I DO BELIEVE YOU'RE TRYING TO GET ME DRUNK!"

"AFTER ONLY THREE DRINKS, SWEET THING? YOU MUST HAVE A LOW THRESHOLD."

"I THOUGHT YOU WANTED TO CHECK OUT MY PORTFOLIO, MA'AM."

AMONG OTHER THINGS. JUST THOUGHT YOU NEEDED TO GET COMFORTABLE FIRST--!

MMM-- YOUR CHEST HAIRS TICKLE MY TOES.

THIS IS SUPPOSED TO MAKE ME RELAX?

GOD, SWEET THING-- I CERTAINLY HOPE NOT.

"MOM? HEY, MOM!?"

"HEY YOURSELF! WHAT IS IT, VANESSA?"

LIGHT JUST WENT OUT IN MY ROOM-- SOME KIND'A SHORT OR SOMETHIN'!

I CAN'T SEE WHAT I'M READING!

YOUR ROOM DOESN'T HAVE A TV SET!

SO GO INTO MY ROOM AND STUDY.

BESIDES, I SAW SPARKS! WHAT IF MY ROOM CATCHES FIRE OR SOMETHING?

WITH MY WALKMAN ON, I MIGHT NOT HEAR IT TILL IT WAS TOO LATE!

PLEASE, MOM-- JUST COME LOOK AT IT, OKAY?

21

HONESTLY, VANESSA-- HOW DOES ONE MANAGE TO *SHORT CIRCUIT* A WHOLE ROOM WHILE *STUDYING?*

BEATS *ME!* I JUST *LIVE* HERE!

MAYBE SOME *MICE* ATE THE *WIRING!*

I HAD THE WIRING *CHECKED* JUST LAST MONTH.

MAYBE IF YOU'D SIMPLY *STUDY,* INSTEAD OF WATCHING *MTV* AND FILLING YOUR HEAD-PHONES WITH *JON BOVIE--!*

BON JOVI!

WHATEVER!

ANYWAY, ONCE I FIX THIS *LIGHT,* YOUNG LADY--

--YOU AND I ARE GOING TO HAVE A NICE LONG *TALK* ABOUT YOUR *STUDY HABITS* AND YOUR--

--YOUR--

... OH... MY... GOD...

HELLO, JULIA.

HOW *ARE* YOU?

SEE? *SEE?*

I *TOLD* YOU SHE'D BE *SURPRISED!*

SURPRISED? I'M *FLABBERGASTED!*

OH, HONEY, IT'S SO GOOD TO *SEE* YOU AGAIN!

I'D BEGUN TO THINK YOU WERE *NEVER* COMING BACK!

I HAVE SO MUCH TO *TELL* YOU, JULIA-- SO MUCH TO *DO!*

MAY I *STAY* HERE AGAIN?

AS IF I'D *LET* YOU STAY ANYWHERE *ELSE!*

"WELCOME HOME, DIANA...

"WELCOME HOME!"

22

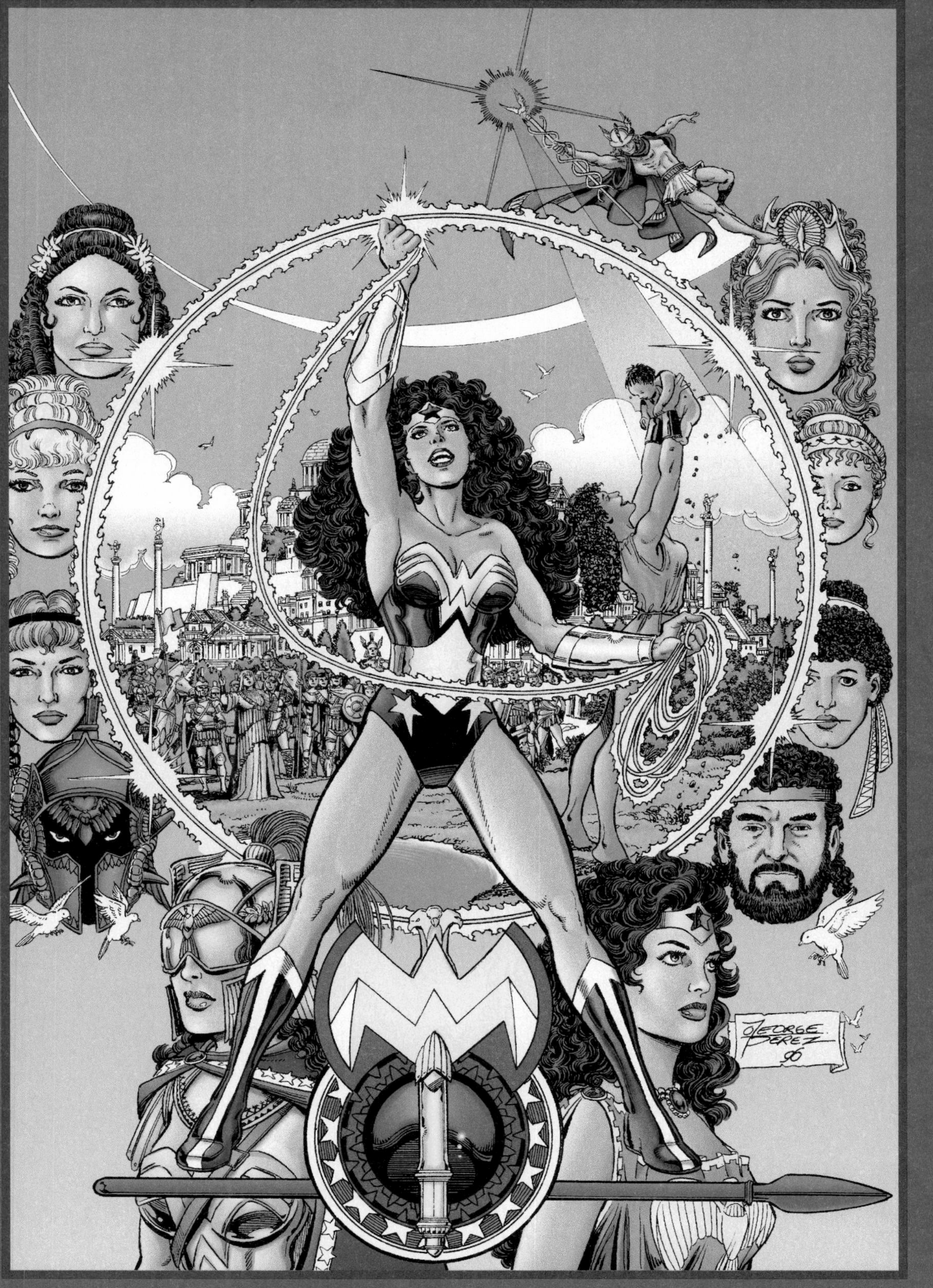
GEORGE PEREZ
96

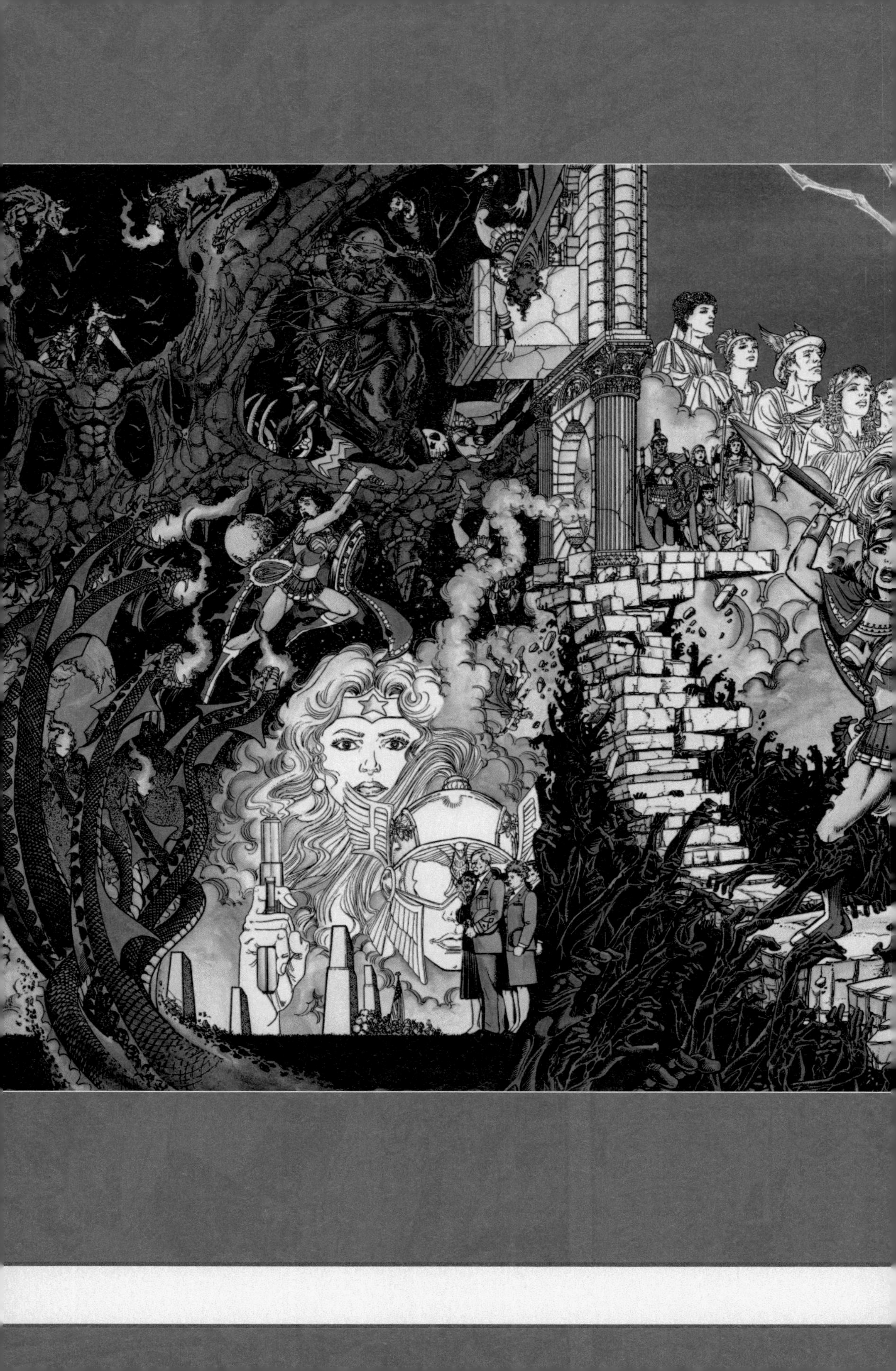

Gatefold cover art from WONDER WOMAN #10,
released as a retail poster in 1987 (color by Tom Ziuko).

WONDER WOMAN

ALTER EGO: Princess Diana
MARITAL STATUS: Single
KNOWN RELATIVES: Hippolyte (mother), Antiope (aunt)
GROUP AFFILIATION: None
BASE OF OPERATIONS: Paradise Island; Boston, Massachusetts
FIRST APPEARANCE: (historical) ALL STAR COMICS #8, (modern version) WONDER WOMAN (second series) #1
HEIGHT: 5' 11"   **WEIGHT:** 135 pounds   **EYES:** Blue   **HAIR:** Black

OCCUPATION: Ambassador, Teacher

HISTORY

In 30,000 B.C. a brutal caveman, made an outcast from his tribe for losing his left hand to a sabertooth tiger, murdered his pregnant wife in a fit of rage. The souls of the woman and her unborn daughter were taken by the Earth goddess Gaea to the Cavern of Souls, which lies within Hades, the realm of the dead known to the people of ancient Greece. Over the following millennia, Gaea brought the souls of other women who died before their designated time.

In 1200 B.C. the goddess Artemis proposed to the Olympian gods that a new race of mortal human beings be created. All of them would be female, and Artemis intended that this new race would set an example to the rest of humanity as to what the proper relationship between men and women should be, one of equality between the sexes. Artemis'

proposal was vehemently opposed by the self-proclaimed war god Ares, who sought to reduce humanity to utter submission through force, and ultimately to rule Olympus himself.

Together Artemis, goddess of the hunt; Athena, goddess of wisdom, Aphrodite, goddess of love; Demeter, goddess of fertility; and Hestia, goddess of the hearth were guided by Hermes, messenger of the gods, to Hades itself. There the goddesses went to the Cavern of Souls, where they caused the thousands of souls of the dead women that had been gathering there to be reincarnated on Earth as adult women. The first to be reborn thus became known as Hippolyte and was designated by Artemis as the queen of this new race. Artemis decreed that Hippolyte's sister Antiope rule beside her, and that both sisters always wear Gaea's girdles as symbols of the goddesses' trust in them. Artemis called this new race of women Amazons.

The Amazons founded a city-state called Themyscira, where compassion and justice reigned. But the male rulers of ancient Greece grew jealous of the Amazons, and through false tales alleging that the Amazons committed crimes and atrocities, it caused the Amazons to be regarded as threats and outcasts.

Ares, feeling the Amazons an obstacle to his quest for absolute power, had a pawn taunt the demigod Heracles (later known as Hercules) with false reports that Hippolyte was besmirching his reputation. Enraged, Heracles led warriors to Themyscira to defeat Hippolyte and her Amazons. But, meeting in single combat, Heracles was himself defeated by Hippolyte instead.

Heracles now professed respect and friendship for the Amazons and, on his suggestion, a celebratory gathering of both his warriors and the Amazons was held. But with the Amazons off-guard, Heracles and his men treacherously attacked, defeated, and enslaved them. Hippolyte was placed in chains and Heracles departed, taking Gaea's girdle from her as a prize.

Hippolyte prayed to the goddesses for forgiveness. Athena appeared to her and said she would be free if she rededicated herself to her ideals. Hippolyte escaped her cell, freed the other Amazons, and led them in defeating their captors. Unlike Hippolyte, Antiope took pleasure in killing their enemies. As a result, once the battle was over, the Amazons divided into two groups: one led by Hippolyte (to whom Antiope gave her girdle of Gaea) and the other led by Antiope, who forsook the Olympian gods.

The goddesses decreed that Hippolyte and her Amazons do penance for failing to lead humanity to establish new ways of justice and equality. Therefore, the goddesses sent Hippolyte's Amazons to a distant island, beneath which lay a source of great evil. As long as Amazons served to keep that evil from menacing humanity, the Amazons would be immortal.

Hippolyte's Amazons established a new city-state on Paradise Island, and the Amazons renewed their sense of purpose and self-discipline as the centuries passed. Various Amazons were killed over the years in carrying out the difficult task of keeping the great evil confined underground. During all this time, the Amazons of Paradise Island had no contact with the outside world.

Hippolyte was the only one of the Amazons who was pregnant when she was killed in her previous incarnation. The soul of Hippolyte's unborn daughter still inhabited the Cavern of Souls. Recently, on Artemis' instructions, Hippolyte formed the image of a baby from the clay of Paradise Island. The five goddesses who were the Amazons' patrons, along with Hermes, endowed the unborn soul with various gifts, including super-human strength and speed and the power of flight. Then the unborn soul entered into the clay image, which came to life as a real baby. The child was named Diana, after a revered warrior who had died to save the Amazon race.

After Hippolyte's daughter had grown to adulthood, the gods revealed to the Amazons that Ares had gone insane and might destroy all of Earth with a terrible source of power. The gods decreed that the Amazons choose through a tournament a champion who could confront Ares in the world outside Paradise Island.

Diana asked to participate in the tournament but was forbidden to do so by Hippolyte. Nonetheless, urged on by Athena, Diana entered the tournament, concealing her identity, and won. Unable to defy the gods' will, Hippolyte agreed to let Diana be the champion to be sent against Ares. Diana was given a costume bearing the standard of her deceased namesake.

Hermes transported Diana to Boston, Massachusetts, where she met a professor of classical Greek history named Julia Kapatelis, who taught her how to speak English and serves as her guide to contemporary civilization. Diana presented herself as an ambassador from Paradise Island to the rest of society, here to teach the ways of her just and peaceful civilization to a violent world. The media have dubbed her "Wonder Woman." Although she does not actively seek to fight crime, Wonder Woman had already found herself pitted against threats masterminded by Ares.

POWERS & WEAPONS

Wonder Woman possesses super-human strength and the ability to fly. She also has super-human speed and reflexes, and can move swiftly enough to deflect bullets with her silver bracelets. Wonder Woman is another extraordinary hand-to-hand combatant, trained in all the methods of combat of ancient Greece.

She was given the "Lasso of Truth," remolded from the girdle of Gaea by Hephaestus and presented by Hestia. The unbreakable lasso forces anyone within its confines to tell the absolute truth.

Entry from 1985-1986's WHO'S WHO: THE DEFINITIVE GUIDE TO THE DC UNIVERSE (text by Bob Rozakis; color by Tom Smith).

HISTORY

One of the three children of the supreme Greek Gods, Zeus and Hera, Ares is the God of War, loving battle for its own sake. Ares never favors one city or party over another, fighting on either side, as inclination prompts him, delighting in the slaughter of men and the sacking of towns.

Ares is hated by all his fellow immortals, from Zeus and Hera downward, except for Eris, and Aphrodite, who nurses a perverse passion for him, ultimately bearing his children, Deimos, Phobos and Harmonia.

Ares opposed the plan of his half-sister Artemis to create a new race of mortals on Earth, a race that would make men worship the gods as never before. Ares was outvoted by the other gods and, through the efforts of Artemis and the other goddesses, the new race was created from the swirling souls of women whose lives had been cut short by man's fear and ignorance. This new race was called the Amazons. From that moment on, Ares became the Amazons' sworn enemy.

Recently, when the Amazon oracle Menalippe sensed a tremendous surge in Ares' power and influence that threatened to consume the very Earth itself, the Amazons were commanded by the other gods to choose a champion to confront Ares in the World of Man. The winner of this tournament was the Princess Diana, daughter of Amazon Queen Hippolyte.

After confronting Decay, an agent of Ares' son Phobos, then Phobos and Deimos themselves, Princess Diana finally confronted the God of War himself, and after battle, defeated him.

At this writing, Ares has withdrawn himself from the affairs of men, to recover from his battle with Wonder Woman and to scheme anew.

POWERS & WEAPONS

As the God of War, Ares is obstinate, hateful, wicked, and untrustworthy. He is the living personification of the savage side of War, an almost unparalleled master of combat, possessed of super-strength and complete command over any weapon.

The vulture and the dog, as scavengers of the battlefield, are his favored pets.

A R E S

ALTER EGO: None
OCCUPATION: God of War   **MARITAL STATUS:** Divorced
KNOWN RELATIVES: Zeus (father), Hera (mother), Hephaestus (brother), Eris (sister), Harmonia (daughter), Deimos (son, deceased?), Phobos (son)
GROUP AFFILIATION: Olympian Gods
BASE OF OPERATIONS: Areopagus, a hill near Mount Olympus
FIRST APPEARANCE: WONDER WOMAN (second series) #1
HEIGHT: 6' 10"   **WEIGHT:** 359 pounds   **EYES:** Red   **HAIR:** Unknown

---

Entry from 1985-1986's WHO'S WHO: THE DEFINITIVE GUIDE TO THE DC UNIVERSE (text by Len Wein; color by Tom Smith).

HISTORY

In the year 1200 B.C., the Greek goddess Artemis proposed the creation of a new race of mortals on Earth, females who would set an example to make humanity worship the gods as never before. Despite the opposition of the War-God Ares, Artemis and the other goddesses went ahead with their ambitious plan.

Transported by the fleet-footed god Hermes to the underworld called Hades, the goddesses were met by Charon, he who ferries the souls of the dead across the River Styx. There, in the Cavern of Souls, the goddesses stood before the Well of Rebirth, which was also the womb of the Earth-mother Gaea, and beheld the swirling lights that were the souls of women whose lives had been cut short by the ignorance of man.

When the female race had been completely reborn, the goddesses appeared before them, and Artemis told them of their great destiny, to lead humanity in the ways of virtue always. To this end, the Amazons were granted wisdom by Athena. Artemis granted them skill in the hunt. Demeter made their fields fruitful. Hestia built them a city, while the goddess Aphrodite granted them the great gift of love. Finally, Artemis designated the first soul to be reborn, Hippolyte, to be Queen of all the Amazons.

Though Hippolyte guided the Amazons in the ways of peace, still Mankind was suspicious of a society composed entirely of women. Goaded by a pawn of the conniving Ares, the warrior Heracles led his troops against the Amazon capital Themyscira. Defeated in combat by Hippolyte, Heracles and his troops became the Amazons' guests, lulling the women-warriors into a false sense of security, then conquering them when their guard was down.

Abused and humiliated by Heracles and his men, the Amazons were freed with the help of Athena, on the condition that the Amazons rededicate themselves to the principles of peace.

After defeating Heracles' troops, the Amazons were transported by the goddesses to an island in the mid-Atlantic, where they were granted immortality so long as no man ever set foot on the island. On this island, the Amazons toiled to build a paradise, and eventually succeeded.

Years later, yearning for a child, Hippolyte formed the image of a child from the clay of Paradise Island, and the final female soul remaining in Gaea's womb possessed the clay figure and gave it life. An ecstatic Hippolyte named her daughter Diana.

Hippolyte remains leader of the Amazons and has given her daughter permission to dwell among humans in order to prevent global Armageddon.

POWERS

As Queen of the Amazons, Hippolyte is possessed of superior strength and immortality and a warrior's heart, though it is all tempered with justice and mercy. As an Amazon, Hippolyte wears the bracelets of submission as a constant reminder that as women, they must never again be subservient to men.

H I P P O L Y T E

ALTER EGO: None
OCCUPATION: Queen of the Amazons   **MARITAL STATUS:** Single
KNOWN RELATIVES: Diana (daughter), Antiope (sister)
GROUP AFFILIATION: The Amazons
BASE OF OPERATIONS: Paradise Island
FIRST APPEARANCE: WONDER WOMAN (second series) #1
HEIGHT: 5' 9"   **WEIGHT:** 131 pounds   **EYES:** Blue   **HAIR:** Black

Entry from 1985-1986's WHO'S WHO: THE DEFINITIVE GUIDE TO THE DC UNIVERSE
(text by Len Wein; color by Tom Smith).

HISTORY

At this writing, little is known of the origin of the new Cheetah save this: Some time ago, archaeologist Barbara Minerva went in search of a legendary lost race of cat-like humanoids. Though she did not find the cat people themselves, in the ruins of their treasure city she found an ancient herb long thought extinct that they had purportedly worshipped and nurtured.

With the aid of her African aide-de-camp, Barbara made an elixir from the leaves of the herb, drank of it from a saucer-like vessel during the reenactment of an ancient ritual, and thus was transformed into the humanoid cat-creature called the Cheetah!

For reasons as yet unexplained, the Cheetah seeks the mystic girdle of the Earth-Goddess Gaea, which has since been transformed by the Olympian God Hephaestus into the golden Lasso of Truth now wielded by the Amazon Princess Diana, known to the world at large as Wonder Woman.

Though the Cheetah appeared to perish during her first battle with Wonder Woman for possession of the lasso, no trace of her body was found, and thus her current whereabouts remain unknown.

POWERS & WEAPONS

A superior hand-to-hand combatant, the Cheetah is incredibly fast, possessing superhuman agility and strength, unerring night-vision, and razor-sharp claws that are able to pierce bricks as easily as they rend her attackers to shreds. She can also control her tail as an extra appendage to grapple with her foes or strangle them.

C H E E T A H

ALTER EGO: Barbara Ann Minerva
OCCUPATION: Archaeologist, Treasure Hunter
MARITAL STATUS: Single
KNOWN RELATIVES: None
GROUP AFFILIATION: None
BASE OF OPERATIONS: Mobile, principally Europe
FIRST APPEARANCE: (As Barbara Minerva) WONDER WOMAN (second series) #7,
(As the Cheetah) WONDER WOMAN (second series) #9
HEIGHT: 5' 9"   **WEIGHT:** 120 pounds   **EYES:** Brown   **HAIR:** Black

*Entry from 1985-1986's WHO'S WHO: THE DEFINITIVE GUIDE TO THE DC UNIVERSE
(text by Len Wein; color by Tom Smith).*

Title page art for 1996's WONDER WOMAN GALLERY (color by Tatjana Wood).

Cover art for the 2004 trade paperback collection
WONDER WOMAN: CHALLENGE OF THE GODS (color by Tom Smith).

BIOGRAPHIES

GEORGE PÉREZ

George Pérez started drawing at the age of five and hasn't stopped since. Born on June 9, 1954, Pérez began his professional comics career as an assistant to Rich Buckler in 1973. After establishing himself as a penciller at Marvel Comics, Pérez came to DC in 1980, bringing his highly detailed art style to such titles as JUSTICE LEAGUE OF AMERICA and FIRESTORM. After co-creating THE NEW TEEN TITANS in 1980, Pérez and writer Marv Wolfman reunited for the landmark miniseries CRISIS ON INFINITE EARTHS in 1985. In the aftermath of that universe-smashing event, Pérez revitalized WONDER WOMAN as the series' writer and artist, re-establishing the Amazon Princess as one of DC's most preeminent characters and bringing in some of the best sales the title has ever experienced. He has since gone on to illustrate celebrated runs on Marvel's *The Avengers*, CrossGen's *Solus*, and DC's THE BRAVE AND THE BOLD. His newest project is *George Pérez's Sirens* for BOOM! Studios.

LEN WEIN

Veteran comics writer and editor Len Wein is the creator of such memorable characters as Wolverine, the New X-Men and the Human Target, as well as the co-creator (with Bernie Wrightson) of the Swamp Thing. In his long and prolific career he has written for hundreds of titles, encompassing nearly every significant character in the medium. He has also built a successful career in TV animation, scripting such hit series as *X-Men*, *Spider-Man* and *Batman: The Animated Series*.

BRUCE PATTERSON

Born in 1953, Bruce Patterson was part of a new wave of talent that broke into comics in the mid-1970s. After honing his pen and brush work on a steady stream of small assignments, he emerged as one of the industry's most in-demand inkers. He has since worked with many of the medium's greatest artists, including Steve Ditko and Brian Bolland, on such classic titles as LEGION OF SUPER-HEROES, BLUE BEETLE, CAMELOT 3000, GREEN LANTERN and *Alpha Flight*.

GREG POTTER

Greg Potter began his comics career as a teenager writing horror stories for Warren Publishing in the early 1970s. He sold his first story to DC Comics in 1978 (HOUSE OF MYSTERY #259's "Do You Believe In...?"), and in 1984 he created the character Jemm, star of the 12-issue DC series JEMM, SON OF SATURN, illustrated by Gene Colan, Klaus Janson, and Bob McLeod. After helping to launch George Pérez's WONDER WOMAN run in 1987, Potter left the industry to focus on his work in advertising.

BOB SMITH

During a visit to the DC offices in 1975, confusion over the names Carmine (as in then-publisher Carmine Infantino) and Conway (as in then-editor Gerry Conway) led to Bob Smith landing his first assignment at the company—inking Ramona Fradon on PLASTIC MAN. Over the next twenty years, Smith became a DC mainstay, working on a variety of titles including SECRET SOCIETY OF SUPER-VILLAINS, SUPER FRIENDS, NIGHT FORCE, DETECTIVE COMICS, CAPTAIN ATOM, and CATWOMAN. Since the late 1990s he has been a regular contributor to Archie Comics.